Anglican Women Novelists

Anglican Women Novelists

Charlotte Brontë to P.D. James

Edited by
Judith Maltby and Alison Shell

t&tclark

LONDON • NEW YORK • OXFORD • NEW DELHI • SYDNEY

T&T CLARK
Bloomsbury Publishing Plc
50 Bedford Square, London, WC1B 3DP, UK
1385 Broadway, New York, NY 10018, USA

BLOOMSBURY, T&T CLARK and the T&T Clark logo are trademarks of Bloomsbury Publishing Plc

First published in Great Britain 2019

Copyright © Judith Maltby, Alison Shell and contributors, 2019

Cover design: Terry Woodley
Cover images: Background: billnoll, iStock and Shutterstock.
Rose Macaulay (Sasha/Hulton Archive/Getty Images), Charlotte M. Yonge (Hulton Archive/Getty Images), Charlotte Brontë (GL Archive/Alamy),
P. D. James (Adrian Sherrat/Alamy).

A catalogue record for this book is available from the British Library.

A catalogue record for this book is available from the Library of Congress.

Library of Congress Cataloging-in-Publication Data

ISBN: HB: 978-0-5676-6585-0
         PB: 978-0-5676-8676-3
         ePDF: 978-0-5676-6586-7
         ePUB: 978-0-5676-6587-4

Typeset by Integra Software Services Pvt. Ltd.
Printed and bound in Great Britain

To find out more about our authors and books visit www.bloomsbury.com and sign up for our newsletters.

For
the Revd Canon Timothy and Mary Hallett
dearest friends, wisest guides
and in memory of
Rachel Boulding (1964–2017)

CONTENTS

LIST OF ILLUSTRATIONS

CONTRIBUTORS

Susan D. Amussen is Professor of History at the University of California, Merced. She is the author of *An Ordered Society: Gender and Class in Early Modern England* (1988) and *Caribbean Exchanges: Slavery and the Transformation of English Society* (2007). *Gender, Culture and Politics in England, 1560–1640: Turning the World Upside Down*, co-authored with David Underdown, was published by Bloomsbury Academic in 2017. Her work on Elizabeth Goudge arises out of her interests in the relationship of religion and literature, and in the cultural politics of masculinity.

Nancy Jiwon Cho is Associate Professor of English Literature at Seoul National University, South Korea. Her research spans the intersection of British literature and religion during the long nineteenth century, with a special focus on gender, poetry and women's biblical exegesis. She has published widely in journals (such as *Modern Language Review*, *Romanticism* and *Journal of Eighteenth-Century Studies*) and contributed book chapters on British women's hymn writing, missionary verse, moral and religious poetry for children and Romantic-era millenarian female prophecy.

Peter S. Hawkins is Professor of Religion and Literature at Yale Divinity School and the Yale Institute of Sacred Music. He has published widely on Dante, on the history of biblical reception and on the place of religion in twentieth- and twenty-first-century literature. Among his publications on the latter topic are: *The Language of Grace: Flannery O'Connor, Walker Percy and Iris Murdoch* (2004), *Getting Nowhere: Christian Hope and Utopian Dream* (1985) and *Naming the Unnameable from Dante to Beckett* (1984). His most recent book, co-written with Lesleigh Cushing Stahlberg, is *The Bible and the American Short Story* (2017).

Ann Loades is Professor Emerita of Divinity, Durham, and Honorary Professor in the School of Divinity, St Andrews. She was the first woman in the history of the University of Durham to be awarded a personal chair, was President of the Society for the Study of Theology (2005–6) and was awarded a CBE for services to theology in 2001. She has published widely on nineteenth- and twentieth-century women theologians, including Evelyn Underhill, and on theology and its relationship to the arts. Her most recent publication is 'Some Straws in the Wind: Reflections towards

Theological Engagement with Theatre Dance', in *Christian Theology and the Transformation of Natural Religion*, ed. C.R. Brewer (2018).

Judith Maltby is Chaplain, Fellow and Dean of Welfare at Corpus Christi College, and Reader in Church History in the University of Oxford. She has written *Prayer Book and People in Elizabethan and Early Stuart England* (1998) and, with Christopher Durston, edited *Religion in Revolutionary England* (2006). She has also published on Rose Macaulay, on the relationship of Anglicanism and literature and on the modern history of the Church of England, particularly in the area of the ordination of women. She is currently researching the twentieth-century American Episcopalian poet and disability activist Vassar Miller.

Jessica Martin is Residentiary Canon for Learning and Outreach at Ely Cathedral. Before moving into full-time ordained ministry she was Fellow and Director of Studies in English Literature at Trinity College, Cambridge. Her publications include *Walton's Lives: Conformist Commemorations and the Rise of Biography* (2001) and *Private and Domestic Devotion in Early Modern England and Scotland* (2012) edited jointly with Alec Ryrie; she has also worked on the early generations of women in higher education and women writers in the nineteenth and early twentieth centuries.

Alison Milbank is Associate Professor of Literature and Theology at the University of Nottingham and an Anglican priest working at Southwell Minster, where she is Canon Theologian. Margaret Oliphant's supernatural fiction featured in her *Dante and the Victorians* (1998) and is also discussed in *God and the Gothic: Romance and Realism in the English Literary Tradition* (Oxford University Press, 2018). Her interest in Anglican women led her to edit a volume of essays on Josephine Butler, and she teaches Jane Austen in the context of virtue ethics.

Charlotte Mitchell is Honorary Senior Lecturer in the English Department at University College London, where she taught for many years. She is editor, with Ellen Jordan and Helen Schinske, of the online *Letters of Charlotte Mary Yonge*, which can be accessed at https://c21ch.newcastle.edu.au/yonge/. Dr Mitchell has published on Yonge and other Victorian novelists, and was a co-editor of the *Oxford Companion to Edwardian Fiction* (1997). Her recent discovery, with Gwendolen Mitchell, of a painting by Joshua Reynolds of Jane Austen's aunt, Philadelphia Hancock, was revealed in the *Times Literary Supplement* in 2017.

Sara L. Pearson is Associate Professor of English Literature at Trinity Western University, Canada. She has an ongoing interest in the classical, biblical and religious influences on English literature, and the fiction, non-fiction and poetry of nineteenth-century Britain, especially the works of

Charlotte Brontë. Most recently she has co-authored *Celebrating Charlotte Brontë: Transforming Life into Literature in* Jane Eyre (2016) with Christine Alexander; previous work on Charlotte Brontë and Anglicanism appears in *Brontë Studies* (2015). Dr Pearson's current research is on Charlotte Brontë's use of classical and biblical allusion in her literary works.

Clemence Schultze taught in the Departments of Classics at Queen's University Belfast and at Durham University. Her specialist interests range from Dionysius of Halicarnassus, Roman republican history, ancient historiography and the material culture of the ancient world to classical reception in nineteenth-century Britain and France. She has published extensively on Charlotte M. Yonge's use of ancient myth and history, is chairman of the Charlotte M. Yonge Fellowship and co-edited *Characters and Scenes: Studies in Charlotte M. Yonge* (2007) with Julia Courtney. She also works on the changing attitudes to Special Providence in Victorian and post-Victorian fiction.

Alison Shell is Professor in the Department of English at University College London. Her work centres on the relationship of English literature and religion from the Reformation to the present day. She has published *Catholicism, Controversy and the English Literary Imagination* (1999), *Catholicism and Oral Culture in Early Modern England* (2007) and *Shakespeare and Religion* (2010); with David Loewenstein, she is currently co-editing a volume of essays for the journal *Reformation* on the topic of the Long Reformation. She has also written on Charlotte Brontë and Charlotte M. Yonge, and contributes to the Church Times and the Times Literary Supplement.

Peter Sherlock is Vice Chancellor of the University of Divinity, Melbourne, and author of *Monuments and Memory in Early Modern England* (2008) and *Practices of Gender in Late Medieval and Early Modern Europe* (2008), co-edited with Megan Cassidy-Welch. He has also published on the role of women in the Anglican Church from the Reformation to the present, especially in the areas of clerical marriage, lay women in church governance and the ordination of women. He is currently completing an analysis of the origins of the theological issues deployed in the modern debate over the ordination of women. In 1994, he briefly met Monica Furlong in Australia.

Francis Spufford teaches on the MA in Creative and Life Writing at Goldsmiths College, University of London, and serves as one of the lay representatives for the diocese of Ely on General Synod. His non-fiction work includes *Red Plenty* (Faber, 2011), which was longlisted for the Orwell Prize, and *Unapologetic* (Faber, 2013), an attempt at an apologetics for post-Christian Britain which was shortlisted for the Michael Ramsey

Prize. His first novel *Golden Hill* (2016) was the Costa First Novel of the Year and is being translated into ten languages; his most recent book is the essay collection *True Stories* (2017).

Jane Williams is Assistant Dean and Lecturer in Systematic Theology at St Mellitus College, of which she is a founder member. She is the author of several books, including *Approaching Christmas* (2005), *Approaching Easter* (2006), *Lectionary Reflections Years A, B & C* (2011), *Faces of Christ* (2011) and most recently *Why Did Jesus Have to Die?* (2016) and the Archbishop of York's Advent book *The Art of Advent* (2018). She and the other founders of St Mellitus College, Bishop Graham Tomlin and Revd Dr Michael Lloyd, appear in a regular theological podcast, Godpod. Her research on Barbara Pym has been particularly inspired by the comedy and community in her novels, and the theological implications of these.

ACKNOWLEDGEMENTS

This book began as a chance conversation some years ago between the two of us at an academic conference in the United States, when we found we had been reading Charlotte M. Yonge (Alison) and Rose Macaulay (Judith) on our transatlantic flights. The idea for a collection of essays exploring a range of authors who shared both a gender and, at the very least, a formative time in the Anglican tradition was hatched. It took us a number of years to return to the idea, but return we did.

We are grateful for the advice we received in the early stages of developing the project from Robin Baird-Smith, Peter Hawkins, Arnold Hunt, Diarmaid MacCulloch, Greg Seach, Francis Spufford and Gill Sutherland, two of whom subsequently contributed to the volume. The readers for Bloomsbury – Matthew Grimley, Charles Hefling, Mark Knight and Emma Mason – gave us an invaluable scholarly steer. Later on, we benefitted from the expertise of Helen King, David Krooks, Kenneth Parker, Marianne Thormählen and Sarah Wootton. We are grateful to our patient editors at Bloomsbury, Anna Turton and Sarah Blake; to Gopinath Anblagan, Vinita Irudayaraj, Seilesh Khumanthem, Angelique Neumann, Integra Software Services-India and all others involved in the book's production; to the organizers and audiences of the various public events and lecture series promoting the book, at Westminster Abbey (2017, 2018), the University Church of St Mary the Virgin, Oxford (2017), and the Bloxham Festival of Faith and Literature (2016); and to our splendid body of contributors, for scholarly insights and practical help going far beyond their original commissions.

Judith wishes to thank Corpus Christi College, Oxford, and the Humanities Division of the University of Oxford for funding a number of visits to archives holding unpublished papers of Rose Macaulay in England and the United States. She is also grateful to Ian Markham and his colleagues at Virginia Theological Seminary (VTS) for an extended visit as 'Dean's Fellow' for writing, which gave her access to a library with extraordinarily rich holdings on the history, culture and theology of Anglicanism. The VTS librarian, Mitzi Budd, and her staff could not have been more welcoming and helpful. This project has also reminded Judith of her debt to the late Dorothy Owen, the formidably learned, yet wonderfully kind, University Archivist of Cambridge who first introduced her to Rose Macaulay, sending her away after a supervision on early modern court records with a well-worn copy of *Letters to a Friend*, sparking a long interest in Macaulay and Macaulay's Anglicanism.

Alison would like to thank her mother, Jean Shell, and her late father, Stephen Shell, for introducing her to so many of the writers in the volume; Arnold Hunt; Giles Mandelbrote; Rupert Shortt; colleagues in the English Department at University College London, especially Juliette Atkinson, Julia Jordan, John Mullan, Charlotte Mitchell, Hugh Stevens and Peter Swaab, and the committee of the Chambers Fund for a grant towards the cost of preparing the index for this volume; contributors to the email list 'History of Women Religious in Britain and Ireland'; the staff of the *Church Times*; The Reverend Prebendary Marjorie Brown, vicar of St Mary's Primrose Hill; the Charlotte M. Yonge Society; the Charlotte M. Yonge Fellowship; the Barbara Pym Society; and Guido Granai, Hilary Morris and the late Henry Harvey for insights into Pym and her circle.

We dedicate this book to dear friends, fellow Anglicans, living and departed.

Judith Maltby
Alison Shell
The Birth of the Blessed Virgin Mary, 2018

ABBREVIATIONS

ODNB   *Oxford Dictionary of National Biography*, online

OED   *Oxford English Dictionary*, online

Unless otherwise indicated, all references to the 1662 Book of Common Prayer have been taken from *The Book of Common Prayer: The Texts of 1549, 1559, and 1662*, ed. Brian Cummings (Oxford: Oxford University Press, 2011). References from the Bible, unless otherwise indicated, have been taken from *The Bible: Authorized King James Version with Apocrypha*, ed. Robert Carroll and Stephen Prickett (Oxford: Oxford University Press, 1997), apart from references to the Psalms, which have been taken from the Book of Common Prayer. Where the wording in a novel differs from these sources, the novelist's words have been retained.

Introduction: Why Anglican; Why Women; Why Novelists?

Judith Maltby and Alison Shell

Admirers and detractors of Anglicanism both agree that it has a remarkable literary heritage. They point to the prose of the King James Bible and the Book of Common Prayer; poets ranging from George Herbert to T.S. Eliot; and novelists such as Anthony Trollope and C.S. Lewis. Women's writing is rarely mentioned. However, looking at the output of the thirteen female novelists covered in this collection of essays, it is hard to see why this is so. All these writers were well known in their time: most for their fiction, a few primarily for their commentary on theological, cultural and ethical issues. Their work varies in literary quality, but includes many books that deserve lifting out of obscurity and many others that have always inspired love and enthusiasm. Anglicans are much given to writing about themselves, but this has seldom been undertaken so entertainingly as within the fiction covered in this book. Our introduction sketches a literary-historical context for this, with a double aim: of identifying family resemblances between our chosen novelists as they reflect on the implications of Anglican belief and practice; and of tracing common themes across the generations. These writers need, above all, to be read in the light of each other. Together with their male counterparts, and those who fall outside the parameters of our study in other ways, they comprise a continuing tradition of the Anglican novel.

* * *

The authors gratefully acknowledge permission to cite works of Rose Macaulay from The Society of Authors as the Literary Representative of the Estate of Rose Macaulay and Durham University Library.

Following the popular and critical success of her last novel, *The Towers of Trebizond* (1956), Rose Macaulay reflected on the problematic place occupied by Anglican writers and intellectuals in post-war Britain, particularly in comparison to their Roman Catholic counterparts. In a letter to her younger friend, the novelist and librettist William Plomer, she complained of the hostile correspondence and reviews she had received from Roman Catholics since the publication of *The Towers of Trebizond*.[1] 'I think they feel it arrogant to exalt the despised ... severed branch of the tree [Anglicanism] into a real Church, with sacraments and grace', she wrote, 'it seems to vex them'. Macaulay conceded that this was not a universal reaction from that constituency to her most Anglican of novels, 'I've had two very nice reviews from [Roman Catholics], though also two fierce ones.' Turning specifically to the problem of exploring Christian confessional identity through fiction, she remarked:

> They can't take Anglican novels as well as we take theirs; Graham Greene and E[velyn] Waugh are admired by us. There is some obscure psychological resistance in this which raises its hackles at the Anglican Church, especially the Anglo-Catholic section of it.

In the world of the British intelligentsia, which she had inhabited so successfully for so long, Macaulay had come to believe that, in the minds of many, the only plausible form of Christianity for an intellectual, writer or artist was Roman Catholicism. She told Plomer that some mutual friends had recently challenged her about her views on the Eucharist: 'She didn't really think she was "eating God"? Did I really? I said I did. They accept Roman Catholicism as a kind of mania that they know & allow for in their friends. But *Anglicanism*; in this apparently sane and civilized friend is more difficult to swallow.'[2]

Macaulay's observations are striking, given that Anglican Christianity has long enjoyed a privileged position among Britain's churches. In the process of drawing together this volume of essays, however, we began to realize that we were challenging some contemporary assumptions not far removed from those observed by Macaulay in the 1950s. The scholarly field is rich in studies of the Catholic novel and the Nonconformist literary tradition, categories familiar as well to readers outside the academy.[3] Nonetheless, in the early stages of this project, we experienced surprise – sometimes bafflement or even hostility – from a few interlocutors. Like Macaulay, we found that 'it seem[ed] to vex' some.

* * *

Macaulay died in 1958, but had she lived into the 1960s and beyond, she would have seen more of the same. Where late twentieth- and early twenty-first-century fiction is concerned, it has sometimes seemed as if only one story can be told about religion, of which Jeanette Winterson's *Oranges Are Not the Only Fruit* (1985) is exemplary. Brought up in a fundamentalist sect, the lesbian heroine of this novel – based on Winterson herself – experiences violent and extreme homophobia and distances herself from her oppressive community and its version of Christianity in her quest for personal integrity. While riffing throughout on St Augustine's *Confessions*, this conversion narrative has the effect of aversion therapy, dissuading its reader from all religious practice. Within mainstream contemporary fiction, it has been too common for religious extremism to stand for all religion; ancient polemical energies have been borrowed from interdenominational and inter-religious conflict to taint all religious belief and practice. Attractive depictions of faith are rare – in part, perhaps, because authors are afraid of being taken for proselytisers. And since contemporary fiction is a lens through which the canon is viewed, this has mattered for our understanding of Britain's literary heritage. Most readers of *Jane Eyre* (1847), the first and best-known novel discussed in this volume of essays, know to condemn the hypocritical Mr Brocklehurst and the fanatical St John Rivers, but need permission to appreciate the saintliness of Helen Burns, the benevolence of Maria Temple and Jane's own devout faith.

We may be moving towards more broad-minded times, though. The Congregationalist Marilynne Robinson's nuanced fictional explorations of mainstream Protestantism in such novels as *Gilead* (2004) have been not only praised but rewarded with an array of literary prizes. As a side effect of the increased public sensitivity to Islamophobia and anti-Semitism in recent years, anti-religious discourse of all kinds has become less acceptable, and even Anglicans now have a greater freedom to challenge discourtesy. Then there is the internet, which – in the field of literature as elsewhere – has facilitated religious encounter. Most of our chosen writers are invisible within university English departments, but they are often read and loved outside them, and thanks to online search engines, the canon is becoming more heterogeneous and democratic than ever before. The body of passionate thinkers whom Virginia Woolf termed 'common readers' can now find each other through blogs and online fora. Out-of-print books are unprecedentedly available, whether through internet sales platforms or downloads. Thanks to digital technology more generally, publishing companies like Persephone Books, Greyladies and Girls Gone By are bringing some of these writers to a new generation, following the example that Virago Press has set from the 1970s. All this is quietly revolutionizing the way that we encounter the past in fiction and giving new purpose to the literary societies which have kept votive candles alight for so many of our writers.[4]

Within the academy too, the editors of this volume are not wholly swimming against the tide. Feminist history and literary criticism have entered the mainstream, and their practitioners – in earlier generations so often hostile to organized religion, or seeing it merely as a way for women to legitimize self-expression – are increasingly willing to acknowledge the diverse world views held by the neglected women they recover. More broadly, departments of religious studies regularly draw on imaginative literature, literary studies have embraced historicization and historians are more at ease with using literature as historical evidence: an interdisciplinarity which can be seen in our contributors' academic backgrounds. Both literature and history have experienced a 'religious turn', and scholarly accounts of how faith shapes ideology and motivation have achieved a new sophistication across the board.[5] Paradoxically, this has been brought about by the secularism so characteristic of the twenty-first-century academy.[6] When teaching the unchurched, and those of other faiths, the imaginative outworkings of Christianity need explaining; thus, they have the potential to become more visible, in relation both to writers long dead and those nearer our own time. What is true of Christianity is true of the Church of England; much literature from the Reformation to the twentieth century, and a surprisingly large amount in the present day, cannot be adequately understood without a working knowledge of Anglican ideas and culture.

* * *

All collections of this kind are acts of exclusion as well as inclusion. To create manageable boundaries – and a book of publishable length – we decided to limit our selection to women writers who were British and deceased. By doing so, significant and popular authors have been excluded, such as the gifted Madeleine L'Engle, an American Episcopalian who died in 2007. Pushing our boundaries beyond England to include the British Isles is a first step towards recognizing that this is not a parochial and Anglocentric field of study. Rather, since modern Anglicanism is a global branch of Christianity – the typical Anglican of today is female, black, African and does not speak English as a first language – we indicate straight away that our book is not canonically definitive.[7] We invite future scholars to extend the reach: geographically and at both ends of the chronological spectrum. Jane Austen was perhaps the greatest Anglican woman novelist of them all, certainly an inspiration to several writers in this volume: many share her intense concentration on practical ethics played out within an Anglican context, with – more often than not – a female protagonist at the heart of the narrative. Had this been a multi-volume project, she and her contemporaries would certainly have gone in. However, she is more peripheral within the historical trajectory that has shaped this particular collection.[8] Charlotte Brontë, the first writer covered below, lived at a time when England was moving away from the world of Austen's Georgian Anglican ascendancy, and when membership of the Church of England was embarking on its transition from a default position to a positive choice. For several centuries, and to varying degrees, parliamentary legislation had penalized Protestant Nonconformists and Roman Catholics in the exercise of their faith, as well as constraining their involvement in civic society. The repeal of the Test and Corporation Acts

(1828) and Catholic Emancipation (1829) began the process of opening up participation in public life for Nonconformists and Roman Catholics – or at least for the male members of those denominations. In this new landscape, the established Church still enjoyed certain privileges but had lost, or was to lose, its exclusive hold on key national and local institutions.[9]

Charlotte Brontë and the second of our chosen novelists, Charlotte Maria Tucker, responded to these changes in different ways in their fiction. For Brontë, realism about the changing religious context for Anglicans needed to be met with renewed pastoral commitment by the clergy; the nostalgic Tucker saw her novelistic mission as warning her readers against the dangers to Christian verities presented by a newly liberated Roman Catholic population, whose attempts to move into the mainstream she saw as papal aggression. As this implies, greater religious toleration and decreasing confessionalization in political, educational and social arenas were liberating for adherents of other Christian denominations.[10] But while religious toleration was increasing in the Victorian era, intellectual and scientific developments were feeding agnosticism and atheism, presenting new challenges for all churches and faith groups. Eastern religions were becoming more visible too, thanks not only to the endeavours of missionaries intending to extirpate them, but to scholarly engagement with the indigenous peoples ruled by the British Empire and to immigrant communities in Britain. It is hard not to see an awareness of world spiritualities behind Evelyn Underhill's remarkable journey from the Order of the Golden Dawn to commemoration in the Church of England lectionary.[11] Turn-of-the-century occultism, for all its elaborate secrecies, had an ecumenical openness in its view of all religions as containing elements of truth and must have contributed to the wider acceptance of Eastern beliefs in the British mainstream.

Underhill's supernatural fiction recalls some of Margaret Oliphant's work – though not all, since Oliphant is the most imaginatively polarized of our chosen writers. Her 'Chronicles of Carlingford' come from a different cosmos, drawing on the Anglican careerist comedy of her contemporary Anthony Trollope's 'Barchester' series. But for religion with the supernatural consciously omitted, it is Barbara Pym, writing many decades later, towards whom one must reach: here, for instance, is Mildred Lathbury, the narrator of *Excellent Women* (1952), hesitating sleepily between the devotional and cookery books on her bedside table: 'My hand might have chosen *Religio Medici*, but I was rather glad that it had picked out *Chinese Cookery*.'[12] Pym's books are more engaged than this might suggest with the ethical demands of professing Christianity – as often with mid-twentieth-century middlebrow novels, frequently written by women, where the Anglican faith shapes a social milieu.[13] Her work – unpublishable in the early 1960s, acclaimed again in the late 1970s, consistently in print thereafter – was critically underrated for the same reasons that it is now so popular: because it was funny, because it gave space to religion and because it focused on women. Increasingly, too, her reception has benefitted from nostalgia for the world she depicts.

Anthropologists are committed to documenting traditional societies in the light of modern pressures, and Pym, as a participant observer, has preserved for all time a disappearing parochial culture.

Pym would have been aware, as the readers of this volume are, that Anglicanism faces many challenges within the country of its inception: ebbing congregations, religious pluralism, many practising Christians' scepticism about the value of denominational allegiance, the ever-increasing respectability of unbelief, and the practical outworkings of secularism.[14] Against this, one must set the facts that Anglicanism remains England's established church to this day, continues to permeate the ethical and cultural landscape of English-speaking countries, and at the time of writing has some 85 million adherents worldwide.[15] But this global presence has brought about diversity and fragmentation, with regard to both faith and literature. It is a long time since Anglicanism has signified a common spiritual and literary inheritance – if, indeed, the two can be distinguished for bookish churchgoers – and since Anglicans, whatever their background, have had a common frame of reference in the various incarnations of the King James Bible and the Book of Common Prayer. P.D. James, the last writer in this volume, deplored this loss of England's literary heritage: one reason why her later work frequently modulates into state-of-the-nation polemic.

Charlotte Maria Tucker's *nom de plume*, 'A Lady of England', could have been borne by more than one of our writers. The Englishness of Anglicanism and how this can be conveyed within fiction are among the thematic continuities in this volume. In this and in other ways, these novelists examine how the Church of England has mattered within the formation of personal identity: for good and ill, for women and men, for adults and children. Brontë's *Jane Eyre* in the nineteenth century and Streatfeild's *A Vicarage Family* over a century later draw elliptically on childhood experience to imagine a spectrum of formative incidents connected to religious belief and practice: some yielding grace, charity and comfort, others chronicling what would now, rightly, be called spiritual abuse. Writing about children is not the same as writing for them, but the two categories overlap to a high degree, and given their role as educators within the home, women have always been strongly represented among children's writers. It is not surprising that the Church of England should so often have pressed them into service in this capacity; Charlotte M. Yonge, writing for the financial benefit of the Church's Anglo-Catholic wing and the moral and spiritual formation of its membership, did much to inaugurate the young adult fiction of our own time.[16] Thus, she can be seen as a distant foremother of a writer like Monica Furlong, whose novel *Wise Child* (1987) is a distinguished example of the genre. Furlong's world view was more eclectic and radical than Yonge's, to put it mildly – the latter might well have been disconcerted by a story of witches, written by an author who led the Movement for the Ordination of Women in the 1980s. Yet both women were dedicated activists for the renewal of the Church of England and shared other preoccupations; Yonge's

Ethel May, as she wrests her vocational urges towards home-making, and Furlong's Juniper, as she initiates Wise Child into ancient traditions of female wisdom, both engage with comings-of-age and the godliness of the everyday.

The latter theme permeates the work of Elizabeth Goudge, whose sense of a world 'charged' – in Gerard Manley Hopkins's phrase – 'with the grandeur of God' comes over as almost hallucinogenic.[17] For Goudge, if you walk with God, he will see to it that you live in glorious Technicolor. But she is a keen casuist, constantly making readers aware of her characters' success or failure in the micro-challenges of everyday life – which is how her novels, like the best movies of her contemporary Walt Disney, manage to avoid sentimentality while still being joyously kitsch. Susan D. Amussen's essay in this volume demonstrates how this moral alertness plays out in relation to the doctrinaire gendered expectations so typical of the post-war era when Goudge was writing. One of Goudge's characters, the Anglican priest John Wentworth in *The Rosemary Tree* (1956), is depicted as suffering from extreme charitable dyspraxia; his right hand never knows what his left hand is doing, which creates endless problems for his household. He is not excused, yet he functions as an ethical touchstone both for the other characters and for the reader. Rendered vulnerable through this holy incompetence, he subverts hierarchies not only of gender but of class – he is the squire as well as the parson – and of the clergy in relation to the laity.

Other novelists in this collection depict women compensating for the failures and shortcomings of men in holy orders: within *Jane Eyre*, for instance, St John Rivers's sisters Diana and Mary smooth over difficulties caused by their rebarbative brother. But Barbara Pym might have argued that a clergyman's personal qualities matter less than the symbolic function he fulfils, as the central figure of the parish. Pym brought her day job at the International African Institute to bear on the Anglican parish, seeing opportunities for anthropological fieldwork in the heart of England. Émile Durkheim, whose thought influenced the anthropological scholarship Pym would have known, saw religion as 'something eminently social', consisting in practice rather more than belief.[18] This makes a lot of sense in relation to Pym's work, where comedy regularly arises out of compulsory social interaction between parishioners individually ill-assorted but representative of the wider community *en masse*. Pym is arguably the most comic and, as mentioned above, the least devotionally engaged of our novelists – but even she can, as Jane Williams's essay describes, be read as having a pastoral message, given that her later novels depict the bleak fates of those who hold themselves aloof from communal interaction.

In Pym's fiction, the spinster devoted to church work – a stock character in any Anglican scenario – occasions a necessarily female, necessarily Anglican take on platonic love.[19] Harriet Bede in *Some Tame Gazelle* (1950) lavishes asexual pampering on a succession of curates – again it is the role, rather than the individual, which matters here – while her sister Belinda yearns after a married archdeacon with what we are meant to recognize as a parody of

Petrarchan desire, so attenuated and sublimated that we never seriously see it as adulterous. Because Anglican clergy are allowed to marry, they can be envisaged as sexual beings. And because Anglo-Catholic clergy come from a tradition where celibacy is highly prized, the bachelors among them give rise to a specifically Anglican kind of amorous suspense – exacerbated, in Pym's *A Glass of Blessings* (1958), when the handsome curate Marius Ransome toys with the idea of going over to Rome. All is resolved when he marries the church-worker Mary Beamish, quintessentially dowdy and eager: seemingly a dream resolution for her, though – as Pym implies – her life after marriage will still remain a round of voluntary church duties.

For Yonge, there could be no more glorious calling for an unmarried woman than this. But even then, what was a vocation for some would have been *faute de mieux* for others, and either way would often have been misogynistically interpreted. The so-called superfluous women of twentieth-century England, where similarly engaged, would have run the gauntlet of popular psychoanalysis as well. Pym, writing after Freud, always has in her sights the idea that an unmarried woman's penchant for priests is not just sad, but sick. Her riposte is to stress the spinster's lack of repression and her imaginative agency: in love, but also in understanding and controlling her environment. Anthropologically attuned to kinship ties, she acknowledges that her unmarried women are outsiders. Yet they see most of the game, even standing in for the author herself – Pym makes a Hitchcockian appearance in more than one of her novels.[20]

Pym's protagonists, like many others in this collection, give us the view from the pew. Fiction written by women engaged with the church, dating from before the period when ordination to the priesthood was an option for women, is almost bound to focus on lay experience. It can also manifest lay freedoms: as Alison Milbank points out, Margaret Oliphant's ghost-story 'The Open Door', which hints that damnation may not be eternal, evokes ideas outside the Victorian Church of England's official parameters.[21] This suggests how, for all the impediments women writers suffered, they – and, for that matter, laymen – must often have been imaginatively aided by not having to think and write as priests. Monica Furlong campaigned for the ordination of women, but her novel *Cousins* (1983), with its explicit depiction of an adulterous relationship where one of the parties is a clergyman, would have been harder to get away with if she herself had been in holy orders – not least because it is based on the premise that the relationship yields spiritual illumination. Adulterous quandaries which foreground a clash between conflicting ethical imperatives crop up regularly in the work of a novelist with whom Furlong has much in common, Iris Murdoch: an expression of how the latter drew on many philosophical sources in her idiosyncratic search for the good.[22]

In practice, if not in theory, most religious denominations have a penumbra where the orthodox rub shoulders with the partially committed, the fellow-travellers, the slightly interested and the eclectic. This is highly enabling in the case of the established Church of England, given its cultural visibility, and also mattered for Murdoch, brought up in the more marginal Church of Ireland.[23] But a position on the margins is a source of pain for the self-excluded: for Laurie, who narrates Macaulay's *The Towers of Trebizond*, her bond to her married lover means estrangement from the church, reflecting Macaulay's own circumstances for many years. As the novel's near-tragic ending shows, the walled city of Trebizond becomes a symbol for this exile:

> Still the towers of Trebizond, the fabled city, shimmer on a far horizon, gated and walled and held in a luminous enchantment. It seems for me, and however much I must stand outside them, this must for ever be. But at the city's heart lie the pattern and the hard core, and these I can never make my own: they are too far outside my range.[24]

Adam Dalgliesh, the policeman who figures in many of P.D. James's detective novels, also haunts the borders.[25] A clergyman's son saturated in Anglicanism, he is an agnostic who experiences frequent promptings towards Anglican belief and practice. Anglicanism makes regular incursions into detective fiction, a genre which has been hospitable towards – even dominated by – female authors. This book includes essays on James and on her precursor Dorothy L. Sayers; Agatha Christie, Margery Allingham and Ngaio Marsh are among the queens of crime who await treatment in this light.[26] The fact that so many Golden Age detective novelists were practising Anglicans is less striking than it would be now – but still, as we have seen Macaulay complaining, men and women of letters seldom self-identified as religious in the mid-twentieth century either. Then, as now, genre fiction often accommodated the residue of religious world views: the idea that a detective, rather than God, can bring about justice at the end of a story can be seen as the culmination of a centuries-long departure from the idea that crimes could be discovered by providential revelation.[27]

But if God was no longer appealed to directly, detectives could be the agent of providence. In G.K. Chesterton's 'Father Brown' stories, written at a period when detective fiction was evolving rapidly, faith is even seen as a necessary condition for rational deduction: characters asserting *bien-pensant* secularism are regularly misled by superstitious trains of thought when they encounter inexplicable events, while the Catholic priest-detective displays exemplary common sense. This is a reassuring vision, perhaps even slightly smug: more so than that found in either Sayers's work, which overlapped chronologically with Chesterton's, or later in James's. Sayers and James regularly bring us up against the problem of undeserved suffering, especially with regard to the damage that compromises all attempts to deliver justice, and they chronicle the effect this has on their neurasthenically sensitive detectives. As Jessica Martin puts it in her essay on Sayers, 'justice, while sought by human beings, is inadequate to its task and has to be established through the intervention of powers somehow beyond human reach'.[28] Can one see Sayers and James, both so well aware of Anglicanism's history, as channelling the Church of England's predestinarian Reformation inheritance, with its emphasis on God's inscrutable power to dispose human affairs as he wishes?

* * *

The novelists featured in this collection demonstrate the range of theologies, convictions and devotional practices that the members of any one denomination can hold, while still being part of the same church. Yet, as the foregoing paragraphs have demonstrated, these writers manifest a strong pull towards particular themes and genres, and show marked family resemblances across generations: one reason why they manifest considerable coherence when looked at as a group. It is all the more remarkable, therefore, that scholars have been slow to recognize this. One reason is that academic studies on 'Church feminism' in the nineteenth- and twentieth-century Church of England have largely concentrated on institutional, rather than literary or intellectual, aspects of the movement. The struggle to expand both the lay and ordained participation of women over two centuries, both in the emerging forms of parochial and synodical government and the authorized ministries of the Church, has been a key concern.[29] For most of the period under consideration, women would not have had equal access to the professions and, in particular, would not have been able to seek ordination as priests. Thus, though women have always been participants in the Church of England, they have – as with other religious traditions – figured less prominently than men in narrative accounts of its history. Indeed, apart from royalty, they have been less well served than in accounts of Nonconformity or Roman Catholicism: the former offering more scope for leadership and preaching, and the latter providing an institutional focus through studies of religious orders and foundations.

The recent five-volume *Oxford History of Anglicanism* is instructive here. Anglican women and questions of gender receive only one bespoke chapter each in the two volumes covering 1829 to 1914 and western Anglicanism from 1910 to the present: they barely feature, unless ruling the country, in the first two volumes examining the periods c.1520–1662 and 1662–1829. The editors of the later volumes, which map onto our own timespan, had the advantage of numerous significant institutional developments in the Church of England, which made it less of a challenge to include women in an Anglican narrative: the re-establishment of the deaconess order and religious sisterhoods, missionary and educational societies, female enfranchisement into new forms of church governance from the local Parish Church Council to the national General Synod and – most recently – the admission of women to the orders of deacon (1987), priest (1994) and bishop (2015).[30] Over the same period, novel-writing – an activity which permitted self-fashioning as a professional – was practised by both women and men on more equal terms than any to be found within the Anglican establishment, and many Anglican women exercised a public voice within and without their church through fiction.[31] But, as a freelance calling, such literary activity is largely invisible within narratives which concentrate on institutional aspects of the church.

This points to a wider issue. Evaluations of fiction, whether by men or women, are almost entirely absent from what one might call 'Anglican confessional scholarship' as well. Novelists sometimes appear, but overwhelmingly it is their non-fiction that is cited or anthologized. For instance, the standard-setting anthology *Love's Redeeming Work*, edited by three distinguished male Anglican bishops and published as recently as 2001, has no recourse to the novel – poetry, yes, but fiction, no. While novelists appear in the anthology (Underhill, Sayers, C.S. Lewis, Charles Williams) only their non-fiction is drawn upon, indicating that the absence may stem from misgivings about the novel form. The episcopal editors inform their readers:

> If the collection seems heavily male and clerical, we can only plead that this reflects the history of the Anglican tradition, certainly until relatively recent times … An anthology published at the end of the present [twenty-first] century would be likely to redress this imbalance.[32]

One of the anthology's editors, the late Geoffrey Rowell, remarks on how often the connection is made between literature and Anglican spirituality, yet he finds this link weaker in the period 1830–2001: it is 'not in many ways as obvious in this later period as in earlier centuries, [although] there are still significant poets and powerful prose writers'.[33] However, it is precisely that period that we draw upon for the subjects of this study, when Anglican women were exercising a public voice in their Church through the novel. Our chosen authors challenge the idea that the dominant Anglican voice is 'heavily male and clerical' – and given the depth of these novelists' engagement with their religious tradition, the editors of this volume concluded that they need not wait until the late twenty-first century to foreground them.[34]

But if the tradition of Anglican women's fiction has been ignored by establishment-focused scholars, it may well have been more effective than official Anglican apologetic in portraying the Church of England to the world outside and has been very visible indeed to novelists who see themselves as part of it.[35] In Pym's *Jane and Prudence* (1953), Jane Cleveland reflects of her existence as a clergyman's wife that 'somehow it hasn't turned out like *The Daisy Chain* or *The Last Chronicle of Barset*'. It is a rueful comment, and – as such – even more ironic than Jane intends; the families depicted in these novels are far from ideal.[36] Linking Yonge and Trollope, its conscious literariness functions on several levels: it reminds us both that Jane was a tutor in English literature before her marriage, and that she herself is

a character in a novel. Again, thinking about her only child Flora, Jane
muses that 'her picture of herself as a clergyman's wife had included a large
Victorian family like those in the novels of Miss Charlotte M. Yonge' (8).[37]
There is a kind of daughterhood in how Pym recalls her predecessor.

* * *

As Pym looked back to Yonge, Anglican novelists of today continue to be
inspired by their literary predecessors, both female and male. Catherine Fox,
for instance, channels Trollope in her 'Lindchester Chronicles'.[38] Another,
Francis Spufford, speculates about future directions for the Anglican novel
in his 'Afterword' for this volume. As he writes, novelists can tap into the
'muddled and complicated soul of a nation', and this has a lot to do with
the intrinsic messiness of the novel-form: multi-voiced, pulling away from
exemplary characterization, deriving narrative interest from imperfect
behaviour.[39] Perhaps it is appropriate that the Church of England, begotten
in scandal, should have been so good at producing writers who can give us
insight into human flaws and limitations; perhaps it is understandable that
this has not been more widely celebrated as a strength. In both their lives and
works, one can often see the novelists in this volume as presenting muddled
and complicated souls for our inspection. In some cases their partisanship
may look dated and their views embarrassing. Nonetheless, they train us
in redemptive compassion, and give us so many ways of explaining what
Anglicanism and Christianity have to offer: to the bemused and dismissive,
and also to the sympathetic. As academics, we have found this project
even more intellectually rewarding than we had imagined at the outset. As
Anglicans, we have come to appreciate what a rich resource these writers are
for understanding, developing and deepening our religious tradition.

FIGURE 1 *Charlotte Brontë.*

1

Charlotte Brontë (1816–55): An Anglican Imagination

Sara L. Pearson

Charlotte Brontë is an Anglican novelist. Although this statement is true, it seems a bold claim in light of the current critical conversation about her works. Discussions of religion in Brontë's fiction tend to focus broadly on 'Christianity'; there is no monograph on Charlotte Brontë's Anglicanism, as there is for her predecessor Jane Austen.[1] There are several insightful considerations of how Brontë's religious faith helped to shape her fictional works;[2] however, there are hardly any investigations of how her participation in the Church of England influenced her fiction. Brontë herself is partly responsible for this state of affairs, since Anglicanism does not feature prominently in three of her four novels: *Shirley* (1849) is the notable exception. Nevertheless, in her fiction she consistently depicts the Church of England as an active and essential influence upon the social and spiritual condition of the country. Two other factors have contributed to the perception that Brontë is not a particularly 'Anglican' author: first, she held theological views that transgressed the boundaries of orthodox Anglicanism, and second, she was frequently critical of the Church of England and its clergy. But as we shall see, in common with a number of the authors explored in this volume of essays, despite divergence from and criticism of the Church, she neither rejected nor repudiated it. She was firmly committed to the reform of an institution about which she cared deeply and passionately throughout her life.

Charlotte Brontë's belief in universal salvation is her best known divergence from orthodox Anglicanism of the nineteenth century. She shared this belief with her sister Anne: that after death, 'even the vilest sinner will eventually, by God's grace, be purified and made fit for Heaven'.[3] With characteristic vigour, Charlotte writes to a friend that she is 'sorry the Clergy do not like the doctrine of Universal Salvation; I think it a great pity for their sakes, but surely they are not so unreasonable as to expect me to deny or suppress what I believe [to be] the truth!'[4] Her statement demonstrates her commitment to the Church and its clergy, even though she regrets they do not hold to the same beliefs as she does. She also indicates that, despite her loyalty to the Church, she felt free to critique the clergy in her letters and fiction. Critics such as John Maynard interpret Brontë's critical stance as virtually constituting a departure from the Church of England, asserting that although Charlotte 'identified [herself] … as [a member] of the Church of England', she and her sisters' energies 'were devoted to a somewhat subversive project – the subversion sometimes acknowledged, sometimes not – of converting that tradition: most often into secular, usually psychological, tropes; but sometimes … into alternative religious energies moving towards pagan, female, or pagan and female new religion'.[5] Although these ideas might apply to Emily Brontë, my argument in this chapter is that Charlotte Brontë did not subvert or convert the traditions of the Church of England into 'alternative religious energies'; rather, she vigorously criticized and sought the reform of an institution she loved, longing for the Church '[to] be purified, her rites reformed, her withered veins [to] swell again with vital sap'.[6] Her love for the church is evident in her response to a review of *Jane Eyre*: 'The notice in "the Church of England Journal" gratified me much, and chiefly because it <u>was</u> the <u>Church</u> of <u>England</u> Journal – Whatever such critics as He of the Mirror may say, I love the Church of England. Her Ministers, indeed I do not regard as infallible personages, I have seen too much of them for that – but to the Establishment, with all her faults – the profane Athanasian Creed <u>ex</u>cluded – I am sincerely attached.'[7]

An Anglican childhood

The foundations for Brontë's Anglicanism were laid in her childhood, and the most significant influence was her father, the Revd Patrick Brontë, an Irishman by birth. While still in his adolescence, Patrick became a school teacher and later a tutor in the family of an evangelical minister in the Church of Ireland, the Revd Thomas Tighe.[8] Tighe recommended to the aspiring young Patrick his own college, St John's College, Cambridge.[9] Patrick eventually attended St John's from 1802 to 1806 as a sizar – a student who was able to participate in common meals and whose fees were reduced, but one who still needed additional financial support. He was fortunate to find such support from several influential figures in evangelical circles: Henry Thornton, William Wilberforce and Henry Martyn, the curate of the prominent clergyman Charles Simeon.[10] For fifty-three years,

Simeon was the influential vicar of Holy Trinity Church, Cambridge, and was a founding member of the Church Missionary Society in 1799.[11] At Cambridge, he 'attracted a large following among "gownsmen" intending to take Holy Orders', and one of those 'gownsmen' was Patrick Brontë, who was ordained to the priesthood in August 1806.[12] After holding several posts as curate and minister, Patrick's longest tenure as a clergyman was as the Perpetual Curate of St Michael and All Angels, Haworth, Yorkshire, where he served from 1820 until his death in 1861.

Before taking up this post in Haworth, Patrick had married Maria Branwell in December 1812. Maria was from Cornwall, a Wesleyan Methodist who had met Patrick while she was visiting her aunt Jane Fennell at Apperley Bridge, near Bradford, when Patrick was serving the parish of Hartshead-cum-Clifton.[13] After their marriage and the birth of two daughters at Hartshead, Maria (1814) and Elizabeth (1815), Patrick accepted another perpetual curacy at Thornton (also in West Yorkshire), where four more Brontë children were born: Charlotte (1816), Patrick Branwell (1817), Emily Jane (1818) and Anne (1820). Soon after moving to Haworth in 1820, their mother Maria died of cancer in September 1821. Maria's sister Elizabeth Branwell was already resident at the Brontës' home in Haworth during Maria's illness, and 'Aunt Branwell' remained in the household to help raise the six children. Like her sister Maria, Elizabeth was also a Wesleyan Methodist.

In 1825, young Maria and Elizabeth Brontë died of tuberculosis contracted while attending the Clergy Daughters' School at Cowan Bridge, Lancashire.[14] The four surviving Brontë children grew up in the Haworth parsonage, just a few short steps from the church. The church building and graveyard comprised their view from the parsonage's front windows; the tolling of the church bells resounded throughout their day and measured their time; the liturgical seasons, the daily services and the prayers of the Book of Common Prayer provided a rhythm and resource for their outer and inner lives. The family gathered for Evening Prayer each day, and the language of the Psalms from the Book of Common Prayer became so familiar to Charlotte that her literary allusions to the Psalms more frequently echo the Prayer Book than the Authorized Version of the Bible.[15] Their lives were thoroughly rooted in the landscape, language and ritual of the Church of England.

Despite having a Methodist mother and aunt, Charlotte seems to have identified most strongly with her father's denominational loyalties and religious views. In their juvenile and mature literary works, Charlotte and all of her siblings enjoyed mocking Dissenters, and the particular dissenting sect of Methodists was certainly not exempt from ridicule. For example, in *Villette* (1853) Brontë describes the child Paulina Home 'praying like some Catholic or Methodist enthusiast – some precocious fanatic or untimely saint'.[16] The Brontë siblings were also extremely critical of the followers of the Oxford Movement (which began in the 1830s), also called 'Puseyites', a term the Brontës used in a derogatory fashion. Charlotte Brontë opens her novel *Shirley* by sarcastically describing the 'present successors of the apostles, disciples of Dr. Pusey and tools of the Propaganda, [who] were at that time [1811–12] being hatched under cradle-blankets, or undergoing regeneration by nursery-baptism in wash-hand-basins'.[17] Though they were clearly not 'High Church', the Brontës cannot easily be characterized as 'Low Church' or (anachronistically) as 'Broad Church'. Instead of attempting to fit the Brontë sisters into one or more of these categories, Marianne Thormählen argues that what best describes their religious outlook is simply their intrepid search for truth.[18] They were not monolithic in their beliefs: their views on religion were far from simplistic, and they demonstrate a complexity of thought that precludes definitive pronouncements about their opinions.[19]

Charlotte's attitude to Catholicism is a case in point. The Roman Catholic Relief Act (1829), also known as Catholic Emancipation, allowed Roman Catholic men to hold public office, to participate in the militia or to attend university in England. It followed the repeal of the Test and Corporation Acts in 1828 which gave the same liberties to Protestant Nonconformists. Charlotte was thirteen years old in 1829, and Catholic Emancipation was such a significant event in her family that she writes a semi-fictionalized account of it in her 'Tales of the Islanders' (October 1829):

> I remember the day when the *Intelligence Extraordinary* came with Mr Peel's speech in it, containing the terms on which the Catholics were to be let in. With what eagerness Papa tore off the cover, and how we all gathered round him, and with what breathless anxiety we listened, as one by one they were disclosed and explained and argued upon so ably and so well and, then, when it was all out, how Aunt said she thought it was excellent and that the Catholics [could] do no harm with such good security.[20]

The entire Brontë household was strongly in favour of Catholic Emancipation, though mainly because it was seen as a 'security' against 'harm', as Charlotte's Aunt Elizabeth Branwell had stated. Before the event, Patrick Brontë had written three letters to the *Leeds Intelligencer* advocating emancipation, mainly as 'an antidote to the sort of extremism, embodied in the Roman Catholic Association, which could only lead to popular violence', according to Juliet Barker.[21] Patrick believed 'that Catholics, like Dissenters, should have civil rights', provided those rights did not interfere with the Established Church.[22] Charlotte's fiction reveals a similar mixture of tolerance and suspicion, attraction and repulsion, to Roman Catholicism.

Charlotte Brontë's four novels demonstrate that she constructed religious faith in ways that were appropriate to the different cultural settings she envisioned. The first novel she wrote, *The Professor*, was completed in 1846 but published posthumously in 1857. After the publication of *Jane Eyre* in 1847 came *Shirley* (1849) and *Villette* (1853). Both *The Professor* and *Villette* depict an English Protestant protagonist in a (frequently hostile) continental Catholic setting, drawing on Charlotte's own experience as a student at the Pensionnat Heger in Brussels, Belgium, from 1842 to 1843, a time when she felt isolated and ostracized as a Protestant living among Roman Catholics.[23] In these two Belgian novels, true Englishness is defined as being Protestant and not Catholic. However, in the two novels set in England, *Jane Eyre* and *Shirley*, to be English is to belong specifically to the Church of England, rather than being a Protestant of some other denomination. These two novels thus provide the best insight into Charlotte Brontë as an Anglican novelist.

The Church of England in *Jane Eyre*

Perhaps more than most other authors in her time, Charlotte Brontë drew on her life experience to create her fictional worlds, asserting that 'not one feeling, on any subject – public or private, will I ever affect that I do not really experience'.[24] In *Jane Eyre*, Brontë draws upon the setting and backdrop of her own life narrative as a Church of England clergyman's daughter in order to create what she considered a realistic setting for her fictional characters. Without being explicitly didactic, Brontë also employs the novel to explore the limited options for women's lives within the Church of England, to critique certain aspects of Anglican theology and practice and to illustrate how devout and capable women are able to ameliorate the shortcomings of male clergy.

Charlotte Brontë's Anglicanism not only infused her imagination but also contributed significantly to how she set about creating an air of realism in *Jane Eyre*. Much of its Anglican flavour is implicit simply because Brontë assumes that the Church of England is part of her readers' world, a fact of their everyday life. So, for example, she does not define the various church architectural terms she uses, such as 'vault', 'chancel', 'vestry' and 'communion rails': she simply assumes that these terms are common knowledge.[25] However, her daily experience of life in a clergyman's household led her to provide a superabundance of accurate details in her depiction of ecclesiastical scenes. For example, just as Jane Eyre never moves from one place to another without mentioning her trunk being packed and transported, all three wedding scenes in the novel mention the presence of the parish clerk as well as the officiating clergyman. I would imagine that most readers (and authors, too) would not consider a wedding scene deficient if the clerk were not mentioned. But in Brontë's novel, the clerk is always present, because his role was to assist the minister in the performance of his liturgical duties.[26] Even in the game of charades during Mr Rochester's house party, during the mock ceremony marrying Blanche Ingram and Mr Rochester we see 'the bulky figure of Sir George Lynn ...

enveloped in a white sheet: before him, on a table, lay open a large book; and at his side stood Amy Eshton, draped in Mr. Rochester's cloak, and holding a book in her hand' (182). Sir George Lynn is clearly the priest in his white surplice; Amy Eshton, whose office is not explained, must be the clerk. One wonders if Patrick Brontë had experienced trouble on more than one wedding occasion because of an absent clerk.[27]

Just as Jane Austen, another clergyman's daughter, playfully created fictional entries at the front of the marriage register at Steventon (she announced the banns of marriage between herself and three different suitors, Frederick Howard Fitzwilliam of London, Edmund Arthur William Mortimer of Liverpool and Jack Smith, no location) so Charlotte Brontë must have been tempted to answer the question she asks in *Jane Eyre*, when the priest pauses after asking if either party knows of 'any impediment why ye may not lawfully be joined together'.[28] In *Jane Eyre*, Jane muses, 'When is the pause after that sentence ever broken by reply? Not, perhaps, once in a hundred years' (288).[29] One can picture the young Charlotte letting her imagination run free while sitting through a Prayer Book wedding service, visualizing what it would be like to have that pause 'broken by reply'. In *Jane Eyre*, Brontë famously breaks the pause, in which an impediment to Mr Rochester's marriage is declared: he has a 'wife now living' (289). In creating this scene, it appears that Brontë used her remarkably acute memory when writing the words of the marriage service, since there are only minor differences in spelling, punctuation, capitalization and, in one case, a slightly different word order ('lawfully be joined' rather than 'be lawfully joined') between Brontë's final manuscript copy given to the printers and 'The Form of Solemnization of Matrimony' in the Book of Common Prayer.[30] Not only is she intimately familiar with the words spoken during the service, but also with the rubrics, or 'stage directions', prescribed in the Book of Common Prayer. These directions mandate that the clergyman must have the person declaring the impediment 'prove his allegation' and 'the solemnization must be deferred, until such time as the truth be tried'.[31] In *Jane Eyre*, the clergyman Mr Wood follows these instructions precisely, declaring, 'I cannot proceed without some investigation into what has been asserted, and evidence of its truth or falsehood' (289). Brontë's familiarity with the Book of Common Prayer clearly influenced, and perhaps even inspired, her depiction of the fateful marriage service and Mr Rochester's failed attempt at bigamy.

The Book of Common Prayer haunts the pages of *Jane Eyre* in other ways, important not only for its contents, but also as a physical object. Brontë would have used the Book of Common Prayer daily through its set service of Morning and Evening Prayer. Charlotte, Emily and Anne had their own personal copies, Charlotte's being the gift of the Reverend William Morgan of Bradford in 1831.[32] In Brontë's fiction, the Book of Common Prayer serves as an archetypal 'book': it is a touchstone that defines what a book is. Jane Eyre learns Maria Temple's name because it is 'written in a prayer-book entrusted to [her] to carry to church' (47). The word 'entrusted' indicates the book's value, but also communicates Miss Temple's esteem for Jane. Later on, the gypsy (Mr Rochester in disguise) 'seemed [to be] reading in a little black book, like a prayer-book, by the light of the blaze' (195), the simile suggesting that the gypsy, just like the 'little black book', might not be what she appears. When Jane returns to the household of her dying aunt, she observes her cousin Eliza Reed studying a 'little book, which [Jane finds], on inspection, was a Common Prayer Book' (234). Eliza is particularly attracted by the Prayer Book's rubrics, or rules and directions that accompany the words of the liturgical services.³³ The Prayer Book in Brontë's fiction thus serves different purposes in different contexts: as a symbol of trust, of deceit, of religious legalism. Not only the text of the book but the physical book itself lends a sense of realism to Brontë's imaginative world.

Brontë's reliance on her Anglican experience also contributed to her depiction of a clerical network that provides knowledge and assistance across parish boundaries. For example, when Jane describes Lowood Orphan Asylum and asks the question, 'you will have heard of it, Mr. Rivers?' we are not meant to be surprised when St John Rivers responds that he has 'heard of Mr. Brocklehurst' and has seen Lowood School (347). St John later appeals to the existence of this clerical network in order to dissemble about how he knew that Jane was John Eyre's missing heir: 'Oh! I am a clergyman … and the clergy are often appealed to about odd matters' (383). Brontë would have been aware of her own father's numerous letters to other clergymen and to the newspapers, and of his active involvement in the wider Church of England beyond his parish. Though Jane's discovery that the Rivers family are her cousins does qualify as a coincidence of Dickensian proportions, St John's clerical knowledge would not be anything out of the ordinary in Brontë's actual experience, or in the realistic world she portrays in her fiction.³⁴

The fact that after her impoverished wandering Jane takes up residence in a clergyman's household seems natural as well. For centuries, parish priests had a key role in the distribution of local charity and the administration of poor relief – the conscientious and dedicated clergy often going beyond what was required of them by law.³⁵ The clergy provided help to the unfortunate – the homeless, the destitute, those reduced to extreme poverty. When Jane's flight from Thornfield places her precisely in those circumstances, she asks for charity from a number of sources before recalling that she could seek help from the clergy: 'I remembered that strangers who arrive at a place where they have no friends, and who want employment, sometimes apply to the clergyman for introduction and aid. It is the clergyman's function to help – at least with advice – those who wished to help themselves' (327). Again, Charlotte drew on her own experience of parsonage life, where strangers could arrive at the door with various needs and requests.³⁶ Jane knows where to go for help, and she ends up in a household that was not unlike Brontë's own.

In *Jane Eyre*, references to the Church of England provide Brontë with a way to inject realism into her novels, but they also offer a means of critiquing, sometimes explicitly though often implicitly, the Church's practices and its authorized ministers. I will reiterate here that Brontë criticizes failures and abuses in the Church because she desires its reform, not its abolition. One area of implicit critique is the low esteem given to female missionaries. St John Rivers's marriage proposal to Jane, in which he declares, 'God and nature intended you for a missionary's wife ... you are formed for labour, not for love' (402), encourages readers to focus on St John's complete misreading of Jane's character and his attempt to control and dominate her life. However, the view of St John as a cold, controlling character obscures other important aspects of his relationship to Jane. For example, readers might not notice that St John treats Jane as an intellectual and spiritual equal. While training her for missionary work in India, he teaches Jane 'Hindostanee' (397). Not only that, but Jane masters the language! St John views Jane as a missionary with capabilities equal to his. Furthermore, Jane never denigrates the missionary enterprise, nor does she reject a missionary life for herself. At one point she muses, 'Is not the occupation [St John] now offers me truly the most glorious man can adopt or God assign?' (404). Even after Jane hears Mr Rochester's mysterious calling of her name across the miles, she still intends to leave England for the mission fields of India after one final visit to Thornfield. She arranges her room in Moor House for 'a brief absence' (420) and says she has 'some to see and ask after in England, before I depart for ever' (421). To 'depart for ever' suggests she plans to travel to India and end her days there. For Jane, the crux of the problem is not the idea of missionary work; it is the fact that her sex and marital status hinder her from serving as an independent missionary.

Brontë accurately reflects the situation for Anglican women missionaries at the time: the Christian Missionary Society 'did not encourage applications from single women' and although

> the society's printed register of missionaries contains a list of female missionaries from as early as 1820 ... many of these women were sisters or widows of male missionaries who were 'taken up' by the CMS after the death ... of their brother or husband and allowed to remain in the field; others had been recruited as assistants to missionary wives to help them in their work with women and girls.[37]

One of Brontë's implicit critiques of the Church of England is that, although women possessed the intelligence, ability and willingness to serve as missionaries, they could not serve independently from men: they had to be sisters, wives or an assistant to another female. The Christian Missionary Society 'did not count missionary wives as missionaries in their own right',[38] so even if Jane had married St John, she would not have been recognized as a missionary. St John observes that Jane's new fortune makes her 'independent of the Society's aid' (413), implying that obtaining financial support from the Society as a single woman would have been difficult, if not impossible. But even though Jane has the financial resources to be a missionary, St John says that 'while in town, [he will] speak to a married missionary, whose wife needs a coadjutor' (413). Money is not enough – an unmarried woman needed to have a respectable connection with another missionary in order to serve.

While Brontë implicitly criticizes the idea that unmarried women were not allowed to serve effectively as missionaries, she also questions the conventional morality that insists that Jane could only be St John's 'female curate' (413) if she were his sister or his wife. St John asks, 'How can I, a man not yet thirty, take out with me to India a girl of nineteen, unless she be married to me? How can we be for ever together ... and unwed?' Jane replies rather tartly, 'Very well ... under the circumstances, quite as well as if I were either your real sister; or a man and a clergyman, like yourself' (408). St John's argument is that everyone will suspect an immoral relationship if they are not married; Jane's argument is that they would be in an immoral relationship if they were married but not in love. She believes that if, as St John asserts, she is 'formed for labour – not for love' then 'it follows that [she is] not formed for marriage' (416). From Jane's perspective, to force marriage onto a woman for the sake of propriety is more immoral than allowing her to travel as a 'curate' (413) or 'deacon' (415) to assist a male missionary. Ironically, even though Jane is earnestly seeking God's will and trying to make moral choices, she is thwarted by the barriers that social convention, the Church Missionary Society and the Anglican priest St John Rivers put in her way.

Brontë not only critiques the Church's practices, particularly with respect to missionary work, but also criticizes the clergy. Mr Brocklehurst is a full-blown hypocrite; St John Rivers is a more complex character, partially unaware that his religious vocation serves mainly to satisfy his essentially unspiritual sense of personal ambition. Mr Brocklehurst and St John Rivers are both theologically conventional clergymen of the period, espousing Calvinistic doctrines easily recognizable to Brontë's early readers: they preach judgement, condemnation and eternal torment for sinners predestined by God to suffer in this way. Brocklehurst denounces Jane in front of the school as 'a marked character', rhetorically questioning, 'Who would think that the Evil One had already found a servant and agent in her?' (66). When Jane first hears St John Rivers preach, 'stern allusions to Calvinistic doctrines – election, predestination, reprobation – were frequent; and each reference to these points sounded like a sentence pronounced for doom' (352). Yet the failings of these men are usually redressed or ameliorated through the quiet, behind-the-scenes actions of Anglican women.

While she is at Lowood School, Jane finds her antidote to Brocklehurst's toxic theology in Helen Burns, who teaches Jane her 'creed[,] which no one ever taught' her: that everyone will ultimately be redeemed by the Maker

(59). Furthermore, Mr Brocklehurst's ironic failure to provide true charity in what he describes as 'an evangelical, charitable establishment' (63) is remedied by Miss Temple, who provides a lunch of bread and cheese for the starving students after the school serves them an inedible meal (48). After inviting Helen and Jane to her room in the evening, Miss Temple again creates bounty from scarcity – the housekeeper Mrs Harden refuses to provide more bread and butter for evening tea, but Miss Temple notes, 'Fortunately, I have it in my power to supply deficiencies for this once', as she reveals a 'good-sized seed-cake' (72). This shared meal is reminiscent of Holy Communion, and it constitutes a type of 'Last Supper' before Helen's health begins its fatal decline, evoking an image of the 'passion' that the Christ-like Helen undergoes.[39]

Similarly, St John Rivers's less obvious but still real failure to provide true charity is rectified by his sisters Diana and Mary, who care for Jane out of a sense of genuine compassion. Jane herself remarks on the difference, contrasting Diana and Mary's 'spontaneous, genuine, genial compassion' with St John's 'evangelical charity' (348). St John is quick to notice Jane's precise verbal distinction and says that he is 'quite sensible of the distinction drawn, nor do I resent it – it is just' (348). Brontë thus suggests that through their genuine compassion for others, whether in the untaught creed of universal salvation or in the charitable care for others motivated by love rather than by duty, women help to compensate for the shortcomings of the male clergy, providing a truer model of Christian ministry. It is interesting that two of these Anglican women end up marrying clergymen whom Brontë depicts as slightly inferior to these excellent women. Miss Temple marries and moves away with her husband, 'a clergyman, an excellent man, almost worthy of such a wife' (84), in Jane's estimation. Brontë employs similar language for Mary Rivers's husband, a cleric who 'from his attainments and principles, [is] worthy of the connexion' (452). One feels that even though these men are ordained ministers and priests, they are not by any means superior to their wives, who demonstrate quiet, genuine and exemplary Christian virtues.

An Anglican novel: *Shirley*

Charlotte Brontë followed up the success of *Jane Eyre* with *Shirley*, published in 1849. In response to criticism 'that *Jane Eyre* had been too sensational and melodramatic', Brontë chose to write a historical, 'condition of England' novel set in 1811–12, during the Napoleonic Wars and the Luddite riots.[40] She would have known of the Luddite uprisings from her father's memories of that time, while he was a curate at Hartshead, and also 'from her teacher Margaret Wooler, whose Roe Head school at Mirfield was situated in the heart of the wool-manufacturing district affected by the industrial disturbances'.[41] Brontë also conducted her own historical research by reading the *Leeds Mercury* from 1812 to 1814.[42] The industrial strand of the novel follows the fortunes of Robert Moore, a half-Belgian mill-owner whose purchase of new machinery is perceived as responsible for causing increased unemployment among mill-workers in the village of Briarfield. But the novel is not really about industrialization, though it has been read as an industrial novel.[43] In fact, *Shirley* has defied easy categorization: 'history, politics, religion, business, and romance are drawn together into an … uneasy alliance'.[44] Critics view the novel as lacking unity because of this multiplicity of themes. One of the earliest reviews was written by George Henry Lewes (common-law husband of the novelist George Eliot), who describes *Shirley* as 'a portfolio of random sketches for one or more pictures'.[45] When read as a political, industrial or feminist novel, *Shirley* does indeed provide a challenge to anyone looking for a clear explication of these topics. However, when *Shirley* is read as a novel about the Church of England – its central role in society, its shortcomings, its urgent need for reform – the novel's plot becomes more coherent. *Shirley* is quintessentially an Anglican novel.[46]

In the novels of Jane Austen, we find a world in which Anglicanism is normative, the 'default position', as argued in the Introduction to this volume. Charlotte Brontë's Church of England was struggling to understand its changed place in the country's religious economy. Austen's Church had also faced competition from Dissenters and Roman Catholicism. However, in Austen's time all non-Anglican Christians in England operated under an extensive system of legal penalties and exclusions. Although Brontë's Church of England still enjoyed the privileges of establishment, following the repeal of the Test and Corporation Acts and Catholic Emancipation, Christians of other churches were increasingly being freed from legal penalties and exclusion for their non-Anglicanism. In *Shirley*, Brontë displays a passionate concern that the Church of England maintain its status not only as England's established church, but as its truly national church, serving the entire nation. It was an institution that could no longer rely on its privileged past. The Church of England was in desperate need of reform if it were to remain beneficial and central to the lives of English men and women.

By setting the novel in 1811–12, Brontë uses the past to examine how the church has arrived at its precarious state in the present.[47] She aims her main criticism at the clergy, curates and rectors alike. The three curates in the novel, Mr Donne, Mr Malone and Mr Sweeting, prefer to visit each other in order to eat, drink and argue about 'minute points of ecclesiastical discipline' (8), rather than to invest themselves 'in a diligent superintendence of the schools, and in frequent visits to the sick of their respective parishes' (6). In the novel's opening scene, they are dining at Mrs Gale's, landlady of Mr Donne. Mr Gale allows the curates to revel unhindered: he 'had been a churchwarden, and was indulgent to the clergy' (11). Brontë suggests, here and elsewhere in the novel, that this type of indulgence has led to complacency, which has in turn led to clergy 'too often perform[ing] the holy service of our church to bare walls, and read[ing a] bit of a dry discourse to the clerk, and the organist, and the beadle' (13), according to the rector of Briarfield, Mr Helstone. Helstone contrasts the curates' ineffectiveness with the Dissenters' success: Supplehough, a Baptist who has 'dipped sixteen adult converts in a day', and Barraclough, a Methodist tailor who attracts the 'weaver-girls' with his oratorical skills (12).

Shirley depicts Brontë's fears for what England would become if the Church of England disappeared. To leave England to the Dissenters would be disastrous, since they are the source of all political and social disruption – at least in the fictional world Brontë constructs. The Methodist Moses Barraclough is responsible for the initial act of sabotaging Robert Moore's equipment; Mike Hartley, 'the Antinomian weaver' (14), makes an attempt on Moore's life. Brontë implies that England will only be strong and healthy if the Church of England is likewise flourishing. At the heart of the novel (and literally at the centre of the book) the narrator cries, 'Let England's priests have their due: they are a faulty set in some respects, being only of common flesh and blood, like us all; but the land would be badly off without them: Britain would miss her church, if that church fell. God save it! God also reform it!' (254). This longing for the Church of England's preservation and reformation echoes throughout the novel, offering both criticism and praise of the Church's pervasive influence on the lives of those in its parishes.

A mock battle that occurs between the Church of England and the Dissenters in *Shirley* illustrates the close relationship of church and nation. The rectors, curates, Sunday School teachers (who are all women) and Sunday School children of three parishes are assembled into a Whitsuntide procession of 'twelve hundred children, and one hundred and forty adults' (254). Revd Helstone decides to take the parade on a shortcut through Royd-lane, only to be confronted by 'an opposition procession' of 'Dissenting and Methodist schools, the Baptists, Independents, and Wesleyans, joined in unholy alliance' (255–6). As the two lines approach one another, the Church of England procession sings 'Rule, Britannia', while the Dissenters strike up 'the most dolorous of canticles'. England's church emerges triumphant, holding their ground as they march, forcing the opposition to give way; in the comic conclusion, 'the fat Dissenter who had given out the hymn' is 'left sitting in the ditch' (256–7). Brontë thus depicts England and its Church as inseparable, ultimately triumphant over the disruptive forces of the Dissenting sects.

In *Shirley*, Brontë critiques the shortcomings of the Established Church and its clergy while continuing to assert that the Church is vital and integral to England's religious, social and political life. In seeking to write a novel that reflected the truth of her own experience, Charlotte created an intimate exploration of the lives of characters and communities whose very existence is interwoven with that of the Church of England, even to the extent of their time being measured by the church clock.[48]

Conclusion: An Anglican novelist

Brontë's own life was firmly rooted in the Church of England, and in *Jane Eyre* and *Shirley* her imagination, infused by her experience, created an unflinchingly honest but loving portrait of England as inextricably bound to 'her church' (*Shirley*, 254). In writing these novels of social realism, Brontë drew on the reality of the Anglican Church's physical and spiritual presence in England in order to create a fictional world that seemed 'real, cool, and solid' (5). In Brontë's novels, the Church of England is a comforting presence, embodying stability and order in the midst of sometimes chaotic circumstances. However, Brontë's goal of producing a novel of social realism meant that she portrayed the Church as it was in real life: neither perfect nor ideal, but an institution in constant need of reform and renewal. In the imaginative world of Charlotte's fiction, the seeds of reform are often sown by female characters; in the real world, Charlotte Brontë was an Anglican woman novelist who participated in and contributed to the ongoing conversation about the Church of England's past, present and future.

FIGURE 2 *Charlotte Maria Tucker, 'A Lady of England'.*

2

Charlotte Maria Tucker, 'A.L.O.E.' (1821–93): Anglican Evangelicalism and National Identity

Nancy Jiwon Cho

As her memorable *nom de plume* A.L.O.E. testifies, Charlotte Maria Tucker – one of the most prolific writers of juvenile fiction during the latter half of the nineteenth century – self-fashioned her authorial identity as 'A Lady of England'. Promoting a high-minded vision of Englishness conflated with incorruptible Christian faith, her writings became sanctioned reading in Victorian middle-class homes and Anglican schools.[1] Scholars of children's literature have estimated her prodigious literary output as around 150 titles of moral novels, tales and poetry; the exact figure is unknown because, as Kimberley Reynolds explains, 'her stories frequently appeared first in magazines and were subsequently collected to make Sunday school

This work was supported by a Seoul National University Research Grant. An earlier version of some of the material from this chapter can be found in 'Female Biblical Engagement in Charlotte Maria Tucker ("A.L.O.E.")'s *Pictures of St. Peter in an English Home* (1887)', published in *Literature and Religion* [the journal of the Korean Society for Literature and Religion], 23:2 (2018): 111–36; the author is grateful to the journal's editorial board for permission to include this material.

prizes and other books'.[2] As rewards, prizes and charitable gifts, these works were broadly distributed; for instance, 'very large numbers of these books found their way into the homes of working-class families – homes where other books were often a rarity'.[3]

Tucker was one of the most widely circulated authors of juvenile fiction in the Victorian era, and the impact of her art on the genre must have been substantial. Indeed, she has been deemed a 'forerunner' of Victorian children's didactic fantasies such as Charles Kingsley's *Water Babies* (1863) and George Macdonald's fantasy literature, and her mode of the Victorian moral tale has been considered a formative influence upon E. Nesbit's imagination.[4] Yet she remains an under-researched cultural figure. Her disappearance from literary history may be partially explained by Trisha Tucker's observation that 'twentieth-century literary scholarship has ensured that the most famous Evangelical characters from nineteenth-century literature are Mr. Brocklehurst, Nicholas Bulstrode, Obadiah Slope, Mrs. Jellyby, and Mr. Chadband, rather than any Evangelical characters created by actual Evangelicals'.[5]

Although Tucker's reputation has suffered because twentieth-century readers found her overtly didactic religious stories unpalatable, the ambitious range of Tucker's religious projects has started to be acknowledged in the present century. For instance, her writings about Hebrew women from the scriptures have been viewed as examples of nineteenth-century women's exegesis of the Old Testament.[6] At the same time, there has also been recognition among scholars that children's novels – so often treated as 'entirely distinct from other fiction of the period' – participated in many of the same discourses as works for adults, frequently in transgressive ways.[7] This chapter demonstrates that Tucker's writing resonated beyond children's literature. Specifically, as an Evangelical committed to the Protestant identity of England, she used children's fiction to participate in the larger ecclesiological campaign of nineteenth-century Anglican Evangelicals to uphold the Protestant identity of England and its established Church in the face of Roman Catholic emancipation and revival.

The desire for useful ministry

Although Tucker wrote poetry, family magazines and plays in her youth, she did not embark on a professional literary career until after the age of 30. Her father, Henry St George Tucker – a self-made man who rose to the position of Chairman of the East India Company – disapproved of employment for genteel women; because of this, she only wrote privately during his lifetime. After his death in 1851, however, she began writing for the expansion of God's kingdom. Having undergone an Evangelical conversion around 1848, she was driven by an 'anxious desire to add my mite to the Treasury of useful literature'.[8] As Ian Bradley has explained, 'That they [might] be privileged to live useful lives was the most sincere prayer of all Evangelicals'.[9] At a time when women's official roles within the Church were limited, religious writing for children was acceptably within their province. Earlier Christian women writers, including Hannah More and Mary Martha Sherwood, had developed a tradition of using children's literature as 'a calculated part of the Evangelical determination to reform and convert the nation and eventually the world'.[10] As Tucker explained in a submission letter to a publisher: 'My position in life renders me independent of any exertions of my own; I pray but for God's blessing upon my attempts to instruct His lambs in the things which concern their everlasting welfare.'[11]

In her undertaking to proliferate Evangelical faith, Tucker experimented with a profusion of fictional styles throughout her productive publishing career, which exceeded four decades. The mode she returned to most consistently was allegory, drawing from the heroic model of the Protestant literary lion John Bunyan; her works utilizing this genre include *The Giant Killer: or the Battle That We Must Fight* (1856), *The Young Pilgrim* (1857) and *The City of No-Cross* (1872). However, she also experimented with animal adventures (*The Rambles of a Rat* (1857)); the it-narrative (*The Story of a Needle* (1858)); biblical history (*Exiles in Babylon* (1864)); religious history (*The Life of Luther* (1873)); historical fiction (*The Blacksmith of Boniface Lane* (1890)); scientific fairy tales (*Fairy Know-a-bit* (1865)) and Indian tales (*A Wreath of Indian Stories* (1879)). In all these works, Tucker sought to mould her young readers' malleable minds with gospel truths and values.

As an Anglican Evangelical, Tucker particularly sought to instruct English children about Protestant beliefs (such as the supreme authority of the Bible and salvation by faith) and practices (such as vernacular prayer in direct relationship with God, and hard work demonstrative of the Protestant work ethic). In Tucker's view, English moral strength was a fruit of faith and divine grace, not a virtue intrinsic to national character or ethnicity. A.L.O.E.'s consistent message to her readers was that the key to personal improvement and national progress was Evangelical religion with its Reformation emphases. In her aim to advance the Protestant cause, she sought to dismantle Catholic beliefs and practices, affirmed the Protestant identity of the *ecclesia anglicana,* and asserted that English industrial success and international prowess were outcomes of Protestant faith.

Nineteenth-century contests for the Church of England's identity

Tucker's Evangelical mission to uphold Protestantism must be understood within the context of nineteenth-century disagreements within the Church of England on how to define its true identity. Between the origins of Evangelicalism in the middle of the eighteenth century and the 1850s when Tucker began her publishing career, Evangelicals had become a powerful and politically active demographic group in Britain.[12] However, by the mid-nineteenth century, Anglican Evangelicalism was being challenged both within and outside the Church of England. Prior to the rise of the Oxford Movement, the Church of England had been broadly understood as 'a reformed church, confessing with all the Reformers the supreme authority of Scripture, justification by faith, the legitimate role of the laity (embodied in the sovereign and parliament) in the government of the church, and a particular national and regional identity'.[13] However, from 1833, the Tractarians proposed an alternative version of the Church of England's identity, which stressed its Catholic heritage and character; in a series of ninety 'Tracts for the Times' published over a period of eight years, they asked questions such as: 'How were the "golden ages" of the early Church fathers and seventeenth-century Anglican theology to be recovered?'[14] This disagreement about the nature of the Church of England resulted in polarization and contest between church parties.

Also at this time, English Protestants perceived the growing toleration of Roman Catholicism as geo-politically dangerous. As the Elizabethan Act of Supremacy of 1559 had required renunciation of allegiance to the sovereign power of the Pope, to be Roman Catholic had effectively been treasonous, even if the law was spasmodically enforced. To the dismay of Evangelicals, Catholic Emancipation in 1829 allowed Roman Catholics to begin the process of joining English mainstream social and political life, as the repeal of the Test and Corporation Acts had done for Protestant Nonconformists the year before. In 1850, Evangelicals were further angered by the re-establishment of the Roman Catholic hierarchy in England – the distribution of territorial titles to bishops was particularly viewed as an act of papal aggression. This anti-Catholic anxiety was national; as Linda Colley has remarked: 'The absolute centrality of Protestantism to the British experience ... is so obvious that it has often been passed over ... Catholics as a category remained in popular mythology an omnipresent menace.'[15]

Although, as Margaret Nancy Cutt has noted, the 'Tracts for the Times' were written for adults, 'they aroused a furore which was reflected in children's books for the rest of the century'.[16] Tucker's works fervently challenged Catholicism in both its Anglican and Roman forms.[17] Her Evangelical religion is characterized by a privileging of the authority of the vernacular Bible; a belief in the justification of faith rather than works; the importance of a personal and direct relationship with God developed through prayer; and a commitment to bringing non-Evangelicals to a new spiritual and moral life through conversion. Tucker highlights these core characteristics constantly in her fiction. As this chapter will demonstrate, her anti-Catholic strategies include promoting indigenous Protestant beliefs in novels set before the Reformation and telling stories that privilege the transformative power of Protestant practices, including Bible studies and household prayers. Tucker persistently maintained to her Victorian readers that Protestantism was the foundation of a true English moral character and the engine driving the nation's domestic industry and international prowess.

Protestant providential history

One method Tucker adopted to teach Protestantism was to write historical works about Reformation heroes. *Sketches from the Life of Luther. Taken Chiefly from D'Aubigné's History of the Reformation* (1873) – a ninety-six-page biography that explains Martin Luther's rejection of Roman Catholicism and his key theological ideas to young readers – illuminates the anti-Catholic strategies of her historical fiction. Her aim to circulate Reformation thinking is markedly similar to that of the Parker Society, which was established in 1840 by Anglican Evangelicals to promote Protestantism in response to the Tractarians' publishing endeavours.[18] Named after Matthew Parker, Elizabeth I's first Archbishop of Canterbury, the Society republished cheap editions of key Reformation texts for popular circulation. Although the Parker Society ceased publication in 1853, *The Life of Luther* replicates its principles for children, paralleling the Society's circulation of Reformation writings for adult readers. Tucker frequently deployed this strategy of using Reformation history to attack Catholicism in her children's novels, and discussion of her rhetorical strategies in this text illuminates her art as an Anglican Evangelical woman novelist.

Tucker starts *The Life of Luther* by instructing young readers about the errors of pre-Reformation religion. Indeed, although the title page asserts that the biographical sketch is 'taken chiefly' from J.H. Merle Aubigné's monumental *History of the Reformation of the Sixteenth Century* (published in translation in England between 1838 and 1853), her book is not an objective summary. A.L.O.E. expresses her Evangelical condemnation of Roman Catholicism from the first page. For instance, whereas Aubigné depicts Luther's origins as honourable by emphasizing his parents' virtues – John Luther is described as 'upright', 'diligent' and well read for his station, and Margaret as characterized by '[m]odesty, the fear of God, and devotion'[19] – Tucker opens her account by disapproving of his parents' pre-Reformation religion: 'I dare say the man, whose name was John Luther, had never opened a Bible, although he was very fond of reading, and that his wife often knelt down to an image of the Virgin Mary, or said prayers to St. Peter or St. John.'[20] She presents an extensive list of Roman Catholic errors utilizing highly provocative language: 'The very prayers which men were taught to say were in Latin, that they might not understand them! ... Even many of their priests knew nothing of the Bible!' (6) Her dogmatic rhetorical exclamations are clearly intended to rouse the indignation of her juvenile readers: 'affectionate children would half starve themselves, that they might buy their dear parents' souls out of Purgatory' (8). Repeatedly appealing to the readers' sense of pathos, Tucker's didactic text is unquestionably polemical in its narrative interventions rather than historically impartial.

Writing consciously as 'A Lady of England', Tucker takes pains to explain the significance of the German Reformation to contemporary England. Embellishing Aubigné's history, she provides a providential account of the Elector of Saxony's heavenly reward for his allegiance with Luther by highlighting Prince Albert's descent from the Elector's brother's line to assert that God rewards the faithful:

> The Prince of Saxony lost his electorate in the cause of the gospel ... [B]ehold, to his remote posterity God gives the promise of the crown of a mighty empire, the greatest *Protestant* empire on the face of the earth. May the children, and children's children of our beloved sovereign, show themselves worthy of such an ancestor as the Elector of Saxony! (85)

Tucker thus rewrites history to persuade her readers that the distant history of the German Reformation is intimately linked with England's present and future international power. The Church of England is not referred to specifically; as Alistair McGrath asserts, for Evangelicals, 'The notion of "apostolic community" was ... generally interpreted in doctrinal terms, as fidelity to the teaching of the apostles as set out in Scripture, rather than in historical or institutional terms, as fidelity to a specific ecclesial structure or community.'[21] However, Tucker's history asserts that Anglicanism's identity is profoundly Protestant, because Queen Victoria, head of 'the greatest *Protestant* empire on the face of the earth', is the Supreme Governor of the Church of England. Tucker's hope that Albert and Victoria's descendants, engendered of such auspicious Protestant descent, will be worthy protectors of the Reformed faith is an Evangelical Anglican prayer for the Church of England.

Condensing Aubigné's expansive and intricate history, the Reformation principle that Tucker emphasizes most to her readers is Luther's Biblicism – a characteristic which D.B. Bebbington has viewed as a cornerstone of Evangelicalism.[22] Although she uses the biography of the 'Father of the Reformation' for multiple purposes – such as to expound on the errors of the monastic life, critique corruption and condemn ritualism – she concludes that his greatest insight concerned the supremacy of the scriptures and his greatest achievement was to make the Bible available in the vernacular for the use of ordinary Christians. Indeed, while Luther's famous doctrine of justification by faith alone is spelt out only twice in the work, Tucker punctuates the text with Luther's encounters with the Bible from his first reading to translation and printing. She concludes climactically by urging readers to be inspired to action by Luther's example:

> Pity for the nations yet in darkness, Italy, Spain, Portugal, France, and parts of Germany and Switzerland are yet in the chains of superstition ... We must spread the word of God. The Bible Society has already distributed *millions* of copies over the world, in more than one hundred and fifty languages and dialects. Can *we* not assist in this blessed work? (96)

Throughout the text, Tucker has been rhetorically fanning her readers' sense of righteous anger about Roman Catholic error and tyranny, and she finally offers an outlet for release in promoting the vernacular (Protestant) Bible as an instrument for enlightening 'the nations yet in darkness' and unshackling those 'in the chains of superstition'. Thus, she moves from Reformation history to future mission. This conclusion may be viewed as a bookend to the biography's opening paragraph, which highlighted the spiritual ignorance of Luther's parents, for Tucker returns to her opening discussion about Catholic iniquity but then provides her Protestant remedy, the Bible.

Later, Tucker used the genre of children's historical fiction to reiterate her belief in the interconnections between Protestantism and English identity. Whereas *The Life of Luther* tells of a foreign Reformation which eventually became connected with English destiny, *The Blacksmith of Boniface Lane* (1890/1) teaches about the Lollards, who were viewed anachronistically by Evangelicals as 'the first English Protestants'.[23] As Miriam Elizabeth Burstein has observed, Protestant writers of the Victorian era developed a 'counter-medievalism', which attempted to destabilize Anglo-Catholic arguments about an irrefutably Catholic medieval past by highlighting proto-Protestant movements before the sixteenth century.[24] In particular, counter-medievalists used the history of John Wyclif (d. 1384) – associated with the first English Bible and controversially known as the 'Morning Star of the Reformation' – and his followers, the Lollards, from John Foxe's *Acts and Monuments* (more commonly known as *The Book of Martyrs*) to oppose Tractarian arguments about the Church of England's Catholic continuity with the pre-Reformation past.[25] In *The Blacksmith of Boniface Lane*, Tucker fictionalizes the heroic story of one of Foxe's martyrs, John Badby (d. 1410), 'the first layman to be executed as a consequence of anti-Lollard legislation'.[26]

The provenance of Badby's history is significant. *The Book of Martyrs* was widely known in Britain. Colley has suggested that developments in print technology, which enabled the production of cheap abridgements in the second half of the eighteenth century, meant that by the nineteenth century, Foxe's *Book,* 'together with the Bible, [and] John Bunyan's *Pilgrim's Progress* … came to be one of the few books that one might plausibly expect to find even in a working-class [British] household'.[27] As Peter Nockles has discussed, from the eighteenth century onwards, new editions of *The Book of Martyrs* contributed to 'the belief that Catholics persecuted Protestants under Mary and would do so again if they attained power in England'.[28] In fact, the Victorian era saw the publication of four unabridged editions of Foxe's *Acts and Monuments*, the first of which was published between 1837 and 1841 by the Evangelical publishing house Seeley and Burnside. The force behind these new complete editions came from 'the Protestant (albeit not exclusively Evangelical) reaction against the Oxford Movement'.[29] The prominent cultural presence of Foxe's martyrology sustained 'a popular and elite anti-Catholic historical memory … Foxe helped link Catholicism in the minds of English people with religious persecution, foreign interference, arbitrary government and despotism'.[30] Such associations were a new development according to Nockles, who suggests that, in its own time, Foxe's *Book* was part of a 'broad bottomed Protestant internationalist [European] agenda' rather than a domestic project to define an 'elect nation'. Nineteenth-century admirers of Foxe like Tucker, however, viewed the book 'primarily as a founding text of England's national church, as a buttress of the contemporary British establishment and even of the union of Church and state'.[31]

As with *The Life of Luther*, Tucker's publication of the story of Badby's martyrdom shares the objectives of the Parker Society. As the final report of the Society's Council observed, their publications 'comprise[d] the complete works of the most eminent prelates, and others, who suffered imprisonment, exile, or death, in the sixteenth century, for the gospel's sake'.[32] As Mark Chapman has observed: 'Quite clearly [for the Parker Society], the essence of the Church of England was established on the faith of those who were willing to suffer persecution and even death during the Reformation. It was this example that continued to provide the weaponry to combat Roman Catholicism and Anglo-Catholicism in the nineteenth century.'[33] In *The Blacksmith of Boniface Lane*, Tucker similarly uses the earlier history of Lollard martyrdom as a native English weapon against the alien forces of Catholicism. Telling the early fifteenth-century history of Badby's heroic martyrdom, which culminates in his historically documented refusal to recant his rejection of transubstantiation despite the offer of a pardon and pension from Prince Hal (the future Henry V), Tucker both presents a native proto-Reformation that predates Continental reform and connects English moral fortitude with Protestant beliefs. Indeed, the national significance and patriotism of A.L.O.E.'s history is further substantiated by its setting in the world of Shakespeare's celebrated English history plays, *Henry IV, Part 1* and *Henry IV, Part 2*.[34]

As Burstein comments, 'At a time when Protestants felt that Roman Catholics were instituting a counter-Reformation of sorts, tales of ... the Lollards attempted to reconsolidate the "Britishness" in British Christianity ... assert[ing] that Protestantism was not only native but also, in a sense, natural.'[35] Certainly, Lollard faith is homegrown – not imported from Germany or Switzerland – and Tucker's story endeavours to construct a nationalist as well as religious myth. For instance, Burstein has observed that in counter-medievalist novels, 'one of the key charges against Roman Catholicism was that it undermined civic loyalty',[36] and, in Tucker's novel, allegiance to Rome has resulted in the king's disloyalty to his subjects. In the opening chapter, readers learn that, prior to anti-Lollard legislation, 'to burn men for their opinions was then a thing unknown in England'.[37] This new, alien practice is explained as the outcome of the king's desire to appease the pope: 'Henry of Lancaster [Henry IV] has stains – he knows best what stains – on his soul, and he wants Rome's whitewash to hide them' (17). In this context of the corruption of English values and law by foreign Roman Catholicism, Tucker paints the Lollards as champions of nationalist civic freedom as well as true religion. For instance, the narrator informs us that 'Dame Marjory', a Lollard matriarch, 'would never hear of the family going to mass at a popish church, stuck full, as she said, with idols, where folk must say their prayers in Latin instead of their good mother tongue' (102). Here, Roman Catholicism is presented as suppressing the native language as well as the English religion. Moreover, the idea of upright civic rebellion against inequitable oppression is further emphasized by Tucker's invention of a backstory that Badby's father was a martyr of the Peasants' Revolt under Wat Tyler.

The protagonist's labouring identity is highly significant for Tucker, as she uses it to emphasize further links between English proto-Reformation religion, Christian physical manliness and national industry. Although historians remain uncertain about whether Badby was a tailor or blacksmith, Tucker invests much meaning into the profession she selects for her hero. Characterizing the Lollard blacksmith as a physical and moral Herculean, Tucker produces a muscular Christian hero of the type popularized by Charles Kingsley and Thomas Hughes in the 1850s. As T.C. Sandars wrote in the review of Charles Kingsley's *Two Years* (1857) that originated the term 'muscular Christianity': 'His ideal is a man who fears God and can walk a thousand miles in a thousand hours – who, in the language which Mr. Kingsley has made popular, breathes God's free air on God's rich earth, and at the same time can hit a woodcock, doctor a horse, and twist a poker around his fingers.'[38] Tucker's blacksmith is just such a man, and his vigorous male body becomes a metaphor for national as well as religious strength. Unlike the foppish courtiers of the day (aligned with the Catholic king) who wear party-coloured clothes and whose 'Longbeards, thriftless, / Painted heads, witless, / Gay coats, graceless, / Maketh England thriftless' (12), Badby is variously depicted as unaffected, powerful and productive:

Folk said that John could no more tell a falsehood than he could play a juggler's tricks with those strong muscular hands which wielded the hammer so well. Badby is emphatically a man and an Englishman, but he is something more … John from his early days has received gospel truth with the simplicity of a child. There is nothing between him and the Saviour of whom he heard when sitting on the knee of his mother … The smith's faith is of that kind which a well-known preacher [Charles Haddon Spurgeon] has described in a few vigorous words: 'We want workshop faith as well as prayer-meeting faith … – a sound commonplace faith which will be found wearable and washable and workable through life.' Such is the faith of John Badby. (65–6)

Badby's Christianity is thus merged with his Englishness. His proto-Protestant faith is artless, steadfast and industrious, and readers recognize from the contemporary reference to Spurgeon that he is just the kind of Englishman that 'the greatest *Protestant* empire on the face of the earth' needs. Indeed, in the novel's only full page of illustration, it is noticeable that

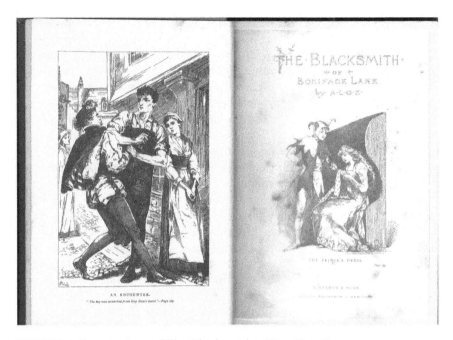

FIGURE 3 *Frontispiece of* The Blacksmith of Boniface Lane.

the titular blacksmith would not be out of place in Victorian England, unlike the effeminate Catholic courtier in stockings.[39] Through her characterization, Tucker maintains that Protestantism is requisite for English industrial success. Badby is not simply a Protestant with a strong work ethic; he is an example of a muscular Christian in whom Tucker, as one critic has said of Charles Kingsley, attempts 'to identify spiritual or moral law with physical law'.[40] For Tucker, national moral fortitude and physical industrial strength are bound up with Protestant English religion.

Family prayers, Protestant mother-teachers and English industry

In several domestic novels, Tucker highlights the role of Protestant practices in cultivating true Englishness. In particular, she makes ideological use of Bible studies and morning prayers as Protestant instruments for developing English values. As Cutt elucidates: 'Evangelical discipline was tied to a strict code of moral conduct. The Evangelical kept himself up to the mark by the constant renewal of his religious life by prayer, Bible reading, and Sunday observance.'[41] English moral courage and true religion are consistently presented as cultivated through these practices in Tucker's fiction.

From her debut publication, Tucker envisaged piety cultivated in domestic morning prayers as imbuing moral fortification. In *The Claremont Tales; Or, Illustrations of the Beatitudes* (1852) – a collection of tales tied together as the collective adventures of one household – morning family prayers are presented as a transformative Anglican practice not confined to the educated classes. Tucker depicts all sections of society as benefitting morally and spiritually from daily observance. Although the stories tend to centre on the titular middle-class Claremonts, Tucker also illustrates the integrity of devout labouring-class Christians. One recurring character is the seamstress Rachel, the virtuous young daughter of Staines, the Anglican parish priest's gardener. Readers are informed that, in Staines's pious home, 'early as was the hour, the morning prayer was never omitted; and Rachel read (for her father could not read) from the large Bible'.[42] In this context, readers understand that Staines is an upright Anglican Evangelical like his employer Revd Ashley (perhaps a nod to the great Victorian Christian hero Anthony Ashley-Cooper, Lord Shaftesbury). As Elisabeth Jay has explained, 'The Evangelical view of the family as a unit particularly favoured by God received its symbolic expression in the ritual of Family Prayers. The practice of praying in a family unit was not an Evangelical innovation … The Evangelicals were, however, responsible for popularizing Family Prayers among the middle-class laity.'[43] The narrative arc implies that the Staines's faithful and respectable observance of morning prayers is instrumental in the expansion of God's kingdom: Rachel, fortified in faith through regular devotion and scriptural knowledge, becomes a channel for conversion when she resolves to teach a poverty-stricken and physically abused Roman Catholic girl, who is forbidden from reading the Bible, 'the blessed light of the gospel' (111). As Jay further elucidates, for Evangelicals '[t]he family provided the most immediate sphere for the exercise of the sense of accountability for one's fellow mortals … Concern for others could act as a kind of thermometer by which to record one's spiritual temperature'.[44] In this context, Tucker implies through Rachel's example that daily family prayers are foundational in the development of socio-spiritual concern for others and bringing saving light to Roman Catholics.

In *Pictures of St. Peter from an English Home* (1887), a family drama centred on one summer at Willowdale Lodge, a middle-class Anglican Evangelical home, Tucker makes intricate use of both domestic Bible studies and morning family prayers as instruments of true Protestant faith. The novel starts with the unexpected arrival of Clarence St Clare, the nephew and heir of 'the Duke of Framlingham, … a Romanist peer'.[45] Piteously unable to return to the family castle because his sister has contracted smallpox, Clarence has been invited by the 14-year-old Harold Hartley (the motherless son of a missionary to India and adopted son of the Evangelical widow Lady Clara Laurie) to spend the school holidays with him. Clarence undergoes conversion during his sojourn, kindled by his attendance at the family's evening Bible studies and morning household prayers led by Lady Laurie.

In fact, Tucker's depiction of Clarence as a vulnerable child spiritually and morally endangered by the Roman Catholic Church was a trope of mid-century anti-Catholic writing; as Diana Peschier notes, 'Actual cases of the dangers posed to the young and defenceless by Roman Catholics became the basis for pamphlets and lectures warning the Protestant public of the menace lurking within English society.'[46]

Clarence first becomes suspicious of his family religion when he attends Lady Laurie's daily Bible studies about the history of the apostle Peter, 'partly from the gospel and partly from his letters' (21). These scriptural texts are the titular 'Pictures of St. Peter' used by Tucker to dismantle Roman Catholicism and propagate Protestant faith. Although Biblicism is a pan-Evangelical trait, engagement with the Bible is a feature of Anglican women's writing; as Marion Taylor has asserted, in the nineteenth century, the 'majority of British women who published on the Bible were Anglican'.[47] Tucker's scriptural focus on St Peter is a strategic outcome of her Victorian Evangelical anti-Roman Catholicism. Because Roman Catholics popularly consider St Peter to be the first pope, Tucker critiques what she views as erroneous beliefs through scrutiny of the biblical figure. Using the mode of the 'double story ... a tale about a family ... and the story their mentor tells them',[48] Tucker teaches and expounds on the scriptures, even providing scholarly contextual information from Josephus about the Lake of Galilee in Peter's time. Participating in the Bible studies, Clarence's Roman Catholic understanding about St Peter is challenged; for instance, he is surprised to discover that the biblical Peter was 'such a commonplace sort of person' as a fisherman rather than the first pope in a 'gold-broidered dress' (27–8).

Clarence's personal transformation is further accelerated when he starts attending the family's morning prayers, a practice which Tucker depicts as revealing sincere faith and true Anglican Protestant worship. In chapter ten, while the other children attend a party, Clarence stays at the Lodge owing to an eye injury. Lady Laurie uses the situation to challenge Roman Catholic doctrines about the Immaculate Conception and the Assumption of the Virgin. Readers are informed that, following a disturbed night's sleep, Clarence 'arose early, and appeared for the first time at morning prayers' (102). Attendance at this family observance allows Tucker to present the virtues of middle-class Anglican Evangelical domestic piety: 'There was something impressive to the Romanist youth in the simple, devout manner in which family worship was conducted at Willowdale Lodge; the service seemed so earnest, so real' (103). Evidently, Tucker uses the occasion to establish the sincerity of Protestant worship as well as the sanctity of the middle-class English home fostered by a Protestant matriarch.

Indeed, Clarence's experience of the family's morning prayers allows him to perceive Lady Laurie's domestic spiritual leadership (in the manner of the Protestant priesthood of believers), which contrasts sharply with his female relatives' Roman Catholic deferral to male clerics:

When Clarence saw how carefully the children of Lady Laurie had been instructed in religious knowledge, he wondered to himself why his own mother had taught him nothing. The lady had left all the religious training of her family to Father O'Brien, of whom Clarence was by no means particularly fond, though the priest exercised boundless influence over Catherine St. Clare (103).

At several points, Tucker offers scriptural proof texts for the priesthood of women in her novel. For instance, explicating the idea that the apostles are the foundation of the Church, of which all believers are 'living stones' (1 Pet. 2:4–5), Lady Laurie teaches that Christ's atonement has made all his believers priests:

> I will read a verse from the first chapter of the Book of Revelation: 'Unto Him that loved us, and washed us from our sins in His own blood, and hath made us kings and *priests* unto God and His Father; to Him be glory and dominion for ever.' There is not the slightest reason for supposing that this word *us* does not include *all* Christians – men, women, and even children. To confirm this, I will turn to what St. Peter writes to Christians scattered in various lands: 'Ye are a chosen generation, a *royal priesthood*, an holy nation, a peculiar people.' (81)

Tucker thus affirms female ministry through explicit propagation of the priesthood of all believers, and Lady Laurie's Anglican religion is depicted as enabling greater spiritual exercise for women than Roman Catholicism.

In fact, Tucker was so convinced about the influential roles of mothers in children's religious formation that the saintly mother-teacher has been identified as a trope of her *oeuvre*. As Bratton has observed of another family-centred novel, *The Giant Killer*: 'The progress of the children depends wholly on the mother's teaching (in almost all her books Charlotte Tucker makes moral training exclusively the preserve of women); when she is absent neither his family nor even his pupils look to the clergyman [her husband] for guidance, and he leaves them to fight their battles quite alone.'[49] Indeed, although Tucker's clergymen are not always ineffectual – for instance, Mr Ashley of *The Claremont Tales* is a worthy pastoral leader who helps a bright and devout working-class boy by raising a subscription for him to go 'to college to study for the Church' (77) – mothers are repeatedly shown to be the true spiritual leaders of children. In this manner, Tucker echoes the belief of Sarah Lewis, who asserted in *Women's Mission* (1839) that while '[male] power is exerted in the shape of authority, and is limited in its sphere of action … [female influence] has its source in human sympathies, and is as boundless in its operation'.[50] Following this pattern, the Bible-centred education that Clarence receives from Lady Laurie is the catalyst in his developing social and national stature.

Certainly, Clarence becomes a more useful member of English society as a result of his Anglican Evangelical conversion. When his paternal uncle – the Duke – becomes a father, Clarence ceases to be his heir and his aristocratic prospects come to an end. However, this personal loss eventually becomes England's gain. Forfeiting his patrilineal position as the head of a blue-blooded Roman Catholic family, Clarence can enter fully not only into the Church of England – after his conversion, he attends 'divine service' (319), while visiting his mother at the St Clares's castle – but also into productive English society.[51] For he rejects not only religious error but also foreign allegiance when he objects to the Duke's consolatory offer to give him 'a liberal allowance', free rein to shoot and hunt with friends on the family estate, and help towards 'a brilliant career' in 'either the diplomatic or political arena', which would require removal from his English public school to be privately tutored by the Duke's foreign chaplain, the Jesuit Padri Benito (207–8). Seeking a Protestant future, Clarence shifts kinship allegiance from his paternal aristocratic Continental Roman-Catholic uncle to a maternal middle-class English Evangelical one (whom he had previously disdained for his bourgeois position as a banker). As such, he relinquishes upper-class leisure for middle-class industry as the adoptive heir of his 'vulgar puritanical' Uncle Cobbs (193). His uncle's salt-of-the-earth name seems to signify English integrity in contrast with the suspiciously foreign St Clare. In fact, a stipulation for Clarence's matrilineal adoption is that he must take on the Cobbs's name; as his uncle explains: 'My good father, on his deathbed, exacted a promise from me which I shall *religiously* [my italics] keep. He had a fancy that the old firm should always retain the old name, and therefore no one can enter it without assuming that of Cobbs' (343).

Humbling himself by taking on the 'utterly plebeian' English name and forsaking the 'euphonious' (344) ancestral Italian one, Clarence becomes entirely English. Throughout the text, the St Clares are continually aligned with the Continent rather than England; for example, the Duke's heirs are born in Paris and he employs an Italian chaplain. As Colley comments: 'The most common slang for Catholics was "outlandish," and this was meant literally. Catholics were beyond the boundaries, always on the outside even if they were British-born: they did not and could not belong.'[52] While the Duke's successor, Clarence is similarly un-English through his patrilineal name and religion. However, when he becomes his Evangelical Uncle Cobbs's heir, Clarence is not only 'naturalized' as a Protestant but also becomes a useful member of English society.

Following in the footsteps of his hardworking maternal uncle, Clarence's partnership in the family bank enables him to play an active part in building England's economy. As Uncle Cobbs explains to Clarence's mother, 'your boy is my nearest, I may say my only male relation in the world, and it seems natural and right that I should make him my heir; but if he is to share the profits he must share the pains. He must put his own shoulder to the wheel, and not do business by proxy' (342). As the Duke's heir, it is likely that Clarence would have replicated his patterns of living a Continental life, financially supporting the Roman Church, employing foreigners and thus contributing to the growth of non-British economies. As the daughter of a chairman of the East India Company, Tucker 'was acquainted with the bustling commercial world of the 1850's [sic] and 1860's [sic] in which Work and Progress became synonymous …. In all her work she was adept at supplying juvenile versions of that mid-Victorian theory of work laid down by Carlyle in *Past and Present* (1843), its "perennial nobleness and even sacredness"'.[53] Casting off the pride and selfishness of the high-born Continental St Clares, Clarence Cobbs matures into a humble, self-forgetful man who works to transform England for the better. Notably, Tucker reassures readers of the permanence of Clarence's Evangelical transformation by explaining at the novel's end that, having sacrificed a prestigious upper-class career for the 'monotonous business in the bank, Clarence threw himself heart and soul into the great work of evangelizing the heathen in London' (429). Clarence's bourgeois work is an antidote for the 'once indolent, self-indulgent young aristocrat' (373), which allows him to participate in English economic advancement and the improvement of English lives.

Conclusion: Bursting out of the domestic sphere

From her stance as an Anglican Evangelical, Tucker was convinced that Catholicism, whether Anglican or Roman, was both dangerous and foreign. However, as an Evangelical woman, she was limited in terms of official ministry owing to St Paul's prohibition on women preaching and teaching (1 Timothy 2:12), and like all women of her generation, she received no university education. She was unable, therefore, to engage directly in the ecclesiological battle over the Church of England's Protestant identity open to university-educated Anglican Evangelicals, whether ordained or lay. However, publishing her ideological and proselytizing writings for children as 'A Lady of England', Tucker fervently defended the English Church's Protestant nature within the sanctioned province of women's care for the young. Like Isaac Watts, who in the Preface to his pioneering work of children's religious writing *Divine Songs Attempted in Easy Language for the use of Children* (1715) anticipated that Christian truths absorbed in youth might 'be a constant Furniture in the Minds of Children', Tucker aimed to disseminate to children an understanding of the Church that would mature into adult conviction.[54] Applying the objectives of the Parker Society to young readers to teach them about proto-Protestant history, beliefs and practices, Tucker crucially aimed to be the first in the race between Protestants and Catholics (of both varieties) to persuade children about the true nature of English religion. Pursuing this mission, although using the feminine, domestic and familial genre of children's literature, Tucker's works exceeded these boundaries and operated beyond the distinct sphere of writing for the young.

FIGURE 4 *Margaret Oliphant.*

3

Margaret Oliphant (1828–97): Opening Doors of Interpretation

Alison Milbank

In Margaret Oliphant's novel, *The Perpetual Curate* (1864), Frank and Gerald Wentworth, two brothers and Anglican clerics, discuss the nature of the true church. Gerald has decided to abandon his Anglican orders to embrace Roman Catholicism, which he has come to believe is the only true authority. Unable to move his brother on the question of doctrine, Frank changes tack to make an appeal to the problematics of human experience:

> 'Perhaps you can reconcile freewill and predestination – the need of a universal atonement and the existence of individual virtue? But these are not to me the most difficult questions. Can your Church explain why one man is happy and another miserable? – why one has everything and abounds, and the other loses all that is most precious in life? My sister Mary, for example ... she seems to bear the cross for our family. Her children die and yours live. Can you explain to her why? I have heard her cry out to God to know the reason, and He made no answer. Tell me, have you the interpretation?' cried the young man, on whom the hardness of his own position was pressing at the moment.

Frank continues:

> 'You accept the explanation of the Church in respect to doctrines ... and consent that her authority is sufficient, and that your perplexity is

over – that is well enough, so far as it goes: but outside lies a world in which every event is an enigma, where nothing that comes offers any explanation of itself; where God does not show Himself always kind, but by times awful, terrible – a God who smites and does not spare. It is easy to make a harmonious balance of doctrine; but where is the interpretation of life?'[1]

For the fictitious Frank Wentworth, the perpetual curate of the novel's title, these questions arise from the experience of his ministry as a priest and from his sister's troubles. Oliphant, the novelist, draws here on her own life and difficulties as expressed so poignantly in her private autobiography.[2] Her husband Francis died in 1859, leaving her heavily in debt and with three small children. After her brother Frank's financial failure and subsequent demise, she brought up and provided for his family as well. She lost her daughter in 1864, which plunged her into deep depression, and she outlived all her children. Much of her writing is therefore concerned with maternal grief, the problem of suffering and the enigmas of life.

Despite her questioning of a God 'who smites and does not spare', Oliphant did believe that there was 'an interpretation' of life, though it is noticeable that she uses a word that describes exploratory ways of reading and analysing a text rather than the more conclusive word: 'explanation'. Writing fiction with this hermeneutic aim in view became a mode of religious exploration as well as a means of making a living and supporting her family. Oliphant wrote fiction in three distinct categories: realistic novels, ghost stories and a new genre focusing on exploration of the afterlife. The first comprises a large number of realist novels which probe human character with a depth and generosity reminiscent of George Eliot; in these, she used a free indirect mode of discourse to layer interpretations upon human enigmas. In a second group of ghost tales, which by their very nature are overlaid narratives seeking an explanation or a discovery of another story, she explored the borders between life and death. A third strand of her writing creates its own sub-genre, where, in a sequence of stories closely modelled on Dante's *Inferno* and *Purgatorio*, a 'little pilgrim' experiences the world beyond the grave directly: as reality, not a problematized liminal in-between space.[3]

It is perhaps surprising that the Tractarian ritualist Frank Wentworth, who knows very well the doctrinal issues at stake for his brother's conversion to Roman Catholicism, should mention free will and predestination in the passage quoted above. Yet although Oliphant worshipped as an Anglican in her adult life, and loved the Book of Common Prayer and Anglican ceremonial, she was brought up a Free Presbyterian by her Scottish parents, and her brother Willie became an English Presbyterian minister at Etal in Northumberland.[4] In the nineteenth century, debates about predestination and universal atonement are usually associated with churches more firmly in the Calvinist tradition than the Church of England, including Oliphant's parents' evangelical wing of the Free Presbyterian Church in Scotland. This chapter seeks to argue that Oliphant moves beyond her Presbyterian allegiance and can be considered an Anglican writer, even though she brings Scottish theological concerns along with her. She is attracted to the Church of England by its breadth and openness, which is precisely what Gerald Wentworth finds problematic, complaining that 'in England it seems to be the rule of faith that every man may believe as he pleases. There is no authority either to decide or to punish' (434). Oliphant is unpersuaded by Gerald's preference for Rome because she feels that this very 'authority' shuts down questioning and does not penetrate to the mysteries that concern her. Anglicanism, by contrast, offers texts – Scripture and the Prayer Book – which allow hermeneutic engagement and act as a key: they are like doors shaping and opening human experience.

The Carlingford novels

The Perpetual Curate is one of a number of novels set in an imaginary English town, Carlingford, several of which have clergy as their main protagonists, in the manner of Anthony Trollope's Barchester series.[5] The clergy contrast with the leisured class that dominates the town, as they are 'the only people who have defined or compulsory duties to give a sharp outline to life'.[6] Here too the image of the doorway is implied: the priest in his duties is like a doorway shaping the sense of community both for the Carlingford gentry and for the reader of these novels. In each case, he offers a knowledge of life beyond their limited experience. It was, as we saw, Frank's pastoral ministry which produced a sense of 'every event [as] an enigma'. For an open door reveals, but also witnesses to a depth beyond its frame: further mystery awaits. The topography of Carlingford is conveyed through an interplay of doors and openings, so that in *Salem Chapel* (1863) the dissenting minister, Mr Vincent, is caught between his duty to attend the endless competitive tea parties of his shopkeeper elders, whose doorways smell of ham and cheese, as the visitor penetrates beyond the shop to the parlour, and the seductive power of the green door which leads to the garden of the beautiful Lady Western. Frank Wentworth in *The Rector* (1863) is in similar romantic thrall to the gate to the Woodhouse garden in Grange Lane, which becomes the entrance to Paradise because it leads to his beloved Lucy Woodhouse.

In the Carlingford novels, the social comedy played out in class terms, through access to particular doors and entrances, is given a metaphysical weight. Mr Proctor, the incumbent of *The Rector*, who has left the comfort of All Souls' College, Oxford, for a parochial ministry for which he is wholly unprepared, experiences for the first time in his life what Oliphant calls 'the secret of discontent': that 'something better, though it might be sadder, harder, more calamitous, was in this world'.[7] This yearning after something higher is expressed in terms of the Garden of Eden, as he has 'something in him more congenial to the thorns and briars outside to be conquered, than to that mild paradise for which our primeval mother disqualified all her children' (34–5). The door here opens outwards to a fallen world, but like Milton's Adam and Eve in *Paradise Lost*, this world is 'all before' him and a Paradise within awaits him, which is 'happier far'.[8] Mr Proctor is being called away from the paradise of All Souls' High Table to the post-lapsarian toil of pastoral ministry. The call fails on this occasion, and he bolts back to Oxford in *The Rector*, but by the end of *The Perpetual Curate* he has actively chosen marriage and a parish.

The Carlingford novels also explore the intricacies of the freehold system in some depth. The rector of Carlingford usually comes from All Souls' as the College holds the patronage of the living, and, once appointed, the rector has considerable autonomy. Frank Wentworth is perpetual curate of a chapel-of-ease, St Roque's, which is within the parish but has its own private endowment, and thus he enjoys more independence than a normal curate.[9] There are disputes with a later rector, Mr Morgan, over his work with the bargees on the canal, about which of them has the right to evangelize these unchurched transient workers. *Salem Chapel*, however, shows how constrained the minister of a 'free' church can be, since Mr Vincent is appointed directly by the elders of the chapel, and paid by them, and therefore they can also dismiss him. Vincent gives a rip-roaring lecture denouncing church establishment, and Oliphant allows his arguments to tell, but they are fatally compromised by his infatuation with Lady Western, his sense of social exclusion and the control the wealthy deacons have over his ministry. The novel ends with Vincent quitting Salem Chapel for a career in journalism, because ministry in a free church, as opposed to an established church, cannot provide the minister with this opening door, enabling desire for something higher. Oliphant may have in mind the experiences of her brother as a free church Presbyterian minister in Etal, where at first she believed that 'the church and parsonage were quite exotic, and the humble chapel the real centre of the place', and regarded Willie as a 'direct successor of the two thousand seceders of 1661', meaning the clergy ejected from their livings during the Restoration of Charles II after the return of the king and episcopacy.[10] She was soon disabused of this fantasy of a continuing 'true' established free church, and before long Willie left in some disgrace, having displeased his congregation, possibly by his heavy drinking.

The ghost stories

This image of the shaped opening carries on into the second strand of Oliphant's writing: her supernatural short fiction. One ghost story is entitled

'The Open Door', and although a ruined and completely open doorway is the site of the haunting, the ghostly voice moans continually, 'Oh, mother, let me in!' and evidently is shut out.[11] The narrator's little son is the first to hear this voice and it has made him ill with worry and concern, so that the life of the child becomes interwoven with the fate of the ghost. The story is set near Edinburgh, and consequently the cleric called in to help is a Church of Scotland minister, Dr Moncrieff; he recognizes the voice and lays the spirit to rest. Significantly, his status as a minister of an established church means he shares the spiritual freedom to act of the Anglican clergy in England. Moncrieff establishes that the ghost is Willie, the housekeeper's prodigal son, who prior to his death had arrived home to find the house empty because his mother had died. Dr Moncrieff had heard the living Willie crying at the door, and he appeals to his shade: 'She's no here. You'll find her with the Lord. Go there and seek her, not here ... He'll let you in, though it's late. Man, take heart! if you will lie and sob and greet [cry], let it be at heaven's gate, and no' your poor mother's ruined door' (154).

Three biblical references frame the interpretation of this story. First, the parable of the prodigal son from Luke 15, whose father comes to greet him and celebrate his return; secondly, the story of the good Samaritan from Luke 10:30–7, with the fearful servant and incredulous doctor in the story playing the priest and the Levite who pass by the man in need, and the minister Dr Moncrieff the Samaritan who rescues him; thirdly, Christ's words to the church at Philadelphia in Revelation 3:8: 'behold, I have set before thee an open door, and no man can shut it'. The dead man's desperation and lack of hope make him see a closed door which is, in fact, open, and he places his only trust in his mother, who is no longer there but in heaven. The three biblical allusions stress forgiveness and acceptance, and are employed to suggest that there is hope for the lost beyond this life. Dr Moncrieff goes on to pray for the dead man, even though such prayer has no validity in Presbyterian doctrine, prompting the doctor to ask him if he believes in purgatory. He replies in the terms of the parable of the prodigal son: 'there is just one thing I am certain of – and that is the loving-kindness of God' (156).

The open door in this story is a rich symbol, standing both for the wideness of God's mercy to all and for the passage of communication between the living and the dead. The non-existent door does indeed open and the mother pulls the lost son through, after the minister prays: 'Lord, let that woman there draw him inower [inside]!' (154). This prayer imitates the Catholic practice of invoking the prayers of the saints. The minister prays to God to enable the mother to effect her son's salvation, acting like a Beatrice to his Dante or perhaps Matilda, the guardian of the Earthly Paradise, who in *Purgatorio* 31 pulls the poet bodily through the river of Lethe.[12] This rescue is important for Willie but equally so for the sick child Roland, who has been drawn close to death's portal by the cries of the ghostly son, and is restored to health only after the visitation is over. Oliphant suggests a psychic pressure on the living from the unquiet dead.

Oliphant was not alone in holding to 'the larger hope' for the damned; such a belief lost the Congregational minister George MacDonald his position at the Congregational Church at Arundel and the Anglican theologian F.D. Maurice his Professorship at King's College London.[13] Maurice had merely suggested in an essay, 'Eternal Life and Eternal Death', that the qualifier 'eternal' is not a measure of duration but belongs properly to God: to be damned is to be without knowledge of God, who is love.[14] He by no means asserted the doctrine of universalism, in which all are saved, but he did go so far as to confess, 'I am obliged to believe in an abyss of love which is deeper than an abyss of death', words not unlike those of Dr Moncrieff.[15] This remark, and others like it, were words of immense hope and comfort to many of Maurice's contemporaries such as Margaret Oliphant.

As I have argued elsewhere, it was a desire to hold together God's loving-kindness with justice which led a number of Victorian Christian writers – including associates of Maurice – to employ Dantesque tropes of educative suffering, which turn Hell into Purgatory.[16] One can identify a specifically liberal Anglican version of Purgatory in George MacDonald's fantastic stories such as 'At the Back of the North Wind' (1871), in which a neglected child is taken to a version of Dante's Earthly Paradise to aid his spiritual development, and Charles Kingsley's *The Water-Babies* (1863), in which the death of young Tom, the chimney sweep, is followed by a mode of rebirth and spiritual evolution. Kingsley's novel also includes the fate of the cruel sweep-master himself, who is punished by being stuck inside a chimney like those he forced child chimney sweeps to climb, until his repentant tears wash away the mortar from the bricks and release him.[17] These Anglican writers elide Dante's Hell and his Purgatory so that the poetic justice characteristic of the fate of the damned becomes a mode of education and spiritual renewal through suffering, more like Dante's mode of purgation. Dante's Purgatory is a site of reconciliation and mutual support, and thus it is Tom who must aid Grimes the sweep in his conversion and restoration, just as the tears of the sweep's mother seek to melt Grimes's frozen heart. Yet the movement of repentance must initially come from the sinner himself.

Dante in the supernatural tales

In the same way, Oliphant quotes from Dante frequently in the third strand of her fiction – her 'Little Pilgrim' stories – where she employs symbolic landscape and social ordering in a Dantesque manner to express the nature of sin and its manifestation as a punishment, in the manner of Kingsley's chimney. Willie's error in 'The Open Door' had been to 'abandon hope' like the lost in the *Inferno* and to view the gate of Hell as closed, but Oliphant's supernatural tales are all in the service of suggesting that the door to salvation remains open, and Hell can morph to Purgatory. These highly popular 'Little Pilgrim' tales, which take place in the afterlife, combine Bunyanesque allegory with Dante and quite a modern Kafkaesque alienation to describe the horrors of Hell. In 'The Land of Darkness', for example, the soul can choose from a capitalist Vanity Fair, pleasure and self-indulgence that will not let one stop dancing in the manner of Hans Christian Andersen's story, *The Red Shoes*; the mines of Demas, which are as illusory as the silver-mines promised in Bunyan's *Pilgrim's Progress*; or a hell of bureaucratic surveillance and control reminiscent of the writings of Michel Foucault. People sacrifice one another in this hellish land, and there are public acts of vivisection on sentient beings. There is, however, some hope in this polity of evil for evil's sake, in the form of a small opening: 'a moving spot of milky whiteness in that dark and miserable wilderness, – no bigger than a man's hand, no bigger than a flower'.[18] A horrendous story offers hope in the form of a physical way out: a light opening out of the darkness, and another of Oliphant's open doors.

What allows the unnamed protagonist of 'The Land of Darkness' to view a way out of this miserable wilderness is an ability to imagine something better than the world he is within. In Romantic and Coleridgean fashion, the imagination is a holy thing and connects us with the transcendent. Similarly, in another tale the aristocratic and well-read subject of the story, 'Old Lady Mary', finds herself with all her wits about her in the afterlife, and her imagination active:

> 'I suppose,' she said rather timidly, 'that we are not in – what we have been accustomed to call heaven?'
>
> 'That is a word,' he said, 'which expresses rather a condition than a place.' … 'It cannot be the – Inferno, that is clear at least,' she added with the sprightliness which was one of her characteristics; 'perhaps – Purgatory? since you infer I have something to endure?'
>
> 'Words are interchangeable,' he said: 'that means one thing to one of us which to another has a totally different signification.'[19]

The afterlife too is a place of interpretation, where those who learn to read it can be saved. Lady Mary voluntarily goes back as a ghost to seek to right the wrong she did to her ward, Mary, in not making a will, impelled by a desire for justice and by love for her. She does not accept the view expressed by other souls that penitence is 'the fire that purges us, – to see at last what we have done, and the true aspect of it, and to know the cruel wrong, yet never be able to make amends'.[20] Instead she goes back through the door between the living and the dead to make reparation, and endures the torment of visiting her old home as a stranger: apart from a baby, no one can see or hear her. She must also witness Mary toiling as governess to the child of a prosperous commercial family, in the very house where she had lived in luxury with her guardian.

A Beleaguered City

Eventually Mary marries well, experiences Lady Mary's presence for a moment and gains her inheritance when a document is uncovered. The two greatest supernatural novellas by Oliphant, however, are less easily resolved. Her most exploratory and questioning fiction is in that second strand of supernatural tale, which explores the boundaries and liminal spaces between the seen and unseen worlds. *A Beleaguered City* (1880) is a narrative *tour de force*, voiced by a French mayor and other contributors to an imaginary official enquiry into events in Semur, an actual French cathedral city near Dijon. As a consequence of having grown worldly and greedy, the inhabitants of the town are enveloped in a pall of darkness and a document is found, attached to the cathedral wall, calling on them all by name 'to yield their places, which they had not filled aright, to those who know the meaning of life, being dead'.[21] It is signed, 'NOUS AUTRES MORTS' (we other dead), as if to suggest that the living inhabitants are already spiritually defunct. The citizens all leave and the dead occupy their former places in the town. For many of the male townsmen, who are associated particularly with *laïcité* (the state as purely secular) and an Enlightenment disdain for religion, the dead are the enemy; they patrol the area beyond the walls of the town, as if laying siege to the dead as invaders of their territory. For the mayor's wife, by contrast, they are the beloved dead: 'our little Marie, and my mother, who died when I was born', and she longs for them.[22] Her husband, however, blames God for taking the dead but is also terrified of them and of their power over the living. There is, for instance, one Paul Lecamus, who has lost all his family, and who longs to join the dead in the city. Lecamus can see the dead because he lives partially in the other world already, and he joins the dead at the end of their visitation.

The mayor, Martin Dupin, and the priest re-enter the city at the invitation of the dead and find it deserted, but with evidence of the visitation of the dead left behind. In Dupin's house, his father's desk has been moved back to its old place in the centre of the study and, more significantly, at the family shrine to his dead daughter there lies an olive branch. Bells ring and the two men approach the cathedral, where the priest says mass and the agnostic mayor goes back to childhood practice by acting as acolyte. The mayor and priest call the townspeople back into the now-empty city, where they worship as one community. From this expression of unity, one might expect that this visitation of the dead would be transformative. During the occupation, the citizens had made a single home at the mayor's country house for the women and children, cared for the aged, and worked cooperatively across class and religious boundaries. Yet this is not the outcome. The mayor himself has to finger the silvery leaves of the olive branch to recall the events, and he loses the fervour that led him to serve at the mass. His secular prejudices come back apace. Yet this failure of the visitation within a carefully accurate presentation of French mores and politics serves only to make the narrative contract stronger and more realistic for the reader. The dead are sad that they cannot communicate directly with their loved ones, yet leave real tangible evidence of their visitation, and their very failure adds to the realism of the story, despite its supernatural themes. The living are shown their transience and mortality as they are decentred from their own lives and expelled from their houses. The barriers between life and death are both breached and affirmed through the medium of the physical houses, the city and its gates. The story affirms that here is an open door, but its interpretation is difficult and its communication only partial.

'The Library Window'

In sharp contrast to Roman Catholic provincial France, 'The Library Window' is set in Presbyterian St Andrews in Scotland, called 'St Rules' in the tale. Written at the very end of Oliphant's life in 1896, it recalls her own youth as it describes the long visit of a young girl to an elderly aunt, and what she sees through the window of a first-storey drawing-room recess, across the street to a window in the college library. Brilliantly structured through sequences of elderly tea parties and formal visits, which take on a liturgical rhythm, the narrative enacts 1 Corinthians 13:12: 'for now we see through a glass, darkly; but then face to face: now I know in part; but then shall I know even as I also am known'. St Paul's image is of a metal mirror, which shows only a shadowy reflection and is an apt figure for earthly perception. Other nineteenth-century ghost story writers employed the double meaning of 'glass' as both mirror and window, to narrate acts of vision beyond the physical. For example, the Irish writer Sheridan Le Fanu entitled a collection *In a Glass Darkly*, and made a false window opening out from a hidden frame central to the Gothic terror of death in his novel, *Uncle Silas*.[23] The unnamed young narrator of Oliphant's tale sees the library window at first only 'darkly', as she sits in her recess looking over the street. She is open and enclosed at one and the same time with regard to the social world, and completely open to the imaginative possibilities of the window opposite, so that she is ready to see further. There is some debate among the characters in the story about whether it is a true or false window, for it was common in days of window taxes to employ the latter. For one viewer it is just 'a very dead thing without any reflection in it'; for another 'the framework is all right, at least', but another notes 'a great want of light'. A younger visitor opines that 'it is not a window to give light', whereupon the formidable and aged Lady Carnbee observes scornfully: 'and who ever heard of a window that was no to see through?'[24] Like the events in *A Beleaguered City*, the sight of the window calls out a flurry of hermeneutic activity, and that is, perhaps, the meaning of the story: 'have you the interpretation?' Lady Carnbee suggests ending the speculation by getting a boy to cast a stone at the window, but Aunt Mary refuses, preferring the mystery to remain.

Prompted by all this discussion to observe this mysterious window, the narrator begins to see further into it, '*through* a glass darkly', and discerns a pale greyness of space beyond the window and visible pieces of furniture. On later occasions, details of a writing desk with papers emerge, and then signs of movement. On St John the Baptist's feast day and the longest day of the year, her vision culminates in discerning a man seated at the writing desk with the back of his head towards her, composing. He is wholly absorbed, and the sight might be taken for a naturalistic one – except that he writes on and on, but the page on which he writes never seems to need turning.

The narrator is presented as the child of a writer so that this vision can be taken to articulate the desire of a woman to enter the male world of professional authorship. It is, however, about much more than this. The man in the room writing, and later getting up and moving about, is a figure for the narrator's desiring imagination, which seeks to move ever outward and beyond and which is represented by the way the girl sits apart in the recess of the drawing room, with her eyes always focused on the world beyond the confines of the domestic space. The narrator does not so much want to be the man writing, or engage relationally with him, as to see as through his eyes.[25] He and the room are the 'glass' through which she will 'see darkly' and yet further with the ultimate aim of coming 'face to face' with ultimate reality.

The medium in which all this occurs is the Scottish 'gloaming', the long twilights of northern summer evenings 'when the light had begun to fail, and the world was full of that strange day which was night, that light without colour, in which everything was so clearly visible, and there were no shadows'.[26] It is the time when the fairies have power and the narrator seems to half believe in them. Her twilight vision is, however, challenged that same evening when she is taken to a party in the college and forced to see that there is physically no space where her window could possibly be. She is taken home in distress, still holding to her belief, and then she sees the man actually open the casement and wave towards her. In delirium she cries to be believed, and to comfort her, her aunt sends down to a small child in the street, who confirms her observation. She also learns that her aunt and other women of her blood have often been similarly haunted: 'it is a longing all your life after – it is a looking – for what never comes'.[27] The desire for something more is baleful because never capable of fulfilment. As in ballads of those taken by the fairies, there is no content in this life for those who have had the uncanny experience. The narrator longs for silence and darkness to cover her as if she desires death. Her aunt mutters softly over her, 'like a dream when one awaketh,' paraphrasing Psalm 73:19, which continues in the Book of Common Prayer 'so shalt thou make their image to vanish out of the city'. The desire for the world beyond the physical can be a death wish.

There is a logic to this haunting in that a scholar was once seduced from his books by one of the narrator's forbears, who signalled to her suitor by means of a hand wearing a certain ring waving from her window. Her brothers killed the scholar, and he takes his ghostly revenge by luring her descendants in return. The plot turns at the tale's conclusion when the narrator, years later, arrives as a widow from India, rather like Oliphant herself, very sad and alone, with small children and no one to welcome her. She sees the man from the window one more time, as he waves from the crowd at the docks. Having experienced marriage and bereavement, she has in a sense passed through the window of death already and can meet him as a spiritual fellow-sufferer beyond the grave. It is significant that the ghostly scholar is no longer confined to the room, but is also moving forward as a fellow-traveller on his spiritual journey.

Yet the baleful ring of her ancestor still survives and has been left to the narrator by Lady Carnbee. It remains locked up in the lumber-room of a country-house also left to her, as if it is still too dangerous to wear. Like the olive wreath in *A Beleaguered City*, the ring is a form of evidence of the force of the supernatural and of life beyond the grave. Whereas the olive branch is a clear religious symbol of reconciliation, the ring and the window are signs asking for interpretation, and the narrator concludes: 'Yet I never knew what Aunt Mary meant when she said, "Yon ring was the token", nor what it could have to do with that strange window in the old College Library of St Rule's.'[28] The gloaming of the long Scottish evening is a figure for this suspension of knowledge, which becomes a blessed thing: living and dead, fact and possibility, are held in balance, and the action of interpretation, even without an explanation, offers a kind of redemptive space.

This last example of Oliphant's writing is in continuity with the rest of her fiction in seeking out an opening – a middle liminal space – where faith and doubt about the afterlife and God's providence may be explored and where religious experience may be interpreted. Her vision is surprisingly ecumenical for the time in embracing French Catholicism, Scottish Presbyterianism and the liberal Anglicanism of F.D. Maurice. Oliphant reviewed Maurice's *Theological Essays* and disagreed with his theology of the Atonement, because he presented the Crucifixion as a proof of God's overflowing love rather than as a test of it.[29] Oliphant was herself tested to the limit by the many bereavements she endured, and for her too easy an Atonement denied this aspect of human suffering. As we have seen, Oliphant shared Maurice's adherence to 'the larger hope' of a possible salvation for all, and she was also influenced by the ecumenism evident in his work.[30] Maurice is perhaps a true key to her thinking in that he offered an 'open door' and found good in all denominations, while claiming in *The Kingdom of Christ* that Anglicanism was broad enough to include the best elements of them all.[31] In the section on Maurice in Oliphant's study of Victorian literature, she commends Maurice's Broad Church party because it 'demonstrate[s] above all the breadth and elasticity of that church, which was so far from any narrow or sectarian temper that the most differing theories, so long as they held their allegiance to Christ and His all-pervading character and personality, might find rest in her bosom'.[32] Oliphant too held implicitly to the Church as a *via media* and, like Maurice in *The Kingdom of Christ*, saw the principles of that Kingdom dispersed and fragmented in the different denominations. She commended Maurice for believing that there was 'no exclusive strand of goodness or certainty of salvation in any framework of ecclesiasticism' but also for his unwavering allegiance to the Church of England.[33]

Oliphant even has the idealistic protagonist of her novel *A Son of the Soil* (1865) advocate a reordering of the Church of Scotland to include the best of Catholic piety and Anglican liturgy. This reflects a general movement for the revival of worship in the Church of Scotland in the nineteenth century, illustrated by the Church Service Society, which was founded in 1865, and a kirk equivalent of the high church revival in the Church of England, which asserted the place of the Genevan/Knox Book of Common Order (which was a set order of service) over against the advocacy of extempore prayer of the Directory of Public Worship.[34] A 'high church' Presbyterian minister, James Cooper, furthermore, advocated not only a use of Anglican liturgy but also a reunion between the two churches, based on the best aspects of each communion.[35] The Catholic Apostolic Church associated with Edward Irving, of whom Oliphant wrote a biography, also attracted much interest and even adherence from Scottish Presbyterians (including Cooper), and one reason for the attraction was its richer and more 'catholic' liturgical practice.[36]

Another reason for the breadth of Oliphant's Christianity is that her vision always reaches out to the world beyond, seeking to include the dead, who also seem to have a narrative trajectory as they purge themselves and learn through suffering to love more truthfully and generously. In different ways, all three strands of Oliphant's fiction make interpretive activity a redemptive spiritual practice, in which the Church on earth and the Church expectant are equally engaged. I use this latter phrase, which is more commonly associated with Roman Catholicism, because it best describes Oliphant's belief about the afterlife as a site of purgatorial testing and development, in which suffering is relieved by expectation. Christ, she wrote in her autobiography, is 'the one thing certain in this terrible problem of human existence', and she believed in him 'as in the only light which throws a little illumination on the darkness'.[37] That light took the form of a questioning spirit for Oliphant, whose Christ was the man praying in torment in Gethsemane as he too sought for the meaning of his imminent death. But Oliphant's quest for illumination on the enigma of human suffering led beyond the grave, to unite living and departed in one ongoing journey towards interpretation of the mysterious ways of God. As her realist novels sought a social space on earth where Anglicans and Dissenters might come together in friendly accord, so her supernatural fiction came to verify a gospel of hope for the future salvation of all humankind, in which the door would always lie open.

FIGURE 5 *Charlotte M. Yonge.*

4

Charlotte M. Yonge (1823–1901): Writing for the Church

Charlotte Mitchell

We had a wonderful visit yesterday from an utterly unknown little American girl of fourteen or fifteen, who bobbed into the room, rushed up to me, shook hands, 'Miss Yonge, I've come to thank you for your books, I'm an American.' … It was odd to be thanked by a little bolt upright mite, as if in the name of all the American Republic, for writing for the Church.[1]

In her day Charlotte M. Yonge was immensely famous all over the world, yet nowadays she needs explaining to many readers, even to enthusiastic readers of Victorian novels and lifelong members of the Church of England. A High Church novelist whose work was addressed to both children and adults, even before her death it was often forgotten that she was never exclusively or primarily a writer for children.[2] Between 1844 and 1900, between the ages of 21 and 77, she published a staggering quantity of literary work in a wide variety of genres, including fiction, biography, history, children's books, textbooks on history, geography and divinity, advice books, journalism and anthologies, of which I am going to mention only a paltry sample. Much of this circulated internationally, but she was also generous with her support of obscure charitable organizations and journals and a tireless worker both in the village and for national causes.[3] She saw all this work as devoted to the service of the Church of England, specifically, of that group within it whose members called it the Church Movement, and whose opponents called them Puseyites.

Now we most often talk of 'the Oxford Movement' or 'the Tractarians'; we no longer talk about Puseyites, but for the present purpose 'Kebleite', if it existed, would be a more useful term: Yonge herself had little to do with E.B. Pusey. The defining experience of her life was being prepared by John Keble for confirmation in her early teens; she was fired by him with the belief that even a young lady of the lesser gentry had a significant part to play in the imminent transformation and renewal of the Church of England. It was this message she expressed in her fiction and other work, and in which a wide audience found inspiration. There is no modern scholarly biography of the Revd John Keble (1795–1866), nor is there a good edition or even a large collection of his letters; his once internationally celebrated poetry is now hardly read even by specialists. This *lacuna* is all the more misleading because of the exceptionally thorough scholarly treatment of his friend Cardinal Newman. Keble had many disciples, most of them men, but through none of them did he reach a wider audience than through Charlotte Yonge.

Origins and context

She was still a child when in 1836 Keble was appointed Vicar of Hursley and Rector of Otterbourne by Sir William Heathcote, Bt., of Hursley Park in Hampshire. Although the Yonges themselves normally attended church in Otterbourne, where the duty was done by the curate in charge, they were quickly drawn into friendship with the Kebles and strenuous participation in the life of the combined parishes. William Crawley Yonge, Charlotte Yonge's father, was an ex-army officer living with his wife and two children in Otterbourne House, outside Winchester, the property of his mother-in-law, Mary Bargus, an old lady with strong opinions of her own. (The family's letters were addressed to them 'at Mrs Bargus's'.[4]) He had plenty of time on his hands, and he became Keble's lieutenant in many projects of social and religious reform, working together, according to his daughter, 'in a manner that always reminded me of the friendship of Laud and Strafford'.[5]

One of her biographers called Yonge's an 'uneventful life'. She was born at Otterbourne House in 1823. In 1862, some years after her brother's marriage, she and her widowed mother moved out to a house in the village, where she lived until her death in 1901. Except for regular visits to her father's family in Devon, she travelled little, though she once went to Ireland and once to France. Living in Keble's parish, however, meant that she and her family were kept closely in touch with the newest developments in the drama of the Tractarian movement. Her life was also rather less safe and prosperous than has been assumed by some, such as one of the reviewers of her life and letters who called it 'an eventless pastoral'.[6] As Charles

Kingsley tried to explain to an undergraduate audience many years later, the 1830s and 1840s did not seem at all innocent and peaceful to those who were living at the time, and the south of England was no rural idyll: 'Then arose Luddite mobs, meal mobs, farm riots, riots everywhere; Captain Swing and his rickburners, Peterloo "massacres," Bristol conflagrations.'[7] Charlotte Yonge was not shielded from knowledge of the riots of 1830/1: two brothers of her own nanny were transported to Australia for sedition, and at Hursley Park the squire's children were shut up in the silver safe when Captain Swing's men appeared.[8] In later years, moreover, life in Otterbourne, as in other places, was affected by the enormous social changes of the Victorian period, and some of these developments caused her much regret. There was a financial crisis in her brother's family, and many of her friends and relations were affected by the relative decline in the fortunes of the landed gentry in the latter part of the century. Almost all her associates were diehard conservatives on most social issues, yet they had imbued her, paradoxically, with the belief that the world required regeneration, and so to the very end of her life she was a generous supporter of diverse projects of reform at home and abroad, from the Society for the Propagation of the Gospel in Foreign Parts to the Girls' Friendly Society. Although she looked back to her childhood and adolescence in Otterbourne as a golden time of aspiration and idealism among congenial friends, and much deplored the growing materialism and secularism of the late nineteenth century, the successes of Tractarianism were a source of great satisfaction to her: she had a characteristically Victorian faith in progress as well as a religious faith in God's providence. Her undoubted social conservatism was, therefore, always flavoured with activism and openness to the spirit of reform.

As I have suggested, the religious and social campaigns which Keble and his friends were waging during Yonge's youth were lent urgency by their fear of actual social revolution. Much of the establishment, however, including the Bishop of Winchester, Charles Sumner, saw the Tractarians as a fifth column whose real goal was the reintroduction of popery. From the point of view of the teenage Charlotte Yonge, their programme therefore had the additional appeal of being tremendously controversial. Christabel Coleridge, looking back in the twentieth century, pointed out how enjoyable it must have been to belong, along with all her pastors and masters, to a campaigning pressure group:

> She had those greatest joys of high-minded and enthusiastic youth, hero-worship, and the sense of being in the van of one of the great movements of the day; but whereas in many cases young people buy these joys by discord with their elders ... in Charlotte's case authority, family ties, faculty, and aspiration all flowed in the same full and powerful stream.[9]

Yet 'Puseyism' was so objectionable that members of her parents' circle felt like a band of beleaguered warriors for the faith, and several sacrificed their careers for the greater good. (This was to be a characteristic move for a Yonge hero for many years.) Keble himself lived in the expectation that at any moment some crisis might require him and his followers to give up their livings for principle, just as the non-jurors had in 1690 and the ministers of the Free Kirk in 1843, and just as, deplorably and agonizingly, so many of their friends were doing in converting to Rome, especially around the times of Newman's conversion in 1845 and Manning's in 1850.[10]

The sacramental vision of the natural world which Keble versified in *The Christian Year* (1827) and other volumes reached an enormous international audience, and he earned significant amounts of money from his early bestseller. The poems always meant a great deal to Yonge. No doubt, too, the intimacy with Keble helped to bring about the surprising situation in which a very young and very shy woman without any urgent need for money became a professional author. Socially, the excuse was that the work was only undertaken '*Pro Ecclesia et Dei*' and the profits benefitted the church. Psychologically, Keble's example and support (for many years he corrected her proofs) must have helped her imagine herself in the role of author. His kind of authorship, combining national fame with continuous residence in a quiet village and the ploughing of the profits into Anglican charities, was a model she and her family could accept.[11]

Yonge's contemporary and later influence

Yonge's friendships throughout her life were centred on a series of family groups, all suffused with Tractarian values, on which she could depend for advice, comment and collaboration. These included the Kebles, the families of the Rt Revd George Moberly, of the Revd William Butler of Wantage and of the Revd Charles Dyson at Dogmersfield, and her Yonge, Coleridge, Crawley and Gibbs cousins. The collective charitable and religious work of this group was done by women as well as men, and Yonge's writings, whether fiction, journalism, histories or textbooks, were in the main conceived as providing examples, inspiration, guidance or materials to help them do so. Keble's parochial circle, like his wider circle of disciples in the outside world, expressed its zeal above all in relation to two institutions, as it were two buildings: the church and the school. After his installation money was raised in his parishes to replace the dilapidated church of St. Matthew, Otterbourne (1839), to build an entirely new one of St. Mark, Ampfield (1841), substantially to rebuild All Saints, Hursley (1848), to build a new chapel and Sunday school at Pitt (1858), and to construct schools for boys (1839) and girls (1842) in Otterbourne and likewise in the other villages. It was this building programme which gave birth to Yonge the novelist, starting with *Le Chateau de Melville* (1839), a privately printed selection of translations into French published to raise money for the girls' school in Otterbourne, and, more seriously, with her first novel *Abbeychurch* (1844), which describes the impact on a clergyman's family of the inauguration of a new church. It links the self-examination of a group of earnest upper-middle-class adolescent girls to the spiritual regeneration of a community. Yonge's fiction returned again and again to this link, perhaps most notably in *The Daisy Chain* (1856), the story of Ethel May, a clever, untidy, bespectacled doctor's daughter who resolves to start a school in a poor village near her home. One of Yonge's most powerful and most popular books, it answers the questions: What can a young lady actually do? What difference does she make? The answer is her slightest actions matter to God, her decisions have huge consequences, the improvement of the world requires nothing less from her than a lifetime of strenuous and committed work. Susan Walton has shown how early this fundamental idea is expressed in Yonge's magazine, the *Monthly Packet*.[12] When the magazine had been founded to provide suitable Tractarian reading for upper-middle-class young people, there had been trouble thinking up a suitable title. Yonge lamented: 'I wish it had found a name; if there was any word to express "for Confirmation girls" it would be the thing.'[13] In the series of dialogues 'Conversations on the Catechism', a message was conveyed which was at the core of her work for the next half century:

> *Miss O.* Well, then, my dear, when we see clouds darkening round our Church … and feel grieved at our weakness and inability to come forward in her cause, let us remember that God can work deliverance by few as well as by many, by the weak as well as the strong, and that to guard ourselves, fight our own battle with sin and temptation, and pray that He will defend the right, may do more good to the cause than if we were the most powerful distinguished men in the fore-front of the battle.[14]

Powerless women reading this message could believe their actions were significant: it was to inspire many.

Nor was this appeal confined to women, although we can be sure that its call had been heard at first- or second-hand by a high proportion of Anglican church workers well into the twentieth century, women like George Orwell's 'old maids biking to Holy Communion through the mists of the autumn morning'.[15] The life of Abraham Kuyper (1837–1920), the Dutch theologian and politician, was changed by reading *The Heir of Redclyffe*;[16] the Archbishop of Canterbury and the Earl of Rosebery, later Prime Minister, were overheard showing off how well they knew *The Daisy Chain*;[17] and Elizabeth Wordsworth remembered 'a lively conversation with Dr. Whewell … on *The Clever Woman of the Family*'.[18] In the mid-1850s, the Revd John Coleridge Patteson, later Bishop of Melanesia and martyr, built, with Yonge's money, a school near Auckland for the young Melanesian converts he had brought back to train as teachers, a single-storey stone barn with a dais one end, like a small Oxbridge college hall transported to New Zealand. (It is now a coffee shop.) Patteson and his team named the college, unexpectedly enough, St. Andrew's, Kohimarama, after the church in *The Daisy Chain*.[19] These men were engaged in missionary work in very demanding circumstances: Patteson would sometimes reach an unfamiliar island inaccessible by boat by swimming across the reef, and commence his ministry on the shore, naked and dripping and unable to speak the local language.[20] Naming the college from the book was an acknowledgement that it expressed symbolically the emotions and beliefs which inspired their work, a sign that they and Yonge had a purpose in common. Christabel Coleridge was getting at the same idea when she wrote of *The Heir of Redclyffe* (1853) that it 'embodied the spirit of the Oxford Movement in its purest and sweetest form'.[21] The book's hero, Sir Guy Morville, is a rich young man in modern England; his task is to imitate Christ as far as possible within the sphere in which he has been placed. By overcoming his natural bad temper and the defects of his upbringing, by charity, self-denial and consideration for others, and acts of bravery (saving lives in a shipwreck) he does this, and dies of fever on his honeymoon in Italy, having sacrificed his life for his greatest enemy. The Revd R.W. Dixon, *apropos* of the novel's impact when as an undergraduate he belonged to the circle of Morris and Burne-Jones, wrote that after nearly fifty years it still seemed to him 'unquestionably one of the finest books in the world'.[22] John Duke Coleridge, the future Lord Chancellor, then a cocky young barrister brimming with intellectual self-confidence, called the novel soon after its publication:

> A book of unmistakeable genius and real literary power, a book to make men pause and think, to lift them out of themselves and above the world, and make them, unless they are hard-hearted and cold-natured, the wiser and the better for their reading.[23]

To the young men and women of the 1850s, then, Yonge's fictions represented more than entertainment for an idle hour: they were expressions of an ardent passion for virtue and reform, a real source of hope and inspiration.

Fictional style and reputation

Yonge had grown up a lonely little girl yearning after the big family of Devon cousins with whom she spent holidays and solacing herself with the invention of imaginary families.[24] Perhaps this is why, when she started to write fiction, she often set herself an unusual, perhaps a unique, technical challenge: the management of stories which include families of ten or twelve children ranging in age between infancy and adulthood.[25] Her extraordinary skill in doing this was recognized by, of all people, H.G. Wells, who, commending the first novel of an avant-garde young friend, wrote, 'you steer your family one among the others as skilfully as that delightful and all too little praised Charlotte M. Yonge'.[26] Despite this self-imposed handicap, her novels are remarkable for their vivid characterization. Any of her fans, required to account for their devotion to a neglected writer, is likely to cite her creation of a host of lovable or maddening characters whom one can follow from sequel to sequel. Yet this aspect of her work, its remarkably convincing depiction of the surface of family life, has probably led to the underplaying of something equally distinctive, which is the extent to which her novels are conceived in symbolic terms.

In Yonge's account of being prepared for confirmation by Keble, a fairly brief document, in which her reverence for him and her fear of profaning sacred subjects very obviously inhibit her writing, she summarizes the work they did together thus: 'he opened to me the perception of the Church, her Sacraments and her foundation, and prepared me to enter into the typical teaching of Scripture.'[27] The key word here is 'typical'. Just as initiation into serious religious teaching involved an appreciation of the typological interpretation of the Bible, so all Tractarian aesthetics were penetrated with alertness to spiritual analogies. As Christabel Coleridge tried to explain in her conscientious, loyal but reticent biography of Yonge, the Hursley circle were very much in the habit of interpreting the books they read allegorically, symbolically and allusively. Tractarian homes maintained enthusiastic cults of Dante and also of Friedrich de La Motte Fouqué, whose mystical allegories of chivalry, such as *Sintram* (1814) and *Undine* (1811), were then at the height of their fame. They extended this exegetical approach to other favourite readings, such as the poetry of Robert Southey and the verse and fiction of Sir Walter Scott. This was the intellectual atmosphere in which Yonge's writing developed, and it affected her deeply. In the same way that *The Christian Year* encouraged its readers to find parallels in everyday life for the mysteries of their faith and the history of their religion, Yonge's fiction was designed to present indirect parables of religious truth. As one of her best-loved characters, Countess Kate, once exclaimed, 'There is no heart or beauty in what is not symboli–.'[28] Keble's Latin lectures as Professor of Poetry at Oxford, from which Philip Morville quotes in *The Heir of Redclyffe,* were the theoretical underpinning of this aesthetic system, and it is significant that the novel early on sets both Sir Guy Morville and his cousin Charles Edmonstone to work at construing them.[29] To miss this dimension is to miss something fundamental, which helps to explain the discrepancy between the initial reception of her fiction and its subsequent reputation; more recently, scholars such as Gavin Budge have begun to appreciate and explore this aspect of her work.[30]

By the end of the nineteenth century, though, Yonge's fiction had been relegated to the class of works which did not require sophisticated reading and were not capable of multiple interpretations.[31] The often patronizing and contemptuous attitudes adopted towards her fiction, especially on the subject of its supposed conformity to patriarchal ideologies imposed on her by her father and by Keble, have blinded even those critics most cautious of belittling women writers. This has led to her fiction being read in simplistic ways which ignore its complexity. I treasure the memory of the late, the formidable Professor Kathleen Tillotson flicking through *Be Good Sweet Maid*, a copy of which had been kindly presented by the author to the Charlotte Mary Yonge Society. The book contains a chapter entitled 'Female Reality and the Christian Ideal: Charlotte Yonge's "Anti-feminist" Novel, *The Clever Woman of the Family*'.[32] She made one of those noises which old-fashioned novelists used to know how to pin down on paper. 'Pah!' she said, or perhaps, 'Faugh!! It's a feminist book!' Well, I agree with her. At any rate, *The Clever Woman of the Family* (1865) is a novel which ventilates the whole question of the desirable scope of women's activities, intellectual and practical. It offers its young women readers a wide range of possible options for women's work, including teaching, social work, charity administration and journalism, as well as marriages which involve new kinds of work as well as companionship and intellectual stimulation. Like many another novel of its period, it ends with marriages, but it is often a mistake to assume that the last page sums up the meaning of a book.[33] In fact there is ample evidence that Yonge's dramatization, in novel after novel, of conflicts between feminine ideology and female aspiration was experienced by her first readers as inspirational, for, as a writer in the *Edinburgh Review* noticed,

> the authoress here [in *Heartsease*] and in all her books keeps a great kindness for the high-spirited girl who rebels against use and wont and scorns feminine subjection.[34]

The publication of Yonge's fictions in uniform editions has tended to obscure, misleadingly, the generic differences between them. *The Clever Woman of the Family* was intended for adults. Although to our eyes it contains nothing very unsuitable for a teenage girl, it was not published in the *Monthly Packet*, from which courtship novels were generally excluded. None of the four major early novels which were conceived as a tetralogy – *The Heir of Redclyffe* (1853), *Heartsease* (1854), *Dynevor Terrace* (1856) and *Hopes and Fears* (1860) – was serialized in the *Packet*.[35] They also fall into the class of adult fiction and require a greater literary sophistication from their readers than *The Daisy Chain* (1856), which did run for a long time in the *Packet* and has a much more episodic structure. However, rather to Yonge's surprise, *The Daisy Chain*, on which one suspects she expended much less care, proved one of her most successful works, a perennial bestseller. An allusion to it is crucial in Virginia Woolf's *Between the Acts* (1941), although the conjunction of the two novelists now seems so unexpected that this fact is hardly known by anyone.[36]

The Daisy Chain also helped to give birth to a whole new category of fiction whose heroine is a teenage girl struggling with her siblings, her schoolwork, her friendships, her physical appearance, her sexuality, the ideology of femininity and the whole business of growing up and discovering her identity. It provided, for one thing, an important model for Louisa May Alcott's *Little Women*, published to instantaneous acclaim in 1868, for all that the latter novel includes so much autobiographical material. Structurally the time frames are similar.[37] Invalidism, the nature of true gentility, the heroine's impatience with the restrictions of young ladyhood, the contrast between the poor and well-born and the rich and vulgar, the necessity of holding a high religious ideal before one – all these themes echo preoccupations of Yonge to the point where one feels confident that the teenage Alcott had read *The Daisy Chain* as enthusiastically as Jo March lies on the sofa weeping over *The Heir of Redclyffe*.[38] Jo also longs for a copy of La Motte Fouqué's stories *Undine* and *Sintram*, the latter tale of which is central to *The Heir of Redclyffe*, the baby born at the end being named Verena after its heroine. Her hero Laurie is, like Guy Morville in *The Heir of Redclyffe*, the orphaned grandson of a rich old man whose son has run away with a singer and died young. *Little Women* and its sequels also use allusions to allegorical works such as *The Pilgrim's Progress* and *Sintram* in ways which are very reminiscent of Yonge's practice.

More generally, of course, the market for Yonge's books in America had helped to create the demand which led Roberts to ask Alcott to write *Little Women*, and which encouraged the production, on both sides of the Atlantic, of so many other fictions about the home life of upper-middle-class girls, and the development of a whole new segment in the market. Very few of Yonge's followers in this genre, however, attempted to depict the miseries of adolescence, its physical and emotional discomforts and social agonies, with anything like the same force that she achieved in her major early novels. The character of Sophia in *The Young Step-Mother* (1861), for instance – plain and awkward, angry despite herself, suffering from a bad back, intellectual frustration and unrequited love – is quite without precedent in English fiction; another powerful depiction of teenage angst is Bertha Fulmort in *Hopes and Fears* (1860). The latter book, about the adoption of two orphans by a sentimental spinster, is even more obsessed with education and teaching than Yonge's books usually are, vivid in its sense that they must be adapted both to the modern world and to the needs of the individual pupil. Yet all her novels are animated by the sense that the transition from childhood to adulthood is a moment of huge social and spiritual significance: she was always thinking about 'confirmation girls'.

There will be those, however, who feel that to have almost invented a kind of novel about and for teenage girls does not give Yonge a strong enough claim on their attention. In order to persuade those people to read her, or to read about her, one would need to explain why she is, ultimately, so tremendously good at writing novels. She possesses, above all, the ability to convince the reader that they are inhabiting her world. Her novels of contemporary life persuade one that they are a record of the habits and preoccupations of the time. This was not because they were (though this is sometimes claimed for them) photographic representations of family life, nor just because they were especially numerous and published over such a long period. More fundamental, perhaps, is the fact that they are perennially interested in education, especially for middle-class girls but also for boys and for other classes, and because they consistently acknowledge and react to change. Practically involved in the delivery of various kinds of education to an extent unusual among teachers, let alone full-time novelists, Yonge was peculiarly aware of the effect on schools and home educators of the changing climate of opinion, government regulations, trends in publishing, the availability of employment and the impact of new qualifications. Never herself in the vanguard of modernity, her novels nonetheless show a sensitivity to developments in the *Zeitgeist*, and nothing is more characteristic of her later works than the acknowledgement that she has revised an earlier position; her writing consistently registers awareness of living in a new world.[39] Weaker as the later novels undoubtedly are, there is no other Victorian novelist whose fiction covers fifty-five years and records so conscientiously the large and small changes which transformed the social and intellectual sphere of women of her class.

Feminism

Modern accounts of the gradual legal and social emancipation of women during the nineteenth century usually cite Yonge, if at all, as a convenient example of the sort of thing their heroines were up against.[40] A short advice book, *Womankind* (1877), which never circulated widely, has proved a useful source of repressive statements. To mid-Victorian women she appeared differently. It is remembered that she refused to help Emily Davies set up Girton College; people seldom quote Anna Richardson recommending her help be sought:

> Do you so entirely abjure Miss Yonge, as to refuse to ask her? Her name is so well known, and so well liked by vast numbers of young ladies, and her own claims to solid culture so real.[41]

Davies replied: 'There are few names I should like better to have than that of Miss Yonge, but I despair of getting it.' They must both have understood what we are now in danger of forgetting, that for the mid-Victorian young lady who wanted to learn Greek and Latin, mathematics or astronomy, Yonge and her heroines were models to aspire to. Her novels were unusual for their time in dramatizing the achievements of those who had overcome educational disadvantages through personal exertion: Ethel May has an old-fashioned governess who still makes her learn by heart answers to Richmal Mangnall's *Questions*, but she learns Greek and Latin from her brother's books, despite being obliged, unlike him, to waste time sewing and learning

French: her appetite for learning is associated with her energetic devotion to projects of reform. That was something her first readers took from the book. An old friend, the Revd William Butler, wrote late in life that it was only due to Keble's influence that Yonge had exerted her powers for the High Church movement rather than on behalf of feminism.[42] When his son published this letter in 1897 it must have seemed an eccentric assessment of her position, yet Butler had observed Yonge closely since childhood, and his opinion is therefore worth listening to. The feminist campaigner Bessie Rayner Parkes put her finger on the problem in the same year, when she commented that justice had never been done to Yonge by literary critics because of her 'loyal devotion' to the 'Anglican Church'.[43] She was pigeon-holed as a pious do-gooder, and the complexity of her readers' responses was overlooked. Ray Strachey, in her early history of the suffrage movement, recommended her readers to read Victorian novels to understand the story of the emancipation of women:

> One author deserves special mention, namely, Charlotte M. Yonge. Her delightful tales were written between 1847 and 1890, and they give pictures of the lives of educated families between those years which are irresistibly convincing. The author was herself a convinced anti-feminist, but her characters lived and developed with the times, and a detailed study of their fortunes is a most agreeable and instructive pastime.[44]

Is it a coincidence that two well-known campaigners for women's rights independently emphasized the value of Yonge's work in recording this particular historical moment? Surely it was because they felt her fiction conveyed, better than that of her contemporaries, the gradual process whereby pressure built up for improved access for women to both work and education. For a 'convinced anti-feminist' Yonge addressed herself energetically for over half a century to precisely the issues with which convinced feminists were concerned, and perhaps it is time to acknowledge that she was nothing of the kind.

As well as writing books about modern girls and their problems, Yonge also wrote a large number of historical novels, being – like so many of her generation – an enthusiastic devotee of the novels of Sir Walter Scott. The uniform edition problem comes up here too, as it is not always appreciated that these fall into various distinct categories: some, such as *The Dove in the Eagle's Nest* (1866), *The Chaplet of Pearls* (1868), *Unknown to History* (1881) and *Stray Pearls* (1883), being full-length novels for young women and adults; and some, such as *The Little Duke* (1854), *The Lances of Lynwood* (1855) and *Two Penniless Princesses* (1891), being aimed at younger children. Very popular in its time, but now little read, Yonge's historical fiction has a fascination of its own: *The Dove in the Eagle's Nest*, for example, whether or not it bears any relation to what life was actually like in the castle of a robber baron in pre-Reformation Germany, is full of romance, vivid characters, striking situations and places which seem real, though of course never visited by Yonge except in her imagination. *The Little Duke*, too, an early work aimed at small boys, has always been one of her best-loved works and is still in print.[45] Undoubtedly, for Yonge and her readers, part of the function of these works was to lend immediacy and human interest to dull lists of kings and dates. Scott had been a great inspiration to many: as a girl in Yonge's first novel exclaims, 'Who would care for Louis the eleventh if it was not for *Quentin Durward*?'[46] In Yonge's historical works she often built on Scott's fictional foundations; the sinister Louis XI, for example, appearing in a younger but equally nasty incarnation bullying his Scottish first wife in *Two Penniless Princesses*; and *Unknown to History* covering areas of the career of Mary, Queen of Scots, which Scott had neglected in *The Monastery* and *The Abbot*. From Scott she took the insight that fiction can express the clash of systems of thought and showed everyday life providing a steady counterpoint to the drumbeat of political history. Far more than he did, though, she looked at history from women's point of view. Just as in 'Conversations on the Catechism', she returned repeatedly to the question: what can a girl do? What difference, for good or evil, can she make in the grand scheme of Christian history? One might think of her historical fictions, which range over an enormous tract of time, as a series of thought experiments in gynocentric history. Old and young, rich and poor, her characters have the potential to do good or evil. The underlying message – that history is not just about men and events, but about women, children, the diurnal and the domestic – is utterly congenial to contemporary historians. Who can wonder that her first readers found this version of history refreshing?

Yonge suffered particularly badly from the wholesale denigration of Victorian culture which gained so much traction in the interwar period. She was despised for being a spinster, religious and a conservative. Yet of all the novelists who entered the Victorian debate about the supposed problem of single middle-class women, she was one of the few who genuinely saw their function in society as multiple and satisfying. For many years she made it a rule (an early version of the Bechdel test?) that fiction in the *Monthly Packet* had to be about more than just getting married.[47] A proper reassessment of her significance will require the abandonment of misogynistic standards of critical evaluation, as well as the idea that it is clever to condescend to 'the Victorians'.

Some years ago our vicar, meandering characteristically away from the ostensible theme of his sermon, mentioned the Jewish principle of *minyan*: the rule that ten adult men must be present for a ceremony to be valid. The idea was quite new to me. Naturally I immediately began scanning the congregation estimating age and sex – not always easy from the nape of the neck – and decided that in our case validity would be a close-run thing, and that, really, the vicar was too tactless to draw attention to it. If a majority of your audience are women and children, need you dwell on the fact that some people would once have regarded them as invisible? Since that Sunday I have often thought about *minyan*, the Church of England,

Charlotte M. Yonge and the question of why the Victorian novelist most influential in the Church is no better known today. The idea that the women and children in the congregation simply don't count is a metaphor for the way in which the history of Victorian Anglicanism, perhaps especially of the Tractarian movement, has been written.[48] The fact that some of Yonge's work is for children has often led to the quite mistaken assumption that none of it is sophisticated, scholarly or original. That it is religious has led to the belief that it is conventional. Its passionate belief in the importance of education for women has not properly been acknowledged, and some have even called her anti-feminist, which is not at all what her first readers felt.

The present volume of essays has many predecessors spanning the whole of Christian history. Yonge herself compiled several group biographies which celebrated saintly men and women, not always but usually Christians: these include *Biographies of Good Women* (1862), *A Book of Golden Deeds* (1864), *The Pupils of St. John the Divine* (1868) and *A Book of Worthies* (1869).[49] Perhaps most comparable to the present project, however, was a book which has lain almost unread in manuscript in the Bodleian Library since 1957. The 'Biographies of Eminent Anglicans' were meant as contributions to a book whose moving spirit was the Revd J.F.W. Bullock (1840–1918), Rector of Radwinter, Essex, for the fifty years from 1865, having, remarkably enough, succeeded both his father and his grandfather in that capacity.[50] Only his *Daily Lections for Every Morning and Evening throughout the Year* (3 vols, London: Rivington, 1902) ever appeared. The fifth volume would have consisted of 'Lections on Anglican Worthies' by Yonge and others. It may seem heroically perverse to draw attention to this late and unknown manuscript, but there seems to be a subtext in Yonge's enthusiasm for this celebration of the individual contribution to church history, a sense that the service she was chronicling was the kind she had performed in her own day:

> I think you should have Frances Havergal – She was most devout and good, though not High Church, but most attached to the church. Also Agnes – the devoted workhouse nurse, and I do think Mrs Trimmer and Hannah More ought not to be omitted.[51]

If any Anglican woman writer can be numbered among the saints of the English Church, then Yonge herself is certainly a respectable candidate.

FIGURE 6 *Evelyn Underhill.*

5

Evelyn Underhill (1875–1941): Mysticism in Fiction

Ann Loades

A walk through the graveyard of the parish church of St-John-at-Hampstead will discover a gravestone for Hubert and Evelyn Stuart Moore, the tablet further identifying the latter as the daughter of Sir Arthur Underhill. This memorial in effect relegates Evelyn Underhill to the roles of daughter and wife, containing no indication that she had received public recognition in her own right for her remarkable career. A major feature of this was becoming a 'retreat director', a vocation which, within the Church of England, she pioneered for women.[1] Another was her range of theological publications, of which *Mysticism* (1911) is the best known.[2] As early as 1913 Underhill was made an Honorary Fellow of King's College for Women (King's having been founded as a Church of England College) and became its first woman Fellow in 1927. On that occasion the Dean of King's commended her as one might expect, rehearsing her career and qualifications, but rather to her surprise the principal described her not just as an 'exponent of mysticism' but as a poet.[3] She had indeed published three volumes of poetry, and also three novels which are the focus of this present chapter: *The Grey World* (1904), *The Lost Word* (1907) and *The Column of Dust* (1909).[4] The principal may have been perfectly well aware that Underhill had long since abandoned her attempts to establish herself as a novelist, instead concentrating on her many publications to commend the living of a distinctively Christian life.[5] At the present time there continues to be much interest in these, which established her as a major Anglican voice. But readers of Underhill's non-fiction, on encountering her novels, may well be startled into a revaluation of Underhill and the development of her spirituality. In her novels, whether she realized it or not, she was working out some of her most fundamental convictions.

Early cultural and spiritual formation

In early life Underhill enjoyed a number of social and educational privileges, not least family holidays to mainland Europe with both parents. These began in 1890, continuing with her mother from 1898 and beyond Evelyn's marriage in 1907, until 1913.[6] They enabled the discovery of forms of religious life unknown to her at home, as well as profoundly moving works of art, and the opportunity to record motifs to be used in her book-binding and Hubert's enamelling.[7] Her diary, sketches and recollections of these journeys provided material for her novels.[8] *The Lost Word* was to be dedicated to her mother 'in remembrance of our adventures amongst architecture'.[9] And it was into this novel that Underhill directly worked her discovery of the Pietà, an image which for her related not simply to the end of Christ's earthly life, but to the possibilities of new life for those who embraced her understanding of mysticism.[10]

Travels to Europe apart, Underhill's formal education was begun at home and enhanced by three years (1888–91) at a school in Folkestone, at which she was prepared for confirmation. The candidates were issued with a 'dear little book' which began, 'My child, your life hitherto has been one continuous Sin, and you are now walking on the brink of Hell.'[11] Confirmed in the Church of England on 11 March 1891 in Folkestone, she made her first communion on Easter Sunday that year. Despite her affection for her father's brother, Ernest, a high churchman who worked in Liverpool, at this stage of her life she seems not to have been able to make any connection between her confirmation and the tradition represented by her uncle and her cousin, Francis Underhill, who was to become Bishop of Bath and Wells in 1937. Just how and why she eventually came to become an advocate of Anglo-Catholicism had much to do with her acquaintance with Baron Friedrich Von Hügel.[12] This most distinguished and learned Roman Catholic layman, domiciled in London, had published work in precisely Evelyn's areas of interest and during the last four years of his life (1921–5) became a significant mentor for her and her work. It was he who encouraged her to remain in and publicly renew her commitment to the church of her baptism and confirmation, despite the fact that it was the Roman Catholic Church which had sustained Underhill for many years up to that point.

While attending the 'Ladies' Department' at King's College, London, she discovered the Roman Catholic Church of Maria Assumpta in Kensington, and the Mass celebrated there. It was not the representations of the Assumption that most gripped her imagination and emotion, however. Instead, on her travels she came deeply to appreciate representations of the

Pietà, showing Mary as a strong, elderly woman, 'enduring the weight of her dead Son laid across her knees, all she could do for him, as helpless as when he lay in her lap at Bethlehem'.[13] In a thirteenth-century carving in Carcassonne, she saw Mary as one who had 'looked life between the eyes' and yet retained a vulnerable heart. Whereas her son lies quiet and at peace, she is content to suffer, knowing it was well with him, 'at the cost of loneliness for her', an image of 'quiet, steadfast, grieving affection'.[14] Underhill rewrote this passage from her travel diary for the experience of Catherine (one of the principal characters in *The Lost Word*), though typically unable to resist some elaboration of it: 'all His long curled hair turned back from the heavy wreath of thorn and falling over her knee' (291–2). Underhill herself was so moved by this representation of Mary that she has 'this all-enduring Mother' address Catherine directly, rescuing Catherine's marriage to Paul whom she is about to abandon on their honeymoon (294). This novel apart, the Pietà came to symbolize for Underhill not only self-giving, a sacrifice made so that another can live, but the 'Son' as the 'soul' slain to make possible a new fecundity.[15]

Initial exploration of the Roman Catholic Church may well have helped to shift Underhill from the 'Society of the Golden Dawn', of which she was a member between 1902 and 1905. With a pseudonym of 'Soror Quaerens Lucem' (sister seeking light), she could pick her way through its eclectic mix of astrology, alchemy, divination, kabbalah, Tarot and whatever other rituals might be employed: the grim and dangerous world which was to inform her final novel, *The Column of Dust*.[16] What she learned from this most non-Anglican Society, however, was to stand her in excellent stead: not only when she described the rituals of Freemasonry in *The Lost Word* but beyond that in her mature understanding of Christian liturgies.[17] To begin with, however, the influence of the group may be detected in the epigraph of her first novel, *The Grey World*. W.B. Yeats, another member of the Golden Dawn, had published his edition of William Blake's poems in 1893, and Underhill quotes a passage from *Jerusalem* where Blake declares that he knows no other gospel than 'the liberty both of body and mind to exercise the Divine Arts of Imagination … the real and eternal World of which this Vegetable Universe is but a faint shadow', claiming that 'we shall live in our Eternal or Imaginative Bodies when these Vegetable Mortal Bodies are no more'.[18] To this Underhill adds a quotation from Yeats's *The Celtic Twilight*: 'Let us go forth, the tellers of tales, and seize whatever prey the heart long [sic] for, and have no fear. Everything exists, everything is true, and the earth is only a little dust under our feet.'[19]

Underhill was also interested in the work of someone else who experimented with membership of the Society of the Golden Dawn: the novelist Arthur Machen, to whom – with his wife Purefoy – Underhill's third novel *The Column of Dust* was to be dedicated. Machen too was eventually to declare himself a member of the Church of England, but one could hardly have predicted this from some of his novels of the occult. One of these, *The Great God Pan*, by his own admission, 'made a mild sort of sensation with old ladies, on the press and off it', as well it might. One review which he cheerfully cited in the 1916 re-publication assessed the book as 'the most acutely and intentionally disagreeable we have yet seen in English', and another, that the book was 'gruesome, ghastly and dull', a likely source of 'utter disgust'.[20] In the novel, a group of 'scientists', of whom Dr Raymond is one, want to lift the veil from the world they inhabit to see the god Pan. Dr Raymond wants to bring into play a group of nerve cells in the brain of a young dependent, Mary: cells which no one so far has been able to explain. Though this brain surgery might easily go wrong, attempts to get Dr Raymond to take the potential consequences seriously meet with the response: 'As you know, I rescued Mary from the gutter, and from almost certain starvation, when she was a child; I think her life is mine, to use as I see fit' (8). Mary is a seventeen-year-old beauty, utterly trusting; after her brain has been tampered with she awakens first in wonder, but then in terror, falling to the floor a hopeless idiot. Dr Raymond's response is simply that this could not be helped, 'and, after all, she has seen the Great God Pan' (15). The narrative continues with a series of suicides after experiences of comparable horror.

The Grey World: The beauty beyond

In her first novel, *The Grey World*, Underhill could be said to be attempting to 'lift the veil' without the possibility of reducing any one of her characters to idiocy, and to commend Blake's perceptions, to which she explicitly appeals towards the end of her novel. Her central character, Willie Hopkinson, finds himself in the Sussex downlands, with a flock of sheep spread fanwise, a benevolent silence and an intimate sense of consolation; in a flash of insight he is shown 'the imaginative Universe shining dimly through the Vegetative World' (198). A question for her readers is whether, in order to have Willie reach this point, Underhill needed a framework for his consciousness as macabre as she made it, if not so horrifying as that produced by Machen. The book opens with a scene in a children's hospital where Willie, a small slum child, lies dying of typhoid fever in October 1878. After his death, he has to endure a period of existence as a new-made ghost, one among many complaining spirits. Willie prays desperately for a return to life and finds himself reborn into a fourth-floor nursery, somewhat sickly, but a joy to his mother who thinks he will be a poet if she can rear him. Through the vicissitudes of this second life, he acquires the artistry and skills of a distinguished book-binder and a home in an earthly paradise. The substance of the novel is about Willie's transition from the early miseries of his reborn life to his adult maturity.

Without the 'grey world' Willie might well have been characterized as a 'normal' child, puzzling over matters beyond himself. But from nursery

days onwards he is an unacknowledged irritant to his father and an enigma
to his sister Pauline, three years older than himself. His terror of being
returned to the 'grey world', as he recovers sensitivity to it, precipitates some
distressing scenes: both in the family when he tries to explain himself, and
on the occasions of his mother's 'At Home' tea gatherings. His last serious
indiscretion takes place when a group of matrons are concocting items for a
charity sale and he recollects his previous existence, which included having
to assist a drunken father get upstairs. Being despatched away to school has
its benefits, since 'the heavy bewilderments of a spirit that lived alone with
occult realities which sapped it of all joy ... had worn the body rather thin'
(46). In the 'At Home' world, however, he finds Elsa Levi, who has inherited
from her mother 'a shining black fringe, a sallow complexion, but few
domestic virtues', despite having been trained 'in all the ritual of Teutonic
womanhood', and with two sons 'becoming more uncompromisingly
Hebraic' on a daily basis (comments which may be Underhill's attempts at
irony at the expense of anti-Semitism).[21] Elsa, in time, becomes both Willie's
advocate and his temptress.

Having resisted death at school from a serious attack of scarlet fever,
Willie comes to realize that there is a possibility of finding salvation and
that the solution is to be found within himself. He comes across a group of
'Searchers of the Soul' – themselves unimpressive, but the source of a firm
friendship with Stephen (another young man, enduring a lowly position in
an architect's office), despite Stephen's terror at Willie's tales of his previous
existence and his time as a ghost. Willie also satisfies his mother's desire
that he should become a 'cultured person' (80) and escapes the miseries of
incorporation into his father's clothing-manufacturing business by learning
the skills of bookbinding. He even risks an unsatisfactory engagement,
which his fiancée has the very good sense to terminate. Stephen, on the
other hand, finds himself in love and invents a benevolent story about Pan
and Pan's Master making a man and a woman to share life together, even
though oblivion seems to be their ultimate destiny.

The crucial point in the novel occurs when Willie accidentally enters the
church of Our Lady of Pity, open on a weekday. His reaction is not to the
architectural plan of the building, but to its scent and stillness. The idea of
a religious building as provocative of emotion is strange to him. There he
watches a woman make the sign of the cross, kneel before an altar, and kiss
the feet of a statue before leaving. The invocation of *Veni, Creator Spiritus*
seems to be what he has been seeking all his life.[22] Willie too kneels ('It is not
easy for an Englishman to kneel in a public place'), and with his deliberate
humility comes a new sense of peace and the purging of his pride (179–
80). He comes to realize that the church, 'where invocation of the Invisible
never ceased' (181), has an existence in eternity.[23] The result of an accidental
meeting outside the church with a young man, a convinced Catholic, is that
Willie sees in the soul of his conversationalist 'an inner light', a reflection of
the 'Beautiful God', which leaves him happier and stronger life-long (198).

And in the National Gallery he discovers the Madonna with her child on her lap, a symbol of reconciliation, love and nurture.

His family circle begin to think that Willie is seriously disturbed, and pack him off to Umbria for a holiday, where he realizes that he is now recovering from a stage of 'Purgation' and on the brink of 'Illumination' (229). He meets a Franciscan friar and is taken to see a painting of 'Lady Poverty' by an anchorite, one Hester Waring.[24] Returning home, his dying mother seems to be threatened by the 'grey world'. Willie, now knowing that 'all things exist because of the loveliness that exists in them', at last discerns 'with a certain sad and tender love some beautiful meaning hidden under his mother's garrulous kindness'; she has never in her life longed for anything but the health and success of herself, her husband and her family (241–2). Willie seeks his mother's salvation as she dies smiling at him, with 'the radiance of a quite unselfish happiness' and a kind of joyful blessing: '*You'll* be all right, dearie' (247). Willie comes to realize both that she fears being forgotten – the one great duty of the living being the loving commemoration of the dead – and that he loves her.

This transformation – eyes wide open – of Willie's consciousness takes place in a family gathering, from which he is awakened by having a glass of cold water thrown in his face. He makes a mistake in trying to consult Elsa, who attempts to seduce him, but in a flight to the woods and a recognition of the paganism of the countryside where Pan and Christ both live, he comes to understand Christ's Incarnation as one of 'Earth-holiness', not 'from the Heavens' (294).[25] There he also stumbles across an exquisite picture of the Madonna in the forest, surrounded by wild creatures, placed in a shrine in remembrance of Francis Waring, Hester's much-loved husband. Hester thrives like the Madonna of her painting, living among wild creatures and healing their damage in an infirmary. Willie at last recognizes that his two tasks are to remember the soul of his mother and to live 'the Imaginative Life' (302). He settles down to live nearby to Hester: working at his exquisite book-binding, wanting to 'trace out the Divine in the world', and thinking that 'the honest artist is very near to God' (319).[26]

The Lost Word: Two versions of Anglicanism

Underhill's first book was reviewed encouragingly, and her publisher, William Heinemann, must have thought sufficiently well of it to take on her second novel.[27] In this, Underhill turned to a markedly different scene, at which point it is worth noticing her antipathy to at least some Anglican clergy. In *The Grey World*, Willie is much irritated by a clergy couple, John Finchley and his wife, on his trip to Umbria; the wife agrees with her husband that a 'spiritual religion' (Protestantism) scarcely needs pictures, and her husband meanly complains that the horse pulling their carriage has taken the hills too slowly (226).[28] This sketch, as will be explained below, is relevant to Underhill's portrait of the Dean in her second novel, *The Lost Word* (1907). The most significant link between the two novels, however, is Willie's first experience in the church of Our Lady of Pity, and his sense of a religious building as provocative of emotion. Underhill's second novel is especially ambitious; to write it must have required not merely visits to a range of ecclesiastical buildings in Europe, but some serious study of what was involved in building, furnishing and decorating a church from scratch.

Her central character is once again a young man, but this time growing up in and around an Anglican cathedral. The major responsibility for the cathedral and its associated buildings is that of her protagonist Paul's father, the Dean, who hopes that his son (freckles, broad shoulders and 'a violently romantic soul') may perhaps become a parson 'with a taste for wood-carving or antiquarian research' (5). Paul, however, displays an annoying turn for mysticism, 'rightly held to be out of place in an Established Church' (5). The Dean, 'a muscular Churchman', regards the Cathedral as a most interesting relic of the past, but for his son it is the home of mystery (5). While such understanding is not readily supported via the family library, quite by accident the Dean provides information for his son in a lecture in which he appeals for pew funds. Describing with zeal and theological disapproval the furniture and ceremonial of the old English church, he congratulates his audience, 'and incidentally the nation', on the virtues of the British character 'which had enabled it to eliminate from its religion matters so repugnant to common-sense', and deems the Reformation to have left 'a religion purged of superstition, which expresses the strenuous temper and practical talents of our race!' (6–7)

Paul, on the other hand, thrives in imagining the ceremonies of the past, which gives him a whole new perspective on the Cathedral. He finds a favourite spot for himself on the transept roof, where he restores to some sort of life a long-forgotten angel image, and carvings from a master craftsman left for the angel's delight. His perception of the different ways in which the Cathedral can be experienced is shared by a verger, Mr Rogers, 'a Freemason of the more imaginative kind', who seeks craft and symbolism in every detail of Gothic ornament (17). Paul becomes a competent stone carver, but when the diocesan architect suggests that he should travel to Italy to train, the Dean instead sends Paul to Keble College, Oxford: 'a college which seemed likely to encourage a well-bred orthodoxy without providing further food for architectural enthusiasm' (18).

Paul is so disillusioned by what passes for religious practice at Keble that for a time he becomes captivated by 'modern science'; but he is shaken out of this by a new friend, Hugh, a man with money and a level of trust in the English episcopate which makes him acceptable to Paul's father (23). Paul realizes that he suffers from a kind of 'spiritual nostalgia' and endures a change of consciousness when blindfolded during his initiation into freemasonry (39). One of Underhill's opportunities for a certain didacticism was thus provided at this point, in a comparison between 'the sacrament of the altar, celebrated before a practical and imperceptive congregation' which may yet bring 'the divine sacrifice back to the visible world', and a Masonic ceremony which broke down 'the rampart of illusion' in Paul, so that he stepped over into 'the real and eternal world' (44–5). He sees colours burning 'like intense flames before the altar of beauty', feels silence, sees paradise and fairyland, the possibility of 'radiant fields and magical forests' (45–6). He comes to the Graal-city, the perfect shrine, 'the image of all the buildings that are made for adoration or for love', and the now living angel from the Cathedral roof (47).[29] What Willie experiences towards the end of his progress, Paul experiences before his life's work has even begun.

Hugh helpfully persuades the Dean that since Paul has no vocation for the demands of the ordained ministry, the next best thing is to let him become an architect, remarking that Anglicans *require* nice churches: they can't worship anywhere, like Dissenters' (55).[30] Hugh funds the church Paul builds, and supports Paul's desire to have 'the Queen of Queens, the Perfect Beauty', over the central door, despite the likely disapproval of the Bishop (58). By contrast, Paul finds in a tiny chapel a font 'endowed ... with a vivid and passionate reality', its rim carved with Pan and his fauns (67). Something from 'the terrible and elemental world, no less actual than the flowery playgrounds of the Love Divine, had been caught and fettered to the stone' (68). Paul employs the carver, Mark, for his own church, and the two attend the Guild of Apprentices of Saint Eloy for the purpose of recruiting craftsmen.[31] Underhill's description of this guild gives her full rein to mock 'bullet-headed vicars, built to withstand the impact of episcopal reproof', 'cadaverous curates' and empty-headed women overheard in ecclesiastical tittle-tattle (76). Paul's most significant recruit, however, turns out to be Hugh's cousin Catherine, back from Paris, a young woman who had 'the aggressive chastity which is often developed by the study of the nude and the constant society of busy young men', but also 'a heightened power of observation which comes from residence in Latin countries' (94, 97). Catherine becomes aware that Paul is 'a real artist and a real man' who in some ways is very ordinary, notwithstanding his 'super-sensual revelation' (97, 122). Paul, in turn, comes to see Catherine as a woman rather than an 'intelligent machine' (103). The development of the relationship between the two of them threads its way through the narrative of the building of the church. A minor accident in the enamellist's workshop where a chalice is being made – the artist becoming alert to its occult meaning as the Graal – results in Paul and Catherine's touching one another: 'Arrogant chastity, amazed, wrathful, very sure of itself, forced them apart; and in that act drew them together ... Each loved the other's manifest hatred of love' (140).

Beyond this, to find an appropriate way of representing the Madonna, Paul both throws a piece of fabric over Catherine's head – a suggestion of elusive loveliness – and also thrusts into her arms a little girl from the street, carried as if she were a king's son. This transfigures Catherine, who finds it overwhelming to be given a child by the man she loves, Paul for his part finding the occasion 'to be in the nature of a mystical experience; an emblem, long sought amongst the stones, now discovered in the flesh' (174). Both desperately try not to pledge themselves to one another, but are shocked into doing so when Paul finds the 'Queen of Beauty' dislodged by scaffolding, and Catherine prostrate in distress at the spot prepared for the altar (256). Once they commit to one another in marriage, their honeymoon in Carcassonne becomes a near disaster. Catherine endures a nightmare experience of Paul's unhappiness, believing him to have been made miserable by the marriage, and she determines to leave him. But, in the Cathedral, Catherine comes to appreciate the Pietà's message – the Madonna supporting her Son at peace while she herself bears the pain – which brings her in turn to desire the increase of her own pain if Paul's wound can be healed. It is at this point that the 'all-enduring Mother' leans towards her and encourages her towards this course of action (294). With her words, and in the Mass – 'a sudden peaceful sense of participation in the eternal sacrifice' – Catherine finds the possibility of true union with Paul (295).[32]

Paul himself then comes to find her, deeply distressed by a letter from Hugh, who without consultation with Paul has introduced a number of items into the church. Worse, he has been influenced by Paul's father, the Dean, to think it an error of judgement to have the Madonna over the central door of the church, since it would offend the bishop: 'He didn't think the baby made it any better; the modern feeling, he said, was against this worship of immaturity' (298). The Madonna has been moved to a side entrance and replaced with an Agnus Dei. As Paul sees later, this piece is distressingly overdone: 'One neatly chiselled foot clutched the machine-made Banner of Redemption; the curly fleece lay in serried ranks from nose to tail, like a colony of well-conducted worm-casts' (304). Paul's mood shifts from anger to sadness, but even while recoiling from the sculpture, he at last realizes that the 'lost word' is 'Sacrifice' (309, 315). Now he is able to see the union of shadow and idea deep in the 'Heart of God', and understand the Christian myth as recapitulating the history of the soul (312).

The Column of Dust: The supernatural, good and bad

Reviews of *The Lost Word* were sufficiently enthusiastic to encourage Underhill further.[33] But the year when it appeared, also the year of her marriage, was one in which she had major decisions to make: not least that of resolving whether or not she would become a Roman Catholic. A decision to do so would have serious implications for where she would be married, the upbringing of any children of the marriage and her relationship not only with Hubert but with both sets of parents and neighbours. As it so happened, the problem of 'modernism' and its condemnation by the papacy dissuaded her from becoming a Roman Catholic. Modernism was admittedly an issue within the Church of England as well, but Underhill herself was unlikely to ignore genuinely new sources of knowledge and their importance for reinterpreting tradition, and was unable and unwilling to accept the condemnation of those who made the attempt. On the other hand, she was never an uncritical 'modernist', having developed a deep distaste for 'exclusivism' of any variety, and fighting symptoms of 'fastidiousness' in religious practice throughout her life.[34]

As mentioned above, whether she quite realized it or not, Underhill was using the novel form to work out some of her most fundamental convictions. She had come to understand the value of ritual and ceremony and the way in which both could awaken religious sensibility. And as she shrewdly perceived with regard to the various Christian ways of promoting holiness, 'ritual, where genuine, is always a dramatic expression of doctrine'.[35] These insights she cherished life long, generously able to commend Freemasons for their ceremonies in which people could be bonded together. She had not only been a member of the Golden Dawn Society for a time, but had learned to appreciate the meaning of the Roman Catholic Mass, and attended the ceremonies of the Byzantine and Armenian Orthodox churches, not only in magnificent settings abroad, but also in obscure venues at home. In this overall context she embarked on the writing of her third novel, *The Column of Dust* (1909). In this, she intended yet again to illuminate for her readers how to distinguish the attempt to know, control and manipulate super-sensible realities from the rites which stimulate religious transformation. It was perhaps unfortunate that she returned to the realm of the occult, as well as to examples of genuine religious transformation comparable to those she had depicted in her first two novels.[36]

The plot of Underhill's third novel revolves around her heroine Constance's dabbling in the realms of the occult and its disturbing consequences. The epigraph for the book this time came from Laurence Housman's book of devotional love poems, *Spikenard*, beginning 'O dust, have faith according to the term / Of this life's lease!' and concluding, 'For fringes of thy darkness feel the Light / Which was ordained to be / When God, the Just, / From shadow shaping thee, / Put trust / In dust.'[37] The first two chapters introduce a lonely spirit who comes across the temporal world and its mortality, symbolized by a small kitten dead in the gutter outside a bookshop. An employee of the shop, the supposedly sane and sensible Constance, has chosen to enact some of the ceremonies found in an ancient text, in what at least some of Underhill's readers must have recognized as an utterly blasphemous invocation of 'spirit' as she proceeds to chant 'the strange old Hebrew spell' (16). Not only does this have some effect upon her own mind, she discovers that she will never be alone again, because she has raised up a 'cobwebby thing' with a sad and frightened voice, to be known as 'The Watcher' (18).

Constance's dreary accommodation also houses Vera, apparently an unattractive, cruel and difficult little girl. Vera is supposedly Constance's adopted child, but is in fact her daughter, the result of a liaison with a man whose name she had never even known. When she decides in all honesty to acknowledge Vera as her daughter, she loses contact with a group of 'ladies' who themselves dabble in occult speculations, her hostess remembering that her father had been an archdeacon of the Established Church (250). Never free from the presence of the unwanted Watcher, Constance takes Vera on a holiday to Westmoreland, and as a result of being hopelessly lost on a pony-and-cart expedition discovers a cottage, a church and its priest living there as custodian of the Holy Graal. Taken into the church so stark in its decoration she thinks it must be very 'Low' Church of England, she falls to her knees, like Willie, 'in an act of profound though involuntary adoration' (138). Importantly, this is the one place in Underhill's fiction where she presents profound advice and reflections on Christ offered to someone by an Anglican priest. Constance undergoes a religious conversion as a result, and comes to realize that the Watcher is being gradually humanized too, being turned from intruder to friend. Astonishingly, when Martin, the priest, knows he is dying, he makes Constance responsible for the Graal by bringing it to her lodgings. And at Christmastide the Cup is 'companioned by that antique symbol of incarnate divinity: a weary, selfless mother wholly concentrated on the well-being of her child' (276).

When Vera falls desperately ill, a bereaved neighbour and the husband of the woman who has rejected her from her drawing-room society mercifully do what they can to support Constance as she fights for Vera's recovery. Then, losing her way when walking in thick fog, Constance finds the chapel of a group of women religious, the 'Helpers of the Holy Souls' responsible for the 'Ritual for the Dead': the Dead being seen as those who wait for the supplication of their friends or of others in their place (287, 295). The ritual also involves the kinship of the saints, the company who would welcome and shelter her too. Constance rises on the wings of one particular supplication from the litany for the dead, 'startling in its supreme assurance', 'That Thou wouldst be pleased to admit them to the contemplation of Thy adorable Beauty, we beseech Thee to hear us!' (294). She makes this supplication her own, as she in turn falls ill in her exhaustion. With her neighbour willing to take care of Vera, she realizes that it is Vera who must live and that she must die. It is her acceptance of her own death which results in the Watcher being released from his own dust-fetters. Even he comes to see, in the moment of Constance's death, 'the crucial moment of transcendent victory and earthly loss': the 'transfigured Spirit – the inmost inhabitant – where it sat, like a Mater Dolorosa, holding upon its knees the slain self by whose death it was redeemed' (302). And as he sees Constance's soul shoot up – 'a penetrating flame of love, straight to that Heart of Being which all creation eternally desires' – he too is redeemed, initiated into heaven, with 'the sacred spirit' of man brought forth from the column of dust (304).

Conclusion

The Column of Dust is something of a reversion to the macabre horrors of Underhill's first novel, and it may be significant that, to get it into print, Underhill had to change publishers. The writer of a scathing contemporary review for *Punch* was, though, more troubled by the novel's unevenness of tone, criticizing the juxtaposition of a Kensington tea-fight and a musical comedy with solemn scenes in a mountain chapel and the death of the novel's main character.[38] It may be that Underhill eventually realized one major reason why this novel was not a success with many of her readers, admitting to a friend that 'I just write what comes into my head and leave the result to luck'.[39] Yet, later in her life, having publicly returned to membership of the Church of England, and exactly at the time when she was establishing herself as a 'retreat director', she could recognize the achievement of another who was as much preoccupied with the 'secret of sanctity' as she was herself.[40] Both Mary J.H. Skrine and her novels are undeservedly forgotten, but in at least one of them, *Shepherd Easton's Daughter* (1925), to which Underhill wrote the foreword, she found, for once, the transformation of a Church of England 'Reverend' brought 'under the influence of a spirit so much greater, stronger and simpler than his own', and praised Skrine for showing a most remarkable 'power of sympathetic interpretation', simply and perfectly expressed.[41]

The novel's main character, Dorcas, has an extraordinary gift of compassion for others, expressed both in her discernment of human sinfulness and in her ability to soothe and heal distressed animal creatures and human beings alike (perhaps akin to Hester Waring in *The Grey World*). Living the life of a contemplative, Dorcas 'holds energies stronger than strength, loves that lie deeper than all conscious love'.[42] Set in the most humble circumstances, the novel depicted neither the 'grey world' nor the conjuring of dangerous 'spirits', nor even knowledge of the great architecture Underhill knew so well, but a sense of the effect of 'creative and protective love' poured out for others in the most humble and obscure circumstances.[43] It may even be the case that Underhill recognized that Mrs Skrine got closer to evoking Underhill's ideal spiritual life in fiction than she had herself achieved. But in choosing to write about 'sanctity' in a quite different mode from the fictional, Underhill had found a way of commending the living of a Christian life which is much more highly regarded than any of her novels. Of her three works of fiction, we might conclude that *The Lost Word* is the one which represents Underhill at her best as a novelist, and which still merits careful attention for the importance she rightly attached to the integration of worship and living distinctively as an Anglican.

FIGURE 7 *Dorothy L. Sayers.*

6

Dorothy L. Sayers (1893–1957): God and the Detective

Jessica Martin

'Do carry on. Have something to drink. It's a poor heart that never rejoices. And begin right at the beginning, if you will, please. I have a very trivial mind. Detail delights me. Ramifications enchant me. Distance no object. No reasonable offer refused.' The speaker is, of course, Lord Peter Wimsey, making an early appearance at the outset of the novel *Unnatural Death* (1927).[1] His interlocutor, a doctor who has questions about the apparently innocent death of an old lady from cancer, is a framing device, straight man to Lord Peter's centre-stage entrance. Lord Peter delivers his narrative invitation *staccato*, with what we quickly learn are characteristically mercurial shifts of register and focus. He dances around his audience, affable, proverbial, colloquial, declarative, dominant. He promises to be frivolous but conceals a serious intention. He concentrates not only on trivial details but on their 'ramifications'. The messy problems of human behaviour are to be solved in orderly deductions from minutiae. This is the detective narrative offered as a kind of *synecdoche,* the figure of speech where the part both stands for and reveals the meaning of the whole.

Lord Peter's voice is, in fact, an enhanced version of his creator's. In this brief, early invitation to set out a narrative are all her characteristic modes and approaches in cameo. Orderly neatness jostles together with an exuberant unpredictability, a sense that a life-giving *something* evades all the logic in the world, however rigorously applied. This complex juxtaposition of deliberate rigour with a (sometimes undeliberate, often delighted) liberation from the bondage of the will is at the heart of Sayers's enduring power as a writer.

Dorothy L. Sayers was born into an Anglican household in 1893, the only daughter to the Revd Henry Sayers and his wife Helen. Sayers became a scholar of Somerville College, Oxford, an unmarried mother, a maker of advertising slogans, a theologian, a dramatist, a translator of Dante; but she is best remembered for her detective fiction and for its insouciant – yet sensitive – protagonist Lord Peter Wimsey. The years during which she mainly concentrated on the detective genre ran from 1923 to 1938. Always engaged by the theatre, she moved towards religious drama from the mid-1930s. The most notable was *The Zeal of thy House* (1937) written for Canterbury Cathedral, in the same series of innovative plays set in sacred space for which Eliot wrote *Murder in the Cathedral* in 1935. She then became a highly influential, if reluctant, writer in Christian apologetics, of which the finest example is *The Mind of the Maker* (1941), an account of the dynamic nature of the Trinity using the artist's creative process as its governing metaphor. Early in the war she also produced an idiosyncratic set of recommendations for post-war civic virtue from a Christian standpoint, *Begin Here* (1940). The peak of her explicitly religious imaginative work, though, was her series of plays for radio based on the life of Christ, *The Man Born to Be King*, broadcast between autumn 1941 and spring 1942. These plays permanently changed popular imaginative perceptions of the life of Christ. Her interpretations of motive, character and context made a wealth of thinking about Christ's life vividly available beyond the academy, and her decision to use colloquial English as her main dramatic medium caused a considerable stir.[2] She is known also for her fine translation of Dante's *Divine Comedy*, upon which she spent the last fourteen years of her life, and which she left unfinished at her death in 1957.[3]

This chapter, true to a book on Anglican women novelists, deals with the novels, and therefore with Sayers's openness to what *cannot* be grasped or fully known, the haunting moments when she is lifted beyond the mechanics of her beautiful constructions and is instead caught and held by an order beyond her own intention. It also thinks about the limitations of the detective novel as a frame for such unpredictability, charting at the same time Sayers's increasing unease with narrative arcs which must privilege orderly acts of justice over the wilder power of mercy. Not until after Sayers has moved from detective fiction to a radio drama centred upon Christ – a criminal, a just man, God himself – is mercy given its full space to overturn punishment.

Detective fiction is about control, about the re-establishment of order and rightness to a transgressive situation, and about the rational pursuit of deductive systems in its service. It attracts the puzzle-solver, the restorer of balance, and in those systems forgiveness is structurally redundant because law restores harmony. In that sense its world is more Old than New Testament. Justice and judgement work together and law is the means towards the re-establishment of right living. Often civil society is represented in miniature:

in a village, a country house, a ship, a school, a train, even a room. Order is reached through the correct identification of an individual so corrupt that he or she must be expelled from the civic body. The golden age of detective fiction, of course, subsists in a world with capital punishment. The hangman is a potent nemesis, himself dangerously vulnerable to miscarriages of justice or failures of detection, keeping the stakes high.[4]

Sayers is very responsive to the medium in this guise. Yet she is not so naive as to believe that human systems perfectly mirror divine justice. Therefore, in her detective worlds, justice, while sought by human beings, is inadequate to its task and has to be established through the intervention of powers somehow beyond human reach. Her plots have an invisible protagonist, and his name is Jehovah.

Murder Must Advertise

Take, for example, *Murder Must Advertise* (1933), set in an advertising agency realistically similar to the one where Sayers herself worked as a copywriter, but with a plot hinged around a standard-issue dastardly drug-running melodrama. It features Lord Peter Wimsey, working under the symbolically charged alias of Mr Death Bredon. Sayers plays with the relationship between the illusive visions of a hedonistic world of cocaine-fuelled partying and the neat, slickly solid invitations of advertising copy, each beckoning towards excess but in completely different ways. As Sayers herself was quick to acknowledge, the attempt didn't entirely work. The scenes in the advertising agency are twice as lively as the druggy scenes, about which Sayers candidly admitted she knew little.[5] Her doped characters take cocaine, but mostly behave as if they had taken laudanum – sleepiness, visions, dreams, irrational fears and prescience – rather as if they had strayed into a Wilkie Collins novel. The plot of *Murder Must Advertise* turns on the eerie equivalence between drug pushing and the advertisement of a patent over-the-counter medicine 'Nutrax for Nerves'. Nutrax is itself just the front runner for a morally ambivalent vision of advertising as a process for corrupting will and decision in the name of pleasure.

Sayers's style of naturalistic realism seems to promise the everyday and the rational. Yet this is only a backdrop for its governing sense of the uncanny. *Murder Must Advertise* shows this in an understated form, through set pieces and a quick-witted readiness to borrow the techniques of theatre and of medieval morality genres. Wimsey, an angel of judgement called Death, switches between *personae* in ways which have nothing to do with realism and much to do with the stage conventions of masks, twins, disguise, ghostly messengers. The book's first chapter sees Death arrive; its last sees him leave on the back of an unlikely wedding.

Between these two book-ends Sayers combines witty, lively and mundane scenes of copywriting life with heightened vistas of dreamlike masquerade which seem to owe more than a little to her admiration for Wilkie Collins.[6] Here, for example, is Wimsey's first solo encounter with the debauched Bright Young Thing, Dian de Momerie.[7] Wearing a harlequin mask, he has beaten her in a night-time car chase; now they are both lost in a dark wood. Dian stumbles into the trees 'among briars and tufts of bracken' when she hears 'no jazz tune, but one she remembered from nursery days:

> Tom, Tom, the piper's son
> Learned to play when he was young
> And the only tune that he could play
> Was: "Over the hills and far away".'

The tune 'so bodiless that it seemed to have no abiding-place' is, of course, being played by Wimsey on a penny whistle from where he sits at ease in a tree, but it terrifies Dian, who runs, trips and falls screaming. 'The terror induced by forests and darkness', says Wimsey mockingly to her from above, 'was called by the Ancients, Panic fear, or fear of the great god Pan. It is interesting to observe that modern progress has not altogether succeeded in banishing it from ill-regulated minds.'[8] As their encounter unfolds, Sayers employs 'Panic fear' as a herald for divine justice, poised ambiguously between different supernaturals. For Dian and her world of parties and nightmare seem to belong to the hybrid classicism of the revenge genre in drama, where the vengeance of the Roman God Jove and the divine justice of the Judaeo-Christian Jehovah melt one into the other. An important consequence is that the arbitrary judgements of the pagan gods become partly domesticated by the rule of law. As order is re-established at the end of such plays, its welcome reappearance, usually on the back of a spectacularly high body count, is supposed to herald a new and more righteous order – though we have the freedom to be sceptical about that.

Ten years later Sayers was to come back to the idea of Pan, but as a figure of mercy rather than a herald of judgement. In *The Man Born to Be King* (1943) it is the righteous man who dies, sinners who are given life. In an extraordinary and haunting scene, Pan becomes the dying Christ, allowing his own destruction for the sake of all.[9] The moment comes in the eleventh play, 'King of Sorrows'. Pilate's wife Claudia has a terrifying dream which impels her to warn her husband to have nothing to do with the condemnation of Jesus. Sayers has Claudia tell her dream, far too late for its warning to save Jesus himself, who as she speaks is drawing his last breath upon the cross:

CLAUDIA: I was in a ship at sea, voyaging among the islands of the Aegean. At first the weather seemed calm and sunny – but presently, the sky darkened – and the sea began to toss with the wind ....

[wind and waves]

Then, out of the east, there came a cry, strange and piercing ....

> *[voice, in a thin wail]*
> 'Pan ho megas tethneke
> Pan ho megas tethneke'

And I said to the captain, 'What do they cry?' And he answered, 'Great
Pan is dead.' And I asked him, 'How can a God die?' And he answered,
'Don't you remember? They crucified him. He suffered under Pontius
Pilate.' ...

> *[murmur of voices, starting almost in a whisper]*

Then all the people in the ship turned their faces to me and said: 'Pontius
Pilate' ...
[*Voices, some speaking, some chanting, some muttering, mingled with
sung fragments of Greek and Latin liturgies, weaving and crossing one
another:* ' ... Pontius Pilate ... Pontius Pilate ... he suffered under Pontius
Pilate ... crucified, dead and buried ... sub Pontio Pilato ....Pilato ... he
suffered ... suffered ... under Pontius Pilate ... under Pontius Pilate ... ']

... in all tongues and all voices ... even the little children with their
mothers.[10]

In her use of the credal words Sayers puts together the baldest, most
historically situated declaration within a Christian statement of faith
with a visionary event indirectly expressed. This dream, part-performed,
part-narrated, becomes a space in which a multitude of times and places
speak together. It shows what liturgy does – and it shows, at the moment
of Jesus's surrender to the violence of the world, what faith does. Sayers's
speaking voices include the Creed in German as well as Latin, French and
English – a bold and compassionate move for the year 1942.

When writing about *Murder Must Advertise* in *The Mind of the Maker*,
Sayers described it as a not very successful attempt to depict 'a contrast of
two "cardboard" worlds, equally fictitious – the world of advertising and
the world of the post-war "Bright Young People"'. She also pointed to an
undeliberate piece of shaping it contained, in offering the observation a
reader made to her: 'Yes; and Peter Wimsey, who represents reality, never
appears in either world except in disguise.' 'It was perfectly true', writes
Sayers, 'and I had never noticed it ... it issued, without my conscious
connivance, in a true symbolism.'[11] Indeed, the book's symbolic logic,
intended or unintended, goes well beyond Wimsey's disguise. Almost
everything in it, in both its main settings, revolves around the relationship
which disguise has with greed and desire. The orgiastic parties are fancy
dress, with masks. The promises of advertising are that buying a given
product will make you richer, more successful or more beautiful than
you really are. The copywriters, who divide into Oxford patrician types
and lower middle-class toilers, have uncomfortable conversations which

ponder, but do not bridge, the gap between the effortlessly entitled and the anxiously aspirational. The murderer, Tallboy, masquerading as a virtuous family man with a passion for cricket and stockbroking interests, is revealed gradually as an adulterer and drug dealer's cat's paw. It's significant that he is one of the aspirational, valuing his education at Dumbleton – a very minor public school – far above its actual social value. He is *jumped-up* – not what he seems to be. Only the cricket is real. The climactic match which reveals Tallboy's power and accuracy with a ball (and thus with a fatal catapult/slingshot) also reveals Wimsey as himself, when his characteristic cricketing style and so his name and true identity are recognized by a bystander.

When Tallboy confesses his crime to Wimsey, he is offered a chance to be authentically patrician in his death, as he has not been in life: he can save his family's reputation by sacrificing himself to the drug gang's executioners. When Wimsey suggests it, he laughs: 'that's the public school way of it. I – yes – all right ... We'll show 'em that Dumbleton can achieve the Eton touch' (242). As Wimsey watches Tallboy go he murmurs the words of execution a judge would have said, but it's not a solution within the rule of law, and he is also morally disturbed by it: 'I don't feel much like celebrating' (243). The reader – perhaps also disquieted by the obduracy of the English class system – is likely to agree.

We see Wimsey at the end, in a conversation with one of the few who is honestly herself, Miss Meteyard, wrestling with another moral difficulty. Miss Meteyard – who resembles her authorial creator in a number of ways, and whose name means proportion in judgement – is a woman who sees a good deal but makes no attempt to intervene in the course of events.[12] Is that moral apathy? Wimsey, on the other hand, makes interference his hobby. Is that moral engagement or something much more compromised? Each recognizes the strength, and the weakness, of the other's position; each measures himself by the other.

This all makes the book a much better artefact than Sayers herself allows, divided and clunky though it is. Like all her really good detective novels, whodunnit is a side issue. The murder is the consequence of a secondary blackmail, whereas the book is more focused on the parallels between the kinds of corruption represented by advertising and drug-pushing. 'Fear not him that killeth', quotes Chief Inspector Parker in a conversation about the relative moral status of drug-dealing and murder (to the latter's advantage), 'but him that hath power to cast into hell'.[13] The words are from the tenth chapter of the Gospel of Matthew, but Sayers shifts their resonance. The drug-peddler possesses, and uses, a power more infernal than the power of life and death over another, hints Parker; and yet this power, the power to corrupt the soul, might (unlike an honest-to-goodness murder) incur no punishment in law.

This is where Sayers indicates the limits of neat justice systems. Parker and Wimsey agree that police work will not redeem anything much, necessary though it might be. "'Tis the Last Judgment's fire must cure this place', quotes Wimsey, 'calcine its clods and set its prisoners free'.[14] Wimsey's remark, too, adapted from Browning's *Childe Roland to the Dark Tower Came,* has a grimly suggestive setting: the stanza begins, 'Penury, inertness and grimace ... were the land's portion'. Is this about the posturing poverty of the addict or the posturing poverty of the consumer? How different are they?[15]

The two worlds are not complete equivalents, of course. The moral condemnation and unreality of the drugs world, the infernal efficiency of its vengeful organization, are too complete to be true. And there is a good deal of affection and tolerance in her depiction of the lively offices of Pym's Publicity. They and we have fun putting snatches of quotation, from mostly Victorian poets, into absurd sales settings, with glorious changes of register, and the daft rhymes are splendid:

A meal begun with Blaggs' Tomato
Softens every husband's heart-oh! (126)

The darker parallels emerge in throwaway comments. 'I wonder why the longsuffering public doesn't rise up and slay us,' remarks one copywriter (50). They have a slightly more extended outing in a discussion of the Whifflets smoking campaign when Wimsey asks idly, 'What happens ... when you've increased sales to saturation point? ... Suppose you push up the smoking of every man and woman in the Empire until they must either stop or die of nicotine poisoning?' Pym demurs, but cannot help responding pragmatically to this beguiling vision:

'We're a long way off that,' replied Mr Pym seriously. 'And that reminds me. This scheme should carry a strong appeal to women. "Give your children that seaside holiday by smoking Whifflets." That sort of thing. We want to get women down to serious smoking. Too many of them play about with it. Take them off the scented stuff and put them on to the straightforward Virginia cigarette ... Whifflets. You can smoke a lot more of them in the day without killing yourself. If we increase women's smokes by 500% – there's plenty of room for it –' Mr Bredon's attention wandered again. (197)

Sayers's towers of slogans, which appear twice, once close to the beginning and once as its final statement, are her climactic demonstration of the ways in which copy distorts the nature of desire. Here is part of the earlier one:

The presses, thundering and growling, ground out the same appeals by the million: ASK YOUR GROCER – ASK YOUR DOCTOR – ASK THE MAN WHO'S TRIED IT – MOTHERS! GIVE IT TO YOUR CHILDREN – HOUSEWIVES! SAVE MONEY – HUSBANDS! INSURE YOUR LIVES – WOMEN! DO YOU REALISE? DON'T SAY SOAP, SAY

SOPO! Whatever you're doing, stop it and do something else! Whatever you're buying, pause and buy something different! Be hectored into health and prosperity! Never let up! Never go to sleep! Never be satisfied. If once you are satisfied, all our wheels will run down. Keep going – and if you can't, Try Nutrax for Nerves! (67)

The slogans reappear at the very end, once the murderer has been himself murdered and Death departed from Pym's Publicity. But Sayers slips in with them a slogan of a different kind:

Tell England. Tell the world. Eat more Oats. Take Care of your Complexion. No More War. Shine your Shoes with Shino. Ask Your Grocer. Children Love Laxamalt. Prepare to meet thy God.[16]

Playful and at times farcical though the book is, it is presided over, beginning to end, by something above and beyond the reach of detective, policeman or any human power.

The Nine Tailors

It is in *The Nine Tailors,* appearing the following year in 1934, that Sayers writes the perfect form of the divine judgement plot, and thus the perfect detective novel. The puzzle presents as a mysterious body buried in a Fenland churchyard, mutilated and unrecognizable – apparently victim to a savage murder. Yet as the book unfolds this death is revealed not to be a murder at all, but something much stranger and harder to categorize. There are other, peripheral deaths, some of them indeed savage murders, and there are acts both of malice and of generosity which initially seem to have no consequences. Yet in the end the book's moral logic is governed by the ways in which various characters are implicated in that central mysterious death of a thoroughly bad man.

Jehovah works through inanimate instruments, unwitting actions, coincidence and carelessness. The Cambridgeshire Fen country itself – inhospitable, unpredictable, liable to flood, to revert to its original sea and marsh – is not only the book's starkly vivid setting but one of its most potent plot movers. So is the church of Fenchurch St Paul, its soul pent in those uncanny and enigmatic speakers-without-language, the bells.[17] Its village is a world within a world, where Lord Protector Cromwell lives on as a potent political force, cut off by weather and culture from the softer though no less treacherous landscapes of London and post–Great War Normandy. Into that world Lord Peter stumbles, 'by what men call chance', when his car crashes on a notoriously dangerous corner in filthy winter weather.[18] The scene is set. Lord Peter will meet the main characters, be told the significant back story (the theft of some fabulously valuable emeralds) and be set a couple of beguiling puzzles in the first twenty pages.

Sayers began *The Nine Tailors* before *Murder Must Advertise*, but finished it afterwards. Having chosen to base her plot clues around the patterns of bell-ringing (a favourite hobby of her own father in the fen parish of Bluntisham) she spent time and care on the theoretical mastery of its intricate mathematics. She was not a ringer herself. Bell-ringing is the book's governing metaphor; each chapter is named for a bell-ringing technique, with a punning second meaning which tells the reader where the plot is going ('Lord Peter is called into the Hunt'; 'The Slow Work'; 'The Dodging').

This is the language of bell-ringing, but not the language of the bells. They speak without words. They speak in the mathematical patterning of a peal, in responsive humming or brazen clang, deafening or threatening. They denote the many deaths of a damp, poor 1920s Fen village – babies, the old, the weak, the ill – when they ring the 'Nine Tailors', as the passing bell for a man is called. They speak through their inscriptions. Last of all they speak through old stories. 'Those bells!' exclaims one suspect, Will Thoday, 'I was expecting all the time to hear them speak. I never have liked the sound of bells ... When I was a boy, I read a story in a magazine about a bell that called out after a murderer ... "Help Jehan! Help Jehan!"' (216). It is, of course, the bells which are in the end revealed as the killers, their fatal sound wielded by unwitting ringers including Wimsey and the unworldly, gentle, virtuous Rector himself, battering an evil man with a long New Year Peal on a snowy night. He dies of a stroke, that death traditionally named for divine vengeance as apoplexy or 'the stroke of God's hand'.[19]

Sense and nonsense, deduction and coincidence, pattern themselves together. A vital clue turns up in the belfry as a dreamlike piece of visionary writing on an old bit of paper. It conceals a cipher, the crucial key to which proves to be bell-ringing patterns, identified by the scholarly Rector because he mistakes what he is seeing when his spectacles are off. Decoded, it becomes three enigmatic phrases from the psalms revealing the location of the emeralds in the roof beams of the church. The part in words makes no sense, the part in numbers reveals the sense, and a double sense both locates us in a part of the church and at the same time firmly locates the presence of God: 'he sitteth between the cherubims', 'the [a]isles may be glad thereof'.[20]

Other verbal clues are offered by a parrot and by a simpleton, Potty Peake, who is not sure what is real and is obsessed by hanging. At times both seem to be channelling messages beyond themselves. 'If you knowed what Potty knows ... I seen him – Number Nine – ... But the tailors was too much for him. Him with the rope – he got him, and he'll get you too. Potty knows. Potty ain't lived all these years, in and out of the church, for nothing' (140). The parrot mutters excitedly, 'Must go to church. Must go to church. The bells. Don't tell Mary' (170). An exchange between Superintendent Blundell, Chief Inspector Parker and Wimsey unravels the whole mystery, but in ways none of them understand as they say it. Blundell begins:

> 'Whoever's got the emeralds did the murder. I'm sure of that.'
> 'Where thy treasure is, there shall thy heart be also',[21] said Wimsey. 'The heart of this crime is down in St Paul. That's my prophecy, Charles. Will you have a bet on it?'
> 'No, I won't', said the Chief Inspector. 'You're right too often, Peter, and I've no money to waste.' (153–4)

The emeralds turn up in the church roof. *Ergo*, the church has done the murder. But we do not see it either. Again, coincidentally (and through human contumaciousness) the lock gates to the local drainage canal haven't been properly serviced, and the cataclysmic flood with which the book closes is the result. It looks (as the Rector would say) like chance, but the Lord sitteth above the waterflood.[22] The Church becomes an Ark of safety, sheltering all the village, and the Rector – a loving portrait of Sayers's own absent-minded and dedicated father – proves to be a strong tower of safety for all under his cure. That same flood kills two men, and one of them, Will Thoday, is drowned trying to save the other one. Though no murderer, Will is so fatally compromised by the events of the plot that his death impresses itself upon the reader as both the natural end of, and the redemptive expiation for, his morally equivocal position. The epigraph for the flood chapter is taken from Psalm 42, 'All thy waves and thy billows are gone over me', a psalm which uses the flood metaphor to stand for profound mental distress. At the end of the whole novel the Rector speaks for the creator's-eye view: 'Perhaps God speaks through those mouths of inarticulate metal. He is a righteous judge, strong and patient, and is provoked every day.'[23]

This is uncompromising stuff. But what about redemption? Tough-minded as she is about consequences, Sayers is also extremely interested in forgiveness – she wrote verse exploring the possibilities of redemption for both Faustus and Judas.[24] Where is there room in the detective novel for the disorderly exercise of mercy? The answer is that there is not much space for it structurally. There is a clear connection between mercy and *mess*. Forgiveness is a different kind of openness to divine intervention, the kind which might go anywhere, do anything, disrupt any pattern. It will have little to do with the shape of the original plan made, and will not necessarily support the civic balance which expels or executes the transgressor. It may undermine it or threaten it. The forces of mercy, truth and divine justice pull Sayers's plots in different directions, so that relationships with human justice systems become complicated and sometimes compromised.

Unnatural Death

Wimsey and even more so those who work for him break the law for the sake of the greater good. And quite often Wimsey's mercurial but dominant masculine presence is given a subversive twist through the roles given to his female companions. This is true not only of the woman with whom he falls in love, Harriet Vane (who is quite a problematic example, for various reasons), but also of the spinsters who do so much detective work on his behalf. They exist within the system's cracks, unregarded, curiously transgressive, and they do the Lord's work in despite of the law.

Miss Climpson, the elderly High Church spinster who appears in several of the Wimsey books, is such a woman. She is employed by Wimsey as a kind of agent, part of the organization he calls 'My Cattery', which gives unmarried 'superfluous women' work exposing fraud and other kinds of criminal or exploitative activity.[25] Blameless in every respect, socially invisible and used to casual contempt, she has a conscience honed by years of Anglo-Catholic spiritual discipline and a sense of what is true and right which exceeds – and is prepared to defy – ordinary secular expectations. We meet her first in the early novel *Unnatural Death* (1927), where she is deployed to make enquiries on Wimsey's behalf precisely because her spinster status makes her unremarkable. In fact, she initiates most of the action, does the detective legwork, makes the significant relationships and exposes the murderer under conditions of considerable danger. Her distinctive epistolary voice, with its comic italic sections, is prominent in the novel, but the comedy cannot conceal her courage or her intelligence.

Unnatural Death seeks to expose a crime which has not come to the attention of the justice system. A significant proportion of the book is spent establishing whether any crime took place at all or whether what appeared to be a natural death from illness and old age was in fact a murder. The case troubles Wimsey's conscience because his interference causes more deaths, and he seeks spiritual advice from a priest, Mr Tredgold, as to how to proceed. That the law considers it a crime is, morally, not enough. Wimsey is told that 'the sin ... lies much more in the harm it does the killer than in anything it can do to the person who is killed ... do what is right ... leave the consequences to God ... and remember that if we all got justice, you and I wouldn't escape either' (220–1). Mr Tredgold's position, derived from the twelfth chapter of Paul's letter to the Romans, sees personal vengeance as spiritually dangerous because punishment is a divine prerogative.[26] Once he establishes that Wimsey's motives are disinterested, the priest is much less troubled about the nature of his intervention.

Discussing the case in a much later book, *Gaudy Night* (1935), Wimsey sums up his own dilemma:

I happened to find out that a young woman murdered an old woman for her money. It didn't matter much: the old woman was dying in any case, and the girl (though she didn't know that) would have inherited the money in any case. As soon as I started to meddle, the girl set to work again, killed two innocent people to cover her tracks and murderously attacked three others. Finally she killed herself. If I'd left her alone, there would only have been one death instead of four.[27]

This discussion, which takes places between Wimsey and a group of women academics, considers the ethics of his intervention in terms which deliberately evade the concept of sin. They wonder whether, for example, the further murders come about through the fear of the death penalty, or whether being a murderer was a treatable psychiatric condition, or even (this being the mid-1930s) whether there might be a eugenic solution to transgressive behaviour. They arrive eventually at the idea that the other victims 'died for the people; sacrificed to a social principle' (355). They further establish that principles always bring about violence, but that having none also deals violence, without any social fringe benefits. It is a moral impasse. Wimsey adds, apparently casually, that had the murderer survived she would have been 'incidentally corrupting one or two people's minds, if you think that of any importance' (355).

The arc of *Unnatural Death* (a book written before political principles dealing in violence had quite so clearly re-emerged on the European stage) makes it clear that this is a fact of singular importance. Miss Climpson, who knows about the twists and turns of women's relationships with each other, sees the murderess exerting herself to dominate a much younger woman who is in love with her. She thinks the relationship unhealthy, not because it is between two women, for elsewhere in the book a relationship between two quite different women is seen as a pattern of ideal mutual love, but because the power relations are unequal. She characterizes the relationship as 'damnable selfishness wearying of its victim' and she makes the discovery that the younger woman has been pressurized into lying for the older one (252). A crucial alibi rests upon this lie. Miss Climpson learns this not directly but through reading a scrap of paper, picked up in the church of St Onesimus, which contains scribbled notes in 'devotional shorthand', *aides mémoires* for the young woman's act of confession.[28] Miss Climpson gallantly decides to confront the murderer – with almost fatal consequences. Fortunately Wimsey arrives in time to save her life. The younger woman, Vera Findlater, becomes one of the murder victims, but, true to the logic of Mr Tredgold's theology, she dies innocent. Her conscience following her confession is clear, and this makes her death more redemptive – a more effective social sacrifice, if you like – than the unrepentant suicide of the murderer herself.

It is striking, though, that this 'invisible' murder is also not visibly punished. The murderer evades the arm of the law and dies through the flawed workings of her sinful heart, strangling herself in her cell. As Wimsey looks at the body, the image of a public execution rises in his mind, and he feels 'cold and sick'. Outside, the June day has gone dark. 'What is the matter with the day?' asks Wimsey. 'Is the world coming to an end?' Parker replies, 'It is the eclipse' (277). Is this too an image of divine judgement, or are we being reminded of the sins which required the death of God, the darkness which fell upon the earth on Good Friday afternoon? The book ends there without further comment. Forgiveness redeems; it does not save life. The book's close is dramatic but weirdly abrupt, almost hopeless in its emotional effect.

Strong Poison

Miss Climpson's next outing is more complex, more prominent and more suggestive. The novel, *Strong Poison* (1930), is the one which introduces Sayers's other major protagonist, the novelist Harriet Vane. Harriet appears not initially as a detective but as a suspect, trapped by a chain of evidence which points inexorably towards her as the murderer of her lover. Of course she is innocent, but as we meet her she is being tried for her life, and the judgement appears to be moving towards her condemnation – except that Miss Climpson is on the jury. Wimsey rejoices: 'She has a fearfully tough conscience – she may stick it out yet' (33). Sure enough, she does, arguing that Harriet does not look like a murderer, that the prisoner's demeanour is part of the evidence and that she is entitled to take it into account. Wimsey's mother, the Dowager Duchess of Denver, backs up our sense that just looking at Harriet Vane speaks her innocence: 'so interesting and a really remarkable face' (30). Miss Climpson brings with her another woman on the jury who thinks medical evidence untrustworthy, has 'no opinion of men in general' and takes 'a dislike to the foreman, who tried to bear her down by his male authority' (37). As the barrister for the defence says drily, 'a person who can believe all the articles of the Christian faith is not going to boggle over a trifle of adverse evidence … we sweat like hell to prepare evidence, then one person makes up her mind on what isn't really evidence at all, and another supports her on the ground that evidence can't be relied on' (36–7). The feminine irrational (as the barrister sees it) has broken into the deductive process. Yet because of it, truth has a chance to prevail.

Sayers has a structural problem in *Strong Poison*. Harriet Vane is in prison for the whole book, which enforces passivity upon her except through the retrospective of the murder story. Also, in order to develop Harriet's relationship with Wimsey, Wimsey too needs to be comparatively static. Consequently much of the detective work is assigned to 'My Cattery' – to Miss Climpson, primarily, but also to another minor player, Miss Murchison, a clever, ugly woman who will infiltrate the real murderer's place of work, a solicitor's office, by working there as a typist. Each of these women finds herself breaking the law in order to obtain evidence for Harriet Vane's innocence. And each of these women, in pursuit of their aim, has a form of 'spiritual' assistance in their lawbreaking activities.

Miss Murchison has to break into a strongbox, for which Wimsey finds her the assistance of a reformed safe-breaker turned born-again preacher. She spends an instructive evening singing revivalist choruses and learning how to use a picklock. As she emerges from the solicitor's offices, having successfully used her skeleton keys and found the crucial evidence, she finds herself singing the song she had first heard at the revival meeting, a song in which liberation and entry merge eschatologically:

> Sweeping through the gates
> Sweeping through the gates of the New Jerusalem
> Washed in the Blood of the Lamb. (128)

Miss Climpson's task is yet more morally ambiguous. Sent down to a small town where she must gain entry to the house of a senile old lady and somehow read her will, she finds that the old lady's nurse is a spiritualist. Versed, through long exposure to shabby-genteel ladies' boarding houses, in the tricks of the spiritualist's trade, Miss Climpson poses as a medium and contrives to convince the nurse that the spirit of the old lady in her stupor upstairs requires them to find her will. The séance she holds is, of course, pure trickery and makes for a sharply comic scene; but there is an aptness, again, in the solution to Harriet Vane's liberation lying in a series of otherworldly messages. Though, as Miss Climpson observes in her letter to Wimsey, 'What excuse I can find in my *conscience* for the *methods* I have used, I *don't KNOW!* but I believe the Church takes into account the necessity of *deception* in certain *professions* ... and *I trust that* my *subterfuges* may be allowed to come under that *category*' (190). The higher justice is served by transgressive female guile (some of it used against other women), fervour and spiritual credulousness, while masculine rational deduction stands helplessly by.

Gaudy Night

Dorothy L. Sayers is almost always resistant to a completely straightforward relationship between the logic of justice and the cause of truth. To some extent that is built into the nature of whodunnits, which are as much about the manipulations of 'what men call chance' as they are about the competent reading of clues. It is striking, though, how often, and especially in the most novelistic of her books, her murders are not murders or her murderers are saved from enduring the full justice process – admittedly usually by suicide. This evasiveness reaches a peak in *Gaudy Night* (1935), set in an Oxford women's college, where there is no murder at all but instead a romantic plot wrapped in an intellectual dilemma about the place of women in the world. The presenting issue requiring a detective is poison-pen letters, and in a way the whole book is more about the corruption of the spirit than anything which can happen to the body. Set in the mid-1930s, its preoccupations are set to a disconcerting extent by the Hitlerian agenda – eugenics, experiments on criminals and the unfit, the abolition of sin by science, the place of women in the home.

Remarkable though the novel is, its determination both to examine the dangerous place of principle in life decisions and to provide a romantic denouement sits together uneasily. Having brought Harriet Vane onto her stage, Sayers was a bit stuck about what to do with her. Clearly as soon as she fell into Wimsey's arms her interest would disappear. Only if their characteristics were kept in tension could they subsist together. Even then, Harriet had to be kept just interesting enough without being so omni-competent as to shove Lord Peter out of the limelight. *Gaudy Night* keeps Wimsey stuck on the Continent for as much of the book as it can get away with, in order to give Harriet a decent outing on her own terms. And it requires her to think hard about her independence – intellectual, physical, financial – and her place in the world: about what she would die for, what she is prepared to live for – about what sacrifices are worth it. With hindsight, this does look like a book written in a time limbering up to a war, and not just because Wimsey is spending his time on ticklish foreign diplomacy. But its romantic cadences do not suit its tougher, more uncompromising features, and it sidesteps the issues both of mercy and of judgement. For the desperate writer of the poison-pen letters when exposed is 'medically dealt with' (475), though what that weasel phrase could mean, in the light of all those discussions about medical experiments on the unfit, is left unelucidated.

Sayers is, in fact, encountering the outer limits of what the detective novel will bear. Her last full-length novel, *Busman's Honeymoon* (1937), began life as a play and its plot, which balances a commonplace murder for a commonplace motive against the moral agony Wimsey experiences for having meddled in the case, makes the difficulties of the punishment-plot very evident. She stopped writing in the genre. She would move towards drama which explicitly placed the terms of salvation in disorderly opposition to the moral accounts human beings keep upon themselves. *The Zeal of thy House* has as its protagonist a brilliant medieval architect, whose redemption is found not in his skill but in his humbling through physical accident and pain. His glorious artefact proves less important than the responsive nakedness of his soul before God.

There is no surprise in Sayers's dedication, in the last years of her life, to translating the toughly salvific journey Dante realizes in *The Divine Comedy*. The shaping art of making order through punishment was not so much left behind as made subject to a profound sea change. The narrative journey upon which she settles in the end proves not to be one of detection, not one of the moves from problem to solution. Instead it is an act of divine sacrifice in the person of Christ: an experience of redemptive change which sidesteps neither pain nor death, nor even despair, but which will end in eternal joy.

FIGURE 8 *Rose Macaulay.*

7

Rose Macaulay (1881–1958): Anglican Apologist?

Judith Maltby

The Towers of Trebizond, Rose Macaulay's last completed novel, begins with what must be one of the most famous opening sentences in twentieth-century Anglophone literature: '"Take my camel, dear," said my aunt Dot, as she climbed down from this animal on her return from High Mass.'[1] The work itself, however, is not widely known to twenty-first-century readers, often relegated to niche status as the perfect gift for a certain kind of Anglican ordinand. Published in 1956, Rose Macaulay's last completed novel was both a popular and critical success; an international bestseller, it won for its author the prestigious James Tait Black Prize. The novel had admirers in high places. Macaulay reported to Father Hamilton Johnson, a member of an Anglican religious order, the Society of St John the Evangelist (known colloquially as the Cowley Fathers), that Princess Margaret read *Trebizond* at Balmoral, 'and laughed so muc[h], alone in a room, that the Queen her sister came to know what was the matter'. Queen Elizabeth 'read it, & also laughed'. Lady Elizabeth Cavendish informed the author that Margaret was 'specially interested ... in the parts [of the novel] about

---

The author gratefully acknowledges permission to cite works of Rose Macaulay from the Society of Authors as the Literary Representative of the Estate of Rose Macaulay; Durham University Library; and the Master and Fellows of Trinity College, Cambridge. In addition, she is thankful for permission to cite from the works of Evelyn Waugh, Copyright © 2019 The Estate of Laura Waugh and the Harry Ransom Center, University of Texas at Austin.

adultery'.[2] Macaulay was made a Dame Commander the following year, which may not be unconnected to the novel's royal reception.

Trebizond, however, was not a late blooming. It was the crown of Macaulay's long, distinguished and successful career in letters: as an author of novels, poetry, travel books, edited anthologies, biographies and literary studies. Elizabeth Bowen's assessment was that Macaulay had 'dazzled more than one generation ... [and] better still she has caused more than one generation to sit up' and called *Trebizond* 'possibly [her] greatest' novel.[3] She was a frequent contributor to the pillars of British public intellectual life: *The Times Literary Supplement, Time and Tide, The Listener*, and *The Observer*. In addition, from the 1930s until her death in 1958, she forged a notable career as both a writer and broadcaster on the new-fangled invention of the wireless and enjoyed a considerable presence on the BBC.[4]

Macaulay was what we would call now a 'public intellectual'. As early as the 1920s, Virginia Woolf sniped at her high profile as a public speaker and commentator in the British and American press. 'Why should she take the field so unnecessarily?' remarked this alleged icon of feminism.[5] If anyone should doubt her right to be called a 'public intellectual', Noel Annan identified her as a living example of England's 'Intellectual Aristocracy' in his influential 1955 essay of the same title – for Macaulay was descended from a formidable line of brainy and distinguished dons and clerics. A chilling piece of evidence for her public stature is her inclusion in a list of British citizens to be executed in the event of a successful Nazi invasion.[6]

We are on safe ground, therefore, in calling Macaulay not only an author of distinction, but also a public intellectual who energetically exploited the new medium of radio. But was she an 'Anglican apologist' – and is *The Towers of Trebizond* a work of Anglican apologetics?

> The camel took aunt Dot to church, but not the Austin me. My aunt was a regular church-goer, which I was not. She was high Anglican, not belonging, therefore, to that great middle section of the Church of England which is said to be the religious backbone (so far as it has one) of our nation. I too am high, even extreme, but somewhat lapsed, which is a sound position, as you belong to the best section of the best branch of the Christian Church, but seldom attend its services. (4)

Macaulay confided to Father Johnson that a friend had been considering 'poping' but 'reading my book about the C.of.E. [*sic*] and its glories, she is now going in for that instead!'[7] Her old friend John Betjeman approvingly described *Trebizond* as 'Anglican propaganda' – as did the anti-apartheid campaigner and Anglican religious Trevor Huddleston, CR.[8]

Despite the denominational partisanship of Betjeman and Huddleston, *Trebizond* demonstrates Macaulay's conviction, which will be discussed more fully below, that the novel is not a form sympathetic to confessional apologetics or propaganda. Francis Spufford, the author of one of the most original books on Christianity and Anglicanism to be written in recent years, tells us that his book is called *Unapologetic* 'because it isn't giving an "apologia", the technical term for a defence of ... ideas' – and also because he's 'not sorry'.[9] In that same way, Macaulay did not set out in her greatest novel to marshal 'arguments' for Anglicanism, or even the Christian faith more broadly, but – as Spufford would do later – acknowledged the importance of emotional intelligence in the life of faith. Perceptively, Bowen praised *Trebizond* 'above all [for its] emotion'.[10] As we shall see, in part through her combative literary relationship with the Roman Catholic novelist Evelyn Waugh over the use of fiction for promoting a *particular* church, Macaulay felt keenly the obligation of the novelist to engage honestly with the complexities of human emotions – an obligation which, for her, would always undermine the use of fiction in matters of faith as a propagandist or even an apologetic tool.

The Towers of Trebizond

As a novel, *Trebizond* brings together many aspects of Macaulay's long literary career, and it was by no means her first fictional treatment of Anglicanism and Christianity. Earlier examples include *Told by an Idiot* (1923) with its mercurial clerical patriarch – introduced to the reader at the beginning of the book by his wife exclaiming to their children, 'Well, my dears, I have to tell you something. Poor papa has lost his faith again' – and her beautifully researched Civil War novel *They Were Defeated* (1932), with its depiction of Robert Herrick's rustic Devon parish and a theologically conflicted Cambridge full of metaphysical poets, Laudians, puritans and papists.[11] Nonetheless, *Trebizond* is certainly her most overtly 'Anglican' novel and references to Anglicanism's history and theology abound. Her correspondence with Father Johnson kindled an interest in its reality as a global branch of Christianity, as did her friendship with another member of the American congregation of Cowley Fathers she met through Johnson, Father Alfred Pedersen, SSJE.[12] The niche aspects of its culture, especially forms of Anglo-Catholicism that even some Anglo-Catholics would see as extreme, are comically explored through the memorable character Father Hugh Chantry-Pigg. In addition, Macaulay's long multifarious interests in travel writing, foreign cultures, gender, international politics, ruins and archaeology are splendidly deployed. A case of plagiarism by one of Laurie's friends raises questions about the integrity of the writer and gay relationships figure in the novel in a matter-of-fact way. *Trebizond* also sits in the genre of the 'cold war' novel with frequent references to Russian and Turkish politics, and aunt Dot and Chantry-Pigg are mistaken for British spies.

The novel's plot is challenging to summarize briefly, and unusually for Macaulay it is narrated in the first person. Laurie (she typically gave her female protagonists androgynous names) is the niece of aunt Dot. The novel is strongly, but not entirely, autobiographical, as Macaulay herself noted that she 'put Laurie at a remove from herself'.[13] Nonetheless, Laurie's long-term relationship with a married man, Vere, mirrors an important episode in the novelist's own life. Macaulay met the Irish novelist and ex-Roman Catholic priest Gerald O'Donovan when they were both working in the Ministry of Information during the Great War. The relationship continued in utter secrecy for decades until his death in 1942. Rose was a friend of the family and became godmother to one of O'Donovan's grandchildren. The intimate nature of their relationship was unknown even to her closest friends and became public only with the posthumous publication of her letters to Father Johnson by her cousin Constance Babington Smith.[14]

As a consequence of her long relationship with O'Donovan, Macaulay excluded herself from the sacramental life of the Church for decades. Her transatlantic correspondence with Johnson began in 1950 and was an important factor in her return to the Church in 1951, although her relationship with Johnson as a spiritual mentor has perhaps been exaggerated.[15] Macaulay, like aunt Dot with Father Chantry-Pigg, was perfectly capable of disagreeing with Johnson and chided him for his excessive Anglican papalism. High Anglican though she was, she became committed to inter-Communion with the Free Churches in the 1950s. She no doubt deliberately meant to needle him, however affectionately, by writing of her support for female servers at Communion, although she spared the monk her views on the ordination of women. Macaulay remarked to her sister Jean in 1956 that 'it is all rather mysterious and wants analysing by intelligent psychiatrists – I mean the male disturbance at the idea of women as priests and deacons'.[16]

Father Chantry-Pigg is in this vein. He 'had run a London church higher than St Mary's Bourne Street and even some inches higher than St Magnus the Martyr' (12). Macaulay was well aware of the pitfalls of Anglo-Catholicism, especially its intellectual rigidity perfectly personified by Chantry-Pigg: 'He believed everything, from the Garden of Eden to the Day of Judgment, and had never let the chill and dull breath of modern rationalist criticism shake his firm fundamentalism' (13). Laurie is drawn to high Anglicanism but feels herself debarred from the communion of the Church because of her relationship with Vere – a 'more successful and prosperous version' of O'Donovan.[17] She undertakes to accompany aunt Dot and Father Chantry-Pigg on a mission to convert the Turks to Anglicanism of an especially baroque kind. Her role is that of companion and artist, and she plans to write a fashionable travel book about Turkey. Yet Laurie yearns to be inside the Church of England again:

> The Church has always had great magnificence and much courage, and
> people have died for it in in agony, which is supposed to balance all the
> other people who have had to die in agony because they did not accept
> it, and it has flowered up in learning and culture and beauty and art,

to set against darkness and incivility and obscurantism and barbarity and nonsense, and it has produced saints and martyrs and kindness and goodness, though these have also occurred freely outside it, and it is a wonder and most extraordinary pageant of contradictions, and I, at least, want to be inside it, though it is foolishness to most of my friends. (196–7)

However, Laurie cannot give up her adultery with Vere and the city of Trebizond becomes a symbol for that eternal city, the church, from which she is excluded. O'Donovan died of cancer; in the novel Vere dies in a car accident with Laurie at the wheel. Macaulay was a notoriously keen, but reckless, driver, as attested by her close friend of later years, Benjamin Britten's librettist, William Plomer.[18]

The novel ends, in contrast to Macaulay's own life, with Laurie still constrained by her guilt and grief from entering the gated and luminous city.

I live now in two hells, for I have lost God and live also without love, or without the love I want, and I cannot get used to that either. Though people say that in the end one does. To the other, perhaps never … Still the towers of Trebizond, the fabled city, shimmer on a far horizon, gated and walled and held in a luminous enchantment. It seems for me, and however much I must stand outside them, this must for ever be. But at the city's heart lie the pattern and the hard core, and these I can never make my own: they are too far outside my range. The pattern should perhaps be easier, the core less hard. This seems, indeed, the eternal dilemma. (276–7)

The novel's moving ending reflects her own Eucharistic theology as it was developing in the previous decade. She wrote to Johnson in July 1951:

I like it [the church] as it is[,] as it has come to be; it has built a City of God round the eucharist; one can enter into it each day and be a citizen of that glorious city for a time, and remember its language and its light through the day, if only at rare intervals in the rackety hustle & business of life as lived.[19]

Father Johnson, however, was not pleased with *Trebizond*'s ending. Following its success on both sides of the Atlantic, he urged her to write to *The Times Literary Supplement* to make it clear that, in contrast to Laurie, Rose did *not* believe the path to heaven was too difficult.[20] Rose did not write the letter and commented to her sister Jean that the priest was 'so unquestioningly devout and single-minded … I don't think [he] has ever been troubled by doubts'. She added, 'He is so old and has been so kind to me' – Johnson was in fact only four years older than Macaulay.[21] Although she had many Anglican, Roman Catholic and Nonconformist clergymen among her friends and acquaintances, she was not the type of woman given to their adoration, as demonstrated by the creation of Father Chantry-Pigg or the Victorian clerical patriarch of *Told by an Idiot*. Her letters are warm but could not be described as deferential, and one suspects that Father Johnson, with his great certainties, was in part the inspiration for Father Hugh Chantry-Pigg, although Rose had known so many clergymen throughout her long life who could fit the part as well.

The question remains, if *Trebizond* is, in the words of Betjeman and Huddleston, a work of 'Anglican propaganda', why does the novel not conclude with a joyful, even triumphalist, return of Laurie to the Communion of the Church? Macaulay herself returned to the sacramental life of the Church in 1951, nearly a decade after O'Donovan's death. To explore this question, we need to examine the problematic nature of fiction as a form of apologetic, alluded to above. Towards that end, this essay will consider Macaulay's critique of another leading twentieth-century novelist, whose fiction became, in her view, an apologetic or even propagandist tool: Evelyn Waugh.

Rose Macaulay on Evelyn Waugh

Ten years before the publication of *The Towers of Trebizond*, Macaulay published an extended essay on the novels of Evelyn Waugh in the arts and literary journal *Horizon*. Cyril Connolly, the journal's eminent editor, commissioned a number of well-known authors to assess the 'best and worst' of their peers.[22] She began with Waugh's first novel, *Decline and Fall* (1928), and concluded with his latest at the time of writing and retrospectively best-known, *Brideshead Revisited* (1945). Macaulay began in a positive vein, remarking that Waugh is 'among the world-creators of our time … the most entertaining, and perhaps the most gifted' (360). *Decline and Fall* is 'funny from first to last' as Waugh depicts the descent of its luckless hero Paul Pennyfeather, a would-be candidate for holy orders in Oxford banished to school-teaching in a fourth-rate public school after being rendered trouserless in the quad by members of the Bollinger Club. Repeatedly the hapless victim of circumstance, his decline continues to include a spell in prison. Friends help Pennyfeather to be declared dead and acquire a new identity, so at the end of the novel he has resumed his life as an Anglican ordinand. *Decline and Fall* is, to Macaulay, free of moralizing and is 'a genuinely original comic work', moving in a world where 'vulgarity, refinement and morality do not apply' (362). What she most admired about the novel is that the 'detachment is complete' (361).

Macaulay proceeded to chart Waugh's career as a non-fiction author and novelist, from *Vile Bodies* (1930), through several travel books and more novels: *Black Mischief* (1932) and *A Handful of Dust* (1934), a novel like *Decline and Fall* with an ill-used hero 'born to be betrayed' but much darker. In Macaulay's view, *A Handful of Dust* 'seems to reach the climax of Mr Waugh's view of life as the meaningless jigging of barbarous nit-wits. Pleasure, sympathetic or ironic, in their absurdities has vanished: disgust has set in' (367). She remarked significantly, especially for our purposes, 'what has also gone from his view is detachment' (368).

Macaulay then turned her attention to his next book, *Edmund Campion* (1935), a short biography of the Jesuit martyr. Her ire was up now and she declared that 'he has come down on a side' lamenting 'in art so naturally ironic and detached as his, this is a serious loss ... it undermines his best gifts' (368). Her sharp criticism of *Campion* falls into two areas. First, she regretted that Waugh's first 'partisan, side-taking' book since becoming a Roman Catholic is a work of history. Macaulay read history at Oxford and maintained that in works of a historical nature 'objectiveness and truth to fact should be a *sine qua non*' (368). *Campion* has little of either in her view, although 'there is interest, brilliance, imagination, and sympathetic interpretation'. However, 'it is like a barrister's brief, omitting all that does not support his case' (368). What most offended her historical sensibilities about *Campion* is that the book was written without recourse to the key resources for the historian of the period which reveal the international effort to assassinate Elizabeth; Waugh 'can write almost about Catholic plots [as if they] ... were an invention of Cecil's' (368).

Her second criticism of *Campion* concerns its author's 'excessive hostility' to the Anglican Church which leads him too often into 'inaccuracies'. Macaulay reflected the scholarly historiography of the English Reformation on the origins of Anglicanism before the revisionism of the 1970s onwards, when she took Waugh to task for accusing the Church of England of promoting a 'crazy, fashionable Calvinism'. He ignored, she said, the 'incessant war' waged against the Church of England established by the Elizabethan Settlement by Calvinists and Puritans – whom she does not see as proper Anglicans.[23] But what really got her goat was Waugh's repeated assertion that the Anglican Church has no sacraments: 'What he of course means is that, in the eyes of his Church, Anglican sacraments were not valid' (368). The Book of Common Prayer, as individuals such as John Milton frequently complained, was chiefly translated out of Catholic missals.[24] The Prayer Book 'earned the undying hatred of the Puritan party, who were persecuted under Elizabeth with severe cruelty. But Mr Waugh dislikes this wary *via media* so much that he relegates it to the outer darkness of the Protestant left wing' (369).

> To dislike the deplorable outrages of the Reformation, and many aspects of the whole business, is natural enough; indeed, it is rather hard not to; but to take ecclesiastical sides is, to a style such as Mr Waugh's, part of whose charm is in ironic objectivity and detachment, fatal. Partisanship should be left to thunderers; one cannot have it both ways, and something must be sacrificed to individual style. (369)

There was much to admire in *Campion*, Macaulay remarked, and she was not herself without 'bias' but her chief praise of Waugh's work – his 'ironic objectivity and detachment' – are attributes much admired in her own work.

Before moving on to the main object of her critical scrutiny, *Brideshead Revisited*, Macaulay could not pass without a scathing assessment, heightened by writing only a year after the end of the Second World War, on Waugh's perhaps most ill-judged work of non-fiction, *Waugh in Abyssinia* (1936). In her view *Campion* 'is mellowness itself compared with it' (370). Waugh was sent to Abyssinia by the *Daily Mail*, a newspaper which was, in Waugh's words, 'the only London newspaper that seemed to be taking a realistic view of the situation' and produced a 'blast of triumph over the Italian conquest of that land' and a blow against the 'whinney of the nonconformist conscience' that had protested against the invasion and occupation. For Macaulay, whose adult life had been dominated by two world wars, it is the same 'whinney from the same conscience that protested against the Nazis' (370).

Waugh maintains in the book that the Italians had 'spread order, decency and civilization', that mustard gas was 'pretty harmless' and that the Abyssinians were, in a breath-taking phrase, 'bored and exasperated with a weapon to which they could make no effective return' (370). Like their imperial ancestors, the Italians were bringing roads along which would pass 'the eagles of ancient Rome, as they came to our savage ancestors in France and Britain and Germany' (370). Macaulay deemed it 'an odd and rather unchivalrous book' (370). The motive? A preference for Italian culture over Abyssinian culture? – that is something Macaulay conceded most Europeans would share but 'it should not, but perhaps does, affect the issue' (370). A dislike of black populations? Too generously (or ironically?) Macaulay pronounces that he showed no such bigotry in *Remote People, Black Mischief* or *Scoop*.[25] Perhaps his Roman Catholicism is a more likely driver, due to a desire to support a policy endorsed by the Italian clergy. Is it driven by his dislike of the League of Nations – something she thinks more likely? Or does he simply back the 'big battalions'; in which case Waugh should be 'crying up … Russian domination', which he is not. Macaulay delivered her final *coup de grâce*: 'This book must be pronounced a Fascist tract' (370). In the context of 1946, it is a biting critique and one echoed by other reviewers and critics at the time of publication.[26]

Macaulay passed over briefly, but warmly, *Scoop* (1938), *Put Out More Flags* (1942) and *Work Suspended* (1943). She then turned her attention to *Brideshead Revisited*, published the previous year (1945). The *Horizon* essay was carefully crafted to deliver a devastating critique of Waugh's most celebrated novel – as if calling *Waugh in Abyssinia* 'a fascist tract' were not enough reputational damage. Her critique of *Brideshead* provides the key to understanding the moving, yet starkly non-exultant, conclusion of *The Towers of Trebizond* published a decade later – the ending that so disappointed Father Johnson, lacking as it did a triumphalist return to the communion of the church for the protagonist Laurie.

Between *Work Suspended* and *Brideshead*, Macaulay observed that Waugh 'underwent development' (372) and the only way of assessing *Brideshead* is through horticultural images: 'The baroque became flamboyant; the style curved and flowered; sentimentality at times cushioned it; a grave lushness bloomed ... The era of brilliant farce was over.' All was not lost, however:

> Irony and humour still remained; there are in *Brideshead* wit of character and some sharply drawn comic scenes; there is also much subtly precise and intelligent writing; but it flowers too often into an orchidaceous luxury of bloom that, in a hitherto ironic wit, startles and disconcerts. Love, the English aristocracy, and the Roman Catholic Church, combine to liquefy a style that should be dry. (372)

Macaulay liked the Oxford section set in the 1920s, twenty years after her own time at Somerville. But she found the central family, the Flytes, unconvincing, as 'none of them has the sharp actuality of the minor and more plebeian figures' (372). With the Flytes, however, there is something 'phoney':

> They belong to a day-dream, to a grandiose world of elegance and Palladian grace, a more than mortal ecstasy. Their conversation is at times incredible; Julia's monologue about her 'sin'; ... Lord Marchmain's about his ancestors on his deathbed ... which [returning to her horticultural metaphor] flower up from naturalism like exotic purple plants in a hot-house. (372–3)

Macaulay went in for the kill: 'Mr Waugh has been charged with snobbishness. I would rather call it self-indulgence in the pleasures of adolescent surrender to glamour, whether to the glamour of beauty, food, rank, love, church, society, or fine writings' (373). Macaulay observed that the narrator Charles Ryder speaks of sexual relations with his lover in the same lush language as an excellent dinner or an outstanding Burgundy. It was unfortunate, she thought, that this 'adolescent approach' which mistakes the part for the whole was not avoided, particularly in a novel attempting, according to Waugh, 'to trace the workings of divine purpose in a pagan world' (375).

> No purpose can well have greater importance ... But Mr Waugh seems to equate the divine purpose, the tremendous fact of God at work in the universe, with obedient membership of a church; the human spirit, if redeemed, must loyally conform to this church and its rules. (375)

She acknowledged that it is a reasonable position for a sincere Roman Catholic and 'it is not for those outside this communion to criticize it' (375). However, Waugh's position

> seems to ... reduce the formidable problems of the universe and the human spirit to a level almost parochial. Divine purpose, human redemption,

must flow through channels larger than those of any church ... The interest in moral issues which ... must in the end impose itself again on novelists, transcends (even if it often includes) loyalty to a church: in Mr Waugh's novel, it is subordinate to and conditioned by this. (375)

Macaulay was well aware of the theological diversity within Roman Catholicism – O'Donovan's sympathies for Catholic Modernism would have ensured that – and she contrasts Waugh with 'that equally convinced Catholic but greater and more sin-haunted moralist, Graham Greene' (375).

For Macaulay, a 'concentration on a church' narrowed the moral scope and added 'a flavour of acrimony, a kind of partisan contempt for other churches, about whose members acid and uncivil remarks are made by persons in the book, voicing, one would say, their author' (375). *Brideshead* is reminiscent of *Campion* but with less excuse, since Protestants and Roman Catholics are now at peace and the latter are shown 'great civility and respect' in England. She was aware that Waugh's riposte would be that other churches 'being in schism, are unworthy of civility in return' (375). Most damaging of all for the novelist:

Gone is the detachment, and with it the bland, amused tolerance, of the early novels. Belief meant for him hatred of misbelievers; no sympathetic effort to understand their standpoint has been evident, still less the urbane culture which recognizes human error to be distributed among all sections of opinion, including that to which oneself belongs. (376)

Brideshead, in Macaulay's view, has 'remarkable qualities' as a novel. Nonetheless, she felt that Waugh's career was at a turning point: 'his genius and his reputation seem to stand at the crossroads; his admirers can only hope that he will take the right turning' (376).

An anti-Catholic?

Do Macaulay's criticisms of Waugh make her 'anti-Catholic'? That view has certainly been expressed, and she did – of course – insist that as an Anglican she *was* a Catholic.[27] The two authors corresponded after the publication of the *Horizon* piece and Macaulay responded to Waugh at length and in a measured way.[28] On Christmas Eve 1946, Waugh wrote to her, thanking her for her 'patient letter' and enclosed a Christmas card which he hoped – one does not feel entirely benignly – 'your agnosticism does not prevent you accepting'. Waugh also maintained that he read 'with distaste' the attack on her *Horizon* article in *The Tablet* by the editor Douglas Woodruff, maintaining that he 'had no hand in it'.[29] Woodruff did not like Macaulay's assessment of Waugh one bit, though he declared admiration for her as one of his favourite writers. He claimed she was 'annoyed with [Waugh] for being a Catholic and even writing like one'.[30]

Was this fair? Writing a month before the publication of the *Horizon* article to her cousin Jean Smith, a formerly devout Anglican who became an equally devout Roman Catholic in 1933, Macaulay related a conversation with her friend, the Dominican scholar Gervase Mathew, over dinner at Christ Church, Oxford. She found they shared the same view of Waugh's work: an 'extreme devotion to his earlier books and some distaste for *Brideshead*'.[31] Her admiration for Graham Greene was constant. Her friendship with both Mathew brothers, Gervase the Dominican and his episcopal brother David, was sincere. David's *Scotland under Charles I* carried the dedication 'For Rose Macaulay in memory of a long friendship' and *Trebizond* begins with a playful reference to the theft of aunt Dot's car outside the Athenaeum by an Anglican bishop while she was dining with David Mathew and the eminent classicist Gilbert Murray.[32] Macaulay reassured Johnson that she was in no danger of conversion from her many Roman Catholic friends: 'no one has tried to pervert or convert me', and as to the Mathew brothers, 'I really believe they almost prefer Anglicans.'[33]

There were hints of spring in the ecumenical landscape in the 1940s and 1950s, but the thaw represented by the Second Vatican Council had not yet arrived.[34] It seems clear that there was a clash of personalities, as well as theologies, between Waugh and Macaulay – the latter over twenty years Waugh's senior – and the combative nature of their relationship long predated the *Horizon* critique.[35] Their diaries and letters reveal their mutual dislike from the late 1920s as they encountered each other at the luncheons, dinners and cocktail parties that engaged the lives of eminent persons of letters. Needless to say the animosity was not softened by Macaulay's very public critique, leaving Waugh to comment on her obituaries in 1958, 'They … spoke of her piety. She was, I think, quite devoid of faith.'[36] When approached by the BBC in 1951 about writing and presenting a fifteen-minute talk for the Third Programme on a subject of her choosing, Macaulay suggested either 'Bathing for Pleasure. An investigation into swimming costumes' (Rose was a keen swimmer all her life) or 'An answer to Evelyn Waugh – if Evelyn Waugh gives the kind of talk that deserves an answer'. The BBC producer wrote to his superior that the first suggestion was 'a safe bet'.[37]

Waugh's gibe of 'agnosticism' from that Christmas card of 1946 persisted in his exchanges with Macaulay. Almost a decade after the *Horizon* article, she wrote to Johnson that she met Waugh at a dinner party and observed that he had 'turned into a rather petulant English eccentric'. Picking up the threads of her argument in the *Horizon* essay, she was more candid in a private letter:

I don't think his writing will ever be what it was in his brilliant & unregenerate youth; his conversion did him no literary good, however spiritually improving. I hadn't seen him for years, & he accused me of agnosticism; I was able to retort that I was now a practising Anglican &

went daily to Mass, which is, I suspect, more than he does. How much of his Faith he believes, I shouldn't care to guess. Of course you are right in your diagnosis of the wholesale attitude R.C.s have towards their religion; though there will always be some few who, like Von Hügel and Acton & Tyrrell, can't believe certain doctrines.[38]

In many ways, it was the biography of *Campion*, rather than *Brideshead*, that most rankled her. She wrote at length about it to a young German Lutheran friend in 1957:

Evelyn Waugh's Campion is a very trivial piece of work really ... Evelyn told me afterwards that he had, in fact, read no State Papers at all [and] had done no research in the [Public] Record Office, but used only modern history books & his own invention. However, the book served his purpose, which was to please the church & secure his annulment of his marriage, which was promptly granted him ... I hope he will return to being funny; no writer can do it better.[39]

At the time of the *Horizon* essay, Macaulay had not yet returned to the full communion of the church, although O'Donovan had died in 1942. Waugh had secured an annulment in 1936 and married his second wife in 1937.[40] One cannot help but feel that Macaulay's long and secretive relationship with O'Donovan – and his views about the theological rigidity and social conservatism of the Irish Church attacked in his first and deeply autobiographical novel, *Father Ralph* (1913) – shaped her view of Waugh's annulment.[41] Writing over twenty-five years later, Monica Furlong perceptively connected Macaulay's relationship with O'Donovan and the religious world of *Brideshead*.

The excessive penitence of 'Letters to a Friend' (a priest) has always worried me; the liaison, though technically a 'sin', had clearly been marvellously creative for Rose Macaulay as woman and writer, and it is difficult not to sense the emotional blackmail reminiscent of that which afflicts the principals in 'Brideshead Revisited'.[42]

Apologetic or unapologetic?

Despite the non-triumphalist ending of *Trebizond*, is it still an *apologetic* work – is Macaulay an Anglican apologist? In the protracted quarrel between Waugh and Macaulay, we see how the latter worked out her understanding of the relationship between apologetic and fiction. Writing in the last year of her life to an unidentified friend, Maisie, who was troubled by aspects of the novel, Macaulay was nonetheless clearly pleased by its positive spiritual impact on readers.

It sounds like conceit to say that many people have told me it changed their religious stand-point & their lives, & that some clergy have read the bits about the church to doubtful ordinands to encourage their faith, which it seems it did. I don't say this to boast, but to show you that I was trying to put something across, & many people received it.[43]

However, writing to William Plomer, she was clear that *Trebizond* did not present an 'Anglican victory':

I *am* glad my Towers gave you pleasure. I too had hoped for an Anglican victory at the book's end; but it ended too soon for that. It took me nine years to come back after the relevant death, & that death wasn't caused by me, which would make another barrier. So I had to leave Laurie in the wilderness, though she would little by little get nearer what was for her the inevitable destination, as I suppose it was for me: – if destination isn't too static a word ... An Anglo-agnostic well inside the walls, instead of outside, that is the difference. Thank heaven for the C.of E., which grants so much license & liberty of thought, so much free criticism, so many reserves & speculations & interpretations.[44]

To return to Francis Spufford, *The Towers of Trebizond* is 'unapologetic', 'because it isn't giving an "apologia", the technical term for a defence of ... ideas', but also because Dame Rose Macaulay wasn't 'sorry'.[45]

FIGURE 9 *Barbara Pym.*

8

Barbara Pym (1913–80): Anglican Anthropologies

Jane Williams

Barbara Pym was born in 1913 and died in 1980. She wrote throughout her life; after a degree in English from Oxford, and a stint in the Women's Royal Naval Service during the war, she published novels regularly from 1950 to 1961. Then, in what was to her a surprising change, her publisher, Jonathan Cape, refused her next novel, and she was not published again until 1977. In January of that year, the Times Literary Supplement had a survey of the 'most underrated novelists of the century', and Lord David Cecil and Philip Larkin both independently named Pym as their choice. Suddenly, she became commercially attractive to publishers again – though, perhaps unsurprisingly, she chose Macmillan rather than Jonathan Cape to publish her next novel *Quartet in Autumn,* later in 1977. It was received with critical acclaim and nominated for the Booker Prize; Macmillan quickly reissued her back catalogue and published *The Sweet Dove Died* in 1978. Pym also gained a following in America and is now translated into a wide variety of languages. Her reputation has continued to grow, stimulated by the posthumous publication of some of her letters, diaries and short stories, and of a biography.[1] Even when she was not being published, Pym continued to write: novels, short stories, diaries and letters. She also worked as an editor for the International African Institute: anthropology and anthropologists are regular visitors to her pages, as are gently comical clergy and faithful churchgoing women. Pym never married and shared a home with her sister for many years, both while working in London and after retirement to Oxfordshire.

Pym was a regular churchgoer, though by no means conventionally devout, and although she did not set out to document the Church of England's changing position in these years, something of its fortunes are visible in the pages of her novels. In her early books, like *Some Tame Gazelle* (1950), the village church is the centre of a world, and there is no suggestion of another: the church is not a bubble within a bigger society, but the natural conduit for all social relations. In *A Few Green Leaves*, published thirty years later, the villagers of the novel have transferred their hope and trust from the church to the doctor's surgery.[2] Pym describes the queue of people waiting on a Monday morning for the balm of medicine as 'devout' in their attendance: 'There was nothing in churchgoing to equal that triumphant moment when you came out of the surgery clutching that ritual scrap of paper', the prescription.[3] Similarly, Marcia in *Quartet in Autumn* is obsessed with her surgeon, rather than with the curate as classic Pym characters might have been. In Pym's last book, *An Academic Question,* written and revised from 1971 but only published posthumously in 1986, no one goes to church, except for a funeral: the church is not even one world among several possibilities, but entirely marginal. That is not to say that it had become marginal in Pym's own life, but that she was trying to write for new audiences. *An Academic Question* is not entirely successful, although it has its delights. There is a strong sense that Pym is not writing about a tribe that she has got to know well: her anthropological notes do not take her far enough into the psyche of a modern young woman who has no clergymen in her life. Caro and Iris Hornblower are such familiar Pym characters in some ways, yet their setting lacks colour, as though Pym has read about their country but never actually visited it.

Pym's style of writing makes it necessary for her to be able to get inside the heads of her characters. She is no omniscient author; her novels read very much like her letters and diaries so that, whether written in the first person, like *Excellent Women*, or the third, like *Some Tame Gazelle*, what we hear is the character's own thought processes.[4] Pym does not tell us what we should think or feel about her characters, but allows them to judge themselves. We come gradually, and almost without noticing, to appreciate the characters who see their own imperfections, laugh at them ruefully and move on. We listen in to Belinda's inner monologue throughout *Some Tame Gazelle* and are glad when she realizes at the end of the novel, as we have perceived all along, that the life she and her sister Harriet are living is far more satisfying than the sentimental adventures they have imagined; they just want 'some tame gazelle, some gentle dove … something to love', but not with too much passion.[5] Women like Marcia in *Quartet in Autumn* and Leonora in *The Sweet Dove Died* are chilling because we hear their thoughts and can see, as they cannot, that they are living in unreality: they do not know themselves and so cannot change. Unemphatically, Pym's writing begins to suggest values: we start to appreciate humorous honesty, gently mocking judgement and a willingness to learn.

The world of the parish

It is easy to assume that Pym's fortunes were linked to perceptions about the place of the Church of England in the popular imagination, waxing and waning with the fortunes of those 'cosy' – a favourite Pym word – times of unexamined churchgoing.[6] But churchgoing is perhaps just shorthand for a whole world that, in the 1960s, publishers clearly felt was not inhabited by enough of the reading public any longer. Pym described Cape's list as full of 'men and Americans', and knew that no amount of editing could make her books fit.[7] Churchgoing had certainly not come back into vogue when Pym was rediscovered, but the literary and cultural climate had changed. As Pym said, 'I haven't done anything different, just plodded on.'[8] Writing in *The Telegraph* in Pym's centenary year, Philip Hensher says: 'to those, like Jonathan Cape in the early Sixties, who demand a po-faced engagement with the vital issues of the day, she has nothing to say'. Hensher's own assessment of Pym verges on the patronizing – he describes Pym's 'unique and unmistakeable comedies of English life', and her 'beautifully modest gift' – but he also toasts the fact that when other more aggressive novelists have faded into obscurity, Pym is still read with love.[9]

The world Pym wrote about was small, well observed and heavily populated with women. Comparisons with Jane Austen abound.[10] Like Austen, she chose largely to ignore the great events of the wider world in favour of the small-scale and wryly humorous. Although Pym had experience of travel in Europe immediately before the Second World War, of service during the war, of love affairs that ended in heartbreak and of a final battle with cancer, she chose to write primarily of domestic life in England, of emotion observed and processed with irony and a kind of detachment. This method is not confined to her novels; her diaries reveal emotional storms, though even here, she generally chose to excise the pages that spoke very directly of passion and pain, and only leave the aftertaste.[11] When writing of a failed love affair, the pain is evident: 'it is no longer anything to do with me what Gordon does ... there are an endless number of months to be got through – a long dreary stretch until it doesn't matter any more'.[12] Yet within a few months, she was already writing of herself and her heartbreak as though she were a character in one of her own novels: 'And what exactly, may Posterity ask, *was* all this "struggle" about. Why this need for Patience and Courage? And the bewildered English spinster, now rather gaunt and toothy, but with a mild, sweet expression, may hardly know herself.'[13] When, in *Less Than Angels* (1955), Catherine Oliphant's anthropologist lover dies 'in the field', Pym observes the way in which Catherine deals with this: after an initial burst of tears, Catherine takes a bus ride and gradually sorts her emotions from the 'spontaneous grief for him' on to 'a more selfish and personal sorrow at the failures of their relationship', until very soon, she is imagining the 'cosiness and security' of the suburban houses the bus is passing, and Tom fades to the edges of her consciousness.[14]

Pym treated faith in much the same way as she treats emotion. Although she was herself a lifelong Anglican, her books and her diaries describe church-related activities with the same anthropological precision, as though with the eye of a cataloguer, rather than a participant. Hers is very much a lay perspective on the church; as her preference was for Anglo-Catholic Anglicanism, that largely meant observed rituals, with only minor roles for the unordained, and even more so if the unordained happened to be women.[15] There are few hints in her writing of the depths of personal faith or religious fervour. That is not to say that such depths did not exist, merely that she chose to write of the structures and patterns of life that church provides, rather than the intellectual or emotional reasons for churchgoing. When interviewed by Roy Plomley on the radio programme 'Desert Island Discs' in 1978, Pym admitted that the church was important to her and that she wrote about it 'more than any other novelist', but she did not volunteer why it mattered to her or make any attempt to explain her faith.[16]

Hilary Pym, Barbara's younger sister, wrote of their childhood, 'Church was a natural part of our lives.'[17] Their mother was the assistant organist at the parish church in Oswestry, their home town, and their father sang in the choir. Harriet and Belinda Bede's habit of entertaining clergy, and particularly young, single curates, was a practice borrowed from Pym's own home.[18] At the very least, it is clear that the church plays a social role in Pym's novels: it provides a setting and a social group in which Pym's characters can interact and be observed. In particular, church life provides the kind of 'cosy' but not intimate relationships that Pym's slightly distant women can comfortably inhabit. Mildred Lathbury observes: 'I sometimes thought how strange it was that I should have managed to make a life for myself in London so very much like the life I had lived in a country rectory when my parents were alive.'[19] Pym's other attempts to create such small-scale communities, where her characters can meet regularly and interact for our observation, are never quite as successful. In *A Few Green Leaves*, the last of Pym's novels to be published before her death, village life fulfils some of the same function, but the academic circles that she attempts in *An Academic Question* are a very poor substitute for church. Caro and her circle simply do not have enough in common; the rituals of academic life do not bind them into the conventions of meeting and relating that the church does in Pym's earlier novels.[20] John Bayley's insightful review of *An Academic Question* says of Pym that she is 'accustomed to live in and *with* [her] characters', unlike many other novelists, who use characters as 'aspects of the structure and convention' of what they want to say.[21] Bayley is talking here about Pym's habit of allowing us further glimpses of characters from one book in another, as though their lives have really gone on, even when we are not reading about them. In this way, Bayley surmises, Pym's heroines ask for understanding for Pym herself and her world: it is real; it lasts, even when we lose sight of it. Pym's dependence on the 'comedies and rituals of a churchy setting', Bayley suggests, shows a 'touching lack of self-confidence'.[22]

This is not to say that Pym could only depict an idealized past in which the Church of England was the natural habitat of the Englishman and, more particularly, the Englishwoman of a certain type. In *Quartet in Autumn*, the first book that Pym published when she was 'rediscovered', she wrote about a group of ageing office workers, heading out into the perilous world of retirement, where the rituals and structures of their known lives are to be dismantled. Only Edwin, who is deeply involved in his Anglican church, has an alternative pattern which will not change when he retires:

> Palm Sunday ushering in the services of Holy Week ... Low Sunday always seemed a bit of an anticlimax after all that had gone before but it wasn't long before Ascension Day and then Whit Sunday or Pentecost ... After that you had Corpus Christi ... and then Trinity Sunday, followed by all those long hot summer Sundays ... That was how it had always been and how it would go on in spite of trendy clergy trying to introduce so-called up-to-date forms of worship, rock and roll and guitars and discussions about the Third World instead of evensong.[23]

Pym's diary entries are often headed with both calendar and lectionary dates, so she shared with Edwin a world in which context and shape do not have to be invented by each individual. She has no illusions about this world, writing at one point in her diaries: 'But are Christians always and necessarily nice people? Who could like the Wise Virgins in the Bible, for example? Is that one of the trials of it all – that one must be prepared to be disliked?'[24] Edwin is certainly not a sympathetic or attractive character, and his churchgoing is a niche interest that suits his fussy and self-important persona, but Pym depicted it as offering a kind of stability that the others have to attempt to manufacture for themselves. His colleague Marcia tragically fails to achieve any kind of life-sustaining rhythm after retirement, and starves herself to death.

This transitional book helps Pym's readers to see that the Church of England is more than just a convenient social setting, with observable rituals that allow her to put her characters under her kindly, ironic microscope. Pym's Anglicanism, though never vulgarly evangelistic, was more than just a choice of a particular tribe to study for fieldwork. It has been described as 'Bakhtinian' in its attention to the body, particularly the body which women minister to, with the shared rites of tea and biscuits.[25] This is a perceptive – if arcane – insight drawing on the work of the philosopher Mikhail Bakhtin, who sought the moral reality of human beings in what they actually do, rather than in abstract theories. For him, it is the world we perform and experience, rather than the world we think, that is real, and this certainly resonates with Pym's concerns. David Cockerell expands this in describing the ordinariness of Pym's settings: 'The world is redeemed, transfigured into the material out of which we fashion for ourselves a world of moral and spiritual meaning and purpose.'[26]

The ordinary world, full of small, daily rhythms, where nothing of any apparent great importance happens, is still a world worth attending to. It is the world we actually inhabit. Pym's characters, like Pym herself, observe themselves dispassionately but with gentle affection: they do not take themselves too seriously but neither do they find themselves negligible. Their thoughts, their lives, are worth writing about with unjudging amusement. There is something profoundly Anglican in this vision: the parish church at the heart of each community, drawing daily life into the stuff of discipleship.[27] Whether consciously or unconsciously, when Pym writes about a world where the church has become peripheral, her characters seem to drift, unanchored by this unassuming meaningfulness. Without any theological drum-beating, Pym's novels display the Anglican parish understanding of the importance of connectedness, the importance of a place or community where people of all kinds are accepted as they are and can be a gift to each other in all their imperfections.

Pym's clergymen

This is perhaps most obvious in Pym's depiction of clergy. Clergymen in Pym's novels never talk about their vocation; Father Ransome in *A Glass of Blessings* (1958) experiences a crisis of faith, but is rescued from Rome by the love of a good and unglamorous woman – and her money. Few of Pym's clergy are found doing any pastoral work, carrying out occasional offices or talking about prayer, although they do preach and preside at the Eucharist. The world they inhabit is very much the world of Parson Woodforde's diaries, where playing fives in the churchyard, providing Christmas lunch for fifteen old people in the parish, brewing his own ale and preaching a sermon at a funeral, to say nothing of staying up all night playing cards with friends, are all noted by Woodforde with a deep contentment and certainty of his place in life.[28] Just so do Pym's clergy operate: their ecclesiastical function is assured; whatever their personal inadequacies, they enable the appropriate rituals. After Marcia's death in *Quartet in Autumn*, Edwin arranges for 'Father G.' to officiate at the service in the crematorium to 'ensure that things were done decently and in order'.[29] The fact that shortly after the funeral Father G. is musing about whether or not it would be appropriate to ask for a dry martini in no way undermines the proper ritual he has enabled.

James Runcie calculates that there are seventy-five clergymen in Pym's work, 'which averages out at 5.76 a novel. Quite what 0.76 of a clergyman might be like would, I think, have amused her'.[30] In fact, 0.76 of a clergyman seems quite a good description of most of the clergy Pym describes. Perhaps the best known of them all is Archdeacon Hoccleve in *Some Tame Gazelle*. Belinda Bede has been faithfully and comfortably in love with the Archdeacon since their student days, protected by the Archdeacon's formidable wife from any fear of having to do anything about this emotion. Even though she is biased in favour of the Archdeacon, Belinda admits to herself 'that he had very few of the obvious virtues that one somehow expected of one's parish priest' (6). The Archdeacon is vain, selfish, lazy and sardonic, and his preaching is usually designed to show off his knowledge of English literature, rather than to edify. There is a particularly fine example of this in his sermon on Judgement Day, which Pym gives us interspersed with the congregation's rather jumbled reflections. Belinda's sister Harriet concludes, at the end of this unusually long sermon, 'I expect many people's Sunday dinners will be ruined' (112).[31]

The Archdeacon is not the only cleric to inspire devotion in the female bosom. *Some Tame Gazelle* pokes gentle fun at the good Anglican pastime of female flutterings about clergymen.[32] Harriet Bede is a devoted admirer of curates, insisting on inviting them to supper at regular intervals and knitting for them. But this attention is clearly understood by all concerned to be almost impersonal: it goes with the job, rather than the individual. The colonial bishop Theodore Grote, the Bishop of Mbawawa, makes a serious category mistake when he assumes that interest in his office coincides with interest in himself. In one of the most gloriously comic episodes in the book, he proposes to Belinda, in a scene reminiscent of St John Rivers's proposal to Jane Eyre, but with none of the stern religious seriousness. '"Perhaps you will not be so ready to accept what I have to offer," he said, though it was obvious that he really thought quite otherwise' (223).[33] But Belinda, like Jane, wants to marry for love or preferably – unlike Jane – not to marry at all, although she is vaguely flattered to be considered worthy to be a bishop's wife: it's just unfortunate that in this case, it would also mean being Theodore Grote's wife.

Fr Neville Forbes, in *No Fond Return of Love* (1961), has also negotiated his relationships with the opposite sex wrongly. He turns up at his mother's hotel:

> But although he said nothing about his reasons for coming, Mrs Forbes guessed that it must be, in her own words, 'trouble with a woman', for it had happened before. What began as a pleasant friendship between priest and parish worker all too often blossomed – or should one say degenerated? – into love on the woman's part. And even now Neville seemed quite unable to deal with it. He should either marry or go into a monastery, thought Mrs Forbes firmly.[34]

But this little glimpse into the stuff of handbooks for pastoral ministry is not pursued: Pym prefers to show us Mrs Forbes's impatience, as she realizes that she can hardly ask her be-cassocked son to wait at the tables in her hotel or, indeed, to do anything useful at all.

In *Crampton Hodnet*, the clergyman Mr Latimer, emboldened by a glass of sherry, proposes to Miss Morrow. '"Oh, Miss Morrow – Janie," he burst out suddenly. "My name isn't Janie." "Well, it's something beginning with J," he said impatiently. It was annoying to be held up by such a triviality.'[35] We, the readers, understand and sympathize with Mr Latimer's desperation, as we have already heard his thoughts as he looks out at his congregation:

> Yes, this was the Church of England, his flock, thought Mr Latimer, a collection of old women, widows and spinsters, and one young man not quite right in the head. These were the people among whom he was destined to spend his life. He hunched his shoulders in his surplice and shivered. The church, with its dampness and sickly smell of lilies, felt cold and tomb-like. He had the feeling, as he mumbled through the service, that he and his congregation were already dead. (86)

Our sympathy for Mr Latimer is subtly undermined by his unconsciously dismissive attitude towards the female element in his congregation and by Pym's use of the word 'mumbled': perhaps his lack of fervour is as much to blame as his congregation is for his depression? Certainly, the reader agrees with Miss Morrow in her rejection of his suit: it is not her job to attempt to compensate him for what is presumably his mistaken vocation. Mr Latimer is later allowed a more hopeful romance with a less intelligent and sardonic person than Miss Morrow, but the doubts about his calling, so gently and teasingly touched upon, remain.

Father Plowman in *Some Tame Gazelle*, from the next-door parish, compensates for his failed degree in theology by wearing a biretta and having elaborate services and is rewarded with 'so many pairs of hand-worked slippers that he gave the Archdeacon a pair' (40). The Archdeacon is not particularly grateful, and only partly because the slippers are not his size. There is an element of clerical rivalry about who can inspire the most devotion among the ladies. While Father Plowman and the Archdeacon have none of the pathos of Mr Latimer, they still raise the question of how they came to be ordained in the first place. But that is not a question that Pym encourages – people are what they are and the world goes on. Pym's treatment of clergy is very much like her Church of England world: it is ironic, comic but ultimately accepting.[36] What's more, the clergy, like the Church of England, are important: not for the reasons that they imagine, to do with their own fascination and status, but because of what they stand for and facilitate, almost in spite of themselves. They enable, through their priesthood, a community of idiosyncratic people: all sinners, all failures, yet in their daily interacting, their low-key kindness and unpretentious forgiveness and acceptance, also a community of quiet transformation. People do move on and change in Pym's novels, seldom in dramatic ways, yet generally in hopeful ones.

Spinsterhood and couples

Pym's world is very much a woman's world. While we occasionally hear the inner monologues in the minds of men, it is far more usual in Pym's novels to see the world through the eyes of women. And while Pym's younger women tend to define themselves still in terms of romantic relationships with men, it is part of Pym's understated subversiveness that the more mature and self-reflective her women are, the less likely they are to be interested in marriage.[37] Laurel in No Fond Return of Love, Deirdre in Less Than Angels and Barbara in Crampton Hodnet are among Pym's young girls who find themselves romantically entangled with older men, and Pym skilfully shows how, both with the girls and with the men, what is really going on is part of an elaborate story that each is telling about themselves, rather than a truthful interaction with another human being. In each case, the novel also has an older woman, who knows herself better and sees her own worth, not bound up with that of a man. So Laurel has her Aunt Dulcie, Deirdre has Catherine Oliphant and Barbara has the inimitable Miss Morrow as an example. It is part of Pym's delicate irony that all the young women view the older ones with a mixture of pity and scorn, little seeing their freedom and self-determination.

Some of these women do in fact marry, but we hear their thoughts and understand their realism, both about themselves and about the man they are about to marry. As Ailwyn Forbes hurries in a taxi to win Dulcie's heart in No Fond Return of Love, he is still seeing himself in terms of the hero of a novel: 'He had suddenly remembered the end of Mansfield Park, and how Edmund fell out of love with Mary Crawford and came to care for Fanny. Dulcie must surely know the novel well, and would understand how such things can happen.' Dulcie, meanwhile, 'opened the door cautiously, wondering why he had brought a bunch of flowers when she had so many in the garden' (286). Catherine in Less than Angels, after the infidelity and death of Tom, says, 'I never mind being alone. And my life isn't quite over yet, you know.' She decides to cultivate the eccentric retired anthropologist, Alaric Lydgate. 'It will be an interest, and it will take me out of myself to study somebody equally peculiar' (252).

Pym is no believer in loneliness and splendid isolation as a necessary concomitant to women's independence. It is very much part of her writer's 'theology' that relationships are always imperfect but, if truthful, can still be life-giving. At the end of Excellent Women, Mildred speaks for many of Pym's characters when she says, 'What with my duty there [in the vicarage] and the work I was going to do for Everard, it seemed as if I might be going to have what Helena called a "full life" after all' (288). A 'full life' might not be quite what young romantics long for, but it is a good life, all the same, and a gift to be treasured. The relationships that Pym gently affirms are generally ones where people are able to be companions and 'helpmeets', to use the old-fashioned word, rather than passionate lovers.

The married couples that Pym depicts are a study in her humorous realism about the world. Jane, one of Pym's array of clergy wives, muses: 'A husband was someone to tell one's silly jokes to, to carry suitcases and do the tipping at hotels ... And although he certainly did these things, Nicholas was a great deal more than that.'[38] Her friend Prudence, unhappily and fruitlessly involved in an affair, sees Jane's life as dull, noticing how Nicholas has aged and how uncomfortable their cold vicarage is. Yet Prudence longs to be married or, at least, settled in a long-term relationship. She has yet to learn what Jane has learned, which is that women can be proactive and not reactive in relationships: 'that was why women were so wonderful; it was their love and imagination that transformed these unremarkable beings ... perhaps love affairs with handsome men tended to be less stable because so much less sympathy and imagination were needed on the woman's part?' (217).

Mark and Sophia Ainger, another of Pym's depictions of a clerical marriage, are rendered with a more melancholy undertone than Jane and Nicholas. It is not just the absence of the wonderful, prosaic daughter Flora in *Jane and Prudence* – one of Pym's most successfully depicted younger characters – it is also Sophia's doting affection for her cat, Faustina. As always, there is no hint of disapproval in Pym's comic depiction of Faustina's insouciant attitude to food, visitors, beds and anything else her heart might desire; but we do wonder about Mark's slightly wistful thoughts on the subject. When Mark and Sophia are about to lead a pilgrimage to Rome, Sophia's thoughts are very much taken up with Faustina's well-being in their absence: 'She's all I've got', Sophia says. 'For a moment Sophia was afraid that Mark was going to speak sternly to her, for his eyes had their rather distant look.'[39] A husband cannot be delighted to hear a wife declare that the cat is all she's got. Yet Mark loves Faustina too, and sees her, as well as Sophia, as part of what keeps him firmly anchored in the Church of England: 'There was Sophia too, his beloved wife, and even Faustina who was, he felt sure, fiercely Protestant' (143). Mark and Sophia are contented, mutually supportive, and share a desire to serve the miscellaneous community that gathers around the parish church. They have enough.

Pym's unemphatic affirmation of the importance of relationships is even more obvious in her sympathetic portrayal of those other than marriage. She herself, after a number of affairs, none of which ended in marriage, spent the last few years of her life living contentedly with her sister, Hilary. She had long and faithful friendships, as evidenced not least by the volume of letters she wrote and received, a correspondence which continued, with friends old and new, until a few days before her death. Her diary records an August walk in 1978, with Henry Harvey, with whom she had been deeply in love as a young woman, and his first wife, Elsie: 'Strange situation dating back over 40 years ... Three elderly people walking.'[40] But even strange and not easily classified friendships are still valued. Although *Some Tame Gazelle* was written before Pym had finished with love affairs, it is hard not to hear Harriet Bede's musings as Pym's own: 'Who would change a comfortable life of spinsterhood in a country parish, which always had its pale curate to be cherished, for the unknown trials of matrimony?' (136) That is not meant to be a universally applicable statement, since many of Pym's unlikely heroines do choose to make that risky change, but it is a gentle reminder that, in relationships, there is no 'one size fits all'.

In *A Glass of Blessings*, Pym describes another relationship that fits none of the conventional stereotypes. Piers and his lover, Keith, seem an unlikely couple at first glance, yet the sardonic and restless Piers is clearly at home with Keith in a way that he has not been in the rest of the novel. '"This having things in common," said Piers impatiently, "how overrated it is! Long dreary intellectual conversations, capping each other's obscure quotations – it's so exhausting. It's much more agreeable to come home to some different remarks from the ones one's been hearing all day."'[41] Wilmet's obsession with Piers is shown up as an essentially self-centred thing, with little true knowledge of its object. It is Keith who makes Piers happy, caring for him and making him a home. Pym's unostentatious depiction of the relationship between Piers and Keith is all of a piece with her interest in truthful, unsentimental interactions between human beings. She depicts Keith and Piers as 'ideal', as Jane and Nicholas are, not because they are perfect, but precisely because they are happy not to be.[42] Wilmet discovers that her husband Rodney, too, has had wandering eyes; when they confess to each other, with shouts of laughter, Wilmet realizes what she has been taking for granted, and how much she has still to learn about herself. It is not too late to learn, even in a marriage. With both couples, Keith and Piers and Wilmet and Rodney, Pym is suggesting new ways of valuing relationships, with less emphasis on conformity to convention, and more on their potential 'for further change and transformation'.[43]

The Sweet Dove Died (1978) revisits some of the themes of *A Glass of Blessings*, but in a more chilling form. Leonora Eyre, still beautiful if no longer young, becomes infatuated with James, a good-looking and much younger man. Unlike Wilmet, Leonora has no other deep and lasting relationships to help her to see herself and learn. Her deepest connection is with her pretty Victoriana and with her own reflection. Pym describes Leonora's exquisite bedroom, where she has chosen to display photographs of her grandparents, rather than her parents, because they were 'more distinguished-looking'. Since Leonora rejoices that she does not have to pretend to enjoy sex any more, it is clear that the bedroom and its display are entirely for herself: the deception she is practising about her photographs is to deepen her fantasy world, not to impress others. So it is hardly incidental that we are told: 'No Bible, no book of devotion ... marred the worldly charm of her bedside table.'[44] Leonora's world is dangerously detached from the anchorage of lasting, if imperfect, relationships, and that detachment is signalled by her absence of faith.

Isolation and community

At the end of the book, Leonora has preserved her pride and detachment, but at enormous cost to her humanity. The book ends with her musing: 'Yet, when one came to think of it, the only flowers that were really perfect were those, like the peonies that went so well with one's charming room, that possessed the added grace of having been presented to oneself' (266). She has become so closed in on herself that she even thinks of herself as 'one'. Leonora would rather be alone than accept imperfection; she has put herself at the centre of the universe, where everything takes its value only from its relationship with her. Subtly but damningly, Pym shows us a lonely, miserable woman, who cannot admit her own imperfections or accept them in others. The book seems to suggest that isolation is much more destructive than imperfection, for it stems from an unwillingness to engage with reality.

The ultimate picture of the dangers of isolation in Pym's world is her portrayal of Marcia in *Quartet in Autumn*. In retirement, Marcia, always a little strange, becomes fiercely private and removed from others; she deliberately cuts herself off from her colleagues and neighbours and retreats further and further into loneliness. Her fantasy life revolves around her collection of tins and milk bottles, and her obsession with the doctor who performed her cancer surgery. She buys, but never uses, a drawer full of new nighties, just in case the day comes when she might return to hospital and be seen by Mr Strong again. But by the time her wish is finally granted, she is on her deathbed and unable to utter a word. Her literal self-starvation mirrors the metaphorical refusal of relationships, the refusal of the commonplace reality of the world. This is Pym's most tragic depiction of the dangers of refusing relationships, the clearest signal she gives of one of the values of her world: reality, in all its imperfections, does matter.

So in Pym's Anglican anthropology, the Church is not just a convenient cipher, a device enabling the novelist to move her characters around and make them perform for our observation. Certainly, churches do provide networks of ritual and relationship that might simply be observed, as they are by the young anthropologist Jean-Pierre Rossignol, who treats churchgoing as a kind of fieldwork exploration of English character. '"Last week I was at a Methodist Chapel – exquisite!" Jean-Pierre cast his eyes up to heaven. "The week before at the Friends' House. Next Sunday I have been recommended to try Matins and Sermon at a fashionable church in Mayfair"' (20). But in Pym's world these relationships are not merely to be observed; they are to be participated in. Pym does not suggest total and uncritical immersion: one of the most characteristic aspects of Pym's heroes, but particularly of her heroines, is their ability to stand outside themselves and see themselves with gently deprecating humour.

Yet Pym is not just describing a way of life but also gently, uninsistently, recommending one, and it is one that takes some of its recognizable contours from the Church of England as Pym saw and inhabited it. From her lay perspective, priests and services are not at the heart of the church – or, if they are, it is only because of what they facilitate, which is a shared space and a shared language of acceptance. Pym served the Church of England faithfully, though without any illusions about it: 'Ghastly PCC meeting in the evening', she wrote on 10 May 1977, 'I must have an organist in my next novel.'[45] She is not much interested in its structures or its disagreements, though she is realistic about these. But what her novels build, in her usual understated and non-directive way, is a vision of a community which encourages the growth of her very Anglican understanding of virtue. In Pym's novels, the characters who achieve most contentment and who clearly learn and grow in the course of the novel do so because they accept themselves and others as they are. They do not look for perfection or demand unachievable devotion; they make room for variety, for eccentricity, for ordinariness and stupidity; they forgive and restore to community and move forward together, not striding ahead but ambling along companionably. Characters like Marcia and Leonora who cannot live with the flawed texture of reality are depicted not as culpable but as infinitely sad and, ultimately, static and sterile.

Pym does not suggest that forgiveness, acceptance, community and reconciliation are only to be found in church: by no means all of the people who attain to Pym's commonplace, daily heaven do so by one route. It is more that the kind of community that the Church just is, for all its imperfections, is to be treasured: it enables us to see what we are looking for, even if we are not going to look for it here. The Church of England parish is by definition a people, a building and a community that welcomes all in the locality, even if not all hear that welcome or feel themselves at home.[46] In a parish church, you might meet anyone and be required to enter into conversation, share tea, begin to build the tenuous connections that lead to relationship, however feeble and undemanding Anglican relationships might be. There do not have to be ties of work or class or leisure activity, and that means that the assortment of people can be richer, stranger and more unlikely than would be found in any more natural setting. That makes for good novels, but it also makes for hopeful people, if Pym is to be believed.

No wonder, then, that Pym found it hard to depict other settings, because there are few others that facilitate those loose, yet lasting, relationships, where people might learn from each other and grow and change, without rejection or judgement. Yet that is what Pym's world is, and it clearly still has attractions, if the reprints of her novels and the success of the Barbara Pym Society are anything to go by. There may well be a hint of nostalgia among Pym's fans, a longing for a bygone age of connectedness. It is interesting that such modern novels as there are that are set in churches now tend to be detective stories, which would seem to imply a community whose flaws are dangerous, rather than one whose flaws are accepted and loved.[47] That may be a sad reflection of the current embattled state of the Church of England, more famous nowadays for its infighting than its inclusive parish life. And if that is indeed the case, then perhaps the Church of England needs to see itself again in the benevolent 'theology' of Barbara Pym and learn.

FIGURE 10 *Elizabeth Goudge.*

9

Elizabeth Goudge (1900–84): Clergymen and Masculinity

Susan D. Amussen

Elizabeth Goudge was, in the middle of the twentieth century, well known as a writer in multiple genres, from journalism and devotional works to children's, historical and contemporary fiction. She was a lifelong Anglican, and Christianity – both its practice and fundamental tenets – plays a central role in the life of her fictional communities. Her novels are characterized by unsentimental portraits of children, depicted as curious, kind, mean and extremely observant. In addition, her fiction frequently features independent single women as complex characters living full and satisfying lives. Finally, her writing is marked by a precise observation of the natural world, and each novel is firmly located in a place that is defined by distinctive landscapes, plants, weather and sky. As an unmarried woman raised in a largely gender-segregated society, and who lived most of her life in a homosocial world, Goudge also frequently offers a critical view of contemporary gender norms in her fiction. Her Anglicanism shaped novels that explore sin and redemption from her belief in the generous love of God for all people, especially those at the margins of society.

Life and works

Goudge was born in Wells, Somerset, in 1900; her father was at the time the vice-principal of Wells Theological College, of which he became principal several years later. Her life was shaped by her father's work as an Anglican educator and theologian: it grounded her in the Church of England. It also provided her with multiple homes. From Wells he moved to Ely as a cathedral canon and principal of the theological college there, and then to Oxford as Regius Professor of Divinity. Her mother was an invalid; while her mobility was limited, she was a gifted storyteller and hostess, and, according to Goudge in her autobiography, had a 'strong streak of extra-sensory perception'.[1] She had grown up in Guernsey, the location of Goudge's childhood summer holidays and the setting for her most popular novel, *Green Dolphin Country*. An only child, Goudge was an avid reader from a young age; she describes herself as reading 'by suction'.[2] In 1914, she went to boarding school in Hampshire, which gave her an abiding love of the coastal landscape. After school, she was sent to art school (her expressed desire to become a nurse ignored), where she studied a range of crafts. While she describes herself as someone who could not draw, her time in art school taught her habits of close observation which she transferred to her writing. She expected to work; before succeeding as a professional writer, she taught crafts privately in Ely, and then, when her father took up the post of Regius Professor, briefly at a school in Oxford, which 'had the wisdom to give me the sack with remarkable speed'.[3]

The move to Oxford changed Goudge's life in several ways. The Oxford climate aggravated her mother's asthma, so after one year, her mother spent six months of the year in a bungalow on the Hampshire coast, where Elizabeth reconnected with the landscape she had first encountered while in school. At the same time, while her mother was in Hampshire, Elizabeth took on the role of hostess – a role which did not suit her introverted personality. She had a nervous breakdown in the 1920s. She also started writing, and by the mid-1930s was publishing short stories in magazines; her first novel, *Island Magic*, based on her experiences visiting Guernsey as a child, was published in 1934. After her father's death in 1939, she and her mother took a holiday in Devon, and then moved there permanently. At that point, her earnings as a writer were a necessary supplement to her mother's small clerical pension. She nursed her mother until her mother's death in 1951. Following another breakdown, Goudge moved to a cottage in Oxfordshire, with a young woman named Jessie Monroe, who was her companion for the rest of her life. She thus lived for significant periods of time in different places, and her homes and the landscapes surrounding them were inspirations for her fiction.

The Goudge family, like many clerical families at the time, was comfortable but not wealthy. Clerical salaries, Goudge observed, were rarely adequate to maintain the large and old houses that clergy lived in. In Ely, her father sold his stamp collection to help pay for repairing the roof of their Norman house.[4] As had been the case at least since the introduction of married clergy in England in the sixteenth century, the clergy inhabited an anomalous place in the social hierarchy, defined by position more than wealth.[5] The financial constraints were, however, relative: Goudge grew up in a household with servants, and, until her father's death, they always had household help. While the family lived in comfort, her father ensured that Elizabeth was aware of the conditions in which the poor lived, and her training in art school was designed to prepare her for employment; her role models were her mother's three unmarried sisters, all of whom worked. She was – like Streatfeild and Furlong in this volume – a *working* writer, churning out magazine articles to earn cash while writing her novels.

Goudge was, as a result, a prolific writer; over the course of the forty-four years from the publication of *Island Magic* in 1934 until a last collection of short stories was published in 1978, six years before her death, she published more than forty works spanning multiple genres – novels, plays, poems, children's books and non-fiction. While some of her novels were historical, others had contemporary settings. The range of her work makes generalization difficult, but there are several recurring themes. First, her work is shaped by a magical sense of the connections between present and past in a particular place. Places, particularly houses, are themselves frequently characters. As one critic noted, she was convinced that 'real life *is* magical'.[6] The porousness of present and past, reality and imagination is central to almost all her plots. For instance, in *The Middle Window* (1937), a young Londoner on holiday in the highlands of Scotland and her Scottish host turn out to be resuming the lives of eighteenth-century inhabitants of the house; tensions between them are resolved after she has a flashback to the events following the Battle of Culloden. Goudge was fascinated by ideas of time travel and communication with the dead: in the early 1970s, she enthusiastically read two short books that purportedly detailed letters dictated by two dead young women to their mothers. Her interest in this – while unorthodox – was connected to her faith; both young women discuss their encounters with Christ in the spirit world.[7]

Goudge's work is also strongly shaped by her Anglican faith and her experience as the daughter of a priest: her non-fiction books include *God So Loved the World: The Story of Jesus*, as well as a biography of Francis of Assisi and a diary of prayer.[8] Many of her novels feature clergy as important characters, but even when they do not, the centrality of the church to the life of a community is a common theme, as are the spiritual journeys of individual characters. And it is a journey: faith is tested and challenged by experience, moving the dutiful churchgoer to a deeper engagement with God. In two different novels, elderly people talk about having time to 'make their soul'.[9] In both cases it is associated with leaving (in one case because of bombing) a large house for a simpler life, a move which allows them to turn from practical and worldly concerns to spiritual ones. Faith is also always about learning new ways to understand the world, and accepting God's loving embrace of all. It is God's generous and inclusive love that is central to bringing those on the margins into a circle of family, friendship and community. The marginal in Goudge's novels include traumatized soldiers, Jewish refugees and people suffering from depression and mental illness.[10] Repeatedly, those who are broken are made whole.

By mid-century, Goudge was widely recognized as an important novelist: her first novel, *Island Magic*, sold well, and *Green Dolphin Country* (1944, *Green Dolphin Street* in the United States) was adapted as a film, and won an Oscar for special effects in 1948. Her 1946 children's book, *The Little White Horse*, won the Carnegie Medal as the best children's book published in the Commonwealth that year. Yet over time, reviewers often struggled with the overtly Christian themes of her work. The *New York Times* review of *The Rosemary Tree* (1956) suggested that 'Mrs. [*sic*] Goudge would have one believe in miracles, but ... it is as difficult to believe [her characters'] complete transformation as it is to believe in their original overburdening sense of guilt': the Christian narrative was no longer compelling.[11] Her insistence on fidelity, and conviction that people could and should grow into happiness where they were, rather than leaving to find happiness elsewhere, were increasingly at odds with modern sensibilities. The drama in her fiction is not the quest, but – as I will show – the embrace of stability. Yet her novels have always had passionate admirers; they gained additional visibility when J.K. Rowling identified *The Little White Horse* as one of her favourite books as a child and an influence on the Harry Potter series.[12] The plagiarism of Goudge's novel *The Rosemary Tree* by the Indian writer Indrani Aikath-Gyaltsen raised important questions about her critical reputation. *Cranes' Morning* was published in 1993 to enthusiastic reviews which suggested that it represented a South Asian version of magical realism, before readers recognized both Goudge's plot and prose. Paul Kafka, who had reviewed *Cranes' Morning* in the *Washington Post*, suggested that Aikath-Gyaltsen had benefitted from 'aesthetic affirmative action'; since he still liked the novel, he suggested perhaps Goudge was 'a writer who hasn't gotten her due'.[13] The critical reappraisal this required has not heretofore been undertaken; this chapter constitutes a contribution to that process.[14]

Goudge's work is imbued with a sense of joy and the beauty of the world, but she did not have a simplistic understanding of joy. In her memoir, *The Joy of the Snow*, she describes melancholia as 'the skeleton in our family cupboard'. Her father and paternal grandmother both suffered from depression; she did too and had several nervous breakdowns. She described living with a demon who 'brought darkness and was determined that I should not write books'. After she 'had disentangled [herself] from him', she determined to write books that were 'happy'. She was well into her 50s and had been a successful writer for twenty years, when she had 'a sudden conviction that my demon had left me for good'. She found that 'a dark background to one's life tends to make the happier times happier still'.[15] Mature joy, in Goudge's experience, emerged from suffering and sorrow: this was a practical conviction as well as a theological one. Reflecting in later life on her fortunes as a young woman who came of age at the end of the First World War, she wrote that parents recognized that 'unless their daughters had exceptional beauty and charm' they would not marry. The impact on her was profound. She writes that 'the few [men] who came home ... were so exhausted that they succumbed easily to the influenza'. That was a 'form of plague'; the winter of 1918 was marked by 'still, dark cold like a pall over the land'. While her perception was exaggerated, at eighteen she was coming to terms with a future as a single woman. In retrospect, she was grateful, having found 'great joy in work'; her remark that 'you have to be fairly old before you can recognize the blessings of a single life' is a reminder that this appreciation was not her first reaction.[16] Goudge's novels repeatedly feature characters who need to make peace with, and find joy in, a life that is not what they would have chosen; they also repeatedly feature characters who suffer depression. Such struggles are presented not as aberrations, but as routine features of life.

While reviewers focused on the attention to nature in Goudge's novels, and what they saw as their sentimental plots, the idyllic settings of her novels coexisted with gentle, but consistent, criticism of conventional social mores.[17] Her central characters, particularly in her contemporary novels, were people of modest wealth; their lovely houses in rural communities, and their anchor in the Church of England, give a deceptive appearance of establishment values. Yet these apparently conventional social worlds provided a framework for challenges to materialism and individualism. Goudge's novels articulated a critique of modern society from the perspective of Christian virtues in general and Anglican Christianity in particular. In her autobiography, she describes herself as a socialist.[18] Her own life, and particularly her mother's dependence on her earnings, had made her familiar with economic anxiety. Her portrayals of servants and working people, while marked by her class background, are sympathetic, and acknowledge both their independence and their complex relationship to their employers. In *The Bird in the Tree* (1940), Lucilla Eliot attributes her learning to be a better mother to the influence of her maid, Ellen, who told her 'to love your poor children a bit more' (189). Even those portrayed as faithful retainers have an inner integrity; the gentry needed to earn their loyalty. The old gardener in *The Rosemary Tree*, Goudge writes, 'did occasionally let fall tokens of respect'.[19] Goudge's respect for servants and working-class people, however, did not extend to writing about social mobility: being part of a web of community also meant remaining in one's social position.

Goudge's Christian faith, like her happiness, did not come easily. As a clergy daughter, she had experienced Anglican worship all her life. Yet both her parents had rejected their own parents' approach to religion: her mother's parents had been atheists, her father's rigid evangelicals. She believed that 'neither a copy-cat religion nor a haunting is faith ... there must have been a moment of conviction'.[20] Her own faith was shaped by a crisis following her nervous breakdown. She had been 'troubled' by her mother's illness all her life – how could God cause such suffering? – but it was her own illness that challenged her 'faith in the love of God'. She found her faith when she saw a blind woman and for the first time perceived the unity of all suffering. With this perception, she realized she 'had to find a

God I could love'.[21] In struggling – like many others – with questions of theodicy, she worked her way around to understanding faith as a mystery in two ways. First, through the mystery of God allowing his Son to suffer; as a result, 'when we suffer, we must be as close to God as we are to the pain'. The second mystery is the way faith comes not through reason, but loving. For her, Christ was central: 'His voice is the beauty of the world and the crying of a hungry child.'[22] In 1982, writing to a friend in anticipation of death, she wrote of what she had learned in old age: 'Then, of course (this should have come first!) there is Christ himself. I've got to know him as never before, and never was there anyone more worth knowing. I think I could put my present faith into one sentence. "There is a glory somewhere, and life goes on, and Christ is a reality."'[23] In *The Dean's Watch* (1960), the Dean tells the determined non-believer Isaac Peabody to 'disbelieve' in his father's terrifying God, and 'believe instead in love'. This, after the Dean's death, is a crucial moment in Isaac's return to faith.[24] It is perhaps not accidental that her own father's last words were 'it is loving that matters'.[25] In her characters, Goudge often described a journey from the performance of faith to belief: they have a moment when they have a sudden perception. Thus, in *The Rosemary Tree*, Daphne suddenly sees her pew in church as 'her own particular cranny' in the rock (35). That journey was ongoing. Lucilla Eliot, the matriarch in the Eliots of Damerosehay trilogy, had, during the Second World War, 'learned really to pray'; she was in her 80s.[26] Goudge's own experience years later mirrored that, as she repeatedly reflected on how much she had learned through her long illness and increasing incapacity.[27] While Goudge's theology was orthodox, her spirituality was not. She ends her autobiography with a prayer from Thomas Traherne, but it follows a passage from the *Bhagavad-Gita* that illustrates her sense of the cycle of life and the ways in which the story both changes and repeats itself.[28]

These ideas are visible in what is now perhaps the best known of her works, *The Little White Horse*, which was the basis for a television mini-series *Moonacre*, and a 2008 movie, *The Secret of Moonacre*.[29] Moonacre Manor sits in a sheltered valley, not far from the sea, near the village of Silverydew; it is at once in the world but not of it. As Sir Benjamin Merryweather, the lord of the manor, says, 'Silverydew is not in the outer world, it's in our world.'[30] The valley is filled with magic and wonder – tame beasts, cats who write, secret tunnels. And the people of Moonacre are tightly bound to the past: the relationship between the heroine, Maria Merryweather, and her eventual husband Robin echoes not just the relationship between Robin's mother, Loveday Minette, and Maria's guardian, Sir Benjamin, but also that centuries earlier between Sir Wrolf Merryweather and his wife. The valley is now (in 1842) plagued by the 'dark men' who live in the pine wood – descendants of Sir William Cocq de Noir, whose daughter had married Sir Wrolf. The difficulties of the valley come, it appears, from two acts by Sir Wrolf, 'centuries ago' (100). First was his successful request to the King to turn the monks out of the monastery on Paradise Hill; the other was his struggle with Sir William Cocq de Noir, who held the land between his manor and the sea. He had married Sir William's beautiful daughter, the Moon Princess, who left him when she realized that he had married her for her property, not for love. Centuries later, Monsieur Cocq de Noir and his men are poaching sheep and cattle, and preventing access to the sea. Maria, the newest Moon Princess, is told these stories by the local parson. She sets these things to rights by undoing the damage of centuries ago: she convinces her guardian to give the profits from the former monastic site to the poor; and she brings peace between M. Cocq de Noir and the Merryweathers. In the process, the mystery of the fate of the first Moon Princess after she left her husband is solved, as is that of her father. Yet the key to the happy ending is the return of stolen property: justice and reparations are more important than wealth accumulation.[31] Justice is intertwined with forgiveness and reconciliation. Materialism is as much an evil as selfishness. The three marriages that end the novel emphasize the critique of materialism, as all cross divides of wealth or status. The parson constitutes the moral conscience of the novel, holding all his parishioners up to his standard of faithfulness to God, and scolding them for their misdeeds (61–2). He is the one who sets Maria on her quest, and who identifies the form of penance that will allow reconciliation.

The Rosemary Tree and the critique of masculinity

Goudge's social criticism is more evident in the novels set in the contemporary world. In the remainder of this chapter, I will focus on one element of that critique, the distortions that come from mid-century norms of masculinity. Romantic fiction at mid-century defined 'the perfect man' as combining authority and consideration, expressed through a benevolent exercise of fatherhood. In such fiction, relationships between husband and wife were affectionate but not egalitarian.[32] At the same time, increasingly female congregations raised questions about Anglican masculinity, and clerical masculinity in particular. There were a variety of models which attempted to 'reconcile ideas of Christian love and service with active forms of masculinity'.[33] These models, like romantic fiction, also anchored authority in fatherhood, supporting conservative models of masculine identity by avoiding discussion of any more egalitarian relationship between husband and wife. Goudge's response to these issues was to emphasize the ways alternative models of masculinity provided a more effective basis for engagement with the world. Her critique of such models of masculinity, even those softened by fatherhood, is presented in depictions of clergymen who are not strong and assertive. She sets their lives, behaviour and values in dialogue with men who apparently conform to conventional masculine virtues. Against expectations of competence and control, she posits the importance of understanding and sympathy. In *The Rosemary Tree*, John Wentworth – clumsy, socially awkward and unworldly – turns out to see more truly than his more worldly wife.

The Rosemary Tree is set in Devon in the 1950s, and has three interwoven plots which all resolve in the transformation of the characters. John Wentworth is both the squire and the vicar. He has refused to live in the crumbling Tudor manor house where his great-aunt Maria still presides. The family fortunes have been declining for generations, most recently laid to waste by John's great-uncle, who – after being blinded in the Boer War – planted extravagant gardens that he could never see. John's mother was killed when he was a baby, and his father had turned to drink; he remarried disastrously and died when John was eight. John has always been a faithful churchman, and after university he was ordained and, like Goudge's father, ministered in urban slums. During the Second World War, he was a naval chaplain, wounded in body and spirit when his ship was torpedoed. It was while he was recovering at a military hospital that he reconnected with his distant cousin Daphne. She was staying with her godmother, having recently been jilted on her wedding day. They marry, but things are not entirely happy; she is conventional and worldly, while he is neither. He is socially and physically inept and easily distracted. But he is also generous: he subsidizes his great-aunt's continued residence in the manor house, and shows charity to any poor person who comes by. His generosity of spirit is recognized by others, as he maintains an extensive correspondence with people he has known at all stages of his life. The Wentworths have three daughters, who attend a private school run by a wealthy widow.

In addition to Daphne and John, and Maria Wentworth, two other adults are central to the novel. The first is Harriet, John's former nanny, housekeeper at the Vicarage until crippled by arthritis. She now rarely leaves her room, but observes and comments on family doings from her upstairs room. She is clear-sighted and plain-speaking, serving as the Greek chorus for the novel. The other person is a man named Michael Stone, who arrives in Devon the day after he is released from prison. Stone had caught a train to Silverbridge following his release because while in the army he had read a story on angling set there and was enchanted by the name; he finds the romance of its name echoed in the landscape. He is taken on as gardener and pigman by Aunt Maria. When first talking with Daphne, he describes the village and manor of Belmaray as a 'paradise of a place'.[34]

How does a novel set in 'paradise' offer a critique of masculinity? In each of the strands of the book, John's perceptions are accurate, and his actions, guided by integrity and humility, are able to navigate and manage change. When Michael describes John to Daphne as 'a great man', she is surprised, but by the end of the novel, she understands that judgement. Almost the first thing we learn about him is that he is clumsy – he 'drove as badly as a man can'; he also lived with 'a lifelong sense of failure'. He is, his congregation thinks, 'tootlish' or simple-minded.[35] When he meets Michael Stone, who is hungry, he gets breakfast for him from a nearby farm, but almost forgets to return the plate. He visits Bob Hewitt, gardener and pigman to Aunt Maria and, when he gives him a small flask of brandy, forgets that Michael has already drunk it. His awareness of his catalogue of failings gives him a humility that shapes his engagement with the world.

Daphne has set up, in her mind, a contrast between John's incompetence and awkwardness, and the man to whom she had previously been engaged, who was successful, charming and worldly. That same man had also jilted her with a brief note on their wedding day. She really wants a husband who is steady and faithful like John, and worldly and sophisticated like her former fiancé. When Michael Stone turns out to be the man to whom she had been engaged, she is forced to reframe her understanding of herself, her husband and her marriage. Daphne comes to recognize the worth of the man who, she had always felt, lacked some key 'masculine' attributes. John's humility and his generosity turn out to make him a stronger man than Michael.

The transformation in Daphne's perceptions of John and the ways in which John's bumbling character demonstrates both good judgement and practical resourcefulness are the result of the intersecting plots: one focused on Michael Stone and his re-entry into society; one on Aunt Maria and the future of the manor house; and the final one focused on the girls' school. It also parallels Daphne's deepening faith: towards the end of the novel, as she admits that she is 'a lucky woman', she describes a 'conversion', which started (as we saw earlier) the morning she saw her pew as her own cranny in the rock and meditated (349). The Michael Stone plot is in some ways the simplest, and it most obviously places models of masculinity in dialogue with each other. In spite of their very different characters, Michael and John feel an immediate connection with each other. John's idealistic and impractical character is illuminated by the fact that, at their first meeting, Michael three times identifies him with Don Quixote.[36] On the other hand, Stone is confronting the ways in which his eagerness to conform to expectations – to demonstrate his cleverness and control – led him to embezzle funds from a client, and thus to prison.

One link between John and Michael turns out to be the way in which both suffered in the war: they both failed in the performance of martial masculinity. John's nervous illness following the torpedoing of his ship was – to him – an obvious failure. Michael had joined the army and fought in Greece; his head wound was self-inflicted, a failed suicide attempt as he struggled with his fears. As a result of his 'cowardice', his closest friend in the army was blinded and severely wounded, and he held himself responsible (317). In fact none of the men in *The Rosemary Tree* who go to war are ennobled by it: John's great-uncle Richard was not only blinded, but suffered from bouts of depression for the rest of his life; John felt his breakdown a failure; and Michael is consumed by guilt at the consequences of his weakness. If war is the ultimate test of masculinity, all these men fail it, and the only difference is the way in which they respond to their failures.

Goudge's concern with the impact of war, particularly on sensitive men, is one that she also explored in the two post-war novels in the Eliots of Damerosehay trilogy. David Eliot, the central male character of the novels, is an actor and a RAF bomber pilot during the Second World War. In the second novel of the trilogy, *The Herb of Grace* (1948), he takes refuge at his grandmother's house because he has suffered a nervous breakdown, 'a thing I've always despised in others' (133). In the third, *The Heart of the Family* (1953), David is still struggling with his sense of failure; he has just come back from a triumphant theatrical tour of the United States, during which he was almost unfaithful to his wife. He has brought back a secretary, Sebastian Weber, a refugee from central Europe; their difficult relationship is resolved when David recognizes Sebastian as a brilliant pianist he had heard play before the war and learns that Sebastian's wife was killed in the Dresden raid in which he had been a bomber pilot. Each saw the deaths from the bombing in starkly individual terms: David had felt himself solely guilty for all those killed, and Sebastian had thought only one man responsible for the bombing. Sebastian's response to this discovery links the critique of modern war to Goudge's theology. 'You saw far enough to recognize instinctively the oneness of men in their guilt. I was able at one time to see the oneness of men in their pain. Neither of us saw far enough to see the oneness of the guilt and the pain. But there is such a union.' He adds, 'Men of your type, and my type, should never fight a war.'[37]

The damage from war, these novels suggest, is spiritual even more than physical. Hilary Eliot, David Eliot's uncle, and a parson, has lost a leg in the First World War, which means that he is 'relegated' to a small parish in the country. His injury shapes his life: as the reader learns at the very end of the last novel, he had wished to be an Anglican monk, but the monastery rejected him because of his injury.[38] In *City of Bells,* the first of Goudge's Torminster novels (set in Wells), Jocelyn Irvin has been injured in the Boer War, and in addition to a game leg, 'the horror of war, its futility and beastly cruelty, had injured his mind' as much as his body, 'leaving it sickened and vaguely aching'.[39] War – especially modern war – was not, in Goudge's view, an ennobling experience. In a letter written during the run-up to the Falklands War in 1982, she refers to 'this nightmare of possible war' and notes that 'since the last war I have been a pacifist'.[40]

In *The Rosemary Tree*, a negative experience of war is not all that John Wentworth and Michael Stone share. They each recognize in the other virtues they lack, but also commonalities. Michael recognizes John's generosity and kindness, and John recognizes Michael's charm and social ease. More profoundly, the two men share a sense of failure. In John's case, this is not just occasioned by his lack of social graces and response to war. His sense of his inadequacy as a priest is deepened by his and his family's connection to the community, 'no one would ever listen to him here'. When writing sermons, he struggles to 'write down what he knew,' to share with others the faith that sustains him.[41] Stone's sense of failure is different: he had been imprisoned for embezzlement, and his shame about the betrayal of his clients is tied to his secret shame about his conduct during the war. He is afraid to 'meet the contempt' of people in London who know his history and recognizes that 'A brave man would have faced it.' Observing the other man, John thinks: 'He was not an adult any more than he was himself. Most probably the child in him had not been able to confront the challenge with which life confronts the man.'[42]

When John describes his family to Michael, he notes that the village thought of his great-uncle as 'mad', and would describe his great-aunt as 'unusual'; he adds that 'we are a rather odd family' (28–9). This oddness enables Great-Aunt Maria to welcome a stranger, Stone, into her home to help with the pigs and the garden while Bob Hewitt, the gardener and pig man, is ill. He helps with the work, but also provides companionship and conversation, which offers some relief from her ongoing financial challenges. He is transformed by the place and by the work; he also meets Miss O'Hara, a teacher at the girls' school, and falls in love. He approaches this new love with an honesty that had been missing – on both sides – from his relationship with Daphne. By the end of the novel, Michael is ready to go back to London and work, while Miss Wentworth has accepted the need to sell the manor house. She, and even more John, who actually owns it, have approved its sale to a Roman Catholic monastic order.

The plot that centres around the girls' school underlines John's insight. John's first comment about his daughter's school is that 'it stank'. He then pulls back, acknowledging that he has only been there a few times, and 'what did he know about it?' Daphne, as a mother, would know more. Their older daughter, Pat, has tried to tell Daphne, but her comments have been dismissed. Then John learns that one of the teachers is picking on his middle daughter, Margary.[43] He identifies the problem as Mrs Belling, the owner: her goal is her own comfort, not the good of the students. After Mrs Belling's sudden death, John helps the two teachers buy a small house and start a new school. Daphne's perception of herself is challenged by the recognition that she had failed to see the problems in the school. She is transformed by two conversations. The first is with Harriet, to whom she tells the full story of her relationship with Michael. Harriet, to her surprise, is curious rather than judgemental. In telling the story, Daphne is forced to see the ways her reactions had been shaped by pride and selfishness. To her astonishment, Harriet does not congratulate her for not going away for the weekend with Michael before their wedding, but instead responds, 'it's a poor sort of virtue that has no roots in love'. This conversation, Daphne recognizes, was 'an indictment against her that she would have to read through and understand before she could plead guilty or not guilty before the tribunal of her own mind' (247–8).

While her conversation with Harriet sparks self-examination, a conversation with Michael forces her to confront her failings more directly and acknowledge the ways her pride damaged their relationship. She recognizes how partial her understanding of events has been. In many ways, she and Michael had known little about each other. He ran away from their wedding because he did not think he was worthy: he had failed in the war. 'Marriage with a decent woman was out of the question.' For years, Daphne had told the story as one about herself; now, she understood, it was not about her. She had wanted Michael to play a particular role, and she had played one herself; neither of them had been honest. In the wake of this new self-perception, Daphne was 'trying to get to know myself'.[44]

Michael's reference to 'marriage with a decent woman' is telling. The whole conversation points to the importance of conventional ideas of masculinity to both Daphne and Michael. Yet those norms fail them both. Daphne – in her relationships with both Michael and John – had wanted a man who fitted the model of the romance novel: strong and competent, as well as charming, and someone who would care for her. While Michael had been apparently successful, strong and charming, he was not in the end able to care for her. Michael accepted those norms, but runs away for fear of being unable to achieve them. He cannot marry, because he cannot be vulnerable. For years Daphne has mentally compared John to Michael: John is faithful and caring, but he is hardly the typical hero of a romance.

What ties each of these plot lines together is the way in which conventional values and behaviour fail people. All the central characters except Harriet have to give up some part of their understanding of themselves in the world. These changes are most dramatic in Daphne and Michael, who have clung most defiantly to typical gender norms. Daphne has to face her own faults in her relationship with Michael, and then with John. She has to acknowledge that her expectations of manliness have been unrealistic. In his courtship of Miss O'Hara, Michael has to admit his faults in order to build an honest relationship: he needs to be vulnerable. But others change too. Maria has to give up being the lady of the house, and leave the only home she has ever known. John not only has to let go of a tangible thing – the manor – but adapt to a happier relationship with his wife. At a time of crisis, he is efficient and competent; he also begins to acknowledge his successes. There is a spiritual dimension to each of these changes: they each require characters to acknowledge failures, and seek healing and forgiveness. The spiritual changes are supported, even provoked, by events: change is not magical, but a response to experience.

These transformations are shaped by John's ministry as a clergyman. It not only provides a structure to his life, but his clerical status sits outside conventional hierarchies of employment. The pattern of parish life is, in many ways, unchanged by time. It does not require engagement with the contemporary economy, or the modern workplace. Like John Wentworth, the clergyman Hilary Eliot in *The Herb of Grace* lacks charm and good looks – he is 'distressingly plain'. He is also a terrible driver, and willing to put up with a cold parsonage and bad food because he believes he should not have more. Yet for both, their modesty and sense of inadequacy are key to their success as parsons. When the itinerant tinker-actor Malony in *The Herb of Grace* discovers that Hilary cannot even light his study fire, he reflects of Hilary: 'He wasn't out to do you good, this chap – he didn't think enough of himself for that – he was simply out to jog along beside you for a little.'[45] Their personal humility and sense of failure enable John and Hilary to connect with a wide range of people. Humility allows the clergy in Goudge's novels to reach outside the norms of masculinity and social hierarchy.

In contrast to her view of modern masculinity, Goudge's account of femininity is far less critical. She depicts married women in conventional ways, and the most 'successful' of them are faithful, loving and domestic, displaying a hospitality anchored in prayer. However, by valuing unmarried women – and almost all her novels have significant unmarried female characters – she broadens the mid-century vision of womanhood.[46] In *The Rosemary Tree*, Harriet and Maria provide different models: Harriet as a working woman who has been absorbed into the family she worked for, Maria as the gentleman's daughter who managed the house as the servants gradually disappeared. *The Scent of Water* (1963) features as its main character a woman who has been a government bureaucrat, before inheriting a cottage in the country. Goudge portrays these women as complete people and important contributors to their communities. As we have seen, Goudge's own acceptance of her singleness was a process, and her single women characters have full lives.

For Elizabeth Goudge, a serious engagement with Christian faith and Christian values provided a critical perspective on contemporary life. Her life as an unmarried woman and her deep roots in the Church of England both provided her with an understanding of alternative values that challenged conventional norms. Religion, for Goudge, challenged not just materialism but also normative models of masculinity. The Church of England had room for clergy who might not succeed elsewhere in contemporary society. While part of the establishment, its values were at odds with commercial and competitive values. The lives and work of her characters in idyllic rural communities provided a critical perspective on manliness and worldliness. The practice of Christian virtues – loving your neighbour and welcoming the stranger – offers a surprising counter to modernity. Too often we assume that traditional rural society supports rigid gender roles. Instead, Goudge shows rural communities that are flexible and inclusive. A world grounded in love and compassion, her novels suggest, is also one grounded in justice.

FIGURE 11 *Noel Streatfeild.*

10

Noel Streatfeild (1895–1986): Vicarage and Other Families

Clemence Schultze

Noel Streatfeild was 80 years old when she appeared on BBC Radio 4's classic programme *Desert Island Discs* to select the eight records she would want as a solitary castaway. One institution was, as it were, paying tribute to another, for Streatfeild's books had been loved by readers for forty years, and she was widely known as a speaker and writer about children's literature. By then she had published some eighty works, sixteen of which were novels for adults. Declaring that she was not very musical, Streatfeild chose her discs on grounds of nostalgia. Most of her choices reflected her theatrical and writing career, while three of them communicated the formative role of her vicarage childhood and the Anglican adherence to which she had returned. If only allowed one single record, she would keep the hymn 'All people that on earth do dwell'; and on the imaginary island she would take the opportunity to 'read the Bible properly'.[1] By middle age Streatfeild had

---

recovered a faith that sustained her, but she did not forget the girl who chafed at the restrictions that class, convention and narrow means imposed on an Edwardian clergy family: in all her works she drew repeatedly upon the experiences of her early years.

Family and families – both natural ones and those created by circumstance or deliberate choice – are the stuff of Streatfeild's writings for both adults and children. Her books often challenge the conventional family model but endorse the supreme importance of empathetic nurturing, however and by whomever it is carried out. Streatfeild, who identified herself as a difficult child, handles the problems of the misfit and the excluded with particular insight. Each individual, whether clearly creative or seemingly not so, is important; and it is repeatedly emphasized that love and care entail a cost – often willingly undertaken, sometimes enforced. The numerous Anglican priests portrayed in her books impose upon themselves heavy duties of service and prayerfulness but also require from their families standards of conduct and compliance which frequently become burdensome. The resulting tension between personal affection and the need for individual assertion pervades the depiction of such clergy families. But by no means all Streatfeild's leading characters are Anglicans or, indeed, believers: nevertheless, they generally share a strong ethical code and an acute sense of duty towards others. Accordingly, several of her adult books interrogate the limits of love and self-sacrifice and raise moral issues. One novel, indeed, has at its core the theological issue of sin and reparation, addressing the possibility of taking upon oneself the sin of another.

The present discussion begins with a brief examination of Streatfeild's first adult book and her first for children; in both of these the orthodox family of parents plus offspring is challenged through the creation of 'artificial' or informal families which prove able to offer to children the loving care and the opportunity for development which constitutes successful nurturing. No greater contrast can be imagined than Noel Streatfeild's own upper-middle-class background and her conventional vicarage upbringing; her career then took her away to the stage before she became a writer. The second section surveys the many aspects of nurturing to be found in her works. The role of nurturer can be taken by a range of people – related and not, employed and not, male or female, and of all ages. Families, as Streatfeild shows, may both cherish and warp. Women and men alike may prove inadequate, for various reasons, at providing the necessary love and care; the lack of imaginative insight is a particular grievance in the case of the 'difficult' child. Streatfeild looks bleakly upon the clergy fathers who impose an idealized view of familial perfection, but she also conveys how the family members themselves collude in maintaining such an ideal. The final part examines the 1939 novel *Luke*, in which Streatfeild explicitly deals with the question of sin and its expiation, in a double context: firstly as to divorce and sexual continence, and secondly with regard to a child who has committed the crime of murder.

Alternative and conventional families

Readers acquainted with Streatfeild's first children's book, the bestselling *Ballet Shoes* (1936), who later encounter her debut novel *The Whicharts* (1931), are in for a surprise: the first words, the first page and the whole situation are virtually the same.[2] Three unrelated orphan girls are foisted by an absent male upon a youngish woman, who undertakes the task of bringing them up.[3] With the help of her own old nanny, she keeps the home going by taking in boarders. While this entails a loss of caste and of privacy, the boarders' input into the children's education proves crucial.[4] It leads to their being trained at a stage school as professional dancers, ensuring the survival of the family unit. This career requires hard work and dedication; finances are tight and treats rare; clothes have to be saved for; hand-me-downs and sharing are the order of the day. The adult novel (deemed quite daring in its day) naturally puts more stress on the seamy side of theatrical life and has a less optimistic conclusion, for the Whichart family splits up.[5] In *Ballet Shoes*, the closeness and family cooperation of the three Fossil 'sisters' triumph over the various difficulties to sustain a continued joint aim.

But even allowing for these differences of emphasis, it is apparent that Streatfeild's first adult novel and her first one for children depict 'alternative' family structures – ones in which women (siblings, mother-substitutes and friends) play by far the most important roles and are shown as capable of achieving economic security. Apart from a congenial male lodger in each book to foster the middle girl's love of machinery, the significant men are either absent or dead. It is also striking that the Fossils and the Whicharts in no way resemble the bohemian musical family in Margaret Kennedy's influential bestseller *The Constant Nymph* (1924).[6] The indiscipline and sexual licence of 'Sanger's Circus' (as the children in Kennedy's novel term their ménage) foster talent in a few of the offspring but are the ruin of the others. Their milieu is utterly unlike the careful economies and relentless hard work of Streatfeild's theatrical families, in both her adult novels and those for children. On the one hand, the alternative family set-ups depicted by Streatfeild subvert the kinship tie which lies at the heart of the families typically represented in Victorian novels. In portraying an alternative (often feminine) and modern domesticity that proves itself capable of supporting and fostering individual talent and diverse dispositions, Streatfeild is making a move characteristic of her generation: the idealized Victorian patriarchal family was outdated, potentially damaging, and might be better dead or done away with.[7] On the other, the values of saving, sharing and mutual supportiveness still have a great deal in common with the ideals expressed in fictional families such as those of Charlotte M. Yonge.

Noel Streatfeild herself was a late Victorian who grew up within the orbit of this ideal. She was born on Christmas Eve 1895 into an entirely conventional upper-middle-class family. No prophet at her birth was likely to have foreseen that this daughter of the vicarage would initially train as an actress and then turn to novel writing. The first of these developments met with shock among the extended family at 'the distinguished name of Streatfeild [being] dragged in the mud', and the second with 'isn't it very unpleasant seeing your name in print?'[8] It was not at all what the Victorian Streatfeilds (Kentish parsons and landed gentry) or the Venns (her mother's evangelical family, linked to the 'Clapham Sect') expected for a young woman.

Her father William Streatfeild had followed his father into the church, and the wider family mostly lived in the Weald of Kent. William met his future wife Janet Venn when he served as curate in her father's church; his own first parish was a remote village in Sussex, where Noel lived happily until she was six. St Leonard's, where the family moved in 1902, was a very different place: the seaside resort's stylish facade hid a good deal of poverty, and William's unsparing efforts for his people impinged on his family. A transfer in 1911 to the more important parish of Eastbourne added to this. A character in Streatfeild's *Myra Carrol* (1944) describes life in a home where – just as in a boarding house – the public realm intrudes upon the private one.

> Now I hated rush and tear and flap. Vicarages are full of it. Bishops dashing in for confirmations and losing buttons off their gaiters. Men's societies meeting at the same moment as Communicant's [*sic*] Guilds and only one room free. A never-ending roar for buns for school treats fetched by the vicar's children on bicycles. Urgent notes to be dropped, parish magazines to be dropped, rows of desiccated females sitting with their feet on oilcloth in a roaring draught in the vicarage hall. No peace, no elegance of living. (218)

The same picture recurs in Streatfeild's 1950s and early 1960s tales about the Bells, and in her fictionalized memoir, *A Vicarage Family* (1963).[9] Janet Streatfeild had a difficult time running a household consisting of family plus two servants on inadequate means but in a style befitting a clergyman's position. She was largely indifferent to clothes, and Noel recalled with acute embarrassment the shabby or unsuitable dresses she was obliged to wear. This made any formal occasion an agony, and in any case social life was limited by strict rules about whom it was possible for the Vicar's family to visit. Reserved and unforthcoming, Janet was no great presence in the parish; moreover, William's High Church practices were not to her taste. Her maternal care was chiefly spent on her delicate older and younger daughters, and the youngest, a boy. Noel, the middle daughter, a robust child, appears to have missed out on the attention for which she yearned. She was a show-off, but also believed herself to be plain, stupid and naughty. The only sphere in which she shone was performing in and organizing parish entertainments; the greatest treat was a very occasional trip to the theatre. At Christmas

1913, aged 18, Noel made her social debut at a local Hunt Ball, and enjoyed a few months of dances and mild flirtations before this kind of life ended with the outbreak of war in August 1914. Noel did various forms of war work, including a spell in a munitions factory. After the war, her family agreed to let her train as an actress at the Academy of Dramatic Art. At some sacrifice, they covered the fees, but Noel's career proved relatively unsuccessful. Repertory, touring, some chorus and pantomime work – all of it was hard to come by, and in it she made no impact. Lively and attractive, she enjoyed a busy, even a wild, social life. But by her early thirties she came to realize that she had no future in the theatre. When her father – recently made Bishop of Lewes – died in 1929, Noel was abroad on tour. She returned to England determined to become an author. Her decade on the stage provided authentic background for her tale of sibling interaction, and *The Whicharts* appeared two years later. Its favourable reviews encouraged her to continue, and authorship became her profession.[10]

Nurturers and nurturing

All Streatfeild's novels draw heavily on her own experience. For her second book, *Parson's Nine* (1932), she turned from the theatre to vicarage life. The 'nine' are children born in the years from 1894 to 1902, each named after a book of the Apocrypha. This is the fancy of their father David Churston, prototype of a line of unworldly vicars in Streatfeild's fiction.[11] If a family of this size resembles the mid-nineteenth-century ones of Yonge, Streatfeild's portrayal of the mother's reaction to the arrival of baby number nine does not, for it expresses a knowing hint about birth control.[12] Told by her husband that it depends on God whether there are any further babies, Catherine stoutly asserts that no, it depends on her – and indeed, to her husband's surprise, their family proves complete (8). It may seem improbable that in 1902 the wife of a village clergyman would possess the knowledge or resources to acquire, unknown to her husband, the quite recently devised female barrier contraceptive, but for a 1930s readership, the episode neatly sums up the difference between the couple. Catherine is practical and pragmatic; the saintly David trusts to God for everything.

Parson's Nine depicts the shared nurturing of this large family by parents, servants (especially Nannie), governess and grandfather. Catherine Churston ranks as one of Streatfeild's more effective mothers, able to perceive her children as individuals and trying to do her best by them. She is wise enough to know that she needs time to herself and acknowledges her own limitations: a tendency not to want to worry, and an inability to understand certain things about her children. This applies particularly to the uncannily close bond between the twins Susanna and Baruch, the key pair of children. Catherine's good qualities (attentiveness, insight and recognition of individuals' needs and talents) are shared by the many successful nurturers in Streatfeild's books. Alex Wiltshire in *Saplings* (1945) is one notably perceptive parent, far more so than his wife Lena. His insight into the temperaments of his four children is neatly conveyed through the appropriate tone of his conversations with each of them. But when Alex is killed by a bomb halfway through the book, the family is dispersed, and all the children are damaged by the disruptions of war. In the early wartime book *The Winter Is Past* (1940), Sara, depressed after a miscarriage, gradually achieves the ability to participate in mothering some evacuee children from Deptford.[13] Parental care cuts across class, for their mother and father – both equally concerned for the children's well-being and needs – provide an example to self-centred Sara.[14] The book ends with her reconciled to her husband and ready to try for another baby.[15] Grandparents too are often depicted as taking an active part in nurturing, as in *The Bell Family* (1954). In *A Vicarage Family* it is apparent from her treatment of her *alter ego* Victoria that Streatfeild's own experience shaped her positive view of grandparental input. Their very house is in physical terms a different world from the busy, shabby town vicarage (107–10), and in moral terms it constitutes a realm of affectionate understanding: Granny's tactful and supportive explorations of individual failings recall the behaviour of the best of Yonge's fictional parents (129–36).

But kinship by blood is not everything. The unconventional or self-chosen families in Streatfeild's fiction prove just as competent as the natural ones at raising children. In *The Whicharts* and *Ballet Shoes*, the substitute mother-figures rise to the demands of the family, aided by the stalwart nanny and the various boarders. Nannies are usually depicted positively: they represent comforting routine and reliability and tend to have stock sayings for comfort or closure.[16] And in the later books for children there is usually a mother's help or daily woman, warm, supportive and full of good sense, though sometimes with a limited or conventional outlook. In the adult novels there is, unsurprisingly, more subtlety and more ambivalence in the handling of characters thrust by chance, choice or the need for employment into the role of carer and/or educator. Again, the most effective ones either possess by nature or gain by experience the insight that enables them to deal successfully with the children in their care. Sarah, the governess in *A Shepherdess of Sheep* (1934), is one such: impulsive but empathetic and determined, she can cope with the problems of a seriously disturbed child. In *Saplings* (1945), the governess Ruth Glover ascribes her 'profound understanding of children' from 'bitter school years' spent at a clergy boarding establishment (19).

An important aspect of Streatfeild's depiction of nurturing is siblings' care for each other. Children are often shown as more perceptive than adults in recognizing the needs of a delicate or sensitive one of their number. Vicky, trying to fend off an impending attack of asthma in her elder sister Isabel, is discounted by her mother.[17] The twins Susanna and Baruch in *Parson's Nine* share a complex imaginary world which protects the intensely squeamish Baruch from adult toughening up. During the First World War, Baruch commits suicide by jumping out of a window in order to avoid being called up. To prevent an inquest verdict of suicide, his mother Catherine virtually hypnotizes Susanna into saying that Baruch had recently taken to sleepwalking – which Susanna then realizes is the last and best lie she can tell for Baruch's protection. Children are often aware of suffering in their siblings that simply must not be revealed to adults. Tony's nightmares of bombing in *Saplings* are concealed by himself and his sister;[18] in *Luke* (see below), children's suffering is mute. But children can also be tormentors, operating in an underworld hidden from the grown-ups. In *Saplings*, the Smithson cousins – vicarage children – mock and exclude Tony (303–4), conducting themselves normally when adults are present but, in private, inflicting psychological tortures on the child victim.

Disrupted or unhappy families make a more compelling topic, and Streatfeild is by no means so unrealistic as to show all carers as perceptive and capable. Far from it: the majority of adults in her books fall significantly short of this ideal, ill-suited by temperament or holding romanticized expectations about parenting. Sylvia Strangeway in *A Vicarage Family*, a successful mother to her other children, largely fails to acknowledge Vicky's dissatisfactions. Another factor which impedes nurturing is an intense sexual bond between husband and wife, as with Freda in *Luke* (discussed below). Similarly, Lena, wife to the caring father Alex in *Saplings*, puts her physical relationship with him first (16–17), regarding her children as delightful accessories easily handed over to others. After Alex's death, Lena's priority is to enjoy herself with a succession of new partners rather than make a home for the children.[19]

Fathers too can fail as nurturers. Manly men, like Charles Lane in *Shepherdess*, may lack the imagination to understand a child's fears and needs (59, 313). Others leave such matters to their wives and/or have fixed notions of gender roles to which their children must conform (see below on *Luke*). But most sharply handled are the clergy fathers who embarrass their children by an unwanted degree of emotional intercourse or who blindly assume that their families share their own beliefs. This is invariably undercut by another character or the authorial voice. Fasting for Lent is 'a sublime opportunity' for David Churston in *Parson's Nine*, and (as he believes) for his children too, whereas the governess's unspoken judgement is 'Couldn't he see the smug little hypocrites he was making of them?' (52). The same applies to Sundays: 'the myth ... that the whole day was something special, a kind of treat' (54). Although Streatfeild later asserted of this novel that 'the parson was totally unlike father', the recurrence in the semi-autobiographical work *A Vicarage Family* of imposed Lenten fasting and boring Sundays suggests otherwise.[20] Allowed (most exceptionally) to attend a children's party during Lent, the youngest girl believes that by eating a sugar rose she has 'sinned against the Holy Ghost' (65). Sundays in these households combine embarrassment with tedium:

All the children, especially the boys who sang in the choir when they were home, detested Sundays. But it was an underground detestation never spoken of in front of a grown-up because Daddy must never know. He thought his children loved Sundays just as he had loved them when he was a boy, and this was why their Sundays were modelled on Sundays in their grandparents' house. (37)

Collect and catechism, special Sunday clothes (that were in the Strangeways' case actually *less* good than everyday clothes), two services, Sunday books and no toys – many of these features recall Yonge's novels. And the clergyman father looks back at his own childhood as idyllic, totally unaware that his offspring lack this feeling (85). Streatfeild's narrative voice, however, drily comments, apropos the hot Sunday lunch, that 'church-going was a class affair', and for the servants the day of rest began only at teatime (49). But one element that Streatfeild evidently recalled with warmth was hymn-singing in the evening, for the only hymn specified, 'Glory to Thee My God This Night', was later one of her Desert Island Discs choices (55).

Truth about Sundays is not the only thing the clerical families conceal. Time and again it proves impossible to tell a father something that will hurt him. The Strangeway family hide their dislike of dreary holidays in unsuitable rented houses (179–81). Andrew Smithson in *Saplings* must not know that his children go out to dances or tennis:

Mother and daughter would gaze at each other, both seeing with horrible clarity Andrew looking white and suffering. Andrew, at some time between services, holding out a hand and opening the study door. There would be protestations and penances. Andrew would suffer acutely because of the sin, his daughter merely from embarrassment. (301)

Instead of confronting her husband, Sylvia connives at keeping him in the dark, creating pretexts which allow the children to participate in the social life of their peers. Her lies on behalf of her children render truthful family relationships impossible, and yet her motive is to protect a husband whose innocence she is not prepared to shatter. Andrew Smithson, David Churston, Jim Strangeway and Alex Bell in *The Bell Family* are cut from the same cloth. All are ardent in the spiritual life, devoted to their parishes and at the service of all in need – hence they are frequently termed saintly and are recognized as being unlike other people. Not wholly without insight, they nevertheless tend to idealize the family as a concept and to ignore the particular characteristics or views of individuals. Thus, Jim Strangeway in *A Vicarage Family* is characterized as much more High Church than his wife (281–2) but

[his daughter Isabel] did not believe her father noticed how her mother felt or, if he did, that he cared, for in his philosophy a wife believed what her husband believed. The point was above argument. (45)

Similarly, David Churston in *Parson's Nine* discounts any possibility of their brilliant daughter Judith going to college:

> 'I feel sure that the only career our Judith wishes for is to help you here and me in my parish, and some day, if God should so will it, have a husband, and children, and home of her own to look after.'
>
> Catherine looked at him in amazement. It seemed to her incredible that anybody could live in the same house as Judith and acquire such a remarkably incorrect vision of her.
>
> 'I don't think,' she said drily, 'you'll find those are exactly Judith's views.'
>
> 'Then Judith must learn,' said David sternly. 'God intended women to be wives and mothers.' (103–4)

Streatfeild's narrative underlines the damaging effect of this extreme lack of perception about one's own family. In the event, Judith marries the first intellectual she meets, and is disappointed when he ridicules her participating in his studies: he wants an adoring, adorning wife and future mother (146–8). In ironic fashion, therefore, her father's wishes for her are fulfilled.

Confirmation is an issue that heightens awkwardness and conflict between children and parents. Judith in *Parson's Nine* plans to refuse to be confirmed, and ends up agreeing so as not to hurt her father (94–6). Vicky in *A Vicarage Family* has the resolve to tell her father that she does not feel suitable, but he overrides this: '"You have a more difficult nature ... so you need special help" ... [N]ow he was dedicated to giving this much-loved but wayward child the spiritual help he was convinced would change her life ... [T]o Victoria, nothing was bearable on that embarrassing day [of confirmation].'[21] The last straw comes when the governess relates (in her 'special confirmation day voice') the story of St Dorothea, and Vicky, goaded beyond endurance, hurls an inkpot at her (285). No consequences ensue, for someone (possibly a perceptive grandparent) sees to it that the incident is ignored.

In the same year as she published *A Vicarage Family*, Noel Streatfeild edited *Confirmation and After* (1963), providing linking introductions to essays by various church people.[22] In this and its successor, *Before Confirmation* (1967), she demonstrates her insight into the difficulties likely to be encountered. The later book is addressed as if to a godchild:

> You know that we who are fond of you want you to be confirmed. Our reason is that, if you are anything like I was at your age, you need help. Perhaps you don't fail in trying to do right as often as I did, but even if you do not need help just now, you will need it in the years ahead of you. (4)

This initial greeting recalls her father's statement of some fifty years previously. Perhaps the words she had attributed to Vicky were also in her mind: 'I wonder if God knows how difficult it is being a saint's family' (101). Lack of imaginative perception is the chief shortcoming which Streatfeild identifies in parents and carers generally. And when manifested by a loving, yet controlling, clerical father, this failing evokes reactions ambivalent between compliance and challenge.

Crime and sinfulness

Problems of greater moral complexity arise for the parents and carers of a backward or disturbed child. *Luke* (1939) gathers together all the issues of multiple nurturing, sibling concern and parents' sexual lives and stands out among Streatfeild's works for making a religious issue the core of a novel.[23] The deviant child here is Luke, a musical genius of thirteen, emotional and highly strung. His parents are divorced; his conductor father, the person who understood him best of all, has started another family. His mother Freda, a High Anglican, frivolous, highly sexed and reliant on others, has long been reluctant to agree to a divorce but has finally done so, contrary to the views of her priest on the marriage sacrament. She has then herself remarried, to a bluff hearty widower called Andrew Dawson, father of two children. Dawson's views about Luke's education differ from Freda's: he holds that a conventional boys' prep school would toughen the child, and he also ends Luke's training with the famous musician (chosen by his father) on the grounds of the man's homosexuality. Freda has come gradually to believe that her remarriage was wrong; and her priest tells her that as long as she continues to have sexual relations with her husband, her penance is not to present herself for Holy Communion.[24] Physically obsessed with each other, the couple are incapable of doing this, and in any case such views simply do not enter within Andrew Dawson's range of comprehension.

The book opens just after the discovery of Dawson's body, poisoned, it transpires, by strychnine. The melodramatic plot has a background of the utmost banality: comfortable middle-class life in a village.[25] But this is not a whodunnit, and the reader very soon realizes that Luke is the poisoner. He is the one character whose voice we never hear at first hand and to whose thoughts we are given no access. Streatfeild set herself a considerable technical problem here: she uses conversation, reported speech and free indirect discourse to convey the situation. None of the characters (family, servants, friends, doctor, policemen, lawyer) knows everything, but through their individual contributions the reader gradually learns this backstory, and is also made privy to the investigation into the poisoning and the ongoing reactions of those involved. Luke is never even considered by the police, but several people know or come to suspect that he is the guilty one. A number of them describe his illnesses, his tantrums and his secretive, often malicious, behaviour, and take into account too his broken home and his mother's indulgence. His stepbrother and stepsister are terrified of his spiteful teasing but will not say a word to the grown-ups, not even admitting their own fear to the friendly doctor who is hoping to identify the trouble:

> It was obvious that the boy was wrestling with himself, longing to speak. Then even while he watched he knew that the doors were shut. The appalling reticence of childhood had won, the reticence which allows tortures of physical and mental pain to be endured in silence. (171)

The household servants deeply dislike Luke. His nanny recognizes him as the most difficult child she has ever dealt with but deliberately restrains any further thoughts as they come 'peeping from their holes' (173). His mother Freda likewise has suspicions which she will not admit, even to herself. As the likeliest suspect, she is induced to have counsel to represent her at the inquest. Interviewing her beforehand, he suggests that her husband understood her distress at being banned from Holy Communion and committed suicide in order to free her. Even though part of Freda knows that Dawson was a no-nonsense man who would have ridiculed any such notion, she succeeds in persuading herself of this. In the witness box, her sworn evidence convinces the jury to return a verdict of suicide. The situation is a reversal of that in *Parson's Nine*, when Susanna lies about Baruch's sleepwalking to save his reputation from a suicide verdict; here, one will safeguard Luke's continued freedom.

That Luke committed the murder is clear to the reader via the combination of perspectives. He had found and concealed a packet of strychnine lost by the doctor, then used it on his stepfather. If Freda's assertion in the witness box is true – that she had already told him of her intention to remove him from his much-disliked school – he killed Andrew Dawson even after knowing that this release was coming. Or if Freda has invented this in order to reduce the possibility of anyone ascribing a motive to Luke, then he might be held to have acted in a desperate bid to get free from his stepfather's control. The varying points of view give no answer to this; nor do they assert definitively why Luke is as he is. One of the most insightful is his former governess who, while admitting that he is difficult, spoilt and a show-off, nevertheless refers to him as 'a lovable boy' (133). She holds that his birth father handled him well, always distinguishing between tantrums and real distress, whereas his mother's regime of spoiling and exhibiting him as a genius was damaging, especially when followed by acquiescence in the stepfather's conventional scheme of education (128–43). That is as close as the reader comes to understanding the springs of Luke's actions. Streatfeild makes it clear that he has done a murderous act but does not judge what degree of responsibility lies with him.

The core theological issue, however, relates to Luke's mother and the possibility of reparation for sin. This had initially arisen for Freda some years previously, over whether to allow her first husband a divorce, a phase presented from the viewpoint of Freda's friend Margaret: 'How she'd talked about sin and that strange thorny creed of Father Candon's, reparation, atonement' (47–8). The priest Robert Candon describes to his bishop how, observing in her a potentiality for spiritual growth, he had shown her that she could take her (first) husband's sin upon herself:

> Mrs. Dawson ... is not a strong character, but she could be capable with God's help of greater heights than a less physical type. ... I showed her a way ... That since her husband was committing a sin for which he was not repenting, to atone for him would be her cross. That as Christ carried His on His back, so she on her back could carry her husband's sin. (77–9)

Freda has since fallen short through her own remarriage (hence her ban from Communion), but later she recalls the idea, envisaging the possibility of taking Luke's sin upon herself. As Father Robert watches her in the witness box,

> his words to the bishop came back to him. 'If she could be made to feel the power of God in her life, to take the place of physical love, then something fine would be born.' Wasn't there a change in her? Didn't her whole manner and the lift of her head have a quality of fineness that had not been there before? (230)[26]

Later, he offers her help and prayer:

> In that second Freda faced a future when some knowledge had to be her own. When she, who confided in everybody, could have no confidant.
> 'No.' She sat up. 'Do you really believe one can carry somebody else's sin?'
> 'I know it to be true.'
> She stared in front of her.
> 'All one's life?'
> He laid his hand on her arm.
> 'Mrs. Dawson –'
> She shook her head.
> 'It's all right, I don't need any help.' (241)

The novel ends with George the doctor discovering a hidden hoard of Luke's, including an eyebath lost in the same package with the strychnine; he now knows beyond doubt that Luke is guilty. In the concluding paragraphs he ponders whether to reveal the evidence:

> In the drawing-room Freda was sitting by the fire, she looked ill but at peace. Luke was at the piano, his head was raised, and, listening to the music he made, his eyes gleamed as if they saw Paradise.

George stared at the two of them through the french windows. His fingers rolled the eye-bath in his pocket. How easy it would be to put it in an envelope and drop it off the pier. But should he? Luke was nearly fourteen, in a few years he might be a father, creating others like him. Even now was he safe? Was this the answer to [his step-sister] Viola's terror? His mother was weak; even if she guessed as she must, was she fit to look after such as he? Wasn't this a case for locks and bars? Over and over he turned the eye-bath. What was right to do? (258)

Luke's not unusual faults of temper, wilfulness and spite are partly fostered by circumstance and by adults' decisions; his overpowering need is to create the conditions necessary for him to flourish. To this extent he resembles Streatfeild's other gifted performer children, self-driven to achieve their peak, often at some considerable cost to the siblings and carers who love them. But by placing Luke at the genius end of this spectrum, and making the cost of his flourishing his stepfather's life and his mother's voluntary reparation for sin, Streatfeild moves the question to a wholly different plane from the other 'talented child' novels. Luke himself (never termed 'evil') is ultimately opaque to the reader's understanding. The practical and even the moral concerns mooted by the doctor are not of the same order as Freda's willed decision to take her son's sin upon herself. And among the unanswered questions at the end is not only how the doctor will decide to act, but – were he to remain silent – whether Freda (who was unable to last out in 'carrying the sin' of the divorce) has the resolution this time to do so from her love for Luke.

Luke, published just as hostilities began in September 1939, was little noticed. Unsold copies were lost when the publisher's warehouse was bombed. The narrative technique in *Luke* recalls that of Daphne du Maurier's bestseller *Rebecca* (1938), where descriptions and reactions of others combine to create a picture of the eponym. But the issues treated resemble those of another notable book of 1938: Graham Greene's *Brighton Rock*, the first of his mid-career 'Catholic' novels.[27] Streatfeild, engaging with gender roles, problems of authority and spiritual growth in *Luke*, may well have observed the impact this book made.[28] Charles Péguy's notion of 'voluntary damnation', adumbrated by Greene at the end of the novel, resembles the 'reparation' to which Robert Candon invites Freda.[29] The High Anglican priest is one of Streatfeild's near-saintly clerics. His unwavering certainty that divorce is sinful rouses indignation among the jurors: 'popish talk … if the law [of England] said you could be married by a registrar, then you could. Impertinence' (223–4). But: 'It's his sort and not mine that has kept the faith alive', reflects his bishop (86). Celibate himself, Candon regards Freda's intensely sensual nature as something to be sublimated, while the bishop acutely remarks: 'To divide up where one ecstasy begins and the other ends is beyond most of us' (79–80).[30]

When reading *Luke*, it is hard not to suppose that Streatfeild, who by the 1950s was again a practising Anglican, had in 1939 already started on her return journey.[31] In *Confirmation and After* (1963) her description of the agnostic position, though impersonally expressed, conveys imaginative sympathy:

> It is easy to come back to God at any time but to a lapsed Christian it does not look that way. It looks intolerably difficult. Yet a lapsed Christian need not be an agnostic; he probably can still remember how much richer life seemed when he was part of the Church. (4)

William Streatfeild, as a High Anglican, would have applied the doctrine of reserve in speaking of religious matters.[32] In her published works his daughter adheres to this practice, making it all but impossible to chart her journey. Streatfeild, whose sexuality is ambivalent, may well have used her imagination in depicting Freda and Andrew's intensely sexual relationship, just as she imagined Luke's neatly planned act of murder, but the triggering factors in the situation are less significant than the issue raised: can an ordinary sinful person act in a Christ-like way so as to make reparation for another's sin?[33] In *Luke*, Streatfeild seems to be moving towards an Anglican novel of religious ideas, addressing a test case not of crime but of sin, in an attempt to explore the intersections of human and divine love.

The immediate outbreak of war deflected Streatfeild's work towards topical matters, with the socially optimistic *Winter Is Past* (see above). In three subsequent novels, however, *I Ordered a Table for Six* (1942), *Grass in Piccadilly* (1947) and *Mothering Sunday* (1950), Streatfeild again depicts mothers of criminal sons, but with considerable differences from *Luke*. These are adult men, not geniuses and not murderers, who either have paid or are about to pay their debt to society by imprisonment. The problems arise from the mothers' and other family members' reactions, ranging from rejection to loving support. Repeatedly the question is how far love and protection can – or should – extend; in these later works it is approached in moral and practical terms rather than theological.

Conclusion

Before Nicola Beauman's groundbreaking *A Very Great Profession* (1983), the only women's novels of the 1920s to 1950s deemed to merit discussion were modernist works, but the last generation has seen numerous treatments of all but forgotten books from this period.[34] The novels of manners, of domesticity, the 'middlebrow novel', and women's war novels have all received attention. Only under the last heading does Noel Streatfeild make anything of a showing.[35] Her name is still recognized as a children's author, and the recent reissue of several of her novels for adults is a welcome development.[36]

Many elements of Streatfeild's novels fall at least partially into the categories above, but no single description suits them all. There is humour and social observation, but they are not comedies or what is usually meant by 'novels of manners'. They are not romantic or escapist or exotic. Domestic and middlebrow they undoubtedly are, but they do not share the reflexivity identified as characteristic of middlebrow novels: the characters' self-affirmation through reading.[37] Few of her novels are distinctively 'Anglican' or 'churchy', a term sometimes applied to Barbara Pym's fiction.[38] Rather, they deal almost obsessively with personal growth, empathy and understanding within families, so perhaps 'family novel' – granting the widest possible definition of what makes a family – best approximates to the scope of her work. In *Luke* alone, she addresses theology and a particular kind of churchmanship to engage with the relationship between human love (marital and maternal) and divine love.

Noel Streatfeild, unmarried, partnerless and childless, worked from and with her own upbringing. She replays the events and emotions of her childhood, never, in a sense, getting 'away from the vicarage.' She returns repeatedly to the question of the qualities required in parents and carers for successful nurturing, engaging with the issue from one angle after another. The answer is always the same – love, attentiveness, understanding – and its corollary the same too: fail or succeed, there is a cost entailed.

FIGURE 12 *Iris Murdoch.*

11

Iris Murdoch (1919–99): Anglican Atheist

Peter S. Hawkins

To an extent unmatched by any other British writer of her time, Iris Murdoch devoted her creative life to thinking about religion, and in particular about the decline of Christianity within the UK in the post-war period. 'Christianity is not abandoned so much as simply unknown,' she wrote in 1970. 'A generation has been growing up outside it.'[1] Many of her twenty-six novels approach this crisis through the indirection of fiction, with characters who have lost their faith and vocation – several are clergy or religious – and who subsequently struggle with the absence. The crisis itself, however, is also addressed overtly in her philosophical writing, most extensively in the 500-page expansion of her 1982 Gifford Lectures that became *Metaphysics as a Guide to Morals* (1992). One can get quickly to the heart of the matter, however, by looking at a single exchange in Jeffrey Meyer's 1990 *Paris Review* interview.

> INTERVIEWER: In your work you consider what religion means for people who do not believe in God. Can you say something about this?
>
> MURDOCH: This question interests and concerns me very much. Looking at western societies I think that if we have religion, we shall have to have religion without God, because belief in a personal God is becoming increasingly impossible for many people. It's a difficult question actually to know what believing in a personal God is. I know that I don't believe in one. I don't want to use the word 'God'

in any other sense. I think it's a proper name. I don't believe in the divinity of Christ. I don't believe in life after death. My beliefs really are Buddhist in style. I've been very attached to Buddhism. Buddhism makes it plain that you can have religion without God, that religion is in fact better off without God. It has to do with now, with every moment of one's life, how one thinks, what one is and does, about love and compassion and the overcoming of self, the difference between illusion and reality.[2]

Here Murdoch says explicitly what she does not believe in – a personal God, a divine Christ, an afterlife – but also hints at the kind of religion she stands by: mindfulness, attention, love, compassion, liberation from the ego and its self-serving fantasies. In short, inveterate Platonist that she was, she affirms 'the Good' rather than 'God': Goodness is her 'transcendent magnetic centre'.[3]

And yet for all this, Murdoch did not want to lose too much by asserting too little: 'I want there to be religion on this planet.'[4] Matthew Arnold's notion of lofty morality plus emotion was not enough to live on. The 'old literal beliefs' had to be discarded, but she wanted, somehow, to keep the structures and the stories, the particularities of the church's earthen vessel, the 'picturesque', the sonorities of the Authorized Version and Thomas Cranmer's Book of Common Prayer. Perhaps for this reason *Metaphysics* ends with her citation of Psalm 139:6 ('Whither shall I go from thy spirit, whither shall I flee from thy presence?') notwithstanding its 500-page call to abandon the divine Thou. She even wanted to keep Jesus Christ – provided he could 'become like the Buddha, both real and mystical, but no longer the divine all-in-one man of traditional Christianity of the West'.[5] Murdoch herself dreamed of such a Christ in January 1947 and gave him an appearance thirty years later in *Nuns and Soldiers* (1980).[6] Under the right conditions, he could continue to be a 'saviour'.

The tide of faith was clearly at an ebb, and yet Murdoch hoped for 'a Buddhist style survival of Christianity', for a Christ 'who can console and save, but who is to be found as a living force within each human soul and not in some supernatural elsewhere'.[7] She wanted new Eastern wine to fill old Western skins, and hoped for a Christianity that could 'demythologize itself'.[8] But could this renewal happen before sheer unbelief took over? Although her *Metaphysics* calls for change, it does not offer a concrete vision for what might follow. The doctrinal affirmations of the past are no longer tenable, but it is unclear what kind of affirmations awaits the future. 'Is there a God?' – a question she posed in life as well as in her fiction – is no longer the question of choice. Instead, we get these: 'Can western religion survive?' 'Can the Christian mythology thus transform itself in front of our eyes?' 'Can the figure of Christ remain religiously significant without the old god-man mythology somehow understood?'[9]

Numerous times Murdoch appeals to an assertion of T.S. Eliot (who certainly affirmed 'the old god-man theology' as dogma) 'that Christianity has always been changing itself into something which can be generally believed'.[10] What she referred to as 'recent Anglican theology' was making moves in this direction: J.A.T. Robinson and Don Cupitt are the controversial theologians she mentions.[11] She worried, however, that their demythologization was too severe and colourless. It was in danger of offering only 'an unadorned moral asceticism' that for most people would be 'intolerable', 'unnecessarily extreme', 'oddly abstract'.[12] A 'denuded existentialist faith' had lost touch with the 'old familiar mysterious world' in which we still live and which was crucial to the dictates of her imagination as both novelist and philosopher:

> The idea of 'the world as full of images of God and of hierarchies pointing to God' is, as I see it, fundamental in religion and (*mutatis mutandis*) in morality. I think this is what (if we put Good for God) the world *is* full of! The affirmative way, which can find the divine everywhere in all the desire-driven burrowings of cognition, relates spirituality to the whole of our being.[13]

The world, in other words, is charged with the grandeur of the Good. But how to make the Good compelling and, indeed, explosive? How 'to invent new religious imagery (or twist old religious imagery) in an empty situation', 'to live a religious life without illusions'?[14]

Murdoch's religion

For all the importance Murdoch accorded religion, there is no easy way to characterize what kind of believer she was, or how she imagined that the austerity of the Good could gain the magnetic force once exerted by God. Although technically an atheist – her personal religion had no use for 'God' – she was in another sense a composite of religious self-identifications. She called herself 'Buddhist in style', a 'neo-Christian or Buddhist Christian or Christian fellow traveller'.[15] She was also unapologetically an Anglican of a sort. 'I grew up in Anglican Christianity and I feel in a way I am still inside the Anglican church'.[16] She attended services but without receiving the sacrament ('Something inhibits me from doing this – I'm not quite sure what'). 'I still myself use the Christian mythology. I am moved by it and I see its religious significance and the way in which ordinary life is given a radiance.'[17]

The Anglican House famously has many mansions and ways to be 'inside' it. Murdoch's own background suggests a range of those possibilities.[18] What she inherited by birth and upbringing reflects the divisions within her own Irish Protestant family. (There is no evidence of the Roman Catholic ancestors she also claimed.) On her father's side, the Murdochs were members of the ecclesiastically low Anglican Church of Ireland, to which was added a strong dose of Belfast nonconformity among the aunts and cousins who were Church of the Brethren, Presbyterians, and Quakers. Her mother's Dublin relations represented a more easy-going Church of Ireland sensibility. Although neither parent was particularly pious, Murdoch reports that they met one another on a Dublin tram while going to services at the same Mount Street church where Rene Murdoch (née Richardson) sang in the choir.[19] It was from her mother, rather than from her adored father, that she learned prayers ('Jesus teacher: shepherd hear me') and hymns ('Tell me the old, old story of Jesus and His love').[20] By Murdoch's account, her parents were 'cheerful, relaxed Anglicans'; they 'did not object to religion in others, but did not go in for it much themselves, even at Christmas and Easter'.[21]

Other relatives were more urgently religious. Following her family's move to England shortly after Murdoch's birth, summer holidays were spent in Ulster, where she came in contact with the fiercer Protestantism of her Brethren relations. With them she attended Revivalist meetings at the Anglican Mariners' Church (now closed), an event later recalled in *The Red and the Green* (1965).[22] Andrew, a character in the novel, complains that 'in Ireland religion was a matter of choosing between one appalling vulgarity and another' (62). Murdoch herself was less withering. What she took away from her exposure to evangelicalism – along with a Belfast cousin who as late as 1997 importuned her to 'return to Christ' – was its music: 'singing was the best part of the thing where some light shone'.[23] Musical memory enters her fiction close to the beginning of *The Red and the Green* when 'several hundred youthful voices' enthusiastically peal forth the words of a gospel chorus: 'Over and over, like a mighty sea, Comes the love of JESUS, rolling over me!' (62) Andrew is repulsed by these 'horrible sounds', but in a journal entry from January 1985 Murdoch recalled without disdain the lyrics of those Belfast rallies: 'Wide, wide as the ocean, high as the heavens above, deep, deep as the deepest sea is my saviour's love.'[24]

Well into her adulthood, relatives on both sides of the family gave Murdoch inscribed gift copies of the Bible or devotional works (*Daily Light on the Daily Path*), which she held onto in later years.[25] Both scripture and the Prayer Book left an early mark on her imagination. While at the Badminton School in suburban Bristol she attended the headmistress's Quaker meeting along with her schoolmates and in 1934 was confirmed in the Church of England. There was nothing fervent or concerted in an upbringing of 'cheerful, relaxed' observance. That said, she later told her friend Philippa Foot (to whom, along with John Bayley, she dedicated *Metaphysics*), 'I got religion in childhood, which I think you didn't.' She had, she said, an essentially religious nature and '[t]hese germs in the blood must be confessed to'.[26]

Whatever Murdoch took away from childhood and adolescence, her involvement with Christianity became more serious at Somerville College

(1938–42). She read Classics at Oxford and during the second part of the course – known as Greats – studied philosophy under her tutor Donald MacKinnon, later Norris-Hulse Professor of Divinity at Cambridge. His Anglo-Catholic faith introduced her in a new way to 'J[esus] C[hrist]'; he also, during a time of turmoil in the mid-1940s, sent her on retreat to the Anglican Benedictine Malling Abbey in Kent, later to be reprised fondly in *The Bell* (1958).[27] MacKinnon wanted her to meet its renowned Abbess, Dame Magdalene Mary Euan-Smith, who was well known for 'being good with difficult cases'.[28]

During Murdoch's undergraduate studies, Marxism and the Communist Party provided one kind of inspiration, religion another. The latter seemed to come to her almost as something of a surprise. In a 1942 letter to Frank Thompson she wrote, 'Christianity, you know, when you get away from it a bit and really see it, is a most amazing and almost incredible phenomenon. How does it look from Galilee? What a beautiful, queer, unexpected world it is.'[29] A few years later in 1948, when she was a philosophy tutor at St. Anne's, Murdoch participated in an informal study group, 'The Metaphysicals', convened at Oxford by such Anglo-Catholic luminaries as Eric Mascall, Austin Farrer and Basil Mitchell.[30] She remained in this all-male clergy company until 1952, when it seemed an appropriate time to leave. She did not share the intense Anglican affiliation so important to the others; when it came to church, she was, she said, 'more a fellow-traveller than a Party member'.[31] This remained her stance, notwithstanding cordial relations with clergy and Divinity School academics throughout her life.[32] Intrigued rather than persuaded, she relied on a deep inner knowledge of Christian images, texts and spiritual experience to imagine a world of thought and feeling outside the church. In her fiction, moreover, she showed a remarkable ability to articulate the faith she was determined to move beyond.

In keeping with her critical analysis of post-war Christianity in decline, a number of Murdoch's most vividly drawn fictional characters find that they no longer 'fit' within the church that shaped them: priests Cato Forbes and Brendan Craddock in *Henry and Cato* (1976); a recently cloistered nun, Ann Cavidge, in *Nuns and Soldiers* (1980); and a passionate, if erratic, seeker, Bellamy James, in *The Green Knight* (1993).[33] In different ways, all of these figures were 'soaked in Christianity and in Christ, sunk, saturated, stained indelibly all through'.[34] At some point, however, whether through the loss of faith or because of its deepening, they find that they are 'in the wrong place' and must move on.[35] The novels explore these times of transition.

It is interesting that someone who was raised in the Anglican Church, and who throughout her life believed that she was 'still inside it', should choose to explore the life of faith so vividly through the imagined experience of Roman Catholics. This may have been because the Established Church, with its vicars, parish councils and jumble sales, was far removed from the heightened drama (and spiritual elitism) of English Catholicism. There was more for a novelist to work with, in other words, in a Continental tradition more comfortable with extremes of faith and experience than an English *via media* largely intent on avoiding them.

Other novelists in the present collection, of course, found the Church of England rich fodder for the imagination. Murdoch largely did not, choosing to linger instead with the highs and lows of the celibate life, mysticism, the Mass. She conjured characters who were products of the Protestant English bourgeoisie who had chosen a more intense religious life in a demanding *Roman* church. Joining it, they had much to lose. To be a convert (as all of these figures are, save for the Downside-educated Brendan Craddock) meant in some sense to leave the family fold. With renunciation, moreover, came an impassioned new identification: to be a Catholic is to be 'sunk, saturated, [and] stained' with Christ, to belong to *The* Church whatever the cost. It is no wonder that a religious novelist with a taste for the baroque should find so much to mine and treasure in the spiritual odysseys of its adherents.

Was Murdoch herself, like many another post-war British writer, drawn across the Tiber to Rome? Conradi cites various reports of the author telling her beads in Westminster Cathedral and carrying a Latin missal to Oxford's Blackfriars.[36] In a 1993 letter to Sister Marian (Lucy Klatschko) at Stanbrook Abbey, she wrote, 'I am attached to Buddhism, but am not "practising". I am still with Julian of Norwich and *Cloud of Unknowing*, etc. A pal (A.N. Wilson actually) said to me that Christianity (in the next century) will only be in the Roman church (This can seem plausible.).'[37] It is safest to say that Murdoch 'fellow travelled' in both Anglican and Roman churches, belonging to neither.

The Time of the Angels

Apart from Murdoch's novels of Roman Catholic loss and discovery, however, there is a specifically Anglican equivalent in her fiction. It is not a pretty picture. On the basis of one novel, *The Time of the Angels* (1966), the Church of England looks to be on its last legs. At the heart of darkness in this unrelievedly dark novel stands an atheist quasi-Nietzchean vicar, charming and abusive, with a will to power that holds sway over everyone in his orbit. Transferred from the Midlands to an all but defunct London parish, Fr Carel Fisher has, by the time we meet him, essentially taken up the mantra of Milton's Satan, 'Evil, be thou my good'.[38] For him, God is dead and in his absence the 'principalities and powers' wreck their havoc: 'When I celebrate Mass I am God. *Nil inultum remanebit*'.[39]

Ironically, there is actually no Mass to celebrate: his ruined (unnamed) London parish is presently without congregation or public worship, its building massively damaged in the blitz so that only the rectory and a Christopher Wren tower remain. Yet even the little of the past that does endure is about to fall victim to the developer's wrecking ball. This wreckage comes none too soon after Fr Carel dies at his own hands, his abused, shell-shocked daughters flee the scene, and whatever had once been the ministry of the place – non-existent as far as we can tell – grinds to a halt. Nor is there any reason it should continue, since the heart has gone out of it. It comes as no great surprise in the novel's final pages that a pastoral representative of the bishop, sent to investigate the vicar, should confess, 'I'm not even a proper Christian any more I'm afraid. I suppose I'm a sort of Buddhist now really' (229).

How has the glory departed so thoroughly, and why have the angels of destruction seized the day?[40] The novel offers one diagnosis in the course of a small dinner convened to deal with Carel Fisher, in which the bishop instead holds forth on what he takes to be the spirit of the age. Murdoch turns it into a kind of symposium:

> We have to think of this time as an interregnum. It is a time when, as one might put it, mankind is growing up. The particular historical nature of Christianity poses intellectual problems which are also spiritual problems. Much of the symbolism of theology which was an aid to understanding in earlier and simpler times is, in this scientific age, simply a barrier to belief. It has become positively misleading. Our symbolism must change. This after all is nothing new, it is a necessity which the Church has always understood. God lives and works in history. The outward mythology changes, the inward truth remains the same. (93)

Much of this is vintage Murdoch, but given the novel's circumstances the bishop seems, on the face of things, to be sidestepping the urgency of the issue. Brought in to discuss the parlous state of the parish, he is blithely unperturbed by the reports of Carel Fisher's behaviour and views. 'The Anglican Church has been noted for its eccentrics', he says: 'Let him who is without neurosis cast the first stone!' (91). His dinner-table interlocutors, expecting something brisk and jovial from a London prelate, end up disturbed by what he has to say. The hostess, a model of no-nonsense practicality and also no Defender of the Faith, is disappointed by his vagueness and complacency. She rolls her eyes with his discussion of the 'interregnum': 'The Church will have to endure a very painful transformation ... But the Lord will turn again the captivity of Zion' (93). When he opines that the nihilistic vicar is 'a passionately religious man', her response is 'Oh rubbish!' (93).

Her other guest, however, is shaken rather than merely annoyed. He happens to be Carel Fisher's brother, a scholar working on a very Murdochian book, 'Morality in a World without God', who only half-realizes that 'the era of superstition was over' (71). He is uneasy with the interregnum's 'growing up'. He wants other people to hold fast to a religion to which he himself no longer adheres and is appalled by how diminished the 'deposit of faith' has become even for those, like the bishop, who are meant to be its ecclesiastical custodians: 'behind the scenes it was all being unobtrusively dismantled.

That they should be deciding that God was not a person, that they should be quietly demoting Jesus Christ, this made him feel almost frightened' (94). Despite the bishop's vague confidence that 'the inward truth remains the same', it is unclear that this is at all true. Is there, in fact, any 'inward truth', anything left at the end of the day?

'The death of God has set the angels free', says Carel Fisher. 'And they are terrible' (173). The action of the novel supports his position. By contrast, the angels of a Russian icon of the Trinity, which figures in the novel in various ways, speak to another reality altogether. They evoke a beautiful, if lost, spiritual world, one that is distinctly Christian but coming from the czarist Orthodox East. Murdoch describes this anonymously painted devotional work with the kind of descriptive reverence she otherwise accords the Old Master paintings that appear elsewhere in her fiction. Usually these pictures are encountered in the 'sanctuary' of the National Gallery – a Titian, a Gainsborough, a Piero della Francesca – where they offer focus and peace to frantic, self-absorbed people who are momentarily spellbound by what they see.[41] This Russian icon of the Trinity, although taken out of its intended religious context, nonetheless does what an Orthodox icon is meant to do: it opens a window into another world. More particularly in this novel, it casts a ray of light that shines into the perpetual night-time of a fog-bound London and a sepulchral rectory. Holding it in his hands, not even Carel Fisher is immune to its beauty:

> The solid wooden rectangle glowed golden and blue. The three bronzed angels, weary with humility and failure, sat in their conclave holding their slender rods of office, graceful and remote, bowing their small heads to each other under their huge creamy haloes, floating upon their thrones in an empyrean of milky brightness. (175)

These 'graceful and remote' figures suggest a paradisiacal realm of haloes and thrones, an Empyrean that is eternally '[glowing] golden and blue'. But in truth they belong to another country and to the past. They no longer have a home in a belated 'time of the Angels'. Nor is there a church left to house them.

A Word Child

In another Murdoch novel, however, there is an Anglican Church that continues to function and with it a famous believer who carried the tradition into its uncertain future. In A Word Child (1975), for instance, Hilary Burde – an anti-hero if ever there were one – takes refuge from the accumulated disasters of his life in the Anglo-Catholic darkness of St. Stephen's, on London's Gloucester Road. He goes there for rest only. He is not looking for God after the punishing Evangelicalism of his orphanage childhood; nor as an adult does he have any interest in 'bloody theologians'.[42] But perhaps he stops at this particular church not only because its doors are open but because, literary man at heart, he'd heard that T.S. Eliot served for many years as its churchwarden. Would the poet, if not his God, offer him some kind of consolation? 'I sat in the obscurity of the church and stared at the high golden wall of the reredos and watched the little baffled lights flickering in the dark' (378). Filled with remorse for things done and left undone, Hilary finds in St. Stephen's a place to reckon honestly with himself. But by the end of his time there, he may also have encountered more than that thanks to the association with Eliot:

> I got up to leave the church ... At one end of the aisle under a tasseled canopy the Christ child was leaning from his mother's arms to bless the world. At the other end he hung dead, cut off in his young manhood for me and for my sins. There was also, I saw, a memorial tablet which asked me to pray for the repose of the soul of Thomas Stearns Eliot. How is it now with you, old friend, the intolerable wrestle with words and meanings being over? (383–4)

Hilary can no more pray for the poet's repose than he can accept the blessing of the Christ child or the redemption of the 'god-man'. Still, both the iconography of the place and the faith of its long-time churchwarden move him. He can, as he says, feel grateful for the poet's words, even if he can scarcely understand their sense. As his reverie continues, a specific passage from Eliot's 'Burnt Norton' comes into his mind. 'If all time is eternally present all time is unredeemable. What might have been is an abstraction, remaining a perpetual possibility only in a world of speculation.'[43] The lines seem to confirm the stoic resignation he has come to at the end of his saga of disasters, his acceptance that the past cannot be 'folded up and in the twinkling of an eye everything changed and made beautiful and good' (298). In short, the past *cannot* be redeemed. And yet, if one reads further in the *Four Quartets*, Eliot takes the reader beyond this impasse, away from 'all time is unredeemable' to a resounding affirmation in the last movement of *The Dry Salvages*:

> The hint half guessed, the gift half understood, is Incarnation.
> Here the impossible union
> Of spheres of existence is actual,
> Here the past and future
> Are conquered and reconciled[.][44]

For Eliot, the incarnate 'here' where time is redeemed is none other than Christ, the divine union of newborn child and crucified man before whose image Hilary momentarily stands at attention but in whom he does not believe. He does not go the distance of the *Four Quartets,* neither to the words from *East Coker* inscribed on the poet's actual memorial plaque in St. Stephen's –

> We must be still and still moving
> Into another intensity
> For a further union, a deeper communion
> Through the dark cold and the empty desolation[45]

– nor to Dame Julian of Norwich's famously ringing assurance at the end of *Little Gidding*: 'And all shall be well and / All manner of thing shall be well.'[46] To take all these texts into account is not to claim that Murdoch has become a 'neo-Christian apologist'; rather, she bears witness to the endurance of the old myth and the faith of those who continue to wrestle with it. She juxtaposes religious alternatives, both Hilary Burde's denial of Christ's redemption and Eliot's embrace of it. The reader is left, then, in a 'world of speculation', caught between the conviction that time is unredeemed and the hope of its being conquered and reconciled. Eliot points in one direction, Murdoch in another. The goal for both, however, was to move 'through the dark cold and the empty desolation' of the twentieth century to discover a 'deeper communion' – with or without God.[47]

The Bell

The search for a deeper communion is precisely what draws an odd assortment of Anglican laypeople to Imber Court in *The Bell*, Murdoch's fourth novel and, among all the other works concerned with religious figures, the only one to focus on a community. It was the best received of her works and, coincidentally, the most Anglican. The gathered souls are an inclusive example of the Prayer Book's 'all sorts and conditions':[48] 'You must think we're a proper collection of otherworldly crackpots', jokes its director, Michael Meade, to the earnest teenage newcomer, the 'keen practising Christian' Toby.[49] Imber Court is Meade's ancestral Gloucestershire family home, repurposed by him as an intentional community of Anglicans who can live neither in the world nor out of it, 'whose desire for God makes them unsatisfactory citizens of an ordinary life, but whose strength or temperament fails them to surrender the world completely' (81).

Those who have made that surrender live in an enclosed convent of Anglican Benedictines, Imber Abbey, which was dissolved under the Tudors in the sixteenth century and restored in the late nineteenth century after the Oxford Movement. It is a 'great storehouse of spiritual energy across the lake', located behind high walls and an imposing gate (112). But though a world apart from the Court and its motley crew, it is not inaccessible to them. There is a visitors' chapel adjacent to the worship space of the nuns, albeit separated by a grille and set at an angle to the high altar. The more

Protestant among the fellowship are unnerved by its scent of incense and the 'hideous purity and austerity' of the sisters' plain chant, the more Catholic duplicate the Abbey rite as best they can – women veiled, everyone at prayer on their knees – in the shabby makeshift chapel of the Court's former dining room (175).

What no one can doubt is the power and integrity of the Abbess, as idealized a figure as one can find in Murdoch's fiction, and someone for whom she felt a personal affinity. If, as her *Metaphysics* would have it, 'Good is the reality of which God is the dream', then this nun has real dreams.[50] She also has a large measure of what counts for sanctity in Murdoch's book – unfantasized, modest common sense delivered to people she attends to seriously. The Abbess understands that for intense folk 'disturbed and hunted by God', such as Imber Court's Michael Meade, the best course may be the middle flight between the highs and lows (81). At least this advice is what Reade takes away from his occasional conversations with her:

> Our duty, the Abbess said, is not necessarily to seek the highest regardless of the realities of our spiritual life as it is, but to seek that place, that task, those people, which will make our spiritual life most constantly grow and flourish; and in this search, said the Abbess, we must make use of a divine cunning. 'As wise as serpents, as harmless as doves.' (81)[51]

The novel's cast of characters is comprised of a variety of recognizable Anglican 'types', clergy and lay, as well as a pair of temporary guests, Paul Greenwood (an art historian studying medieval manuscripts at the Abbey) and his wife Dora. She comes to Imber Court attempting a half-hearted reconciliation with her husband and is wholly at odds with its religiosity: 'She had never in fact been able to distinguish religion from superstition, and had given up her own practice of it when she discovered that she could say the Lord's Prayer quickly but not slowly' (14). Aside from one officious extern sister who regularly comes to the Court, the enclosed Abbey nuns glimpsed in passing (at prayer, at work and play, and in one spectacular moment at swim) are of good humour and cheer, in no way suffering as a result of what Dora takes to be their incarceration, 'shut up like that' in a 'dark hole' (69).

Added to this religious mix is a member of the Anglican hierarchy, no sophisticated worldly bishop as in *The Time of the Angels* but a chatty, portly man who steps slowly out of his Rolls-Royce 'with the affable leisureliness of the great personage who knows that whenever and wherever he arrives he is immediately the centre of the scene' (248). Arriving at Imber to preside at a ceremonial christening of a new chapel bell, the bishop is a figure of fun. With no clue as to what is happening around him – the usual Murdochian intrigue of eros and psyche that makes the novel a page-turner – he plays an essentially comic part in the proceedings. He is 'dressed in full regalia, with mitre and crook', concerned primarily about how his churchmanship and pleasure in Latin may appear to those in attendance: 'I'm glad you didn't think I was being too archaic and popish!'[52]

The ancient convent bell that disappeared at the time of the Reformation but is retrieved in the course of the novel plays a role similar to the Russian icon of the Trinity in *The Time of the Angels*. Discovered in the Imber lake by Toby, '[it] was a thing from another world', its uneven bronze surface replete with scenes from the life of Christ, 'strangely shaped crosses', and a Latin inscription revealing its archangelic name and its identity as the annunciation of love: '*Vox ego sum Amoris. Gabriel vocor*' (220–1).[53] Eventually, Dora turns to the bell 'for help … as if supplicating' (266). A dilettante artist, she is dumbfounded by the integrity of the work she sees and envies the seriousness of the craftsman who embellished it: 'The squat figures faced her from the sloping surface of the bronze, solid, simple, beautiful, absurd, full to the brim with something which was to the artist not an object of speculation and imagination … [but] more real to him than his own childhood and more familiar' (267).

Resurrected from the lake's mud and poised to enter the psychological murk of Imber Court's present day, Dora recognizes that the bell 'called Gabriel' is 'the truth-telling voice that must not be silenced' (267). What she does not realize is the sheer cost of truth-telling. As the novel ends, a man commits suicide, a woman on the brink of entering the Abbey suffers a nervous breakdown, the lay community is disbanded after a journalist describes the sequence of events as 'more reminiscent of a witch's Sabbath than of the sober goings on of the Anglican church' (283) and Michael Meade finds that faith in a divinity that shapes our end – a notion forged in his own 'romantic imagination' – is over with: 'There is a God, but I do not believe in Him' (309).

What he does continue to believe in, like Anne Clavidge in *Nuns and Soldiers*, is the Eucharist. Hearing the ring of the new Abbey bell (the ancient one lost again to the mud of Imber lake), he feels himself summoned by its early morning call – not to worship but to understanding:

> The Mass remained not consoling, not uplifting, but in some way factual. It contained for him no assurance that all would be made well that was not well. It simply existed as a kind of pure reality separate from the weaving of his own thoughts. He attended it almost as a spectator, and remembered with surprise the time when he thought that one day he would celebrate Mass himself, and how it had seemed to him that on that day he would die of joy. That day would never come, and those emotions were old and dead. Yet whoever celebrated it, the Mass existed and Michael existed beside it. (309)

Michael comes through the refining fires of his great tribulation bearing all the marks of one who has embraced Murdoch's notion of true religion. The Mass, like some masterpiece in the National Gallery, takes him out of himself – his comforting illusions, his intoxicating weave of thought and emotion – so that in its presence he can pay attention to a pure reality, to a fact. The Real Presence, then, is what *he* brings to the consecrated bread and wine – his attention. Because the Mass exists, so does he, and so too do other people, all of them otherwise foundering in the welter of this human comedy.

'Gabriel' calls the faithful to divine love and calls those who do not believe in God to attention. But one senses that for Michael Meade (as for the author of *The Bell*), it is the Abbess who has the most resonant 'truth-telling voice' of all:

> Good is an overflow. Where we generously and sincerely intend it, we are engaged in a work of creation which may be mysterious even to ourselves – and because it is mysterious we may be afraid of it. But this should not make us draw back. God can always show us, if we will, a higher and better way: we can only learn to love by loving. Remember that all our failures are ultimately failures in love. Imperfect love must not be condemned and rejected, but made perfect. The way is always forward, never back. (235)

For the author of *Metaphysics*, going forward, never back means leaving 'God' behind and advancing to a chastened apprehension of the 'Good'. Nonetheless, it is impossible to deny the eloquence of the Abbess, the consonance of her words with Murdoch's own thought, or to dismiss as pure happenstance the fictional fact that whereas Imber Court comes to nothing in the end, the Abbey itself is growing. Thanks to Michael Meade's largesse ('They've needed more space for a long time'), the monastic enclosure will shortly take over 'the whole thing, the house, the lake, everything' (314). Whereas the cloister had once been the curiosity of the house, the tables are about to be turned. The days of the old religion may be numbered – how long will the nuns carry on? – but at least in this novel the convent rings for Sext and Nones, the sisters keep the faith, and the Anglican Abbess's words continue to overflow the confines of their traditional bounds. She speaks as one who has authority.

FIGURE 13 *Monica Furlong.*

12

Monica Furlong (1930–2003): 'With Love to the Church'

Peter Sherlock

Monica Furlong pushed the boundaries of what it meant to be Anglican. She came to prominence in the 1960s and 1970s as a journalist and writer on religion, spirituality and theology. In the 1980s and 1990s she was admired, disdained, perhaps even feared, for her radical leadership of the Movement for the Ordination of Women, including the organization of public protests inside and outside churches.[1] Upon her death in 2003, she was described as 'the most influential and creative layperson' in the post-war Church of England.[2] Throughout her writing, she explored and interrogated the Christian tradition in the light of modern thought and experience, in search of a deeper knowledge of God and self.

Furlong's extensive publications are distinctive for the provocative honesty with which she wrote about herself and the church: whether directly, as in her autobiography and spiritual counsels, or indirectly, as in her novels for adults and children. Although Furlong was physically inhibited from childhood by an occasional, but pronounced, stammer, her literary voice was disconcertingly articulate and candid. She was fearless in critical self-examination, whether of her own Christian pilgrimage or the failure of her marriage, and in 1971 published an infamous account of taking LSD in order to compare drug-induced and spiritual ecstasies.[3] Her most stinging criticism was reserved, however, for the Church of England on the many occasions when she believed it was failing to follow the wisdom and precepts of Jesus – truths that were meant to be at the heart of the church's purpose and being.

Yet Furlong was in many ways deeply traditionalist; why else did she remain a profoundly engaged Anglican, despite her trenchant criticisms? She was a surprisingly robust apologist for what she believed was the essence of Christianity. Her work espoused the hope of many of her generation, coming of age immediately after the Second World War, that the Church of England might recast itself in the prophetic tradition. If only the church could relinquish the restraints of establishment culture, it might call attention to the transformative power of Christian teaching and spiritual experience for a world possessed by selfishness, greed and violence. An impassioned advocate for handing on the great Christian drama of salvation conveyed in the biblical narratives, Furlong mourned the rapid disappearance from English culture of the peculiarly Anglican investment in parochial communities. As she wrote in 1965, 'If *we* have lost our revelation about love and meaning, then we are of no use to the world whatsoever.'[4] Her commitment to local Christian congregations was expressed in diverse ways throughout her life, whether in forming the feminist St Hilda Community in the 1980s or editing her south London parish magazine in the final years of her life.[5]

Furlong attributed her interests and passions to a single, potent question: what would it mean to live as if love were true?[6] She allowed this question to take her where it would, irrespective of disruption or cost. Her journey encompassed monastic experience, ecstatic glimpses of the divine, meditations on Christ and diverse expressions of Christian community. Answers were always critically assessed, for the principle of love was all too often dominated by self-preservation, greed or just plain poor thinking. Such sins stood in the way of mystical union with God, nature, other people and self. The goal of union was reached not through an unthinking obedience to text or ritual but in the flow of everyday life lived as if love were true.

This chapter is the first major evaluation of Furlong's works of fiction. It examines three novels published between 1976 and 1987, a period when the church's claim to moral authority was tested and largely found wanting in British society. These books were written alongside many non-fictional works – for which she is now chiefly remembered – that engaged in an extensive, if sympathetic, criticism of the Anglican Church, especially in relation to gender and sexuality. The chapter argues that Furlong set forth a remarkably consistent vision in both her fiction and non-fiction of a Christian community bound together by the passionate search for truth in all aspects of life. This search necessitated both handing on divine wisdom received in the past and contemplation of the new things God might be doing in the present. The three novels considered here were deliberately provocative, pushing readers into uncomfortable spaces to explore contradictions between personal experiences and social expectations of marriage, divorce, sex and love.

Biography and work

Monica Mavis Furlong was born in 1930 in Kenton, a new suburb on the outskirts of London, and baptized in the Church of England, as was still conventional between the wars, despite the fact that her Irish-born father had been raised Roman Catholic and her mother had little sympathy for religion.[7] Discouraged from attending university, she followed a well-trodden path for middle-class women of her generation: a secretarial course, office work, marriage in 1953 and two children. Always an avid reader, what she really wanted to do was write. She began submitting articles to magazines and newspapers, and in time, enough were published to enable her to give up office work. Regular employment as a journalist followed in 1961, commencing with the *Daily Mail*. Due to her incisive, passionate and thoroughly grounded approach to contemporary spiritual issues, she soon built a significant following for her regular columns on religious affairs in the *Spectator* and *Church Times*.

In the late 1960s, when Furlong's family moved to Norfolk, she took a break from regular paid employment and focused on writing. In 1965 she published the first of over thirty books she authored or edited, or for which she provided an introduction. *With Love to the Church* was a manifesto criticizing the Church of England's failure to engage with modernity. A series of popular devotional collections drawn from her regular columns soon followed. There is some evidence that these collections had an enduring impact on a generation of Anglicans; in 2015, for example, the Bishop of Norwich, Graham James, reflected on the significance of Furlong's collection *Christian Uncertainties* (1975) for his spiritual development.[8]

In 1974 Furlong accepted employment as a producer in the BBC's Religious Department and purchased a London flat, giving her a new measure of personal and financial independence. The next decade saw her publication of several spiritual biographies, beginning with a book on John Bunyan and culminating with an acclaimed account of the life and spirituality of the Trappist monk, Thomas Merton.[9] Her two novels for adults, *Cat's Eye* (1976) and *Cousins* (1983), brought Furlong to the attention of a wider readership, although they have not developed an enduring following.[10] Furlong and her husband divorced in 1977, and her sense of failure about her troubled marriage profoundly affected her writing. Propelled to speak out on behalf of others whose alleged failings were frowned on by the church, she wrote pamphlets on divorce for the Mothers' Union and on homosexuality for the Society of Friends.[11] She also experienced a new sense of responsibility, even where her decisions had painful consequences, as she was freed from compliance with institutional or social convention for its own sake.[12]

In 1979 Furlong was involved in the foundation of the Movement for the Ordination of Women (MOW), becoming its Moderator from 1982 to 1985.[13] Media-savvy, familiar with how the Church of England actually operated and unintimidated by establishment culture, through MOW she challenged the church to act on its convictions rather than accept the passive restraint of institutional inertia. A series of essays and edited collections on feminism and theology followed, beginning with *Feminine in the Church* (1984) which summed up the case for the ordination of women. In the 1990s her writings ventured further afield into prayer, poetry and liturgy, attempting to create non-sexist languages for worship and extending her lifelong passion for the integration of the sacred and the everyday.[14]

In 1987 Furlong published her first novel for children, *Wise Child*, followed by a prequel *A Year and a Day* (1990, also released as *Juniper*) and a posthumously published sequel *Colman* (2004). Set in the kingdom of Dalriada in the seventh century on the Isle of Mull, in the Scottish Inner Hebrides, the trilogy follows the adventures of a young girl Wise Child, her guardian and teacher Juniper, and her friend Colman.[15] These books explored how life ought to be lived in an imagined Celtic past, drawing on the revival of popular interest in Celtic spirituality and Furlong's previous work on monasticism and mysticism. A fourth, highly popular children's book, *Robin's Country* (1994) narrated the tale of a boy who, having lost his memory and voice, joined Robin Hood's company.[16] These reached audiences in North America as well as Britain and were reprinted. In these books, the constraints of argument and the complexities of psychological insight deployed in her novels for adults gave way to a simpler style of narrative and character delineation.

Furlong's final books included an autobiography and an exploration of Indigenous spiritualities through an Aboriginal community in the Kimberley, Australia.[17] Both contributed to her spiritual quest to understand how humans could encounter God and reach out to each other, even as the Western world became more secular and individualist in its preoccupations. She continued to write and publish up until her death in 2003. In a commemorative collection of poems and prayers published in 2004, Clare Herbert argued that Furlong's writing connected with so many people because of her ability to perceive and articulate spiritual experiences in a time of great social, cultural and technological change.[18] This included a zeal for honest speech, calling out hypocrisy, and an openness to insights from diverse traditions and disciplines: everything from the spirituality of a John Bunyan or a Teresa of Avila to Zen Buddhism and Jungian psychology.

Being Anglican

Although Furlong was an Anglican for most of her adult life, institutional loyalty was not at the heart of her faith. In 1995 she wrote on her childhood memories of religion and its influence.[19] It was her sister and not her parents who took her to Sunday worship, first at St Mary's Kenton and then at St John's Greenhill. Religious education was provided at the local grammar school through hymns, carols and bible stories, and through radio broadcasts, such as Dorothy L. Sayers's famous religious drama *The Man Born to Be King*.[20] Furlong deeply valued the traditions, rituals and relationships she gained from growing up in a culture that took Christianity for granted, and she frequently regretted the loss of this opportunity for subsequent generations in an increasingly secular Britain.

Furlong's critical suspicion of institutional religious conformity was shaped in her adolescence. She found school 'intensely pious' and 'sensed a good deal of hypocrisy behind the bland façade'. Religion 'seemed fatally linked with "being proper"'.[21] The formative influence on her faith in this period was the energetic Anglo-Catholic priest Joost de Blank, vicar of St John's Greenhill (later Bishop of Stepney, then Archbishop of Cape Town), a close friend until his death in 1968. When Furlong was eighteen, she told de Blank outright that she couldn't believe in God. Two years later, following a mystical experience, she returned, to be advised by de Blank that she should start attending church regularly. She did, discovering that de Blank's advice 'made it possible to digest the experience and not to expect to go on having grand experiences all the time'.[22] This approach – taking seriously an experience of God, but emphasizing everyday life – shaped Furlong's writing; she declared that de Blank 'had made me aware of a different possibility, which was a faith that was not about convention, morality, or keeping the lower classes in order, but about a giving of the heart'.[23]

Furlong loved the church, despite many misgivings, and her literary output was bookended by critical works on the Church of England. *With Love to the Church* savaged the church's instinct for self-preservation and its failure to engage with a rapidly changing world: 'how easily, how wickedly easily, Christians turn from love to the most arrant kind of self-seeking ... Neither the inner light, nor authority, neither scripture nor tradition, neither orthodoxy nor unorthodoxy, can overcome this subtle and disturbing form of corruption.'[24]

C of E: The State It's In (2000) was published thirty-five years later and symbolized Furlong's return to full engagement with Anglican parochial life, after decades engaged in the movement to ordain women in the Anglican Communion and a period of worship with a feminist liturgical community. While it provided a more comprehensive historical account of what it meant to be Anglican, ultimately Furlong's conclusions were not so very different from her first book. As she wrote in the preface, *With Love to the Church*

> was a 'young woman's book', slightly wild in its criticisms it seems to me now, but nevertheless written with love as the title suggested. In the intervening thirty-five years, although I have had my ups and downs with the Church, the love has not abated. It has changed, however, as love does in long-haul relationships, and my changed views are what this book is about.[25]

Furlong's fascination with the institutional culture of the Church of England centred on how the church communicated, inhibited or betrayed its theological vision. The idea that an institution could be the body of Christ, however imperfect, made the church unique among human forms of association. As she wrote in 1995,

> Can any institution similarly reflect truth and love? I don't myself believe it can – working together we multiply the danger of ego-trips, and plain error. Yet the Christian institutions ... seem, for all their faults, to have acted as vessels for much that was precious.[26]

Christianity could draw people towards God, and into relationship with each other in the complex, lifelong exercise of seeking to live as if love were true. Christian life was not about adherence to a moral code but the experience and expression of a vital force. The particular value of the Church of England was its capacity to distil the wisdom of tradition, challenge individual greed and adapt to new insights from other Christians and other disciplines. Furlong had much in common with twentieth-century liberal Christian thought but retained a primary focus on the transforming power of divine encounter.

The Cat's Eye

Each of Furlong's novels for adults was grounded in her sexual and spiritual experiences. Her first novel, *The Cat's Eye*, drew deeply on her experience of marital breakdown and the difficulty of reconciling this with Christian teaching on marriage. It tells the story of Bridget Riley, an Irish-born Catholic woman whose marriage to Hugh, an archaeologist, is disintegrating. Bridget encounters Nell Wilbraham, a successful psychotherapist, and is invited to spend the summer with the Wilbraham family. After a miscarriage, and the absence of a child who might knit the fraying marriage together, Bridget accepts Nell's offer, leaving Hugh behind in London. She holidays in Cornwall alongside Nell and her barrister husband, Sydney, and their children Clare, an undergraduate, and Ivo, a twelve-year-old wise beyond his years. The family's friend Paulinus appears: a disruptive, sexual, Pan-like figure whose powerful presence soon complicates Bridget's emerging equilibrium. A simple plot unfolds, ending in disintegration of the group with Ivo's tragic, accidental death and Clare's elopement with Bridget's brother, an IRA operative. The novel is primarily focused on Bridget's emotional, spiritual and sexual experiences, and her infatuation with her companions.

The Cat's Eye includes several passages in which Bridget struggles with her Catholic faith and her marital situation, as she tries to decide whether her marriage has any hope of redemption. These passages undoubtedly draw on Furlong's experiences, even as she distances herself from her protagonist: Bridget is Roman Catholic and childless; Furlong was Anglican and a mother; Bridget's marriage is of a brief duration whereas Furlong's lasted many years. In the novel Nell highlights this latter distinction, pointing out the difference between Bridget's short marriage that had never really become a marriage, and a long marriage where the ending implies a rejection of all that has gone before. Bridget's institutional guilt is focused when she makes her confession to a priest, after an intense sexual encounter with Paulinus. The priest uncovers her lack of repentance for this forbidden pleasure, and reminds her that she has committed adultery because she is still married to Hugh. When Bridget challenges this judgement the priest asks why she married in the first place. She replies, 'Because my friends were getting married. Because I was lonely. Because he was a distinguished man, or going to be. Because I felt sorry for him' (83). Bridget later remarks that she thought Hugh was lonely too, because he pushed people away, and that in marrying him perhaps she 'liked the thought of consoling loneliness' (97). Furlong, here and throughout her writing, argues that the struggle to love God, church, partner or even self is fundamentally about wrestling with loneliness, accentuated by the isolation of modernity. Loneliness can lead to misguided love, as in the case of Hugh and Bridget. Christianity, properly understood, is intended to lead humans out of this isolation into the heartbreaking reality of God's love. It is not supposed to imprison people in permanently fractured or harmful relationships.

In the middle of the novel, Hugh visits Bridget in Cornwall. As they argue they discover their concepts of marriage are wildly divergent. Bridget conceives of marriage as a bloody fight, a drama, where even hate and anguish between a couple may be exposed to light. But for Hugh, marital love is supposed to displace or suppress mutual dislike and disagreement. Love conquers all; but what is love? Is it a state of being created by the couple's struggles and entanglements with each other, or – as Hugh would have it – does it appear out of nowhere like a chivalrous knight to rescue the couple from themselves? Mired in despair after the confrontation, Bridget claims dramatically that 'the real horror of a marriage was that you *saw*, far more effectively than any medieval hell, the way cause and effect worked, your faults and fears and neuroses and worse, what you had meant for virtues, writ large in letters you couldn't miss. No wonder married couples hated one another' (107). Here Furlong demolishes the fairy-tale myth of marriage. She wrote elsewhere of the need for marital advice that 'starts from the position that most people are complete failures, if not at sex (which after all is a learnable skill) at least at relationships', for 'love, far from being the easy achievement we are brought up to believe it is, is the most difficult thing any of us are ever asked to do'.[27]

The only remedy to the problem of love is what Furlong would come to describe as a responsible love, one that does not displace other emotions, one which can bear suffering, rather than love as a form of social compliance. True love might even require stepping out from under the wings of Mother Church. Furlong wrote of herself that the decision to get divorced turned into a crucial stage in my growing up and learning to take responsibility for my own life. Since the Church, at least officially, could not support my decision, then I must learn to carry it for myself, to take the scary step of defying it because I believed this was the right and truthful action.[28]

Furlong argued that whenever the church promoted absolute rules or social conformity over human need, it failed its people and suppressed life. In *The Cat's Eye* Bridget wants to quarrel passionately with God about the misadventure of her marriage and the loss of her unborn child. When she attends confession in Cornwall she encounters a church like

> a shoddy supermarket … The powerful odour of furniture polish and the dahlias arranged in vases completed the atmosphere of suburban vulgarity, which was what? Not so much material ostentation, though there was that, as a soul-destroying compulsiveness. This church chose to know nothing of man in extremity. It had no message for those in agony; not surprising that suicide was the only remedy this generation knew. (82)

In this somewhat snobbish passage Furlong appears to require all spiritual and sexual experiences to reach beyond the ordinary, beyond the suffocation of mystery in middle-class culture. The sterility of the suburban church is in complete contrast with the sense of being fully alive that Bridget experiences in sexual intercourse with Paulinus. Despite the fact that she feels no love for him, she declares that 'I had become for a moment part of the heartbeat of the world, knowing myself part of the life that in fact sustained me every second' (72).

Clare Herbert wrote of Furlong that 'there grew in her a contempt for inhuman beliefs of all kinds within all the churches, and a love of Christ not because he shows us the way to be right but because he suffers with us the human life we live'.[29] This captures the kind of love which Furlong perceived to be at the heart of Christianity. This love, born of suffering and compassion, is revealed towards the end of *The Cat's Eye*. After Ivo's death, Bridget returns to the church where she made her confession to release another extremity of human passion. Unable to pray, 'all I could do was hold out my agony, afraid even to look at it myself … Then I did release it. There in the church of my fathers, in front of that foolish doll, it was possible to cry, to let the dry sobs force themselves up, and finally, to cry tears' (148–9). Despite human foolishness, the suppression of desire and 'soul-destroying compulsiveness', the church is still the place where anguish born of love is poured out before God.

Cousins

Furlong's interest in Anglicanism is foregrounded in her second novel, *Cousins*, which traces the course of an affair between Laura, a sculptor, and her cousin Hugh, a priest and theologian destined for academic advancement. During the novel Laura completes two highly challenging artworks, a bronze sculpture called 'Wings' and a set of minimalist Stations of the Cross for a new church. Through Laura, the reader encounters Hugh's family: his perfect, but icy, wife Rachel; his disabled and adoring sister Susie; and his awkward adolescent son Oliver. Written in the first person, *Cousins* draws directly on Furlong's experiences, including her relationship with 'F.', a married man, that was unexpectedly fulfilling emotionally, intellectually and sexually before it came to an end in 1976.[30]

Cousins is a vehicle for the exploration of human relationships, love and sexuality, and the ingredients necessary for artistic creation and theological insight. The novel contrasts Laura's slightly shabby, hand-to-mouth world with the ordered, expensive perfection of Hugh's. While Hugh delights in the good things of life, and writes learned tomes on Christology, Laura achieves theological and spiritual revelation through the physical demands of her craft. These contrasts are made apparent at the very beginning of the novel in three ways. Laura's childhood memories juxtapose her ordinary upbringing and chaotic home with those of her cousins: Hugh, trained to be coolly perfect at all times, and Susie, whose unspecified mental disability makes it impossible for her to hide her desperate need for displays of affection and love. Second, Laura's ambitious, soaring design for her winged sculpture can be brought into being only through the use of toxic materials requiring the application of barrier creams and protective clothing; her creative output threatens to corrupt and destroy her flesh, much like a mystical experience. Finally comes Laura's disregard for her body, home and surroundings, in contrast to her passionate delight in Hugh's physicality, 'his face and his prick, each intolerably eloquent' (9).

The premise of *Cousins* is transgressive: Anglican clergymen are not supposed to commit adultery, and Hugh is a serial offender. The depiction of sexual pleasure is striking – not the sort of thing expected from the author of devotional columns. Given Furlong's relationship with 'F.' in the years in which *Cousins* was written, this exploration of sex as a sacred act has an element of autobiography about it; does Furlong, through Laura, seek to reconcile her theology with her passions?[31] Furlong not only reports Laura's uninhibited delight in sex but also Hugh's attempts to comprehend the contradiction in his sexual and priestly activities. Laura asks, 'How can you be part of an institution that says you must be faithful to your wife and then sleep around?' to which Hugh eventually replies: 'I suppose my only excuse is that I feel sex is far more than the Church sees or knows; it is a holy thing, it is where I find God, it is how I survive. But it does not seem to be where the others find God. Or else they do not speak the truth in public.' Laura astutely retorts, 'But then neither do you' (47–8). Here sexuality is depicted as holy whenever it is life-giving and unbound by dogma, yet Hugh's lie and Laura's complicity in it taint their relationship. The novel sharpens this dilemma in its presentation of Hugh's wife Rachel as a distant and impenetrable character.

Cousins provides a counterpoint to the theme of erotic love in the relationship between Hugh and his sister Susie. Unhindered by social mores on account of her disability, Susie unashamedly expresses pure devotion. Yet as Hugh says to Laura in describing his and his mother's desire to be distanced from Susie, 'Maybe neither of us can forgive Susie – Louise and me. For being able to love.'[32] The novel highlights the disjuncture between Hugh's irrepressible sensuality and the ordered worlds of academic theology and ecclesiastical hierarchy, while suggesting that one requires the other. Furlong develops this paradox by contrasting Hugh the theologian with Laura the artist. In an early discussion of theology and art, Hugh observes that 'words have obsessed me all my life ... I talked in long sentences in my high chair. I think it's a sort of defence.' 'Against what?' 'Against vision. Your sort of wordless vision.' Laura ponders this, suggesting that 'sometimes I think sculpture is all about sound ... It's like a response to some music I can hear all the time, which I try to copy as I carve' (33). Later they discuss Hugh's priestly vocation. Hugh reports that

> When I was young it seemed a way of changing something, of altering the Church, and making it more livable. Now I'm not interested in the Church but the world, and it seems irrelevant. And I think perhaps priests are like artists – they choose themselves rather than having to be officially ordained. So lots of people have a priestly function without knowing it. (79–80)

The implication is that Hugh has lost the authentic connection with his priesthood. His sexual passions are hidden, altogether at odds with his public image of professional and domestic success. This creates an impossible constriction and contradiction for Hugh, his family and his lovers.

Cousins also contrasts the financial and professional stability of Hugh's academic career with the uncertainty and mild chaos of Laura's life, a situation she tolerates for the fruit it bears:

> The world was full of people eking out their time, well paid for doing jobs that they did without love or interest. I cared passionately about what I did, asked little but to be free to do it, and always there was this humiliation of never quite having enough to be sure I could keep a roof over my head, or eat properly or keep warm. (17)

Laura's vocation as a sculptor depends on an ascetic, penitential discipline, perhaps reflective of Furlong's experience as a writer. Discipline is crucial, not only to the quality of the final product but also as a lifebelt in moments of unbearable intensity:

> A deep boredom had settled upon me as it always did towards the end of any major piece of work, just before the final burst of energy and

enthusiasm and the delight of finishing. I had mentioned this once to a fellow-sculptor who had said, in the most matter-of-fact way, 'It's to save yourself from the ecstasy, isn't it?' (82)

Cousins concludes with Laura's work on the Stations of the Cross. This device knits together the book's themes: the vocation of artist or priest, the balance of ecstasy and boredom, the nature of love and the search for mystical union in everyday life. Laura, despairing after Hugh ends their relationship, contemplates suicide as she works on a Station. Theological truth uplifts her at this darkest moment as she ponders the Stations she has fashioned:

> What they spelled out to me was no transcendent truth, but something surprising in its matter of factness. The crucifixion was sold as a once-for-all event, and Jesus as the most special of men. But maybe what was special about Jesus was that he was us, was that his suffering was simply a copy, a meticulous carbon copy, of the suffering of humankind … if what happened to him resonated for ever it was because he copied it with love and not with hate and bitterness … he surrendered to it for the compelling reason that he was forced to. Only there was something more graceful in his surrender. (152–3)

Laura apprehends the death of Jesus not only as a moment of universal salvation, but also as one man's personal crucifixion. She is drawn to surrender her own pain and feels love flowing into her, 'transfixed' by the meaning of her own work. The novel concludes with a meditation on the challenge of redemptive living:

> Was there, in fact, any way out, through all the mazes of craving and possession, of cruelty and passivity, of loneliness and hunger? I did not know. Only, in the slow meditation of my work I felt schooled to the patience which works at every possibility, which never relinquishes hope. (172)

Wise Child

In *With Love to the Church*, Furlong argued that 'Christians, it seems to me, have to choose between the safety of "morals" and the danger of love'. If Christians followed Christ's example of risking love, she claimed, 'then morals would take care of themselves'.[33] This precept informed *Wise Child*, her first book for children. *Wise Child* naturally avoids the exploration of sexuality and amorous relationships of *The Cat's Eye* or *Cousins*, but shares with them an interest in how life is meant to be lived. In contrast to the anguish and despair of the novels for adults, *Wise Child* presents an attractive vision of the merits of a simple, ordered life. Furlong saw the novel as an attempt to reconcile paganism and Christianity, for 'Christianity, cut off from the tap-root of the beliefs that had nourished our primitive ancestors, was wilting because of its alienation from nature'.[34] The book broadly reflects Furlong's concerns about the future shape of religion in Britain:

> I am a 'religious person' if that phrase still has meaning; in some sense I believe in God and I am moved to my depths by the meaning I perceive in Christianity. Yet I am saddened by the deadness, the lack of imaginative power and, above all, the self-consciousness, of public religion in Britain, and I am even more saddened by a restlessness and hunger within myself.[35]

The central character of *Wise Child* is Juniper, known locally as a doran or witch, who takes a young girl – 'Wise Child' – into her care. Juniper is utterly consistent, always doing what she says, and living independently of men's help. Initially shocked by the severities of Juniper's pattern of life, Wise Child becomes enamoured of the beauty and order of discipline. Joy is found in being attuned to the seasons, in reaping the fruits of one's own labour, and discovering the benefits of each of Juniper's rules. As Juniper tells Wise Child when instructing her on her chores,

> 'keeping yourself clean, preparing the food you are going to eat, clearing it away afterwards – that's what life's *about*, Wise Child. When people forget that, or lose touch with it, then they lose touch with other important things as well.'
> 'Men don't do those things.'
> 'Exactly.' (45–6)

Here Furlong reflects broader feminist concerns in the 1980s about women and work, including women's capacity to live autonomously from men, and the challenges faced by female workers in capitalist societies.[36]

The spiritual insights Wise Child learns under Juniper's tuition bear striking similarities to those gained by the subjects of Furlong's biographies. She wrote, for example, that Merton

> began to see that the highest spiritual development was to be 'ordinary,' to be fully a man, in the way few human beings succeed in becoming so simply and naturally themselves. He began to see the monk not, as he had believed in youth, as someone special, undertaking feats of incredible ascetic heroism for the love of God, but as one who was not afraid to be simply 'man,' who, as he lived near to nature and his appetites, was the 'measure' of what others might be if society did not distort them with greed or ambition or lust or desperate want.[37]

Furlong's spiritual philosophy develops further in the novel when Wise Child learns to fly. The young girl is humiliated when Juniper asks for her trust and then douses her thoroughly with a smelly, greasy ointment. But the result is the ability to fly on a broomstick to an ancient stone circle far, far away. Here, Wise Child has a mystical experience of oneness with nature:

'I am it,' I heard myself say out loud, though at once I knew it would have been equally true to say 'It is me.' The movement of the blood within me was part of the same pattern that moved the sap in the oak tree to my right. The decay of the food in my stomach was the same as the autumn decay of the plants and trees. When Juniper and I shovelled earth upon our human droppings I knew that the flies and the little earth creatures fed upon them; this was their food as the fish and animals and roots and berries and seeds were ours. I began to weep at the beauty of this, to say a psalm ... praising the good God. (81)

This sense of mystical unity and divine praise was drawn directly from Furlong's memory. She wrote in her autobiography that:

Experiences of the numinous, the sacred, have been important in my life, not because they were numerous or particularly unusual ... but because they lent purpose and order to a not particularly orderly or exemplary life. Perhaps they also made it difficult to lead an orderly or exemplary life – there was always the sense of something more cosmic being at work than the tedium of everyday concerns comprehended.[38]

Furlong presents Wise Child's ecstatic experience as continuous with the dullness and labour of daily life, handing on the wisdom Joost de Blank had once imparted to her. As she wrote in 1971, 'Mystical experience was a way in to loving human beings. If people are frightening it is easier to love God, easier to have a transcendental experience ... I don't want transcendental experiences now. I do desperately want to enter into the ordinary, the present moment.'[39]

Just as Wise Child experiences bliss, so too is she exposed to the terrors of hatred and persecution. Towards the end of the novel, in the midst of a famine and a smallpox epidemic, Juniper's life is threatened by a witch-hunt fuelled by the village priest, Fillan. Wise Child asks, 'Why does he hate you so much?' to which Juniper replies,

I think he misunderstands. He thinks that I am working against the new religion but it is not so. I love and revere Jesus as he does – how could one not? But in the new religion they think that nature, especially in the human body, must be fought and conquered – they seem to fear and distrust matter itself, although in the Mass it is bread and wine that is used to show how spirit and matter are one ... Jesus did not tell them this – it is all their own invention. (199)

Persecution arrives with an inquisitor and a trial, but Juniper and Wise Child escape in a voyage to the land across the water. The painful experience causes Wise Child to recognize her deep love for Juniper and her way of life: 'I could see the love that was woven through every fibre of the world, a love that no amount of cruelty or misunderstanding could pull out of the fabric of life' (200–1).

Conclusion

Monica Furlong was, in some ways, an unlikely Anglican woman novelist. She clung deeply to the experience of Anglican communities wherever they embodied the richness of Christian wisdom and reached out for God and each other in fellowship. Yet the label 'Anglican' sat lightly with her. As a woman who had felt the weight of church doctrine on her own life, she was deeply troubled by the church's separation of spirituality and sexuality.[40] Her spiritual counsel and her advocacy for the ordination of women were driven by a fundamental principle, articulated as early as 1965, that humans had a 'desperate yearning for meaning, for love, for hope, for assurance'.[41] The church's role was not to regulate this yearning, or suppress it, but to be a conduit for union with the source of all desire, the living God. Her novels therefore keep the institutional trappings of the church at a critical distance. Truth is found instead in ordinary things, in nature, in honest dealings between people.

It is no accident that women play the leading roles in most of Furlong's novels. Throughout her work, she identified a profound cultural shift in Western concepts of womanhood, changing not only the attitudes of men towards women, but also women's regard for themselves:

> Women have developed a new sense of existing in and for themselves in the same way that men do, not primarily, as in the past, as someone's daughter, wife or mother, not first and foremost as a 'helpmeet', even though some may be glad to be helpmeets to a beloved other person, but as persons in their own right.[42]

In her biography of Thérèse of Lisieux, she wrote of the peculiar conundrum of women and Christianity, for

> quite why women should be drawn to a religion that treated them so woundingly is an interesting question ... Forbidden all leadership, not permitted to raise their voices in public, to perform rites, to preach or teach, women still clung to the religion which spoke of love, sharing and compassion, faithful in prayer, religious devotions, and acts of charity.[43]

Furlong developed this theme in her novels as her protagonists – none of them Anglican – explored love and compassion. She argued that there was nothing to be gained in pursuing power for its own sake, and everything to be lost if love were destroyed in the process.

Furlong did not write novels for an Anglican audience, though many Anglicans benefitted from her books. Rather, she hoped to extend the wisdom of Christian tradition and the experience of love beyond the walls of the church. Towards the end of her life she was deeply concerned about the loss of religious wisdom in contemporary Western societies, and the alienation of younger generations from even the possibility of a passing encounter with Christianity, leaving them bereft of spiritual wells or common cultural foundations. It is surely no accident that she produced several children's novels in the latter part of her career.[44]

In 1995 Furlong wrote: 'I wish I could say that I thought religion had made me better at loving – it has mostly made me aware that I am not very good at it, though I am still very interested in how it may be achieved.'[45] Nonetheless, throughout her novels and other writings she exercised a remarkable capacity to help others to live as if love were real.

FIGURE 14 *Phyllis Dorothy James aka P. D. James.*

13

P.D. James (1920–2014): 'Lighten Our Darkness'

Alison Shell

Veteran novelists often become moral arbiters. In her later years, the detective novelist P.D. James assumed this role, combining it with a championship of traditional Anglican liturgy and an unusual willingness to speak about her Christian faith in public.[1] As a Tory peer, she presented an attractive and responsible version of conservatism even to those who disagreed with her politics; as an Anglican, she was able to make non-Anglicans take her seriously. It can be a struggle to reconcile her public persona with her fiction: how could a woman of such rectitude, gentility and warmth have dreamed up such bleak and violent novels? Yet a dissonance is not a contradiction, and this essay will argue that both James's public utterances and her fictional worlds reveal an unruly theological imagination.[2]

My thanks to Bev Botting, Alison Felstead, Clare Flook, Beatrice Groves, Carol Heaton, Arnold Hunt, Simon Jones, Julia Jordan, Oliver Mahoney, Judith Maltby and Eileen Roberts for help in completing this chapter. Versions of this paper were given to the Barbara Pym Society and the 'Excellent Women' lecture series held in Westminster Abbey, both in 2017, and I would also like to thank the audience members on those occasions for their interest and suggestions. Quotations from James's work are reproduced by kind permission of the copyright estate of the late P.D. James.

Anglicanism in detective fiction

It seemed appropriate to have James as the final novelist in this book, given that her career and writings often recall her predecessors. As both writer and pundit she could be called the Dorothy L. Sayers of her generation, theologically informed and unapologetically learned, and the bleak East Anglian landscapes in her fiction consciously recall Sayers's classic evocation of the Fenlands, *The Nine Tailors* (1934).[3] James also offers interesting points of correspondence with another mid-twentieth-century female Anglican intellectual, Rose Macaulay; her best-known detective, Adam Dalgliesh, hovers on the threshold of the church in a manner reminiscent of Laurie in Macaulay's novel *The Towers of Trebizond* (1956).[4] Sometimes James used her precursors' treatment of Anglicanism to point up differences between past and present, as when Father Barnes, the ineffectual parish priest in *A Taste for Death* (1986), harks back to the time when the clergy were lionized simply because of their office:

> His most recent library book had been a Barbara Pym. He had read with envious disbelief the gentle and ironic story of a village parish where the curates were entertained, fed and generally spoilt by the female members of the congregation.[5]

The reference – as James's ideal reader would instantly recognize – is to *Some Tame Gazelle* (1950), making light-hearted use of a theme which preoccupied James throughout her career: the decline in Anglicanism's social centrality and status.[6] Here and elsewhere, James's work demonstrates the persistent three-way relationship between the Anglican Church, detective fiction and women novelists: a tradition of which she was very aware.[7] Her engagement with the receding fortunes of Anglicanism may owe something to Agatha Christie's sense in her later works that she was chronicling a transitional period, well illustrated by a comment of Miss Marple's in *Nemesis* (1971): 'In my own village, St Mary Mead, things do rather revolve around the church. I mean, they always have. In my young days, that was so. Nowadays of course it's rather different.'[8]

Nemesis marks Miss Marple's last appearance in a full-length novel; *Murder at the Vicarage* (1930), in which she is introduced to the public, epitomizes the importance of the Anglican Church within Golden Age detective fiction, and the imaginative tradition to which James is responding. Christie's title is suggestive in itself: murder at the vicarage, the centre of a parish community, is a social outrage as much as anything. In Christie's hands, whodunnits contain strong elements of comedy: one can compare Philip King's farce, *See How They Run* (1945), set in a vicarage living room, and containing a memorable scene where four clergymen – some real, some bogus – are threatened with arrest.[9] Perhaps the similarity is only to be expected; farces and murder mysteries both show the temporary disruption of respectability and normal social rhythms, while reimposing order at the end. Christie, who saw herself primarily as an entertainer, would probably have acknowledged that comic resolution was part of her agenda.

But she is now valued at least as much for another, more accidental solace. Christie's work, like other Golden Age detective fiction, has taken on a nostalgic glow in retrospect; this, combined with her downplaying of graphic violence, has given a blueprint to present-day writers of so-called 'cosy' detective novels, marketed as suitable for those who dislike hard-boiled crime fiction. In the world of the cosy whodunnit, bloody murder is as toothsomely English as strawberry jam on a scone.[10] The Anglican Church figures prominently, sometimes just to evoke, as Christie did, a world of parochial order ruptured by murder and reinstated by the detective.[11] But in an age where Christian communities tend to be ignored or treated stereotypically within mainstream novels, the genre also provides opportunities for writers wishing to undertake more ambitious depictions of church life.[12] Here, James does have points in common with the authors of cosy detective fiction, yet she is the least cosy of writers herself. For all her own homage to Christie, her novels are far more violent and desolate than her predecessor's; if Christie is the quintessential Golden Age detective novelist, James's fallen world locates her within an Iron Age of crime fiction.[13]

The Church of England and the Gothic imagination

James's novels could also be thought of as exercises in Anglican Gothic. Within literary criticism, the term 'Gothic' refers both to a literary fashion of the late eighteenth and early nineteenth centuries, and a more general imaginative fascination with the ruined, the haunted and the moribund.[14] At its outset, Gothic fiction drew inspiration from the history of Catholicism in England, both its medieval past and troublingly half-concealed present. But in the late twentieth and early twenty-first centuries, it has been Anglicanism's turn to be cast into part-shadow. As the introduction to this volume has shown, this is not a simple story of decline.[15] But it has meant that outside clearly delineated contexts, such as BBC Radio 4's 'Thought for the Day', expressions of belief have long been discouraged within England's public sphere.[16] James nods to this in A Taste for Death, in which a murdered politician, Sir Paul Berowne, experiences an abrupt religious conversion before the novel begins.[17] A Tory stalwart in Berowne's constituency describes to Dalgliesh the embarrassment of a conversation with the dead man:

He said that it wouldn't be right for him to continue as our Member. It was time that his life took a different turn. Naturally I asked what he meant by a different turn ... He said that he didn't know yet. He hadn't been shown. 'Hadn't been shown by whom?' I asked. He said 'God'. Well, there's not much a man can say to that. Nothing like an answer like that for putting a stopper on rational discussion. (280)

While this constraint affects all denominations and faiths, it has had an especially pronounced effect on the Church of England because of its previous cultural dominance: which is where the notion of Gothic comes into play. If, as Freud put it, 'the uncanny is that species of the frightening that goes back to what was once well known and had long been familiar', the current position of Anglicanism has considerable power to generate uncanniness.[18]

James's densely imagined church buildings are a focus for this kind of disquiet – and, often enough, a location for murder. In *Death in Holy Orders* (2001), an unpopular archdeacon set on modernizing a theological college is found battered to death beneath a medieval painting of the Last Judgement, as if he too is hell-bound. But not all James's Gothic catastrophes occur within a medievalizing *mise-en-scène*. In *Death of an Expert Witness* (1977), a stately home repurposed as a forensic science laboratory has a chapel by the classical architect Sir Christopher Wren in the grounds, largely unused under the new regime; when asked about its security, the laboratory director comments, 'There's nothing left there of real value', a comment which functions more broadly as a secularist dismissal.[19] Later in the novel, Brenda Pridmore, a young employee of the laboratory, believes she is being followed by the murderer and rushes there for safety:

And now there was a belt of trees before her and, gleaming through the autumn branches, the Wren chapel, lit from within, beckoning and holy, shining like a picture on a Christmas card. She ran towards it, palms outstretched, as hundreds of her forbears in the dark fens must have rushed to their altars for sanctuary … She threw herself against the oak, and the great door swung inwards into a glory of light.

At first her mind, shocked into stupor, refused to recognise what her dazzled eyes so clearly saw … Stella Mawson's face, dreadful in death, drooped above her, the eyes half open, the palms disposed outwards as if in a mute appeal for pity or for help. (315–16)

This startling scene, focusing on the corpse's gesture of unanswered prayer, subverts any sense that churches yield sanctuary – and a similar point is made about the building itself. We learn that it has hosted an adulterous liaison and that it was a safe place for this because the locals avoided it: 'The fen villagers … would have a half-superstitious dread of visiting this empty and alien shrine' (322). In this and other ways, it appears spiritually void; reflecting on her experience there, Brenda comments, 'It's a funny chapel, isn't it? Not really a holy place. Perhaps it hasn't been prayed in enough' (336), while Dalgliesh ponders, in a passage which dispels any idea that his creator might be indiscriminately nostalgic for the Anglican past:

Its formal classicism rejected emotion. It enshrined man, not God; reason, not mystery. This was a place where certain reassuring rituals had been enacted, reaffirming its proprietor's view of the proper order of the universe and his own place in that order. (321)

Exploring, Dalgliesh finds a copy of the Book of Common Prayer which, tellingly, 'looked unused'.[20] It falls open at the passage from Psalm 39 which forms part of the burial service: 'For I am a stranger with thee, and a sojourner, as all my fathers were. O spare me a little, that I may recover my strength: before I go hence, and be no more seen.'[21] These words, and the book from which they are taken, constitute the chapel's only source of spiritual efficacy; in the following chapter, we are shown Dalgliesh 'sitting quietly in one of the stalls, apparently engrossed by the Book of Common Prayer' (331). Discreetly, James leaves us to ponder whether he is praying or just reading.

When Dalgliesh first handles the Prayer Book, he finds some human hairs under it. As if to frustrate simplistic expectations of providential intervention, this clue proves inconclusive. Providential implications, though, do undergird a later novel, A Taste for Death, again in the context of the Prayer Book. Dalgliesh has been listening to 'Evensong, that most neglected and aesthetically satisfying portion of the Anglican liturgy', in an Anglo-Catholic church where he is investigating a double murder:

Father Barnes's voice, as if from a far distance but very clear, perhaps because the words were so familiar, was speaking the Third Collect for aid against all perils: 'Lighten our darkness we beseech Thee, O Lord; And by Thy great mercy defend us from all perils and dangers of this night for the love of Thine only Son, our saviour Jesus Christ.' (434)[22]

The Collect's plea for enlightenment and defence, so appropriate for policemen and detectives, heralds the moment just after the service when a crucial clue – a silver button from the murderer's jacket – is found in a money box for votive candles by a statue of the Virgin and Child. This recalls an earlier episode when, just after Dalgliesh's first inspection of the bodies, he lights a candle in front of the same statue and leaves payment for it, conscious of how strange the action might appear to his junior colleagues:

On impulse he felt in his pocket for a tenpenny piece and dropped it into the box. The clatter was unnaturally loud. He half-expected to hear Kate or Massingham moving up behind him to watch, unspeaking but with interested eyes, his untypical act of sentimental folly ... He stuck the candle upright in a socket then sat and gazed at the flame, letting it mesmerize him into memory. (78)

At the very least, Dalgliesh is meditating – James suggests more, not least because the chapter section stops here – and the clue emerges later as if in response to an unspoken, barely articulated prayer.

James was well used to burying clues, James's readers are primed to look for them, and once noticed, the convergence between these two moments is hard to ignore. Indeed, it could seem obtrusive, verging on the idea that prayer is a slot machine. But James has anticipated this problem by suggesting that there is nothing supernatural about how it happens. The button probably gets in the box because Darren, a ten-year-old boy who is one of the first to discover the bodies, substitutes it for a coin. As he walks up to the church with his friend Miss Wharton, she hands him 'the usual tenpenny piece' for a candle: 'now she heard a faint tinkle and watched while he stuck his candle in the socket' (9), a noise that could, of course, be made by both a coin and a metal button. We learn later in the story that Darren is badly brought up and a habitual pilferer, even more likely than most children of his age to see no contradiction between lighting a votive candle and stealing from the church. Readers looking for a material explanation can stop there; those searching for a providentialist outcome are given the option of one, though in a way which is anything but glib. On the one hand, we are invited to speculate on the contingent, subterranean workings of a providence that can redeem Darren's petty crime in a way that brings a far worse criminal to justice; on the other, it is hinted that an answer to prayer may bring additional horrors in its wake. When the button is discovered, it leads directly to the murderer, but because of Darren's action, this key piece of evidence emerges too late to avoid an extra death. If this borderline-providential moment stretches Ronald Knox's famous tenet that all supernatural agency should be ruled out in detective stories, it also challenges the idea that God necessarily brings about happy endings.[23]

Confession and death

As this episode illustrates, James writes about prayer the way the Victorians wrote about sex, with the utmost delicacy and indirection.[24] This is entirely in keeping with Dalgliesh's character: a vicar's son, he is shown as comfortable within Anglican surroundings, but also as intellectually fastidious, emotionally inhibited and equivocal towards religious faith. James may have had pragmatic reasons for this, given that depicting Dalgliesh as a paid-up Christian would have compromised his cleverness for some of her readers. But this sceptical distancing from belief makes him, if anything, an especially authoritative witness to the evil he encounters. For a genre that foregrounds the process of rational deduction, detective fiction often has a lot to say about supra-rational perceptions of good and evil. For instance, when it is suggested to Miss Marple that she has a 'very fine sense of evil', she responds:

> Yes, perhaps. I have at several different times in my life been apprehensive, have recognised that there was evil in the neighbourhood, the surroundings, that the environment of someone who was evil was near me, connected

with what was happening … It's rather, you know … like being born with a very keen sense of smell. (113)

James echoes this idea in her portrayal of Michael Baddeley, the priest whose murder precipitates the plot in *The Black Tower* (1975). Chaplain to Toynton Grange, a nursing home run by a bizarre Anglican religious community, he dies because he correctly suspects that the organization is being used as a front for criminal activities: not because of tangible clues, but 'a deep-rooted instinct for what he would describe as evil' (266). On the face of it, suspicion of this kind is a strikingly inadequate reason for murder. While this testifies to the murderer's unbalanced state of mind, it also conveys a vivid impression of Father Baddeley's spiritual perceptiveness, made all the more suggestive by the fact that the reader never encounters him directly.[25]

Suspicions about Father Baddeley's death first arise because his corpse is found wearing a purple stole, as if he has been interrupted in administering the sacrament of confession: a practice that is often useful to the detective novelist. An early instance, which James surely knew, occurs in Dorothy L. Sayers's *Unnatural Death* (1927); here, the high-church piety of Lord Peter Wimsey's assistant Katherine Climpson is crucial to the finding and interpretation of one particular clue, which she happens upon as the result of a minor accident after vespers:

Miss Climpson gathered up a quantity of little manuals, and groped for her gloves. In doing so, she dropped her office-book. It fell, annoyingly, behind the long kneeler, scattering as it went a small pentecostal shower of Easter cards, book-markers, sacred pictures, dried palms and Ave Marias into the dark corner behind the confessional. (359)[26]

Back home, she goes through her devotional books reinserting the prayer cards and finds something she has picked up by accident: a sheet of notes made in preparation for confession, which contains a vital pointer to the identity of the murderer. This puts her in a dilemma as to whether she should disclose it or not – after all, it was not intended for her eyes, and could be seen as affected by the seal of the confessional. She asks to put a case of conscience to the Vicar, and writes a letter to Lord Peter and his collaborator Inspector Parker 'so obscure and mysterious and so lavishly underlined and interlined that it was perhaps fortunate for their reason that they were never faced with it' (364). Providentially, perhaps, the identity of the murderer later becomes clear for other reasons.

In *The Black Tower*, the practice of confession is differently revelatory, not least because Father Baddeley is killed when his priestly obligation to provide it is exploited by the murderer. In the end, it is Dalgliesh who hears the confession instead, reminding the reader that detectives and priests have overlapping concerns. The murderer triumphantly recounts their final confrontation to Dalgliesh as follows:

When he accused me of … using Toynton for some purpose of my own, I said that I would tell him the truth, that I wanted to make my confession. He must have known in his heart that this was death, that I was only amusing myself. But he couldn't take the risk. If he refused to take me seriously, his whole life would have been a lie. (267)

Fr Baddeley is murdered because of his terrifying spiritual insight, and we are invited to believe that he goes to his death living out his faith and vocation. Within a literary genre so concerned with bad and violent deaths, this discreet martyrdom is unusual. But the idea that, despite everything, a murder victim can achieve a good death is explored elsewhere in *The Black Tower* through the fate of Grace Willison, a resident of the nursing home. A high Anglican spinster from the same stock as Sayers's Miss Climpson, Grace is killed because she is responsible for sending out the community's newsletter – the quintessential task of an 'excellent woman' – and has perfect recall of the names and addresses on the mailing list; the fact that some of these contacts are criminal means that she would be able to compromise the murderer. Father Baddeley is Grace's spiritual director and close friend – a relationship which James sympathetically distinguishes from that recurrent theme in mid-twentieth-century English fiction, a spinster's crush on a clergyman – and his death leaves her emotionally desolate.[27] As she reflects: 'She had hoped to be able to feel that [he] was close to her; but it hadn't happened, it just wasn't true. They are all gone into the world of light. Well, gone away; not interested any more in the living' (187).

James is using free indirect discourse here; Grace's thoughts are conveyed to us without inverted commas, and so too is a quotation she recalls from the work of the seventeenth-century Anglican religious poet Henry Vaughan: 'They are all gone into the world of light.'[28] While it is perfectly possible to read the passage without picking up on this quotation, it is one of the best-known lines from a well-known poem, and given James's conscious literariness throughout her career, she would have expected at least some of her readers to notice it. In turn, this recognition could operate at several levels: recalling the line, identifying its author and recognizing the relevance of the entire poem to Grace's present and future situation.[29] Vaughan's speaker starts by celebrating the memory of dead friends, apparently the only positive feature of his life, and ends by longing for the unity with God that death will bring.

Half a page after this quotation, Grace herself is killed, seemingly by a personification of death: '[a] cloaked figure, hood well down obscuring the face, moving swiftly towards her on silent feet like an apparition' (188). Explicable on a literal level by the fact that members of the community wear monks' habits, this passage unashamedly channels the Gothic element in the novel, and with it a twinge of superstitious fear. Yet the atavistic horror of this is mitigated in several ways. As James's narrator reports, '[Grace] did not die ungently, feeling at the last through the thin veil of plastic only the strong, warm, oddly comforting lineaments of a human hand' (188).[30] The notion of a 'veil' is simultaneously sinister and reassuring; it describes the murderer's method of suffocating victims, but also evokes a familiar metaphor for the thin division between life and death, often used to comfort the bereaved.[31] At a more overt level too, the passage reminds us that death may be welcome, even though the act of murder is shocking. Grace is terminally ill, with nothing to live for; as a devout Christian, she has everything to die for; and she has recently been shriven, one of Father Baddeley's last acts before being murdered. Even a bringer of death can be given the kind of welcome expressed in a later verse of Vaughan's poem: 'Dear, beauteous Death! the jewel of the just, / Shining nowhere, but in the dark; / What mysteries do lie beyond thy dust / Could man outlook that mark!'[32] James's ideal reader, able to recall the metaphysical poets in detail, would appreciate the appositeness of this sentiment to a detective novel, a genre centrally engaged with the mysteries lying beyond death.

God's absence

Another quotation within Grace's final musings is even more ambivalently deployed. 'Lighten our darkness; her mother had always liked that collect; and by Thy great mercy defend us from all the perils and dangers of this night. Only there was no peril here, only sleeplessness and pain' (187). The Book of Common Prayer's Collect Against All Perils, drawn on here, has already been discussed in relation to *A Taste for Death*.[33] There it heralds enlightenment; in *The Black Tower* the allusion is inevitably more ironic, given that Grace is about to be murdered. As discussed above, many features of her death are presented as positive, but the reader cannot help noticing that, on a literal level, the collect's plea for divine defence is not answered. Consequently, this exemplary death stimulates notions of God's own death or absence, which have a double purpose in discourse about religion. On the one hand, they are impeccably orthodox: Jesus dies on the Cross lamenting in the words of Psalm 22 that God has forsaken him, while apophatic theology overturns conventional concepts of God, attempting to describe him through what he is not.[34] But such ideas can also be used as shorthand for an agnostic or atheist position, which is how they usually function in writing not undertaken by theologians. Though neither agnostic nor atheist, James can certainly be called apophatic at times. In a field-defining work on female detective novelists, Susan Rowland argues: 'Dalgleish acts as the sign of the absence of God. He is the representative of cultural authority plagued by his awareness of the inability of the police to substitute for God in healing pain and providing justice.'[35] This inability is, of course, not complete – Dalgliesh and his team do bring about resolutions – but James never shrinks from showing how imperfect and compromised these are. The denouement of *A Taste for Death*, discussed above, is one illustration of how, in James's fictional world, human attempts to bring about justice can result in appalling collateral damage.[36]

In the same novel, another of James's high-church spinsters, Emily Wharton, apprehends a divine dispensation to which violence is intrinsic. After the traumatic discovery of a corpse in church, her night-time Bible-reading leaves her 'burrowing and scurrying like a tormented animal':

> The passage from St Luke's Gospel had been the parable of the good shepherd.[37] It was one of her favourites, but tonight she had read it with a sharpened, perversely questioning mind. What, after all, was a shepherd's job? Only to care for the sheep, to make sure they didn't escape so that they could be branded, sheared and then slaughtered. (164)

Prima facie, Miss Wharton is a character from whom one might expect platitudinous piety, making the violence of the passage all the more striking. For her Christ, the existence of cruelty and slaughter is a given; he looks after his sheep with the ultimate aim of preserving them for suffering and death. While this is completely in keeping with the notion of sacrifice set out in both the Old and the New Testaments, which Christ himself exemplifies, it is too biblical to be comfortable.

More immanent, and almost as painful, is the low-key rejection Miss Wharton experiences at St Matthew's. At the end of the novel, her young companion Darren, whom she has done much to support, drifts away from churchgoing. Miss Wharton says to him, 'I miss you at St Matthew's.' He replies, 'Yeah. Well, I reckon I won't have time for that now', and the narrator comments: 'she had glimpsed in his face a curiously adult embarrassment and had suddenly seen herself as he saw her, ... a pathetic, rather silly old woman' (510–11). Darren's is an understandable childish reaction, and readers empathize with his discomfort – yet James also intends them to be angered by those, whether children or adults, who see only the dowdiness in the Miss Whartons of this world, and are blind to their virtue. Humble to the point of slavishness, Miss Wharton projects this rejection onto the congregation as a whole: noticing how the church's numbers have swelled thanks to its notoriety, she wonders 'how long there would be a place in it for her' (511). James often uses her characters' spatial relationship to buildings to reflect their psychological state, and at the end of *A Taste for Death*, Miss Wharton locks herself out of church but gazes in at the sanctuary lamp through a grille in an entrance passageway. The final paragraph gives us her thoughts: at first bleak, then drawing strength from the Gospels.

> [God] wasn't any longer in the church. Like Darren, he had gone away. Then she remembered what Father Collins had once said in a sermon when she first came to St Matthew's: 'If you find that you no longer believe, act as if you still do. If you feel that you can't pray, go on saying the words.' She knelt down on the hard floor, supporting herself with her

hands grasping the iron grille, and said the words with which she always began her private prayers: 'Lord I am not worthy that thou shouldest come under my roof, but speak but the word and my soul shall be healed.' (512–3)[38]

Liturgy and the presence of evil

As the archaic language signals, Miss Wharton – unsurprisingly for someone of her generation and churchmanship – is drawing on the King James Bible for her devotions. This choice, as well as fleshing out her character, echoes James's own advocacy of traditional Anglican worship. During James's lifetime, as part of a move towards liturgical modernization, the King James Bible and the Book of Common Prayer had ceased to be standard provision in Church of England services, even in revised form: a move that was deplored by many, both inside and outside Anglicanism.[39] The non-believers who voiced their disapproval saw the sidelining of Anglicanism's literary heritage as an act of cultural philistinism, and James would have agreed.[40] Within her fiction, she seldom misses an opportunity to advocate what she saw as liturgical soundness. *The Skull Beneath the Skin* (1982), for instance, features a service of Morning Prayer commissioned by an obsessive Victorianist, Ambrose Gorringe, but after James's own heart; we are told that it uses 'the 1662 Book of Common Prayer without deletions or substitutions', and that the congregation 'proclaimed themselves miserable offenders who had followed too much the devices and desires of their own hearts and promised amendment of life in a slightly ragged but resolute chorus'.[41] Afterwards the detective Cordelia Gray, whose charge Clarissa Lisle has just been murdered, reflects that

> for the first time since [Clarissa's] murder, her restless, menacing spirit was subdued. For a few precious moments the weight of guilt and misery lifted from her own heart. It was possible to believe, innocently talking in the sun, that life was as well ordered, as certain, as austerely decent and reasonable as the great Anglican compromise in which they had taken part. (254)

The service may be a historical re-enactment, but it is also a cathartic event, simultaneously soothing and disturbing. On the one hand, it provides psychological reassurance for the members of a house party after a shocking murder; on the other, the fact that the killer may be one of their number gives the congregation's self-accusation an urgent pertinence. The liturgical phrases quoted by James are from the Book of Common Prayer's General Confession, which at the time the novel was published had been generally superseded by the version in the

Alternative Service Book; within the latter, the congregation declare that they have sinned against God and their fellow men 'in thought and word and deed, through negligence, through weakness, through our own deliberate fault'.[42] Though a comprehensive admission of imperfection, this contrasts markedly with the Book of Common Prayer's requirement for a body of worshippers to call themselves 'miserable offenders' who have 'followed too much the devices and desires of our own hearts'. At the time when the earlier prayer was written, as James would have been well aware, the choice of the word 'miserable' would have indicated the speakers' need for mercy, recalling such Latin terms as *misericordia*.[43] Yet this does not exhaust its overtones, and semantic shifts between the seventeenth and the twentieth centuries have served to foreground suggestions of self-hatred and human inadequacy.[44] As an exemplary collective affirmation, 'miserable offenders' would have been much more acceptable in the seventeenth century than in the twentieth. But it speaks far more strikingly than its modern equivalent to the evils presented in James's novel, giving us one good reason why James's dislike of liturgical change went well beyond belles-lettrism, pedantry and nostalgia. She was sensitive to its religious implications, and deplored the passing of a time when liturgy engaged with the dark.

This, in turn, demonstrates how James's thought was permeated by apprehensions of evil. When she was asked in 2012, 'Do you believe in good and evil in a Manichean way or do you see human nature as much more murky and ambiguous?' she replied: 'I believe in good and evil in a Manichean way. Evil is a positive force ... to me, this seems close to human experience.'[45] An off-the-cuff interview comment should not be taken as a credo, but James was scholarly enough to know what was implied by her self-identification as a Manichean: a dualistic view of the world, governed by the perception of conflict between light and darkness. Sometimes described as a Christian heresy, at other times as a religion in its own right incorporating elements of Christianity, Manicheanism is characterized by the notion that evil has a material existence; mainstream Christianity, following the formulation of St Augustine – a Manichean in early life – defines evil differently as the privation of good.[46] In non-theological discourse the idea of Manicheanism is often used in a looser sense, typifying a tendency to see good and evil as binary opposites.[47] This dualistic way of viewing the world is very well suited to murder mysteries, and the notion of Manicheanism is a helpful way of approaching James's novels. Detective fiction was too highly evolved by the late twentieth century, and James was too sophisticated a writer within the genre, for her novels to deploy caricatured murderers and flawless sleuths. Yet evil drives the story in detective fiction, which – it could be argued – gives the genre an intrinsic bias towards the Manichean heresy. James even features two self-confessed adherents to it in a late work, *The Lighthouse* (2005): an alcoholic priest, Adrian Boyde, and his carer, Jo

Staveley. Jo and Dalgliesh talk about Boyde's struggles with his vocation as follows:

> '[He] came to believe that God couldn't be both good and all-powerful; life's a struggle between the two forces – good and evil, God and the devil. That's some kind of heresy – a long word beginning with M.'
> Dalgliesh said, 'Manichaeanism.'
> 'That sounds like it. It seems sensible to me. At least it explains the suffering of the innocent, which otherwise takes some sophistry to make sense of. If I had a religion, that's what I'd choose. I suppose I became a manichaean – if that's the word – without knowing it the first time I watched a child dying of cancer. But apparently you're not supposed to believe it if you're a Christian and I suppose particularly not if you're a priest.' (278–9)

James's fascination with evil goes well beyond the narrative demands of a detective story; as this exchange illustrates, the problem of undeserved suffering is ubiquitous in her work. So is a near-apocalyptic vein of social disenchantment, especially in her later novels, where political arrogance is identified as evil. Often enough, James's anger cuts across policies typical of the Conservative party she knew. For instance, in *The Murder Room* (2003), the knock-on effect of cuts in welfare drives a desperate wife caring for a husband with Alzheimer's to kill him and take her own life. Because heresies throw up points of tension within Christianity, they have a history of reinventing themselves when new difficulties arise; the fierce topical commentary in this novel indicates how the Manichaean tendency in James's writing could be stimulated by contemporary problems.

But, paradoxically, it could also suggest the desirability of taking flight from the ordinary world. Manicheanism is a form of gnostic belief, and like all Gnosticism, it is characterized by the idea that spiritual enlightenment can be achieved only through knowledge.[48] During James's lifetime, modes of thought with a gnostic ancestry had some currency among commentators – notably the critic Harold Bloom – who shared her keen respect for England's literary heritage and her distrust of populism.[49] In James's fiction, her leanings towards this position are played out against the backdrop of Anglican modernization, nowhere more insistently than in a late novel, *Death in Holy Orders*. Its plot revolves around St Anselm's, a conservative and intellectually elitist theological college, being threatened with closure by Archdeacon Crampton, an insensitive modernizer. Crampton's *grand guignol* death has already featured in this essay; earlier in the novel, he passes the remark that the college has become 'irrelevant to the new age', and the college principal, Father Sebastian, replies:

> What is it that you want? A church without mystery, stripped of that learning, tolerance and dignity that were the virtues of Anglicanism? A Church without humility in the face of the ineffable mystery and love of Almighty God? A

service with banal hymns, a debased liturgy and the Eucharist conducted as if it were a parish bean-feast? A church for Cool Britannia? (180)[50]

James has no time for Crampton, while Father Sebastian's views echo her own well-publicized ecclesiological conservatism. Yet the novel does not endorse the members of St Anselm's uncritically. In one scene, for instance, the learned Father Peregrine comments dismissively of a scholar researching the Oxford Movement: 'I sought his views on the effect of the Gorham case in modifying the Tractarian belief of J.B. Mozley and it was apparent he had no idea what I was talking about' (49). Most of James's readers would have been similarly ignorant; the reference is to a Victorian controversy over whether infant baptism was only efficacious if the baptized individual committed to Christianity in later life, notorious in its day, but now familiar only to specialists. Moreover, one can have an interest in the Oxford Movement without having heard of J.B. Mozley, not a household name even as nineteenth-century churchmen go.[51] We are meant to think that Father Peregrine is showing off his own mastery of the field – but there is more to the speech than that. On the one hand, James is signalling to the fogey coterie within her own audience who are familiar with the detailed contours of the Oxford Movement; on the other, she is teasing them for being Father Peregrines themselves and warning that they should not despise those less well up in nerdy church-historical minutiae.

If we think James is writing from inside a bubble, the joke is on us. Yet self-parody is a risky business, and James's use of it renders the novel vulnerable to misreading. The characters' lengthy dialogues on the state of Anglicanism read like the dramatization of James's personal concerns and displace the plot at times, rather as if the Church of England were the real murder victim. Yet this, in turn, encapsulates the paradox of James's career: that, in feeding an appetite for Gothic narratives of Anglican decline, she gave new life to its literary heritage. Using a mass-market genre, the detective story, she may well have done a better job than her clerical contemporaries in disseminating knowledge of the King James Bible and the Book of Common Prayer: not just because she was unusually sensitive to their stylistic merits, but because, in her view, they spoke to a fallen world, succeeding where modern translation and liturgy failed.

Conclusion

At the Reformation, Anglican vernacular texts were intended to popularize the faith; the passage of time has done much to render them the exclusive preserve of the educated. Nevertheless, one of James's characters, the housekeeper Tally Clutton in *The Murder Room* (2003), illustrates her creator's belief that they remained accessible to the well affected. Tally is uneducated but intelligent and sympathetic, returning to her Anglican roots in old age and even visiting the famous Anglo-Catholic church All Saints' Margaret Street in a pilgrimage inspired by Simon Jenkins's popular gazetteer, *England's Thousand Best Churches*.[52] When she searches for solace after finding a burned corpse, James gives us, yet again, the Collect Against All Perils:

> It was a prayer [Tally] had not heard for sixty years, but now the words came as freshly to her mind as if she were hearing them for the first time. *Lighten our darkness, we beseech thee, O Lord; and by thy great mercy defend us from all perils and dangers of this night; for the love of thine only Son, our Saviour Jesus Christ.* She held the image of that charred head in her mind and spoke the prayer aloud and was comforted. (173)

This contrasts with Dalgliesh's response to the same scene, more spiritually inhibited than within the earlier novels quoted above. Looking at the body, he reflects that Father Sebastian of *Death in Holy Orders* would have made the sign of the cross, while his own clerical father would have 'bent his head in prayer':

> The words would be there, hallowed by centuries of use. Both, he thought, were fortunate in being able to call on instinctive responses which could bestow on those awful charred remains the recognition that here had been a human being. (138)

Both Dalgliesh and Tally feel that prayer is appropriate, but only the latter is able to pray; we infer that James thinks her wiser than Dalgliesh. Yet Dalgliesh's reaction reminds us that perils and dangers continue despite prayers for deliverance, sometimes climaxing in violent death. These two responses to a victim of murder span the full complexity of James's approach to pain and evil, acknowledging both the believers and unbelievers within her readership. Typically for James, they also hark back to the past, and show the desire for God stimulated by abjection and horror.

In her lifetime, James was thought the consummate Anglican novelist, yet she herself was aware of being imaginatively goaded in a direction incompatible with orthodox Christianity. For one of England's most prominent lay Anglicans to call herself a Manichaean illustrates the gulf between eras in the period covered by this book: in the Victorian age such an admission would have sparked public controversy, in our own time it comes across as recondite, quaint and harmless. Yet, as articulated by James, it reminds us that detective novels are shaped by the formal acknowledgement of sinfulness, embodying the Manichaean idea that evil is a positive force. Dealing, as any detective novelist must, with extreme human wickedness, James finds no adequate secular response to it; instead, she uses the Anglican literary heritage to recall a time when evil was, at least, explicitly confronted in public liturgy. Her advocacy of traditional Anglicanism taps into the vein of cultural and political conservatism within her writing; but it transcends simple nostalgia, through a sense that language and practice hallowed by generations of believers can act as both a consolation for human failure, and a partial bulwark against the world's cruelty.

Afterword

Francis Spufford

'One of the good things about a Catholic church,' says a character in Rumer Godden's *In This House of Brede* (1969), 'is that it isn't respectable.[1] You can find anyone in it, from duchesses to whores, from tramps to kings.' The Church of England, however – at least until its loss of cultural legitimacy over the last forty years – was always hopelessly respectable. It was part of the definition of what respectable England *was*. It couldn't offer writers the Roman Catholics' counter-cultural take on English society and institutions, mostly conservative, sometimes radical, but always at an oblique angle to the settled grain of things. It couldn't offer them as human subject-matter congregations whose spectacular mixtures of aristocrats and immigrants seemed to point to a principle of human gathering separate from class and place. It couldn't offer an excitingly oppositional reading of national history, in which the stereotypical villains had been really heroes and the stereotypical heroes had been really villains. It couldn't provide a priesthood whose detachment from family life and social status made them look otherworldly compared to the parsons in parsonages and the rectors in rectories. Instead, for most of the three centuries since the novel in its modern form was invented, the Church of England has been a social church, a societal church, embedded in English power structures and social relationships, and tending to reproduce them at prayer, unrolling a vision of the city of God which closely mapped the city of humanity, down to the questions of who sat where, and who got to talk and who got to listen. Ideally, and sometimes even actually, Anglicanism aimed to sanctify its England, to tilt all those familiar relationships that made it up away from their this-worldly ends, and towards redemption and resurrection. In practice, though, it was hard for novelists who consciously wrote as Anglicans during the years of the church's prestige to have access to a completely visionary rhetoric, any more than they could reach easily for wholly corrosive satire or entirely bitter humour. Their Catholic counterparts from Godden to Muriel Spark, Graham Greene to Antonia Forest, could feel that they were measuring the fabric of English life by a standard that came from elsewhere, from heaven or from Douai. The Anglicans were exploring a fabric of which they were part, testing it for its ironies and its hypocrisies, for the always-nuanced, never-quite-total wandering of practice away from theory. They were writing the almost constant failure of Scunthorpe to behave like Jerusalem the golden, and the occasional instants when it did. They had the great advantage of reach – there have been much larger samples of humanity and of human experience in Anglican congregations than in English Catholic ones, covering far more of the interesting ground in between the tramps and the kings, the duchesses and the whores – but the corresponding disadvantage too, of complicity.

Yet, as this book has shown, a critical gap was reopened when it was a woman writing the Anglican novel. The Church of England has been dependent on lay female piety and lay female labour ever since the Reformation, and in that sense it has always had women's experience at its centre. But until 1994 Anglican women could not be priests, and therefore could not participate in the visible, official, explicit processes by which the church taught, worked, celebrated the sacraments and defined its public being. Like almost all the novelists in this book, they could be clergy daughters, clergy sisters, clergy wives, clergy mothers: but not clergy. In tension with the undoubted class and cultural privilege of many of them, there was always the intersectional complication of their gender, limiting the perspectives from which in life, as opposed to fiction, they were ever able to witness the life of their church. There was always the complicating truth that their loyalty to the institution was, in this respect, one way. They maintained the church, they nourished it, they supported it, but they did not decide for it. They interpreted it from the position of the acted-for and the acted-upon, not of the actors. They viewed it, if not from below, then at least sidelong: at an angle to the grain of power in the church, even if the church were not, like Catholicism, angled obliquely in relation to the surrounding society. The novelists in this book were Anglicanism's intimate outsiders, its observant and vitally necessary second-class citizens.

Even a writer as determinedly propagandistic as Charlotte Tucker, committed to a narrative in which imperialism and Protestantism and Englishness fused together into a single triumphant destiny, was doing something a little radical in claiming to speak for it. And a much larger space for female subjectivity was claimed in Charlotte Brontë's portrait of evangelical men as reefs on which a voyaging young woman might wreck herself if she were unwary. Turning from survival to vocation, Charlotte M. Yonge found a case for the dignity and moral significance of women's idealism that was so persuasive that idealistic young men read *The Daisy Chain* and *The Heir of Redclyffe* in search of lessons for themselves: the reverse of the usual Victorian pattern in which girls struggled to extract a viable inspiration from male literary heroics. Margaret Oliphant, freed by her Presbyterianism to find Anglicanism a trifle exotic, an object of curiosity rather than an automatic affiliation, saw in its cultural breadth both a potential for generosity and a doorway through which a non-sectarian grace might flow. Evelyn Underhill, primarily to be influential as the great re-invigorator of twentieth-century mysticism, used her early experiments in fiction to make a case for Anglicanism on imaginative grounds, with the Yeatsian occult and Roman Catholic devotion as the other options, to be considered and rejected entirely on her own idiosyncratic terms. Daughters of the vicarage in the early twentieth century, Noel Streatfeild, Dorothy L. Sayers and Elizabeth Goudge testified in very different ways in popular fiction to its potent peculiarity as a human environment. Streatfeild drew out the emotional costs, and threadbare flipside, of its compulsory high-mindedness; Goudge, re-imagining male spiritual authority figures on her own terms, made them sacrificial heroes able to recognize the spiritual stature of women; Sayers used the micro-worlds of church and congregation as domains for the insatiable human curiosity of the detective story, and looked beyond them, and beyond the play of roles, to the ineffable. In a later generation, P.D. James took onward the use of the church as criminal setting, adding a darkened credal seriousness about what crime *was* and meant. Meanwhile, Rose Macaulay's fiction danced around the ironies of Anglican history and Anglican subcultures, denying itself a secure arrival in the metropolis of faith, yet unwilling to be without 'the City of God you can enter every day' in the Eucharist. Barbara Pym's career spanned the sudden death of Anglican churches as 'the natural conduit for all social relations', meaning that she preserved as observational comedy what turned out to be the last era in which a male clergy served as unwitting objects of female entertainment, observation and fantasy. But even for those who intended to replace Anglicanism with a post-religious philosophy could find, like Iris Murdoch, that the Good did not quite banish the affective pull of remembered liturgy, remembered church, remembered God. As both novelist and activist, Monica Furlong is a transitional figure, both reflecting in the distanced form of fantasy on women's lives under the codes of faith, and in her own life as one of the prime movers of women's ordination in England, helping to bring about the end of the regime of intimate outsiderhood.

From now on – we hope – women need no longer write the Church of England from the angle of disadvantage. But the result, for the Anglican women novelists of the present and the future, cannot be a comfortable fiction of establishment, because the drastic dwindling of the church's share in English attention and cultural assent means that Christianity as such, in its Anglican and all its other forms, has now receded into strangeness for most readers. One angle of estrangement closes; another yawns open. All Christian churches are counter-cultural now. All are unrespectable. Time will tell whether this creates an Anglican fiction with a Roman Catholic adversarial bite to it; or whether it will require writers who want the social reach of the old C of E, the access to the muddled and complicated soul of the nation, to do quiet and implicit apologetics in their work, educating the reader again to see what Christians see.

NOTES

Introduction

1 Macaulay and Plomer appeared together on the arts programme 'The Critics' on the BBC Home Service in the late 1940s and became friends. Plomer returned to being a communicant Anglican in his 50s, and told Macaulay that he had started going on retreat to the Anglican religious community at Mirfield in West Yorkshire, as she sometimes did. Durham University Special Collections, Plomer 6/1, 'Constance Babington Smith to William Plomer' (10 Dec 1961); William Plomer, 'The Way Back', *The Listener* (26 Oct 1961).

2 DUSC, Plomer 132/7/1–2, 'Macaulay to Plomer' (6 Nov 1956). One Roman Catholic convert complained to Macaulay that she had intended the famous camel in the novel to stand for the Church of Rome, a charge which completely baffled the author. Macaulay's engagement with Roman Catholic novelists such as Greene, and especially Waugh, is explored above, 108–14. Though Muriel Spark is often mentioned in the company of Waugh and Greene, her first novel, *The Comforters* (1957), was published only a year before Macaulay's death.

3 On the Catholic novel, see Thomas Woodman, *Faithful Fictions: The Catholic Novel in British Literature* (Milton Keynes: Open University Press, 1991) and Marian E. Crane, *Aiming at Heaven, Getting the Earth: The English Catholic Novel Today* (Lanham, MD: Rowman and Littlefield, 2007). For a recent overview of the Nonconformist literary tradition, see 'Nonconformity and Culture', ch. 16 in Robert Pope (ed.), T&T *Clark Companion to Nonconformity* (London: Bloomsbury /T&T Clark, 2013); see also Valentine Cunningham, *Everywhere Spoken Against: Dissent in the Victorian Novel* (1st ed. Oxford: Clarendon, 1975) and Jane Shaw and Alan Kreider (eds), *Culture and the Nonconformist Tradition* (Chicago: Chicago University Press, 1999). John Bunyan's work, especially *The Pilgrim's Progress*, was definitive within this tradition and an important influence on the novel in its modern form: see W.R. Owens and Stuart Sim (eds), *Reception: Appropriation, Recollection: Bunyan's Pilgrim's Progress* (Oxford: Peter Lang, 2007). For the Unitarian novelist Elizabeth Gaskell, an especially important point of comparison for many of the writers covered in this volume, see Jill L. Matus (ed.), *The Cambridge Companion to Elizabeth Gaskell* (Cambridge: Cambridge University Press, 2007).

4 E.g. the Charlotte M. Yonge Society (no website at present) and Fellowship, www.cmyf.org.uk; the Evelyn Underhill Association, www.evelynunderhill.org;

the Dorothy L. Sayers Society, www.sayers.org.uk; the Barbara Pym Society, www.barbara-pym.org; the Elizabeth Goudge Society, www.elizabethgoudge.org. Charlotte Brontë – a securer canonical presence – is celebrated by the Brontë Society, www.bronte.org.uk, while the University of Chichester houses the Iris Murdoch Society, the Iris Murdoch Research Centre and *Iris Murdoch Review*.

5   See Lori Branch, 'Postsecular Studies', in Mark Knight (ed.), *The Routledge Companion to Literature and Religion* (Abingdon: Routledge, 2016), ch. 8; and Sarah Foot, 'The Church and Its Past', *Studies in Church History* 49 (2013), 1–24.

6   For a critique of the common idea that modernism necessarily entails a departure from religion, see Matthew Mutter, *Restless Secularism: Modernism and the Religious Inheritance* (New Haven, CT: Yale University Press, 2017).

7   Information supplied by the Anglican Communion Office, London and cited in Judith Maltby, *Prayer Book and People in Elizabethan and Early Stuart England* (Cambridge: Cambridge University Press, 1998), 237.

8   See Sara L. Pearson's essay below, ch. 1.

9   Excellent background to British Anglicanism's history in the past two centuries is provided by Rowan Strong, 'Introduction', in *The Oxford History of Anglicanism, Vol. III: Partisan Anglicanism and its Global Expansion, 1829-c.1914*, ed. Rowan Strong (Oxford: Oxford University Press, 2017), 1–23, as well as numerous other chapters; and Jeremy Morris, 'Historiographical Introduction' and 'Anglicanism in Britain and Ireland', in Jeremy Morris (ed.), *The Oxford History of Anglicanism, Vol. IV: Global Western Anglicanism, c.1910-present* (Oxford: Oxford University Press, 2017), 1–21.

10 Confessionalization: the fixing of religious belief into denominational and dogmatic categories.

11 See Ann Loades's essay in this volume, ch. 5.

12 *Excellent Women* (Harmondsworth: Penguin, [1952] 1987), 21.

13 See Nicola Humble, *The Feminine Middlebrow Novel, 1920s to 1950s: Class, Domesticity, and Bohemianism* (Oxford: Oxford University Press, 2004) and Alison Light, *Forever England: Literature, Femininity and Conservatism between the Wars* (London: Routledge, 1991).

14 For the period up to the millennium, see Keith Robbins, *England, Ireland, Scotland, Wales: The Christian Church 1900–2000* (Oxford: Oxford University Press, 2008), ch. 7. According to the latest available figures from the British Social Attitudes Survey, the proportion of the British population identifying as Anglican declined from 40 to 20 per cent between 1983 and 2010 (*BSA* 28:12, 173). Our thanks to the Research and Statistics Unit at Church House, Westminster.

15 Figures from www.anglicancommunion.org (accessed 26 June 2018). See also David Goodhew (ed.), *Growth and Decline in the Anglican Communion, 1980 to the Present* (Oxford: Routledge, 2017).

16 See Kirstie Blair, 'The Influence of the Oxford Movement on Poetry and Fiction', in Stewart J. Brown, Peter B. Nockles and James Pereiro (eds), *The*

Oxford Handbook of the Oxford Movement (Oxford: Oxford University Press, 2017), ch. 29.

17 Quoted from Gerard Manley Hopkins, *Selected Poems*, ed. Peter Feeney (Oxford: Oxford University Press, 1994, this ed. 2006), 31.

18 Émile Durkheim, *The Elementary Forms of the Religious Life* (1912: first English translation, London: George Allen & Unwin, 1915). Pym is discussed in Tim Watson, *Culture Writing: Literature and Anthropology in the Mid-Century Atlantic World* (Oxford: Oxford University Press, 2018). See also Charles Burkhart, 'Barbara Pym and the Africans', *Twentieth-Century Literature* 29:1 (1983), 45–53.

19 Given the exodus of women volunteers from parish work in our own time, this may seem as unfamiliar within a generation or two as any mid-Victorian practice: Abby Day, *The Religious Lives of Older Laywomen: The Last Active Anglican Generation* (Oxford: Oxford University Press, 2017).

20 See Orphia Jane Allen, *Barbara Pym: Writing a Life* (Metachen, NJ and London: Scarecrow Press, 1994), 94–5.

21 On universalism, see Sara L. Pearson's essay above, 15–16.

22 See Peter S. Hawkins's essay below, and Gillian Dooley, 'Iris Murdoch's Novels of Male Adultery: *The Sandcastle, An Unofficial Rose, The Sacred and Profane Love Machine*, and *The Message to the Planet*', *English Studies* 90:4 (2009), 421–34. For a broader study of the topic, see Tony Tanner, *Adultery in the Novel: Contract and Transgression* (Baltimore, MD: Johns Hopkins University Press, 1977).

23 She described herself in later life as 'in a way … still inside the Anglican church'. See Peter Hawkins's essay above, 163.

24 See Judith Maltby's essay above, 107.

25 See Alison Shell's essay above, ch. 13.

26 The ordination of women has allowed for the development in detective fiction of the clergywoman as amateur sleuth, Kate Charles's Callie Anson and Phil Rickman's Merrily Watkins being two examples.

27 Joanne Holland-Barnes, 'From Providence to Police: The Development of the Literary Detective Figure in the Long 18th Century' (PhD diss., McGill University, 2013). However, on the view espoused by Ronald Knox that 'all *supernatural* or *preternatural* agencies are ruled out as a matter of course' in legitimate detective fiction, see Alison Shell's essay above, 196.

28 See Jessica Martin's essay above, 89.

29 Key studies of these earlier institutional issues remain Brian Heeney, *The Women's Movement in the Church of England 1850–1930* (Oxford: Oxford University Press, 1988) and Sheila Fletcher, *Maude Royden* (London: Basil Blackwell, 1989). See also Henrietta Blackmore (ed.), *The Beginning of Women's Ministry: The Revival of the Deaconess in the Nineteenth-Century Church of England*, Church of England Record Society 14 (Woodbridge: Boydell, 2007); Susan Mumm, *Stolen Daughters, Virgin Mothers: Anglican Sisterhoods in Victorian Britain* (London: Leicester University Press, 1999).

For the more recent history of the ordination of women to the priesthood in the Church of England, see Monica Furlong, *The C of E: The State It's*

In (London: Hodder & Stoughton, 2000), 134–7, and *Act of Synod, Act of Folly?* (London: SCM, 1998); Margaret Webster, *A New Strength, A New Song: The Journey to Women's Priesthood* (London: Mowbray, 1994); Susan Dowell and Jane Williams, *Bread, Wine and Women: The Ordination Debate in the Church of England* (London: Virago, 1994). We await a history of the consecration of women to the episcopate in the Church of England. However, on the relationship of Parliament to the ordination of women as priests and bishops, see Judith Maltby, 'Gender and Establishment: Parliament, "Erastianism" and the Ordination of Women 1993–2010', in Mark Chapman, Judith Maltby and William Whyte (eds), *The Established Church: Past, Present and Future* (London: T&T Clark, 2011), 98–123.

30   See chapters by Susan Mumm, 'The Feminization of Nineteenth-Century Anglicanism' (III, 440–55) and Cordelia Moyse, 'Gender Perspectives: Women and Anglicanism' (IV, 68–92) in *The Oxford History of Anglicanism*, gen. ed. Rowan Strong, 5 vols (Oxford: Oxford University Press, 2017–8). Both Mumm and Moyse provide a valuable context for our authors, but neither of them explores the way Anglican women used novel-writing to reach a large audience with their critique of the state of the Church of England, or to promote particular theological, spiritual or church party perspectives.

31   See Kryriaki Hadjiafxendi and Patricia Zakreski (eds), *Crafting the Woman Professional in the Long Nineteenth Century* (Farnham, Ashgate, 2013).

32   Geoffrey Rowell, Kenneth Stevenson and Rowan Williams (eds), *Love's Redeeming Work: The Anglican Quest for Holiness* (Oxford: Oxford University Press, 2001), xiv. This has an ecumenical companion volume, *Firmly I Believe and Truly: The Spiritual Tradition of Catholic England*, eds John Saward, John Morrill and Michael Tomko (Oxford: Oxford University Press, 2013). Interestingly, its editors include a greater number of women and a few extracts from novels, though nothing from Muriel Spark.

33   Rowell et al., *Love's Redeeming Work*, 374.

34   A survey of handbooks, essay collections, and anthologies of Anglicanism reveals that *Love's Redeeming Work* is not atypical. Evelyn Underhill and Dorothy L. Sayers are by far the most referenced of female Anglican authors, but as writers of non-fiction and apologetics. What follows is not an exhaustive bibliography but the works cited support this general argument. Stephen Sykes and John Booty (eds), *The Study of Anglicanism* (London: SPCK, 1988), an older book which does better than newer works in including a handful of Anglican women thinkers; G.R. Evans and J. Robert Wright (eds), *The Anglican Tradition: A Handbook of Sources* (London: SPCK, 1991); Geoffrey Rowell (ed.), *The English Religious Tradition and the Genius of Anglicanism* (Wantage: Ikon, 1992); Richard Schmidt (ed.), *Glorious Companions: Five Centuries of Anglican Spirituality* (Grand Rapids, MI: Eerdmans, 2002); Rowan Williams, *Anglican Identities* (Cambridge, MA: Cowley Publications, 2003); Mark Chapman, *Anglicanism: A Very Short Introduction* (Oxford: Oxford University Press, 2006); Mark D. Chapman, Sathianathan Clarke, and Martyn Percy (eds), *The Oxford Handbook of Anglican Studies* (Oxford: Oxford University Press, 2015), which does include, however, an excellent chapter on 'Gender' by Kathryn Tanner. A compiler who stands out here is the late Raymond Chapman, who edited the anthology

Means of Grace, Hope of Glory: Five Hundred Years of Anglican Thought (Norwich: Canterbury Press, 2005); this includes extracts from the non-fiction of James, Underhill, and Furlong and from the fiction and non-fiction of Yonge. Chapman's *The Practical Mystic: Evelyn Underhill and Her Writings* (Norwich: Canterbury Press, 2012) contains a few extracts from her novels.

35　The essays above yield many examples of this, e.g. P.D. James, above, ch. 13.

36　*Jane and Prudence* (London: Jonathan Cape, 1953), 212.

37　Given the reference quoted above, the name may allude to the character of Flora in Yonge's *Daisy Chain*.

38　Cf. Angela Thirkell's mid-twentieth-century 'Barsetshire Chronicles'.

39　See Francis Spufford's 'Afterword'.

Chapter 1

1　Laura Mooneyham White, *Jane Austen's Anglicanism* (Farnham, Surrey: Ashgate, 2011).

2　The best resource for considering Charlotte Brontë and religion is Marianne Thormählen, *The Brontës and Religion* (Cambridge: Cambridge University Press, 1999).

3　Thormählen, *Brontës and Religion*, 88.

4　Margaret Smith (ed.), *The Letters of Charlotte Brontë*, vol.2 (Oxford: Oxford University Press, 2000), 343.

5　John Maynard, 'The Brontës and Religion', ch. 9 in Heather Glen (ed.), *The Cambridge Companion to the Brontës* (Cambridge: Cambridge University Press, 2002), 196.

6　Smith (ed.), *Letters*, vol. 2, 501.

7　Margaret Smith (ed.), *The Letters of Charlotte Brontë*, vol. 2 (Oxford: Oxford University Press, 1995), 581.

8　Tighe was 'vicar of Drumballyroney and rector of Drumgooland': Juliet Barker, *The Brontës*, rev. edn (London: Abacus, 2010), 5. For biographical information, see also the entry on Charlotte Brontë in the online *ODNB*.

9　Christine Alexander and Margaret Smith (eds), *The Oxford Companion to the Brontës* (Oxford: Oxford University Press, 2006), 98.

10　Christine Alexander and Sara L. Pearson, *Celebrating Charlotte Brontë: Transforming Life into Literature in* Jane Eyre (Haworth: The Brontë Society, 2016), 180.

11　Colin Buchanan, *Historical Dictionary of Anglicanism* (Lanham, MD: Rowman and Littlefield, 2006), 415.

12　Peter Searby, *A History of the University of Cambridge*, vol. 3 (Cambridge: Cambridge University Press, 1997), 332–3.

13　Bob Duckett, 'A Mother and Her Substitutes', ch. 5 in Marianne Thormählen (ed.), *The Brontës in Context* (Cambridge: Cambridge University Press, 2012), 46.

14　Barker, *The Brontës*, 159–60.

15 Alexander and Smith (eds), *Oxford Companion to the Brontës*, 51.

16 Charlotte Brontë, *Villette*, eds Margaret Smith and Herbert Rosengarten (Oxford: Oxford University Press, [1853] 2000), 12. All references to the novel will be to this edition.

17 Charlotte Brontë, *Shirley*, eds Herbert Rosengarten and Margaret Smith (Oxford: Oxford University Press, [1849] 2007), 5–6. All references to the novel will be to this edition.

18 Thormählen, *Brontës and Religion*, 8.

19 Charlotte demonstrated her open-minded approach to ecclesiastical differences by eventually marrying the Haworth curate Arthur Bell Nicholls, who had 'Puseyite tendencies': Alexander and Smith (eds), *Oxford Companion to the Brontës*, 342.

20 Charlotte Brontë, 'Tales of the Islanders, Vol. II', in Christine Alexander (ed.), *An Edition of the Early Writings of Charlotte Brontë 1826–1832* (Oxford: Basil Blackwell, 1987), 100.

21 Barker, *The Brontës*, 183.

22 Ibid.

23 Thormählen, *Brontës and Religion*, 30.

24 Smith (ed.), *Letters*, vol. 2, 23.

25 Charlotte Brontë, *Jane Eyre*, ed. Margaret Smith (Oxford: Oxford University Press, [1847] 2000), 16, 287–8. All references to the novel will be to this edition.

26 See Brontë, *Jane Eyre*, when Mr Rochester asks his recently hired footman to see if the clergyman and the clerk are at the church ready for the wedding ceremony (287), and when Jane describes her quiet wedding where only Jane, Rochester, the parson and the clerk are present (448).

27 Apparently when Charlotte Brontë was married to Arthur Bell Nicholls in 1854, because the wedding was so 'quiet' (virtually a secret), the clerk had to be summoned in haste: 'John Robinson, a resident of Haworth, reminisced about Charlotte Brontë's wedding. As a boy, he was told "to go as fast as I could for Josh Redman, the old parish clerk" on the day of the wedding, telling him "he had to come to church as quickly as possible". There is a touch of humour and reality in Robinson's remembering that "He came immediately. On the way he stopped and said, "I'd better lace up my boots," and he went to the wall and did so"' (Alexander and Pearson, *Celebrating Charlotte*, 135).

28 Mooneyham White, *Austen's Anglicanism*, 53.

29 One wonders if Brontë ever read Frances Burney's novel *Cecilia*, which also has an interrupted wedding ceremony (found in Book 8, Chapter 2): Frances Burney, *Cecilia*, eds Peter Sabor and Margaret Anne Doody (Oxford: Oxford University Press, [1782] 1988), 625–6.

30 The differences between Brontë's fair copy manuscript and the 'Form of Solemnization of Matrimony' in the edition of the Book of Common Prayer that Brontë owned are as follows (with Brontë's version given first):

    both (as ye will answer... disclosed)/both, as ye will answer... disclosed, judgment/judgement

impediment why/impediment, why
lawfully be joined/be lawfully joined
confess it – for /confess it. For
well assured that/well assured, that
doth allow, are/doth allow are
matrimony/Matrimony

Charlotte Brontë owned a Book of Common Prayer published in Oxford by Samuel Collingwood in 1830. All of my references to the Book of Common Prayer are from an edition published by Samuel Collingwood five years earlier in 1825: The Book of Common Prayer (Oxford: Samuel Collingwood, 1825), 168. Available online: books.google.ca (accessed 5 April 2018). For Charlotte Brontë's manuscript of *Jane Eyre*, see Charlotte Brontë, *Jane Eyre: Manuscript*, vol. 2 (Paris: Éditions des saints pères, n.d.), 490.

31 Book of Common Prayer, 168.

32 Charlotte Brontë's copy of the Book of Common Prayer is held at the Morgan Library and Museum, New York. Record available online: http://corsair. themorgan.org/cgi-bin/Pwebrecon.cgi?BBID=111550 (accessed 6 April 2018). Morgan was a friend of Patrick Brontë's and married Maria Branwell's cousin, Jane Fennell. He 'baptized Maria, Elizabeth, Charlotte, and Anne Brontë; and buried Mrs Brontë, Maria, Elizabeth, and Branwell': Alexander and Smith (eds), *Oxford Companion to the Brontës*, 329.

33 Brontë depicts Eliza Reed's High Church tendencies as eventually leading her to Roman Catholicism – she becomes a nun and joins a convent in Lisle (*Jane Eyre*, 242).

34 A letter Brontë writes to her publisher's reader, W.S. Williams, confirms that her depiction of this type of clerical knowledge is actually quite realistic. Brontë describes the response of a clergyman to *Jane Eyre*: '"Jane Eyre" has got down into Yorkshire ... I saw an elderly clergyman reading it the other day, and had the satisfaction of hearing him exclaim "Why – they have got — School, and Mr — here, I declare! and Miss — ["] (naming the originals of Lowood, Mr. Brocklehurst and Miss Temple) He had known them all: I wondered whether he would recognize the portraits, and was gratified to find that he did and that moreover he pronounced them faithful and just' (Smith (ed.), *Letters*, vol. 2, 3–4).

35 Patrick Brontë wrote a letter to the *Leeds Intelligencer* in 1837 calling for the repeal of the Poor Law Amendment Act of 1834 because he saw it as 'unfeeling [and] antiscriptural' in its restricted guidelines for giving help to the poor: *The Letters of the Reverend Patrick Brontë*, ed. Dudley Green (Stroud, Gloucestershire: Nonsuch, 2005), 110–11.

36 Alexander and Pearson, *Celebrating Charlotte*, 150.

37 Brian Stanley, 'Anglican Missionary Societies and Agencies in the Nineteenth Century', in *The Oxford History of Anglicanism, Vol III: Partisan Anglicanism and Its Global Expansion, 1829–c.1914*, ed. Rowan Strong (Oxford: Oxford University Press, 2017), 131.

38 Ibid.

39   Deborah Denenholz Morse also notes the 'gesture of communion' in the scene of Miss Temple's offering tea and seedcake to Helen and Jane: 'Brontë Violations: Liminality, Transgression, and Lesbian Erotics in Charlotte Brontë's *Jane Eyre*', *Literature Compass* 14, no. 12 (2017), 7.

40   Alexander and Smith (eds), *Oxford Companion to the Brontës*, 464.

41   Ibid., 465.

42   Ibid., 464.

43   See, for instance, Rosemarie Bodenheimer, *The Politics of Story in Victorian Social Fiction* (Ithaca, NY: Cornell University Press, 1988).

44   Sara L. Pearson, 'Religion, Gender and Authority in the Novels of Charlotte Brontë' (PhD diss., Department of English, Boston University, 2008), 117.

45   Quoted in Miriam Allott (ed.), *The Brontës: The Critical Heritage* (London: Routledge and Kegan Paul, 1974), 165.

46   J. Russell Perkin also considers *Shirley* an Anglican novel, but he focuses on the novel's anti-Tractarian (Anglo-Catholic) polemic as a 'novel of religious controversy' rather than exploring what it has to say about the Church of England itself: 'Charlotte Brontë's *Shirley* as a Novel of Religious Controversy', in *Theology and the Victorian Novel* (Montreal: McGill-Queen's University Press, 2009), 55–74.

47   The material that follows draws extensively on a previously published article: Sara L. Pearson, '"God save it! God also reform it!": The Condition of England's Church in Charlotte Brontë's *Shirley*', *Brontë Studies* 40:4 (2015), 290–6.

48   Pearson, '"God save it!"', 291.

Chapter 2

1   Dorothy Entwistle, 'Embossed Gilt and Moral Tales: Reward Books in English Sunday Schools', *Journal of Popular Culture* 28:1 (1994), 81–96 (83).

2   Kimberley Reynolds, 'Tucker, Charlotte Maria (1821–1893)', online *ODNB*. Tucker also published works for adults, such as devotional poetry.

3   Entwistle, 'Embossed Gilt', 81.

4   J.S. Bratton, *The Impact of Victorian Children's Fiction* (London: Croom Helm, 1981), 70. Anne Dowker views Tucker's *Fairy Know-a-Bit* (1866) as a 'striking moral precursor to the psammead': 'Five Children and It: Some Parallels with the 19th-Century Novel', in Raymond E. Jones (ed.), *E. Nesbit's Psammead Trilogy: A Children's Classic at 100* (Oxford: Children's Literature Association and Scarecrow, 2006), 170.

5   Trisha Tucker, 'Gendering the Evangelical Novel', *Rocky Mountain Review* 66:1 (2012), 83–9 (84).

6   Tucker's writings about Rahab and Achsah, Caleb's daughter, are excerpted in *Women of War, Women of Woe: Joshua and Judges through the Eyes of Nineteenth-Century Female Biblical Interpreters*, eds Marion Taylor

and Kristiana de Groot (Grand Rapids, MI: William Eerdmans Publishing Company, 2016), 36–40 and 67–8.

7   Alison Chapman, 'Phantasies of Matriarchy in Victorian Children's Literature', ch. 4 in Nicola Diane Thompson (ed.), *Victorian Women Writers and the Woman Question* (Cambridge: Cambridge University Press, 1999), 61.

8   Bratton, *Impact of Children's Fiction*, 71; Agnes Giberne, *A Lady of England: The Life and Letters of Charlotte Maria Tucker* (New York: A.C. Armstrong and Son, 1895), 92.

9   Ian Bradley, *The Call to Seriousness: The Evangelical Impact on the Victorians* (London: Jonathan Cape, 1976), 25.

10 Margaret Nancy Cutt, *Ministering Angels: A Study of Nineteenth-Century Evangelical Writing* (Wormley, Herts: Five Owls Press, 1979), 20.

11 Giberne, *A Lady of England*, 92.

12 For more information, see Richard Turnbull, *Anglican and Evangelical?* (London: Continuum, 2007), 53.

13 Paul Avis, *The Identity of Anglicanism: Essentials of Anglican Ecclesiology* (London: Bloomsbury, 2007), 24.

14 Diana Peschier, *Nineteenth-Century Anti-Catholic Discourses: The Case of Charlotte Brontë* (Houndmills, Basingstoke: Palgrave Macmillan, 2005), 3.

15 Linda Colley, 'Britishness and Otherness: An Argument', *Journal of British Studies* 31:4 (1992), 309–329 (316–17).

16 Cutt, *Ministering Angels*, 45.

17 Turnbull, *Anglican and Evangelical?* 60.

18 For more on the Parker Society, see Mark Chapman, *Anglican Theology* (London: T&T Clark International, 2012), 13.

19 J.H. Merle Aubigné, *The History of the Great Reformation of the Sixteenth Century in Germany, Switzerland, etc.*, vol. 1 (New York: Robert Carter, 1846), 1119–20.

20 'A.L.O.E.' [Charlotte Maria Tucker], *The Life of Luther* (London: The Book Society, 1873), 5. Hereafter, page numbers will be given in the text.

21 Alistair McGrath, 'Anglicanism and Pan-Evangelicalism', in Mark Chapman, Sathianathan Clarke and Martyn Percy (eds), *The Oxford Handbook of Anglican Studies* (Oxford: Oxford University Press, 2015), 320.

22 See D.B. Bebbington, *Evangelicalism in Modern Britain: A History from the 1730s to the 1980s* (London: Routledge, 1989), 12–14.

23 Turnbull, *Anglicanism and Evangelical?* 7.

24 Miriam Elizabeth Burstein, 'Counter-Medievalism; Or, Protestants Re-Write the Middle Ages', ch. 8 in Jennifer Palmgren and Loretta M. Holloway (ed.), *Beyond Arthurian Romances: The Reach of Victorian Medievalism* (New York: Palgrave Macmillan, 2005), 147. Both Burstein and Royal W. Rhodes in *The Lion and the Cross: Early Christianity in Victorian Novels* (Columbus: Ohio State University Press, 1995) have examined Tucker's efforts to present an ancient, native British Christianity in *Daybreak in Britain* (1880).

25   The term 'Morning Star of the Reformation' was coined in 1548 by John Bale:
     Stephen E. Lahey, *John Wyclif* (Oxford: Oxford University Press, 2009), 135.

26   Peter McNiven, 'Badby, John (*d.* 1410)', *ODNB*.

27   Colley, 'Britishness and Otherness', 319.

28   Peter Nockles, 'The Changing Legacy and Reception of John Foxe's "Book of
     Martyrs" in the "Long Eighteenth Century": Varieties of Anglican, Protestant
     and Catholic Response, *c.* 1760–1850', ch. 11 in Robert D. Cornwall and
     William Gibson (eds.), *Religion, Politics and Dissent, 1660–1832: Essays in
     Honour of James E. Bradley* (Farnham: Ashgate, 2010), 222.

29   Ibid., 231.

30   Ibid., 219.

31   Ibid., 247.

32   'The Thirteenth and Final Report of the Council of the Parker Society', in
     General Index to the Publications of the Parker Society, compiled by Henry
     Gough (Cambridge: Cambridge University Press for the Parker Society, 1855),
     no page number [p. 2].

33   Chapman, *Anglican Theology*, 45.

34   Tucker provides a lengthy note quoting from history books about Badby's
     encounter with the prince and refusal to recant (182–3).

35   Burstein, 'Counter-Medievalism', 163. As 'A Lady of England', Tucker writes
     first for England, then Britain and then the Empire.

36   Ibid., 162.

37   'A.L.O.E.' [Charlotte Maria Tucker], *The Blacksmith of Boniface Lane*
     (London, Edinburgh and New York: Thomas Nelson and Sons, 1891), 17.

38   Quoted in Merle Mowbray Bevington, *The Saturday Review 1855–1868*
     (New York: Columbia University Press, 1941), 188, and subsequently in
     Donald E. Hall, 'Muscular Christianity: Reading and Writing the Male
     Social Body', introduction to *Muscular Christianity: Embodying the
     Victorian Age*, ed. Donald E. Hall (Cambridge: Cambridge University Press,
     1994), 7.

39   For more on the relationship between muscular Christianity and Englishness,
     see C.J.W.L. Wee, 'Christian Manliness and National Identity: The Problematic
     Construction of a Racially "Pure" Nation', ch. 3 in Hall (ed.), *Muscular
     Christianity* (66–88).

40   Mary Wheat Hanawalt, 'Charles Kingsley and Science', *Studies in Philology*
     34:4 (1937), 589–611 (603).

41   Cutt, *Ministering Angels*, 51.

42   'A.L.O.E.' [Charlotte Maria Tucker], *The Claremont Tales; Or, Illustrations
     of the Beatitudes* (Edinburgh: Gall and Inglis, 1858), 109–10. Further page
     references will be given in the main text.

43   Elisabeth Jay, *The Religion of the Heart* (Oxford: Clarendon Press, 1979),
     142–3.

44   Ibid., 132.

45 'A.L.O.E.' [Charlotte Maria Tucker], *Pictures of St. Peter in an English Home* (London: T. Nelson and Sons, 1887), 15–16. Hereafter page numbers will be given in the text.

46 Peschier, *Nineteenth-Century Anti-Catholic Discourses*, 20.

47 Marion Taylor, 'Anglican Women and the Bible in Nineteenth-Century Britain', *Anglican and Episcopal History* 75:4 (2006), 527–552 (528). Tucker is included in *Handbook of Women Biblical Interpreters*, ed. Marion Taylor with Agnes Choi (Grand Rapids, MI: Baker Academic, 2012).

48 Bratton, *Impact of Children's Fiction*, 74.

49 Ibid., 75.

50 Sarah Lewis, *Women's Mission*, 2nd edition (London: John W. Parker, 1839), 13.

51 Defined in the Book of Common Prayer as 'the Common Prayers in the Church' (see chapter 'Concerning the Service of the Church', 212–14).

52 Colley, 'Britishness and Otherness', 319–20.

53 Cutt, *Ministering Angels*, 75. Quotation from Thomas Carlyle, *Past and Present* (London: Chapman & Hall, 1843), 264.

54 Isaac Watts, *Divine Songs, Attempted in Easy Language; For the Use of Children* (London: no publisher given, 1775), x.

Chapter 3

1 Margaret Oliphant, *The Perpetual Curate*, intro. Penelope Fitzgerald (London: Virago, [1864] 1987), 434.

2 *The Autobiography and Letters of Mrs M.O.W. Oliphant*, edited by her cousin, Mrs Harry Coghill, was published posthumously in 1899, two years after her death in 1897. A modern edition, edited by Q.D. Leavis, was published by Leicester University Press in 1974. A fuller unexpurgated version of the *Autobiography*, edited by Elisabeth Jay, was published by Oxford University Press in 1990. For biographical information, see also the online *ODNB*.

3 The first two stories, 'A Little Pilgrim in the Unseen' and 'The Little Pilgrim Goes Up Higher', were published together in *A Little Pilgrim in the Unseen* (London: Macmillan and Co., 1882); 'The Little Pilgrim in the Seen and Unseen' (1885) was collected with 'On the Dark Mountains' (1888) and the story 'The Land of Darkness' (1887) in a single volume, *The Land of Darkness* (London: Macmillan and Co., 1888).

4 Elisabeth Jay, *Mrs Oliphant: 'A Fiction to Herself', A Literary Life* (Oxford: Oxford University Press, 1995), 14.

5 The series was mostly first published in *Blackwood's Edinburgh Magazine* and eventually included *The Executor* (*Blackwood's*, May 1861), *The Rector* and *The Doctor's Family* (*Blackwood's*, Sept. 1861–Jan. 1862), *Salem Chapel* (*Blackwood's*, Feb. 1862–Jan. 1863), *The Perpetual Curate* (*Blackwood's*, Jun.

1863–Sept. 1864), *Miss Marjoribanks* (*Blackwood's*, Feb. 1865–May 1866), and *Phoebe Junior: A Last Chronicle of Carlingford* (1876).

6   Oliphant, *Perpetual Curate*, 9.

7   Margaret Oliphant, *The Rector* in *The Rector / The Doctor's Family*, intro. Penelope Fitzgerald (London: Virago, [1863] 1986), 34.

8   John Milton, *Paradise Lost*, ed. Scott Elledge (New York: Norton, 1975), Book 12, ll. 646, 587, 279–80.

9   Jay notes that Oliphant was criticized for her lack of full understanding of the perpetual curate role (Jay, *A Literary Life*, 151). For my purpose here, it is her own view that matters.

10 Oliphant, *Autobiography*, 67–8. Ejections started happening from 1660; Oliphant may be thinking of the Savoy Conference of 1661, which precipitated the Great Ejection of 24 August (St Bartholomew's Day) 1662.

11 Margaret Oliphant, 'The Open Door' [1882], in Merryn Williams (ed.), *A Beleaguered City and Other Stories* (Oxford: Oxford University Press, 1988), 115–60, 126.

12 Dante Alighieri, *Purgatory*, 31: 100–3 in Henry Francis Cary, *The Vision of Hell, Purgatory and Paradise of Dante Alighieri* (London: Bell and Daldy, 1869), 127: 'The beauteous dame, her arms expanding, clasp'd / My temples, and immerged me where t'was fit / The wave should drench me'. Cary was the commonly used translation in this period, although Oliphant had some Italian and may have sometimes read Dante in the original. She was the author of *Dante: Foreign Classics for English Readers* (Edinburgh and London: Blackwood's, 1877), which contained passages of translation.

13 On Maurice's dismissal and Victorian debates about universalism, see Michael Wheeler, *Death and the Future Life in Victorian Literature and Theology* (Cambridge: Cambridge University Press, 1990), 190–8; on MacDonald, see Rolland Hein, *George MacDonald, Mythmaker* (Portland, OR: Wipf and Stock, 2014), 107 (and 178 for his becoming an Anglican under the influence of Maurice).

14 F.D. Maurice, *Theological Essays* (Cambridge: Macmillan, 1853), 442–78 (462).

15 Ibid., 476.

16 Alison Milbank, *Dante and the Victorians* (Manchester: Manchester University Press, 1998), 164–201.

17 Charles Kingsley, *The Water-Babies: A Fairy Tale for a Land Baby* (London: Macmillan, 1863), 326.

18 Oliphant, 'The Land of Darkness', in *A Beleaguered City*, 233–85 (284).

19 Oliphant, 'Old Lady Mary', in *A Beleaguered City*, 163–229 (180).

20 Ibid., 184.

21 Oliphant, *A Beleaguered City*, in *A Beleaguered City*, 3–114 (25).

22 Ibid., 47.

23 J. Sheridan Le Fanu, *In a Glass Darkly*, ed. Robert Tracy (Oxford: Oxford University Press, [1872] 2008); *Uncle Silas*, ed. Victor Sage (Harmondsworth: Penguin [1864] 2000).

24 Oliphant, 'The Library Window', in *A Beleaguered City*, 289–331 (292).

25 Ibid., 314: 'this made my heart expand with the most curious sensation, as if of pride that, though I could not see, he did, and did not even require to come to the window, as I did, sitting close in the depth of the recess, with my eyes upon him, and almost seeing things through his eyes.'

26 Oliphant, 'The Library Window', in *A Beleaguered City*, 314.

27 Ibid., 326.

28 Ibid., 331.

29 See the discussion by Jay in *A Literary Life*, 153.

30 See Jay, *A Literary Life*, 153–4, and M.R. and F.R. Oliphant, *The Victorian Age of English Literature*, vol. 2 (London: Percival and Co., 1892), 2, 23–9 (on F.D. Maurice).

31 F.D. Maurice, *The Kingdom of Christ: Or, Hints on the Principles, Ordinances and Constitution of the Catholic Church in Letters to a Member of the Society of Friends*, vol. 2 (London: Macmillan and Co., [1842] 1882).

32 Oliphant, *The Victorian Age of English Literature*, vol. 2, 335.

33 Ibid., 336.

34 See Douglas Murray, 'Disruption to Union', in Duncan Forrester and Douglas Murray (eds), *Studies in the History of Worship in Scotland* (London: T&T Clark, 1984), 88–92, and Stewart J. Brown, 'The Scoto-Catholic Movement in Presbyterian Worship, c. 1850–1920', in Duncan Forrester and Douglas Gray (eds.), *Worship and Liturgy in Context: Studies and Case Studies in Theology and Practice* (London: SCM, 2008), 152–63.

35 Brown, 'Scoto-Catholic Movement', 160–2.

36 See ibid., 158–60, and Margaret Oliphant, *The Life of Edward Irving, Minister of the National Scotch Church, London, illustrated by his Journals and Letters*, 2 vols (London: Hurst and Blackett, 1862).

37 Oliphant, *Autobiography*, 7.

Chapter 4

1 Christabel Coleridge, *Charlotte Mary Yonge: Her Life and Letters* (London: Macmillan, 1903), 235. Coleridge's book is still the principal authority for information on Yonge's biography and has been used throughout this essay; further details can be found in the online edition of *The Letters of Charlotte Mary Yonge (1823–1901)* edited by Charlotte Mitchell, Ellen Jordan and Helen Schinske, at https://c21ch.newcastle.edu.au/yonge. See also the entry for Yonge in the online *ODNB*.

2 Within a few years of her death a critic opened an article by saying, 'we shall be bold to challenge the common estimate which relegates Miss Yonge to the rank of a mere story-teller for schoolgirls.' 'The Novels of Miss Yonge', *Edinburgh Review* 202 (October 1905), 357–77 (357).

3 As well as editing the *Monthly Packet* and *Mothers in Council* she wrote regularly for the *Guardian*. The Rt Revd George Sumner, Bishop of Guildford, wrote in an obituary: 'it has been a marvel to many how, with all

her engrossing work for the press, she could find time for… taking classes, instructing pupil-teachers, reading aloud at parochial mothers' meetings' (Obituary, *Guardian*, 3 April 1901: 447–8). She served on committees for, among others, the Girls' Friendly Society, the Mothers' Union, the Winchester Girls' High School and the Winchester Diocesan Higher Religious Education Society.

4 Critics of Yonge, such as Elaine Showalter, *A Literature of Their Own: British Women Novelists from Brontë to Lessing* (London: Virago, 1977), 57, have tended to stress the domineering father, and overlook the fact that in the most literal sense she grew up in a matriarchy.

5 Charlotte Yonge, *Musings over The Christian Year and Lyra Innocentium* (Oxford: Parker, 1871), viii.

6 'Charlotte Mary Yonge', *Church Quarterly Review* 57 (January 1904), 337–60.

7 Charles Kingsley, 'Preface. To the Undergraduates of Cambridge' to the revised 1861 edition of *Alton Locke*, in *Alton Locke, Tailor and Poet: An Autobiography* (London: Macmillan, 1895), lxxxix.

8 The sometimes-violent 'Captain Swing' riots by agricultural workers in 1830–1 were formative political experiences for many Victorians; the authorities reacted forcefully to the threat of rural revolution. See Coleridge, *Life*, 81; *Joseph Mason: Assigned Convict 1831–1837*, eds David Kent and Norma Townsend (Melbourne: Melbourne University Press, 1996), 3; Charlotte M. Yonge, *An Old Woman's Outlook in a Hampshire Village* (London: Macmillan, 1892), 66–7: 'probably his descendants are by this time among the aristocracy of Sydney'.

9 Coleridge, *Life,* 145.

10 'He used to speak with great feeling and admiration of the demonstration of those Scottish ministers who left the General Assembly and became the founders of the Free Kirk, and always expected the day might come for acting "the martyr's sternest part"': Yonge, *Musings,* xliv–xlv. (The quotation is from Keble's poem 'Is it a time to plant and build?', for the Eleventh Sunday after Trinity in *The Christian Year: Thoughts in Verse for the Sundays and Holydays throughout the Year,* 2 vols (Oxford: Parker/London: Rivington, 1827), vol. 2, 40–2.) Cf. Charlotte M. Yonge, *English Church History* (London: National Society, 1883), 183: 'They were called the Non-jurors, and among them were some of the very best and most pious and learned of the English clergy.'

11 See also Leslee Thorne-Murphy, 'The Charity Bazaar and Women's Professionalization in Charlotte Mary Yonge's *The Daisy Chain*', *Studies in English Literature, 1500–1900* 47:4 (2007), 881–99, citing Charlotte M. Yonge, *Womankind* (London: Mozley and Smith, 1876), 222, on the way bazaars accustomed middle-class women to earning money: 'I suppose the bazaar system first led to the change of tone.' On Yonge's charitable giving, see Charlotte Mitchell, 'Charlotte M. Yonge's Bank Account', *Women's Writing* 17 (2010), 380–400.

12 *Imagining Soldiers and Fathers in the Mid-Victorian Era: Charlotte Yonge's Models of Manliness* (London: Ashgate, 1996), 196.

13 Yonge to Elizabeth Barnett, November 1850, quoted in Ethel Romanes, *Charlotte Mary Yonge: An Appreciation* (London: Mowbray, 1908), 54. See also Coleridge, *Life*, 164: 'The name was a difficulty. "The Maidens' Manual" was suggested... Among themselves they called it "The Codger", saying that it was intended to please steady old codgers... '. The resulting compromise (*The Monthly Packet of Evening Readings for Younger Members of the English Church*) was both clumsy and non-committal.

14 'Conversations on the Catechism', *Monthly Packet* 1 (March 1851), 129–42.

15 George Orwell, 'The Lion and the Unicorn: Socialism and the English Genius', in Sonia Orwell and Ian Angus (eds), *The Collected Essays, Journalism and Letters of George Orwell*, 4 vols (Harmondsworth: Penguin, 1970), vol. 2, 74–134 (75).

16 John Halsey Wood Jr., *Going Dutch in the Modern Age: Abraham Kuyper's Struggle for a Free Church in the Nineteenth-Century Netherlands* (Oxford: Oxford University Press, 2013), 23, 40, 120. Kuyper was later Prime Minister of the Netherlands, 1901–5.

17 The Ven. H.E.J. Bevan in *Memoirs of Archbishop Temple by Seven Friends*, ed. E.G. Sandford, 2 vols (London: Macmillan, 1906), vol. 2, 21. The date was the 1880s, and they discussed 'the careers of the May family, in *The Daisy Chain*, as though they were living acquaintances'.

18 Elizabeth Wordsworth, 'Charlotte Mary Yonge as a Writer', *Guardian* (3 April 1901): 465–6 (465).

19 John Gutch, *Martyr of the Islands: The Life and Death of John Coleridge Patteson* (London: Hodder & Stoughton, 1971), 124, 127; For the Melanesian Martyrs' Memorial Church of St Andrew, see http://www.standrewskohi.org/my-church/.

20 'Melanesia is my real sphere – on board, in boats on a rolling sea, swimming through surf, landing among wild naked savage fellows' (Gutch, *Martyr*, 146).

21 Coleridge, *Life*, 183.

22 Quoted by J.W. Mackail, *The Life of William Morris*, 2 vols (London: Longman, 1901), vol. 1, 41: 'In this book, more than any other, may be traced the religious ideals and social enthusiasms which were stirring'.

23 'Miss Yonge's Novels', *Christian Remembrancer* 26 (July 1853): 33–63 (35).

24 'An almost solitary child, with periodical visits to the Elysium of a large family', introduction to the 2nd edition of *Scenes and Characters, or, Eighteen Months at Beechcroft* (London: Macmillan, 1886), vii.

25 As noticed by Louisa May Alcott, *Jo's Boys and How They Turned Out: A Sequel to 'Little Men'* (Boston: Roberts, 1886), 287: 'It is as impossible for the humble historian of the March family to write a story without theatricals in it as for our dear Miss Yonge to get on with less than twelve or fourteen children in her interesting tales.'

26 Diana Farr, *Gilbert Cannan: A Georgian Prodigy* (London: Chatto, 1978), 92–3, citing an undated letter from Wells praising Cannan's *Round the Corner* (1913).

27 Yonge, *Musings*, iv.

28 Charlotte M. Yonge, *The Pillars of the House*, 2 vols (London; Macmillan, 1875), vol. 2, 412.

29 Charlotte M. Yonge, *The Heir of Redclyffe*, 2 vols (London: Parker, 1853), vol. 1, 49, 66. The lectures were given by Keble between 1832 and 1841, and published as John Keble, *Prælectiones Academicæ*, 2 vols (Oxford: Parker, 1844). The passage translated by Philip Morville is from the third lecture, I, 27–8; no English translation was published until 1912.

30 Gavin Budge, *Charlotte M. Yonge: Religion, Feminism and Realism in the Victorian Novel* (Oxford: Peter Lang, 2007).

31 For instance, Robert Liddell, 'an immature mind, and undistinguished style, and the values of a pious schoolgirl', in *A Treatise on the Novel* (London: Cape, 1947), 24, cited by Valerie Sanders, '"All Sufficient to one another"? Charlotte Yonge and the Family Chronicle', in Kay Boardman and Shirley Jones (eds), *Popular Women Writers* (Manchester: Manchester University Press, 2004), 90–110 (90).

32 Catherine Sandbach-Dahlström, *Be Good Sweet Maid: Charlotte Yonge's Domestic Fiction – A Study in Dogmatic Purpose and Fictional Form* (Stockholm Almqvist: Acta Universitatis Stockholmensis LIX, 1984). In fairness, the inverted commas in Sandbach-Dahlström's chapter title express her own sense of the novel's feminism and dialogic qualities.

33 N.D. Thompson, *Reviewing Sex: Gender and the Reception of Victorian Novels* (Basingstoke: Macmillan, 1996), 142: 'the actual book seeks to demonstrate that being a "clever woman" leads to anarchy and death': this seems to me to misrepresent its message.

34 'The Novels of Miss Yonge', 374.

35 They represented the four seasons, on the model of Friedrich de La Motte Fouqué's *Die Jahreszeiten: Eine Vierteljahrsschrift für romantische Dichtungen*, of which the four seasons were *Frühlings-Heft: Undine; Sommer-Heft: Die beiden Hauptleute; Herbst-Heft: Auslaga's Ritter* and *Alpin und Jucunde; Winter-Heft: Sintram und seine Gefährten* (Berlin: Hitzig, 1811–14). Yonge made this explicit when the question of the uniform edition came up: see her letter to Alexander Macmillan (29 January 1879), British Library, Add MS 54921: 80–1.

36 The proposal of Edgar to Eleanor in Virginia Woolf, *Between the Acts* (London: Hogarth Press, 1941) is clearly a reconstruction of the proposal scene in Charlotte M. Yonge, *The Daisy Chain, or, Aspirations: A Family Chronicle*, 2 vols (London: Parker, 1856), vol. 2, 264–5.

37 Karen Sands-O'Connor, 'Why Jo Didn't Marry Laurie: Louisa May Alcott and *The Heir of Redclyffe*', *American Transcendental Quarterly* 15:1 (March 2001), 23–41.The first edition of *Little Women* came out in Boston in two volumes in 1868 and 1869. In Great Britain the second volume appeared under various titles but is usually now published as *Good Wives*. The two-volume *Little Women* has a three-year gap in the middle, similar to the gap between the first and second volumes of *The Daisy Chain*.

38 Louisa May Alcott, *Little Women*, 2 vols (Boston: Roberts, 1868, 1869), vol. 1, 39: 'Meg found her sister eating apples and crying over the "Heir of Redcliffe," [*sic*] wrapped up in a comforter'.

39 A classic example is Dolores Mohun's implicitly positive reference to the godless University College London in Charlotte M. Yonge, *The Long Vacation* (London: Macmillan, 1895), 126.

40 For example, the epigraph from Yonge's *Womankind* of Barbara Stephen, *Emily Davies and Girton College* (London: Constable, 1927).

41 *Memoir of Anna Deborah Richardson*, ed. J.W. Richardson (Newcastle, privately printed, 1877) (23 December 1867), 217, quoted in Stephen, *Emily Davies*, 167–8.

42 '[W]e owe to Mr. Keble the absolute firmness of Miss Yonge. I mean her strong grasp of Church principles, in spite of many forces which might have drawn her into the "femme forte" direction': *Life and Letters of William John Butler* (London: Macmillan, 1897), 239.

43 Bessie Rayner Belloc, *A Passing World* (London: Ward & Downey, 1897), 30–1.

44 Ray Strachey, *'The Cause': A Short History of the Women's Movement in Great Britain* (London: Bell, 1928), 419.

45 See Walton, *Imagining Soldiers and Fathers*, 182n.

46 Charlotte M. Yonge, *Abbeychurch, or, Self Control and Self Conceit* (London: Burns, 1844), 133.

47 A character in Alison Bechdel's cartoon strip *Dykes to Watch Out For* (Ithaca, NY: Firebrand, 1986), enunciated this rule in 1985: 'I ONLY GO TO A MOVIE IF IT SATISFIES THREE BASIC REQUIREMENTS. **ONE**, IT HAS TO HAVE AT LEAST TWO WOMEN IN IT, WHO, TWO, **TALK** TO EACH OTHER ABOUT, THREE, SOMETHING BESIDES A **MAN**.'

48 Thompson, *Reviewing Sex,* 107, suggests that the neglect of Yonge's work is explained by its having 'fallen between both patriarchal/sexist and feminist critical agendas'.

49 Yonge also wrote several full-length biographies, numerous obituaries, and shorter articles in the *Monthly Packet* and other journals on saints and heroes of both sexes.

50 Bodleian Library, Oxford: MS Eng misc. d. 1096, e. 1125.

51 Yonge to Bullock, 31 January 1894 (Bodleian Library, Oxford: English Letters: e.174 ff. 165).

Chapter 5

1 The prayer of dedication for Underhill's memorial at the House of Retreat at Pleshey, where she became a retreat director, concludes the 'Introductory Essay' on her writings by Bishop Lumsden Barkway, Bishop of St Andrews, in *Collected Papers of Evelyn Underhill*, ed. Lucy Menzies (London: Longmans, Green & Co., 1946), 30. For her rediscovered prayer books, used at Pleshey, see *Evelyn Underhill's Prayer Book*, ed. Robyn Wrigley-Carr (London: SPCK, 2018). Biographical information on Underhill in this essay comes from the following sources: Christopher J.R. Armstrong, *Evelyn Underhill*

(1875–1941): An Introduction to her Life and Writings (London and Oxford: Mowbrays, 1975); *The Practical Mystic: Evelyn Underhill and her Writings* (Norwich: Canterbury Press, 2012), ed. Chapman, esp. 1–12; Ann Loades, *Evelyn Underhill* (London: Fount, 1997).

2 On Evelyn Underhill, *Mysticism: A Study in the Nature of Man's Spiritual Consciousness* (London: Methuen, 1911), in twelve editions by 1930 and perennially in print, see Harvey D. Egan, 'Evelyn Underhill Revisited', *The Way* 51 (2012) 23–39. Michelle M. Sauer, 'Evelyn Underhill (1875–1941), The Practical Mystic', in Jane Chance (ed.), *Women Medievalists and the Academy* (Madison, WI: Wisconsin University Press, 2005), 183–99, discusses Underhill's contribution to the rediscovery of medieval writers.

3 See the undated letter (written in late 1927/early 1928) in *The Letters of Evelyn Underhill*, ed. Charles Williams (London: Longmans, Green & Co., 1943), 178.

4 Underhill's volumes of verse are *A Bar-Lamb's Ballad Book* (London: Kegan, Paul, 1902), written for the entertainment of the legal profession; *Immanence: A Book of Verses* (London: Dent, 1912), dedicated to her father; and *Theophanies* (London: Dent, 1916). Her novels are as follows: *The Grey World* (London: William Heinemann, 1904); *The Lost Word* (London: William Heinemann, 1907); *The Column of Dust* (London: Methuen, 1909).

5 She is commemorated in the Calendar of the Church of England on 15 June, the date of her death in 1941: see *Celebrating the Saints*, comp. and ed. Robert Atwell (Norwich: Canterbury Press, 1998). Some of her work has been included in anthologies of Anglican writing, e.g. Rowell et al., *Love's Redeeming Work*, 567–75 (see p.11 above). More extensive selections are to be found in *The Practical Mystic*, ed. Chapman. See also Armstrong, *Evelyn Underhill (1875–1941)*, and *Evelyn Underhill*, ed. Christopher J.R. Armstrong, Masters of Prayer Series (London: Church House, 1986); Olive Wyon, *Desire for God: A Study of Three Spiritual Classics* (London: Fontana, 1966), 81–116; *Evelyn Underhill: A Modern Guide to the Ancient Quest for the Holy*, ed. Dana Greene (New York: SUNY Press, 1988); *Evelyn Underhill: Artist of the Infinite Life*, ed. Dana Greene (London: Darton, Longman & Todd, 1991); *Evelyn Underhill: Fragments from an Inner Life. The Notebooks of Evelyn Underhill*, ed. Dana Greene (Harrisburg, PA: Morehouse, 1993); *The Ways of the Spirit: Evelyn Underhill*, ed. Grace A. Braume (New York: Crossroad, 1993); T.E. Johnson, 'In Spirit and Truth: Pneumatology, Modernism and their Relation to Symbols and Sacraments in the Writings of Evelyn Underhill' (PhD diss., University of Notre Dame, Indiana, 1996); Annice Callahan, *Evelyn Underhill: Spirituality for Daily Living* (Lanham, MD: University Press of America, 1997); *Radiance: A Spiritual Memoir of Evelyn Underhill*, ed. Bernard Bangley (Brewster, MA: Paraclete, 2004); *The Making of a Mystic: New and Selected Letters of Evelyn Underhill*, ed. Carol Poston (Champaign: Illinois University Press, 2010).

6 Evelyn Underhill, *Shrines and Cities of France and Italy*, ed. Lucy Menzies (London: Longmans, Green & Co, 1949).

7 *Grey World*, ch. XI (Willie's introduction to the craft of bookbinding), and 317–18 (the beautiful work he produces when he has found his vocation); *Lost Word*, 133–42 ('Translucent Enamel').

8   See e.g. Willie Hopkinson's exploration of Umbria: Underhill, *Grey World*, ch. XIX.

9   *The Lost Word*, ([v]). Subsequent references to this and other novels will be given parenthetically.

10 Underhill, *Shrines and Cities*, contains much criticism of contrasting representations of the Madonna (e.g. 60–3).

11 Underhill, *Letters,* 121–2.

12 Robyn Wrigley-Carr, 'The Baron, his Niece and Friends. Friedrich Von Hügel as a Spiritual Director, 1915–1925' (PhD diss., University of St Andrews, Scotland, 2013). The phenomenon of Anglo-Catholic 'modernism' in Underhill's own family network might well have been a resource for the understanding of Underhill's development, on which Von Hügel himself could draw. See Note 34 below. In the 1920s Underhill worked as reviews editor of *The Spectator* while T.S. Eliot was editor: see Francesca Bugliani Knox, 'Between Fire and Fire: T. S. Eliot's *The Waste Land*', *Heythrop Journal* 56 (2015), 235–48.

13 Underhill, *Shrines and Cities*, 65.

14 Ibid., 87.

15 For Underhill's discovery of Marian devotion, including her attention to the 'mysteries of the rosary', see Carol J. Poston, 'Evelyn Underhill and the Virgin Mary', *Anglican Theological Review* 97 (2015), 75–89. Cf. Grace Jantzen, 'The Legacy of Evelyn Underhill', *Feminist Theology* 4 (1993), 79–100.

16 See Alex Owen, *The Place of Enchantment: British Occultism and the Culture of Modernity* (Chicago: Chicago University Press, 2004), 49–50, 83, 88–9, 136, 221.

17 For Paul's experience of initiation into Freemasonry, see Underhill, *Lost Word*, 38–59 ('The First Degree'). Cf. Michael Stoeber, 'Evelyn Underhill on Magic, Sacrament and Spiritual Transformation', *Worship* 77 (2003), 132–51.

18 *William Blake: Selected Poetry and Prose*, ed. David Fuller (London: Pearson, 2000), 322. On ch. 4 of *Jerusalem*, see also David Fuller, *Blake's Heroic Argument* (London: Croom Helm, 1988), 211–23. W.B. Yeats (ed.) *The Poems of William Blake* (London: Lawrence and Bullen, 1893), 202, could have been Underhill's source.

19 W.B. Yeats, *The Celtic Twilight* (London: Lawrence and Bullen, 1893), 7.

20 Arthur Machen, *The Great God Pan; and, The Hill of Dreams* (Mineola, NY: Dover Publications, 2006). In the 'Introduction' to the former, Machen recalls the reviews of *Great God* (7–8). See also Nicholas Freeman, 'Nothing of the Wild Wood? Pan, Paganism and Spiritual Confusion in E.F. Benson's "The Man Who Went Too Far"', *Literature and Theology* 19 (2005), 22–33. On the tradition of 'Pan fiction' culminating in J.M. Barrie's *Peter Pan* and the search for alternatives to Christianity, see Eleanor Toland, '"And Did Those Hooves?" Pan and the Edwardians' (MA diss., Victoria University of Wellington, NZ, 2014).

21 *Grey World*, 49–50. Like many another Anglican of her time, perhaps, Underhill seems to have had very little knowledge of the lives of even 'assimilated' Jews except for their appearance in drawing rooms (Underhill, *Letters*, 256). She could be said to have made some amends in Evelyn Underhill, *Worship* (Guildford: Eagle, [1936] 1991), Part 2, ch. 10 on 'Jewish Worship', 149–66.

22 Cf. Evelyn Underhill, *The Golden Sequence* (London: Methuen, 1932), commented upon in Nadia Delicata, 'Evelyn Underhill's Quest for the Holy: A Lifetime Journey of Personal Transformation', *Anglican Theological Review* 88 (2007), 519–36. See also Kevin Hogan, 'The Proximity of Doctrine: Underhill and Sayers on the Trinity', *Anglican Theological Review* 78 (1996), 275–89.

23 On a subsequent visit Willie encounters a ceremony during which children throw flowers under the feet of the priest, an indication of one of Underhill's own passions, a 'prostration of the loveliest in Nature' in the presence of 'the mightiest offering in the world' (195). Underhill does not identify the occasion, but it is probably the celebration of Corpus Christi.

24 See 'St. Francis and Franciscan Spirituality', in Evelyn Underhill (ed.), *Mixed Pasture: Twelve Essays and Addresses* (London: Methuen, 1933), 147–68.

25 See also Underhill, *Letters, 57*.

26 See also Underhill's remark about the spiritual element in all good craftsmanship, including the perfectly adjusted home: *The Life of the Spirit and the Life of Today* (London: Methuen, 1922), 218.

27 E.g. *New York Evening Post*, 25 October 1904, and *Athenaeum*, 30 September 1904, 441–2.

28 See also Underhill, *Letters*, 207–8, 265.

29 The Graal, or Holy Grail, returns in Underhill's *The Column of Dust*.

30 Hugh also believes in the 'neighbourly qualities of theology and sanitation' (56): cf. Underhill, *Mixed Pasture*, on housing and living conditions.

31 In addition, in one extraordinary chapter, 'Saint Hubert's Way', Mark tells of his journey to a place where a rite is being celebrated for the presences of the wood, a rite in which atonement is being offered for the healing of creation which involves a penitent.

32 See also Evelyn Underhill, *The Mystery of Sacrifice* (London: Longmans, Green & Co., 1938), 22–3.

33 The novel received generous attention in (e.g.) *Athenaeum*, 16 February 1907, 192; *Punch,* 20 February 1907, 144; *The Bookman* 31 (1907), 273, 'Novel Notes'; *Dublin Review* 140 (January–April 1907), 424–5.

34 Underhill, *Letters*, 126, 143, 171, 182, 255, 272, 295. On her response to modernism, see Grace Adolphsen Brame, 'Evelyn Underhill: The Integrity of Personal Intellect and Individual Religious Experience as Related to Ecclesiastical Authority', *Worship* 68 (1994), 23–45; and Kevin Hogan, 'The Experience of Reality: Evelyn Underhill and Religious Pluralism', *Anglican Theological Review* 74 (1992), 334–47. For the importance of Catholic modernism for another author in this collection, Rose Macaulay, see above, 112–3.

35 Underhill, *Mixed Pasture,* 134.

36 Stoeber, 'Evelyn Underhill on Magic', 145.

37 From 'The Soul Complaineth Against the Body, and Is Answered', in *Spikenard. A Book of Devotional Love-Poems* (London: Grant Richards / Boston: Badger & Co., 1898), 23.

38 *Punch*, 10 November 1909, 342: see also Underhill's reaction in *Letters*, 107. Charles Williams thought the theme of the book to be superb, with possibilities of wit, terror, and sublimity, but only the wit achieved: 'She had not, on the whole, an imaginative style; the reason may be that her imagination moved too near to serious faith to allow itself, in her writings, much leisure' (Underhill, *Letters*, 10).

39 Letter to 'M.R.': Underhill, *Letters*, 106.

40 'To stand alongside the generous creative Love, maker of all things visible and invisible (including those we do not like) and see them with the eyes of the Artist-Lover is the secret of sanctity': Evelyn Underhill, *The School of Charity: Meditations on the Christian Creed* (London: Longmans, Green & Co., 1934), 14.

41 Mary J.H. Skrine, *Shepherd Easton's Daughter* (London: Arnold, 1925), foreword, vii, x.

42 Ibid., 323.

43 Ibid., Underhill's 'Foreword', x; Glen Cavaliero, *The Rural Tradition in the English Novel, 1900–1939* (London: Macmillan, 1977), 29.

Chapter 6

1 Dorothy L. Sayers, *Unnatural Death* (Sevenoaks: New English Library, [1927] 1987), 12.

2 Sayers acknowledges these influences among others: William Temple, *Readings in St John's Gospel* (London: Macmillan, 1942); Sir Edward Hoskyns, *The Fourth Gospel* (London: Faber and Faber, 1942).

3 All biographical information, unless otherwise indicated, is from Barbara Reynolds, *Dorothy L. Sayers: Her Life and Soul* (Sevenoaks: Hodder & Stoughton, 1993).

4 Hugh McLeod comments on the link between an increasing emphasis in Christian soteriology on the Incarnation, rather than the Atonement, among Anglicans campaigning for the abolition of the death penalty between 1918 and 1939: 'God and the Gallows', *Studies in Church History* 40 (2004): 330–56 (345).

5 Reynolds, *Dorothy L. Sayers*, 238, quotes a letter of Sayers's dated 14 September 1932: 'The new book … deals with the dope-traffic, which is fashionable at the moment, but I don't feel that part is very convincing, as I can't say "I know dope".'

6 Sayers wrote a preface to Collins's novel *The Moonstone* (1868), sometimes called the first detective novel and with a laudanum-soaked plot, for an Everyman reprint of 1944 (London: J.M. Dent & Sons / New York: E.P. Dutton & Co.).

7   The name de Momerie, derived from the old French verb *momer,* to disguise oneself, denotes the affectation of a sentiment one does not really hold, and is cognate with the English 'mummery'. Dian, of course, is the chaste and remorseless huntress of the Roman pantheon. Her name seems to have more to do with Wimsey's quest and preoccupations than with any identity she might – had she existed – have called her own.

8   Dorothy L. Sayers, *Murder Must Advertise* (Gollancz: London, 1933), 109.

9   Cf. the linkage of Pan and Christ in Evelyn Underhill's *The Grey World,* discussed in Ann Loades's essay in this volume, p. 78.

10 Dorothy L. Sayers, *The Man Born To Be King* (London: Gollancz, 1943), 310. Sayers, who takes the Greek lament from an anecdote by Plutarch, is probably influenced by G.K. Chesterton, who writes on it in his book of Christian apologetics *The Everlasting Man* (Sevenoaks: Hodder & Stoughton, 1925).

11 *The Mind of the Maker* (London: Methuen, 1941), 62.

12 On 'meteyard', see Leviticus 19:35 in KJV: 'Ye shall do no unrighteousness in judgment, in meteyard, in weight, or in measure.'

13 Sayers, *Murder Must Advertise*, 176, paraphrasing Matthew 10:28.

14 Robert Browning, 'Childe Roland to the Dark Tower Came' in *Men and Women* (1855), quoted from Robert Browning, *Childe Roland to the Dark Tower Came* (Cambridge: Orion, 1996), 19–29 (22).

15 The opening credits of the original 1996 film *Trainspotting,* a list recited deadpan of the consumer goods you could have instead of spending your money on heroin, makes the same point insistently enough for its Deuteronomic strapline 'Choose Life' to resonate with destructive ambivalence. However, telling as the parallels are (as a consumer product heroin is ideal, since like tobacco it has no lasting substance and its very consumption creates increased demand), it seems very important to say that they break down. Shopping is less dangerous than heroin.

16 Sayers, *Murder Must Advertise*, 246, quoting Amos 4:12.

17 Reynolds suggests that Sayers drew inspiration from St Peter's, Upwell, St Wendreda's, March and St Clement's, Terrington for her depiction of Fenchurch St Paul (240).

18 *The Nine Tailors* (London: Gollancz, 1934), 28. The phrase is used by the Rector of Fenchurch St Paul to describe Wimsey's arrival.

19 *OED Online*, 'stroke', 6a.

20 Psalm 99:1; Psalm 97:1.

21 Matthew 6:21.

22 Psalm 29:9.

23 *Nine Tailors*, 237. The Rector is quoting Psalm 7:12.

24 Dorothy L. Sayers, 'The Gates of Paradise' and excerpts from *The Devil to Pay* (1939) in Ann Loades (ed.), *Dorothy L. Sayers: Spiritual Writings* (London: SPCK, 1993), 12–15, 36–50. Cf. Charlotte Brontë's earlier interest in the idea of universal salvation, explored within Sara L. Pearson's essay in this volume.

25 'My Cattery': *Strong Poison* (Sevenoaks: Hodder & Stoughton, [1930] 1993), 47.
    'Superfluous women': a stock phrase quoted by Wimsey in *Unnatural Death*, 35.

26 Romans 12:19.

27 *Gaudy Night* (London: Victor Gollancz, 1935), 355.

28 *Unnatural Death*, 252. Cf. the discussion of this scene in Alison Shell's essay
    on P.D. James in this volume, 197.

Chapter 7

1 Rose Macaulay, *The Towers of Trebizond* (London: HarperCollins [1956],
   1995), 3; all citations are from this edition. I would like to thank Corpus
   Christi College, Oxford, and the Humanities Division, Oxford University,
   for funding research trips to various collections of Macaulay's papers in
   England and the United States, and the helpful staff of those centres. I am also
   grateful to Helen King, David Krooks, Kenneth Parker, Alison Shell and Gill
   Sutherland for their advice on this project and essay.

2 Trinity College, Cambridge (hereafter TCC), ERM 12.194 (12 February
   1957). To her more worldly friend, William Plomer, Macaulay put it more
   strongly, '[Princess Margaret] read aloud the bits she most enjoyed, which
   were about adultery.' Durham University Special Collections (hereafter DUSC),
   Plomer 132/8 (31 October 1956). The reference to adultery is absent from
   the published version of the letter to Johnson. Rose Macaulay, *Last Letters
   to a Friend 1952–1958*, ed. Constance Babington Smith (London: Collins,
   1962), 246. As noted elsewhere in this essay, Babington Smith's editions of
   Macaulay's letters omit some of her more acerbic remarks.

3 Elizabeth Bowen, 'Rose Macaulay, *The Towers of Trebizond*', in Allan Hepburn
   (ed.), *The Weight of a World of Feeling: Reviews and Essays by Elizabeth
   Bowen*, 301–3 (Evanston, IL: Northwestern University Press, 2017), 301.

4 An examination of papers related to Macaulay at the BBC Written Archives
   Centre, Caversham, reveals the extensive nature of her broadcasting work,
   and I am grateful to the archivist, Louise North, for her generous assistance.
   Sadly, I have only found a few recordings of Macaulay's voice: for example,
   BL, Sound and Moving Image, C1398/0105 C11; 1CS0005280. Macaulay
   has been served by three biographies but none engage in any depth with
   this aspect of her public life. Constance Babington Smith, *Rose Macaulay*
   (London: Collins, 1972); Jane Emery, *Rose Macaulay: a Writer's Life*
   (London: John Murray, 1991); Sarah LeFanu, *Rose Macaulay* (London:
   Virago, 2003).The sheer volume of Macaulay's output for newspapers
   and weeklies is captured in Kate Macdonald's impressive annotated
   bibliography and explored in her essay in the same volume. Kate Macdonald,
   'Annotated Bibliography of Rose Macaulay's Works, and Critical Studies'
   and 'Constructing a Public Persona: Rose Macaulay's Non-fiction', in Kate
   Macdonald (ed.), *Rose Macaulay, Gender and Modernity* (London: Routledge,
   2017), 213–320, 118–36. I am grateful to Dr Macdonald for making her work
   available to me. See also the entry for Macaulay in the online *ODNB*.

5   Woolf went on to suppose that 'leading lady novelists' did what they were told, remarking that she herself was 'not quite one of them'. She greeted Macaulay's first bestseller, *Potterism: a Tragi-Farcical Tract* (1920), a surgical dissection of the mass media which now more than ever has a prophetic edge to it, as a 'donnish' book, 'hard-headed' and 'masculine'. Cited in Gloria G. Fromm, 'The Worldly and Unworldly Fortunes of Rose Macaulay', *The New Criterion* 5:2 (October 1986), 38.

6   Noel Annan, 'The Intellectual Aristocracy', in J.H. Plumb (ed.), *Studies in Social History: A Tribute to G.M. Trevelyan* (London: Longmans, Green and Co, 1955), 254–60. See also the fuller genealogy provided in Babington Smith, *Rose Macaulay*, 237. 'Rose Macaulay', *ODNB* (accessed 4 January 2017).

7   Macaulay, *Last Letters*, 234–5 (1 October 1956).

8   Ibid.; DUSC, Plomer 132/8 (31 November 1956).

9   Francis Spufford, *Unapologetic: Why, Despite Everything, Christianity Can Still Make Surprising Emotional Sense* (London: Faber and Faber, 2012), 23.

10 Bowen, 'Rose Macaulay', 303.

11 *Told by an Idiot* (London: Virago, [1923] 1983), 3.

12 Pedersen gave Macaulay a copy of the *Oxford American Prayer Book Commentary*, by Massey Shepherd (New York: Oxford University Press, 1950) which she refers to frequently in her letters to Johnson. Her annotated copy is among her papers at the Harvey Ransom Center, University of Texas, Austin. Rose Macaulay, *Letters to a Friend 1950–1952*, ed. Constance Babington Smith (London: Collins, 1961), 33, 231, 235; *Last Letters*, 170, 172–3, 209, 217, 223, 313. I am grateful to Father James Koester, SSJE for his help in identifying Father Pedersen (1907–76).

13 TCC, ERM 15.72(1), 'To Frank Singleton' (23 September 1956).

14 Emery, *Rose Macaulay*, 160–3, 193–4. The publication of the letters caused considerable controversy: see my '"Oh dear, if only the Reformation had happened differently": Anglicanism, the Reformation, and Dame Rose Macaulay', in Peter Clarke and Charlotte Methuen (eds), *The Church and Literature*, Studies in Church History 48 (2012), 426–7. The recent publication of letters to her cousin Jean Smith reveals that Macaulay had confided the affair to her: *Dearest Jean: Rose Macaulay's Letters to a Cousin*, ed. Martin Ferguson Smith (Manchester: Manchester University Press, 2011), 24, 146–7. I am grateful to Prof. Smith for his advice.

15 See above, 107–8 and my discussion of Macaulay's criticisms of Johnson's Anglican papalism in '"Oh dear"', 427–8, 431–2; also Emery, *Rose Macaulay*, 298–302, 316–17. Cf. Babington Smith, *Rose Macaulay*, 193–7; David Hein, 'Rose Macaulay: A Voice from the Edge', in David Hein and Edward Henderson (eds), *C.S. Lewis and Friends* (London: SPCK, 2011), 105–7, 109–10; Jane Shaw, *Pioneers of Modern Spirituality* (London: DLT Ltd, 2018), 76, 81–8, 91–3, 97.

16 Maltby, '"Oh dear"', 431–2; Constance Babington Smith (ed.), *Letters to a Sister from Rose Macaulay* (New York: Atheneum, 1964), 179–80, 189, 252.

17 Heather Ingman, *Women's Spirituality in the Twentieth Century: An Exploration through Fiction* (Oxford: Peter Lang, 2004), 84.

18 His posthumous appreciation of her is published in Babington Smith, *Rose Macaulay*, 234–5. Macaulay was responsible for a car accident in 1939 in which both she and O'Donovan were injured: Emery, *Rose Macaulay*, 256–7.

19 TCC, ERM 12.40(1) (29 July 1951).

20 Emery, *Rose Macaulay*, 317.

21 Macaulay, *Letters to a Sister*, 202–3.

22 Rose Macaulay, 'The Best and Worst: II – Evelyn Waugh', *Horizon: A Review of Literature and Art* 14:84 (1946), 360–76. Referring to Macaulay's article, Waugh wrote to Nancy Mitford that 'Connolly has fled the country. Some say from his debts. I see he has hired a woman to attack me in his absence' (*The Letters of Nancy Mitford and Evelyn Waugh*, ed. Charlotte Mosley (London: Penguin [1996] 2000), 62). In his diary on 16 December 1946, Waugh remarked that 'This morning *Horizon* arrived with a long article by Rose Macaulay advising me to return to my kennel and not venture into the world of living human beings' (*The Diaries of Evelyn Waugh*, ed. Michael Davie (London: Weidenfeld and Nicholson, 1976), 667). When invited by Connolly to contribute his own piece to the *Horizon* series, Waugh chose Ronald Knox: Martin Stannard, *Evelyn Waugh: The Early Years, 1903–1939* (London: J.M. Dent & Sons Ltd, 1986), 199–200.

23 See Diarmaid MacCulloch, 'Modern Historians on the English Reformation' in Diarmaid MacCulloch, *All Things Made New: Writings on the English Reformation* (London: Penguin, 2016), 239–55, and my '"Neither too mean / nor yet too gay"?: The Historians, Anglicanism and George Herbert's Church', in Christopher Hodgkins (ed.), *George Herbert's Travels: International Print and Cultural Legacies* (Newark: University of Delaware Press, 2011), 27–55.

24 Macaulay knew her Milton well and authored both a biography and a radio play about him. Rose Macaulay, *Milton* (London: Duckworth, 1937). The latter was broadcast on the BBC's Third Programme in February 1947 (https://genome.ch.bbc.co.uk/schedules/third/1947-02-08#at-23.25); the radio script was published in a volume edited by the producer, Rayner Heppenstall: *Imaginary Conversations* (London: Secker & Warburg, 1948), 49–63.

25 Macaulay served on a panel to raise money for the charity Christian Action, led by Canon John Collins for the defence fund of anti-apartheid activists in South Africa. Writing to Johnson on New Year's Eve 1956, she said, 'The world grows more & more dreadful & illiberal & unchristian. What kind of year begins at midnight?' She praised Trevor Huddleston's *Naught for your Comfort* (he had written to her to say that he had enjoyed *Towers of Trebizond*). TCC, ERM 12.193 (31 December 1946). Six months later she concluded a letter to Canon J.A.L. Hardcastle by saying that she was 'just off to a meeting at the House of Lords about the new type of African slave, convened by Fr Huddleston & Michael Scott': TCC, ERM 15.74 (1–3) (26 June 1956). In other words, Macaulay's views and actions on race, although now dated in many ways, diverged sharply from Waugh's and she was an early supporter of the anti-apartheid movement. In contrast, see Waugh's 'Was he right to free the slaves?' for the *Daily Express* (15 July 1933) and reprinted in Donat Gallagher (ed.), *The Essays, Articles and Reviews of Evelyn Waugh* (London: Methuen, 1983), 134–6. Waugh decorated his loo with Ethiopian Christian art: David Pryce-Jones (ed.), *Evelyn Waugh and His World* (London: Weidenfeld & Nicholson, 1973), 157.

26 The editor of *The Catholic Herald*, Count Michael de la Bedoyere, gave it a glowing review whereas David Garnett in *The New Statesman* did not. See Martin Stannard (ed.), *Evelyn Waugh: The Critical Heritage* (London: Routledge, 1984), 185–93.

27 For example, LeFanu, *Rose Macaulay*, 260–1, 283; Emery, *Rose Macaulay*, 305–6.

28 BL, Add MS 81062, fols 13–14v.

29 'Evelyn Waugh to Rose Macaulay' (24 Dec 1946), Original Letter MS, Harry Ransom Center, University of Texas, Austin; for *The Tablet* controversy, see BL, Add MS 81062, fols 15–15v.

30 *The Tablet* (21 December 1947), 342. Woodruff was editor of the Roman Catholic weekly from 1936 to 1967 and had become friends with Waugh from their time as students in Oxford. He shared Waugh's secular and ecclesiastical politics. In the words of Auberon Waugh, Woodruff lived to see, and lament, *The Tablet* 'embrace all the liberal Catholic causes which he found least congenial': Auberon Waugh, 'Douglas Woodruff (1897–1978)', online *ODNB*.

31 Macaulay, *Dearest Jean*, 26, 204 (27 October 1946).

32 David Mathew, *Scotland under Charles I* (London: Eyre & Spottiswoode, 1955); Macaulay, *The Towers of Trebizond*, 3.

33 Macaulay, *Letters to a Friend*, 148.

34 Paul Hedges, 'Anglican Inter-Faith Relations from 1910 to the Twenty-First Century', in William L. Sachs (ed.), *The Oxford History of Anglicanism, Vol. V: Global Anglicanism, c. 1910–2000* (Oxford: Oxford University Press, 2018), 80–3.

35 Macaulay's friend John Betjeman was also drawn into the *Horizon* row: 'The Angry Novelist', *The Strand* (March 1947), 42–4.

36 'To Lord Kinross' (31 Dec 1958) in Mark Amory (ed.), *Letters of Evelyn Waugh* (London: Weidenfeld and Nicolson, 1981), 516.

37 BBC Written Archives Centre, Caversham, Rcont 1, Talks, Rose Macaulay 1949–1962, File II, 'P.H. Newby to Mr Lewin' (10 May 1951). The BBC was the locus of another public row between them that same year. Waugh accused Macaulay of political bias in her role in the production of the National Book League's list of the hundred best novels of the last thirty years: *The Listener* (31 May 1951), 872, 884; TCC, ERM 12.35 (12 June 1951) – again a more barbed account than in the published letter, *Letters to a Friend*, 144.

38 TCC, ERM 12.176 (5 April 1955). This is a fuller version than published in *Last Letters*, 197.

39 Macaulay was caustic: 'Evelyn knows very little of history or theology; when engaged in controversy in a paper, he has to telephone to Fr [Philip] Caraman at Farm Street for information.' TCC, ERM 15.87(1–8), 'To Helmut Rueckriegel' (22 December 1957). Macaulay met the young German diplomat by giving him a lift in London and a friendship developed in which she sought to introduce him to high Anglicanism, although she confessed she was worried that upon his return to Germany he 'will pope soon', which he appears to have done. Macaulay, *Letters to a Sister*, 213, 217, 219, 289.

40 'Evelyn Waugh', online *ODNB*.

41 In *Father Ralph*, the papal documents *Lamentabili sane exitu* and *Pascendi Dominici Gregis* (1907) were the final factors in the protagonist's decision to leave the priesthood. Gerald O'Donovan, *Father Ralph* (Dingle: Brandon Book Publishers Ltd, [1913] 1993), 343–53, 362–9; see Catherine Candy, *Priestly Fictions: Popular Irish Novelists of the Early 20th Century* (Dublin: Wolfhound Press, 1995), 60, 162–70. In private, and no doubt influenced by O'Donovan's own disillusionment regarding the papal condemnation of Catholic Modernism, the Church of Rome was to Macaulay 'that great rigid church': DUSC, Plomer 132/8 (31 Oct 1956).

42 Monica Furlong, 'Joyous Penitent', *The Guardian* (12 October 1972). For Peter Sherlock's discussion of Furlong's own creativity in relation to an extramarital relationship, see above, 183.

43 TCC, ERM 15.82 (23 July 1958). It has been suggested to me by Kenneth Parker and Jane Stevenson that Macaulay's correspondent might have been the Roman Catholic activist and writer, Maisie Ward, but I have been unable to confirm this. Macaulay was familiar with her work: Macaulay, *Letters to a Sister*, 232–3.

44 DUSC, Plomer 132/8 (31 October 1956).

45 Spufford, *Unapologetic*, 23.

Chapter 8

1 Hazel Holt and Hilary Pym (eds), *A Very Private Eye: The Diaries, Letters and Notebooks of Barbara Pym* (1st ed. London: Macmillan, 1984); Hazel Holt, *A Lot to Ask: A Life of Barbara Pym* (1st ed. London: Macmillan, 1990). All biographical information comes from these sources, unless otherwise referenced.

2 See Pamela Osborn, '"The priest and the doctor": Medical Mystique as a Substitute for Religious Authority in the Work of Barbara Pym and Philip Larkin', *Women: A Cultural Review* (online publication) 25:4 (2014), 384–94.

3 *A Few Green Leaves* (London: Granada, [1980] 1981), 18.

4 See also Judy Little, *The Experimental Self: Dialogic Subjectivity in Woolf, Pym and Brooke-Rose* (Carbondale: Southern Illinois University Press, 1996).

5 *Some Tame Gazelle* (London: Granada, [1950] 1981), 252.

6 See, for example, *A Very Private Eye,* ed. Holt and Pym, 197: 'the cosiness of non-intellectual conversation'.

7 Ibid., 213.

8 Quoted in *The Life and Work of Barbara Pym*, ed. Dale Salwak (Basingstoke: Macmillan, 1987), 20.

9 *The Telegraph*, 2 June 2013, http://www.telegraph.co.uk/culture/ books/10071305/Philip-Hensher-toasts-the-novelist-Barbara-Pym.html.

10 E.g. 'Like Jane Austen, Barbara Pym painted her pictures on a small square of ivory, and covered much the same territory as did her better-known predecessor', Alexander McCall Smith, 'Introduction', in *Excellent Women* (London: Virago, [1952] 2009), vii.

11 In *A Very Private Eye*, the editors note that Barbara burned her diaries that
    covered a year in which she had an affair with a married man, 'very serious on
    her part, less so on his' (97).

12 Ibid., 115.

13 Ibid., 122.

14 *Less Than Angels* (London: Granada, [1955] 1980), 232–3.

15 Pym died in 1980, before women could be ordained in the Church of England.

16 BBC Radio 4, 'Desert Island Discs', http://www.bbc.co.uk/programmes/p009mykr.

17 Holt and Pym, *A Very Private Eye*, 3.

18 *Some Tame Gazelle* (London: Jonathan Cape, 1950); Holt and Pym, *A Very
    Private Eye*, 3.

19 *Excellent Women* (London: Virago, [1952] 2009), 8.

20 *A Few Green Leaves* (London: Macmillan, 1980); see also Yvonne Cocking,
    '"Grey and pointed at both ends": The Genesis of *A Few Green Leaves* and
    its Public Reception' (Barbara Pym Society Lecture, 21 March 2009: available
    online at the Society's website, www.barbara-pym.org). *An Academic Question*
    (London: Macmillan, 1986): admittedly, this was published posthumously, and
    not prepared for publication by Pym herself.

21 John Bayley, 'Ladies', *London Review of Books* 8:15 (4 September 1986), 20–2.

22 Ibid.

23 *Quartet in Autumn* (London: Granada, [1977] 1980), 63.

24 Holt and Pym, *A Very Private Eye*, 190. She is referring to Matthew 25:1–13.

25 Judy B. McInnis, 'Communal Rites: Tea, Wine and Milton in Barbara Pym's
    Novels', in Hazel K. Bell (ed.), *No Soft Incense: Barbara Pym and the Church*
    (Hove: Anna Brown Associates/Barbara Pym Society, 2004), 36.

26 David Cockerell, 'What Relevance Does the Church of Barbara Pym Have to
    the World and Church of Today?' *No Soft Incense*, 3–4.

27 See Orna Raz, *Social Dimensions in the Novels of Barbara Pym, 1949–1962*
    (Lewiston, NY: Edwin Mellen Press, 2007).

28 James Woodforde, *The Diary of a Country Parson*, ed. John Beresford
    (Norwich: Canterbury Press, 1999), 19–20. These incidents are all taken from
    1764, between April and December.

29 *Quartet in Autumn*, 152, alluding to 1 Corinthians 14:40.

30 James Runcie, 'Foreword', *No Soft Incense*, 1. Runcie has himself created
    a fictional cleric, Sidney Chambers. Chambers, the flawed but humane and
    perceptive parish priest of Grantchester, has proved immensely popular with
    readers and viewers. See, for example, *Sidney Chambers and the Shadow of
    Death* (New York: Bloomsbury, 2012).

31 Ibid., 112.

32 This point is discussed in the essay on P.D. James in this volume, 198.

33 On this episode in *Jane Eyre*, see Sara L. Pearson's essay in this volume,
    22–3.

34 *No Fond Return of Love* (London: Granada, [1961] 1981), 174.

35 *Crampton Hodnet* (London: Macmillan, 1985, originally written around 1940), 92.

36 On Pym's comedy, see Annette Weld, *Barbara Pym and the Novel of Manners* (London: Macmillan, 1992).

37 This attitude constitutes an ongoing part of Pym's appeal. See Hannah Rosefield's *New Yorker* article of 3 April 2015: https://www.newyorker.com/books/pageturner/barbara-pym-and-the-new-spinster.

38 *Jane and Prudence*, 10–11.

39 *An Unsuitable Attachment* (London: Granada, 1983), 137.

40 Holt and Pym, *A Very Private Eye*, 319.

41 *A Glass of Blessings* (Harmondsworth: Penguin, [1958] 1980), 195.

42 Pym, typically, does not appear to be making a point about sexual politics in her depiction of gay relationships, unusual as she was in her open acceptance of them at that time. It is more that she is questioning what is 'normative' in relationships altogether. For this point, and other insights into Pym as a 'queer' writer, see J.L.J. Kennedy, 'Something Unsatisfactory: Queer Desires in Barbara Pym', *Women: A Cultural Review* 25:4 (2014), 356–70.

43 Ibid., 369.

44 *The Sweet Dove Died* (London: Macmillan, 1978), 14.

45 Holt and Pym, *A Very Private Eye*, 300.

46 Malcolm Torry defines 'parish' as 'territory, people, congregation and building': *The Parish: People, Place and Ministry*, ed. Malcolm Torry (Norwich: Canterbury Press, 2004), 12.

47 See, for example, Kate Charles, *A Drink of Deadly Wine* (1st ed. London: Headline, 1991), and D.M. Greenwood, *A Grave Disturbance* (1st ed. London: Headline, 1996). The place of the Church of England in recent detective fiction is also addressed in the essay on P.D. James in this volume, 193.

Chapter 9

1 Elizabeth Goudge, *The Joy of the Snow* (New York: Coward, McCann & Geoghegan, 1974), 69. Unless otherwise referenced, biographical information comes from this or from her entry in the online *ODNB*.

2 Ibid., 134.

3 Ibid., 198.

4 Ibid., 125. It is perhaps not accidental that both *A City of Bells* and *The Dean's Watch* (set respectively in Wells and Ely) feature a Dean who is independently wealthy, and thus better dressed and more comfortable than his fellow canons.

5 See, for instance, Susan D. Amussen, '"The part of a Christian man": The Cultural Politics of Manhood in Early Modern England', in Susan D. Amussen and Mark A. Kishlansky (eds), *Political Culture and Cultural Politics in Early Modern England* (Manchester: Manchester University Press, 1995), 213–33.

6   Megan Isaac, 'Misplaced: The Fantasies and Fortunes of Elizabeth Goudge', *The Lion and the Unicorn* 21:1 (1997), 86–111 (86).

7   Rosamond Lehmann and Cynthia Sandys, *Letters from our Daughters*, 2 parts (London: College of Psychic Studies, 1972); for the engagement with Christ, see e.g. Part 1, 14–15, 25–7, and Part 2, 3, 26–7; Oxfordshire History Centre (hereafter OHC) P/143/2/C/12, Elizabeth Goudge [hereafter EG] to Madeau Stewart, 14 September 1972. Goudge was so enthusiastic that she was trying to purchase additional copies to share with friends. On negotiations between Anglican theology and spiritualism earlier in the century, see Georgina Byrne, *Modern Spiritualism and the Church of England, 1850–1939*, Studies in Modern British Religious History, vol. 25 (Woodbridge: Boydell, 2010).

8   Elizabeth Goudge, *God So Loved the World* (New York: Coward McCann, 1951); *My God and My All: The Life of St Francis of Assisi* (New York: Coward McCann, 1959); and *A Diary of Prayer* (New York: Coward McCann, 1966).

9   Elizabeth Goudge, *The Heart of the Family* (London: Coronet Books, 1976), 247–8 (here the phrase is followed by a discussion of its possible meaning); Elizabeth Goudge, *The Castle on the Hill* (New York: Pyramid Books, [1941] 1972), 293.

10 These characters include David Eliot in *The Herb of Grace*; Sebastian Weber in *The Heart of the Family*; Miss Brown and Jo Isaacson in *The Castle on the Hill*; the elderly Mary Lindsay, Jean Anderson, and Charles Adams in *The Scent of Water*; Jocelyn Irvin in *A City of Bells*; Isaac Peabody in *The Dean's Watch*.

11 *New York Times*, 27 May 1956, 234. The reviewer was Nancie Matthews.

12 Lindsey Fraser, *Conversations with J.K. Rowling* (New York: Scholastic Books, 2002), 24.

13 Paul Kafka, quoted in Molly Moore, 'A Mysterious Passage to India', *Washington Post*, 27 April 1994, B1. Other reviewers were less kind both to Goudge and Aikath-Gyaltsen: Fawzia Afzal-Khan, 'India *Cranes' Morning* by Indrani Aikath-Gyaltsen', *World Literature Today* 70:1 (1996), 238.

14 The current Literature Online bibliography lists 6 works on Goudge, and two others that deal with her work in passing. The most recent of the former is Cynthia L. Hallen, 'Sacred Realism in the Novels of Elizabeth Goudge', *Literature and Belief*, 32:1/2 (2012): 53–66.

15 Goudge, *Joy of the Snow*, 255, 287.

16 Ibid., 189–90.

17 Reviews are quoted by P. Joan Smith, 'Elizabeth Goudge', *Dictionary of Literary Biography*, online, 191; and *British Novelists between the Wars* (Detroit: Gale Research, 1998), 107–15.

18 Goudge, *Joy of the Snow*, 103: this reference is somewhat incidental, but her father's high-church convictions, and his service in a slum parish, suggest that she may have imbibed Christian socialism from him. In *The Castle on the Hill*, a young man reflects on the disjuncture between the wealth of his family and the poverty of the cities (115–16).

19 Elizabeth Goudge, *The Rosemary Tree* (Peabody, MA: Hendrickson Publishing, [1956] 2015), 267.

20 Goudge, *Joy of the Snow*, 186.

21 Ibid., 235, 241.

22 Ibid., 242, 245.

23 OHC P 143/2/C/45, EG to Madeau Stewart, 1 March 1982.

24 Elizabeth Goudge, *The Dean's Watch* (New York: Pocket Books, [1960] 1961), 265.

25 Goudge, *Joy of the Snow*, 248.

26 Goudge repeats this in two different books: *The Herb of Grace* (London: Coronet Books, [1946] 1976), 44, and Goudge, *Heart of the Family*, 251.

27 OHC, EG to Madeau Stewart, P/143/2/C/45, 47, 48, 53 (1 March 1982, 21 April 1982, 5 July 1982, 16 November 1982).

28 Goudge, *Joy of the Snow*, 314–15.

29 Megan Isaac refers to this as the novel which makes most explicit Goudge's concern with economic justice: 'Misplaced: The Fantasies and Fortunes of Elizabeth Goudge', 98.

30 Elizabeth Goudge, *The Little White Horse* (New York: Puffin Books, [1946] 2001), 55.

31 The idea that holders of former monastic properties were cursed was common in the seventeenth century, and over time, ghost stories were often associated with former monastic properties: Alison Shell, *Oral Culture and Catholicism in Early Modern England* (Cambridge: Cambridge University Press, 2007), ch. 1, esp. 26–8, 47–8.

32 Laura King, 'Fatherhood, Masculinity and Romance in Popular Culture in Mid-Twentieth-Century Britain', in Alana Harris and Timothy Jones (eds), *Love and Romance in Britain, 1918–1970* (Basingstoke: Palgrave Macmillan, 2015), 41–60. Goudge was one of the founders of the Romantic Novelists' Association; the founders were a deliberately varied group. See also Stefan Horlacher and Kevin Floyd (eds), *Post-World-War II Masculinities in British and American Literature and Culture* (Farnham: Ashgate, 2013) and James Gilbert, *Men in the Middle: Searching for Masculinity in the 1950s* (Chicago: Chicago University Press, 2005).

33 Lucy Delap, 'Be Strong and Play the Man: Anglican Masculinities in the Twentieth Century', in Lucy Delap and Sue Morgan (eds), *Men, Masculinities and Religious Change in Twentieth-Century Britain* (Basingstoke: Palgrave Macmillan, 2013), 119–45 (120).

34 Goudge, *The Rosemary Tree*, 177.

35 Ibid., 177, 3, 7, 14.

36 Ibid., 23, 29, 31.

37 Goudge, *Heart of the Family*, 296. Goudge portrayed artists as profoundly affected by war; see also *The Castle on the Hill*, which features a violinist suffering despair in the midst of the blitz.

38   Elizabeth Goudge, *The Bird in the Tree* (Peabody, MA: Hendrickson Publishing, [1940] 2015), 37, 154; Goudge, *Heart of the Family*, 249.

39   Elizabeth Goudge, *A City of Bells* (New York: Popular Library, [1936] n.d.), 26.

40   OHC, P 143/2/C/48, Goudge to Madeau Stewart, 21 April 1982.

41   Goudge, *The Rosemary Tree*, 105, 148.

42   Ibid., 21–2, 26.

43   Ibid., 5, 40, 157.

44   Ibid., 297, 300.

45   *Herb of Grace*, 237; reflections on Hilary as one of the 'plain' Eliots, 35; also Goudge, *Bird in the Tree*, 40–1.

46   Both Alison Light, *Forever England: Femininity, Literature and Conservatism Between the Wars* (London: Routledge, 1991) and Nicola Humble, *The Feminine Middlebrow Novel, 1920s to 1950s: Class, Domesticity, and Bohemianism* (Oxford: Oxford University Press, 2001), discuss the way fiction in the inter-war years re-imagines gender. While some of their arguments apply to Goudge, she seems unusual in the way that her unmarried female characters are not primarily defined by sexual or romantic relationships.

Chapter 10

1   http://www.bbc.co.uk/programmes/p009mtdq, broadcast 17 January 1976. Her chosen book was Galsworthy's *The Forsyte Saga*; her luxury a gardening kit.

2   Angela Bull, *Noel Streatfeild: A Biography* (London: Collins, 1984), 128, 134: the publisher Mabel Carey suggested this plot re-use to Streatfeild. All otherwise unreferenced biographical material comes from Bull's study or the online *ODNB* article on Streatfeild.

3   The fatherless Whicharts create their own surname from 'Our Father Which Art in Heaven'; the Fossils of *Ballet Shoes* have been gathered by a fossil-hunting traveller.

4   Lenore Davidoff, 'The Separation of Home and Work? Landladies and Lodgers in Nineteenth-and Twentieth-Century England', in Sandra Burman (ed.), *Fit Work for Women* (London: Croom Helm, 1979), 64–97; Chiara Briganti and Kathy Mezei, *Domestic Modernism, the Interwar Novel, and E.H. Young* (Aldershot: Ashgate, 2006), 111–30, esp. 119–20.

5   On contemporary reactions, see Noel Streatfeild, *Beyond the Vicarage* (London: Collins, 1971), 54.

6   Nicola Humble, *The Feminine Middlebrow Novel, 1920s to 1950s: Class, Domesticity, and Bohemianism* (Oxford: Oxford University Press, 2001), 152–7, deems the 'dysfunctional' Sanger family in *The Constant Nymph* (neither hierarchically Victorian nor based on modern 'informed loving comprehension') as a significant long-term influence on family novels. Streatfeild's books run counter to this trend.

7   Debates in society generally over women's economic, political and familial roles were especially acute within the Anglican church, where gendered authority had both symbolic and practical significance: see Timothy Willem Jones, *Sexual Politics in the Church of England, 1857–1957* (Oxford: Oxford University Press, 2012).

8   Bull, *Noel Streatfeild*, 74; Streatfeild, *Beyond the Vicarage*, 54, cf. *Away from the Vicarage* (London: Collins, 1965), 67.

9   *The Bell Family* (London: Collins, 1954) and *New Town* (London: Collins, 1960). Streatfeild terms herself 'autobiographer' and refers to 'the facts of my own life': *A Vicarage Family* (London: Collins, [1963] 1979), 1. However, the three 'Vicarage' books adapt and occlude a great deal: Bull, *Noel Streatfeild*, 126, 219–30. Some family members had reservations regarding the mother's portrayal (Bull, *Noel Streatfeild*, 224).

10 Bull, *Noel Streatfeild*, 117–19.

11 She asserts that this parson 'was totally unlike Father' (Streatfeild, *Beyond the Vicarage*, 52).

12 See Angus McLaren, *Birth Control in Nineteenth-Century England* (London: Croom Helm, 1978), ch. 7.

13 Unlike some contemporaries (E.M. Delafield, Angela Thirkell), Streatfeild treats the evacuee situation not as comic material but with sympathy for the clash of values and expectations. Her descriptions of London slum life and lower-class characters draw on her voluntary childcare work in Deptford from the mid-1930s (Bull, *Noel Streatfeild*, 124–5).

14 See Jenny Hartley, *Millions Like Us: British Women's Fiction of the Second World War* (London: Virago, 1997), 25–31, on working-class matriarchs.

15 The traditionally gendered message of this conclusion contrasts with Streatfeild's later wartime and immediate post-war books, where having children is portrayed as problematic: for example, the childless widow Claire in *I Ordered a Table for Six* (London: Collins, 1942); and Penny in *Grass in Piccadilly* (London: Collins, 1947) who, also a widow, has concealed the birth of a child not her husband's.

16 Exceptionally, an Evangelical nanny in *Caroline England* (London: William Heinemann, 1937) terrorizes Caroline's childhood (29–45), and a jealous nanny in *Myra Carrol* (London: Collins, 1944) deliberately widens the gap between Myra and her children (192–4).

17 *A Vicarage Family*, 25, 29–30.

18 *Saplings*, 154, 160, 165.

19 Nancy Huse, *Noel Streatfeild* (New York: Twayne, 1994), refers to the 'moral suicide' of such mothers as Lena in Streatfeild's wartime novels (59); Hartley, *Millions Like Us*, notes Lena as one of the increasing number of bad mothers in later wartime fiction generally (112–22).

20 Streatfeild, *Beyond the Vicarage*, 51.

21 *A Vicarage Family*, 279, 284.

22 Monica Furlong (also featuring in this volume, chapter 12) was the only woman contributor, writing on 'Belonging and a Career' (119–36).

23 Huse, *Streatfeild*, 56–7, sees the book's essence as 'a complex critique of gender codes', treating the religious aspect as one instance among others of gendered authority.

24 Candon's position, standing for Anglo-Catholic views on sacramental marriage, goes further than Lambeth Conference resolutions: Jones, *Sexual Politics*, 21–2, 36–7.

25 Light, *Forever England*, 61–122 on Agatha Christie (esp. 93–9) has much of relevance to the genre and milieu.

26 Streatfeild does not complicate the issue of reparation by making the High Anglican Freda consider the implications of a suicide verdict upon her husband. Her other works (notably *The Silent Speaker* (London: Collins, 1961), concerned with the motive for a seemingly happy woman's self-killing) treat suicides sympathetically.

27 On the post-war Catholic novel, see introduction and ch. 5.

28 A.F. Cassis, *Graham Greene: An Annotated Bibliography of Criticism* (Metuchen, NJ: Scarecrow Press, 1981), 16–18.

29 Graham Greene, *Brighton Rock* (London: Heinemann, [1938] 1947), 331, on which see Mark Bosco, *Graham Greene's Catholic Imagination* (New York: Oxford University Press, 2005), 41–2, and Michael G. Brennan, *Graham Greene: Fictions, Faith and Authorship* (London: Continuum, 2010), 48–55.

30 The Anglican church's changing attitude towards the role of sex within marriage is the background to this issue: Jones, *Sexual Politics*, ch. 5.

31 Streatfeild, *Beyond the Vicarage*, 162; Bull, *Noel Streatfeild*, 222.

32 This is discussed in Emma Mason, 'Christina Rossetti and the Doctrine of Reserve', *Journal of Victorian Culture* 7:2 (2002), 196–219.

33 Bull, *Noel Streatfeild*, 85–9, 103–7.

34 Nicola Beauman, *A Very Great Profession: The Woman's Novel, 1914–39* (London: Persephone Books, [1983] 2008). The footnotes to this article point towards some of her successors.

35 Hartley, *Millions Like Us* (see index).

36 Persephone Books and Greyladies have reissued some, including several money-earners written as 'Susan Scarlett'.

37 Humble, *Feminine Middlebrow Novel*, ch. 1.

38 See Jane Williams's essay in this volume, ch.8.

Chapter 11

 1 Iris Murdoch, 'Existentialists and Mystics', in Peter Conradi (ed.), *Existentialists and Mystics: Writings on Philosophy and Literature* (London: Allen Lane, Penguin Press, 1997), 221–34 (228).

 2 *Remembering Iris Murdoch: Letters and Interviews*, ed. Jeffrey Meyers (New York: Palgrave Macmillan, 2013), 108–9.

3 Iris Murdoch, *The Sovereignty of Good* (New York: Schocken Books, [1970] 1971), 75. See also her essay 'On "God" and "Good"' in Conradi (ed.), *Existentialists and Mystics*, 337–65.

4 'John Haffenden Talks to Iris Murdoch', in Gillian Dooley (ed.), *From a Tiny Corner in the House of Fiction: Conversations with Iris Murdoch* (Columbia, SC: University of South Carolina Press, 2003), 124–38.

5 Iris Murdoch, *Metaphysics as a Guide to Morals* (New York: Penguin, [1992] 1993), 136.

6 Conradi, 252, 554–5.

7 Murdoch, *Metaphysics*, 137.

8 Ibid., 109.

9 Ibid., 135–6.

10 Ibid., 126.

11 See J.A.T. Robinson, *Honest to God* (1st ed. London: SCM, 1963); Don Cupitt, *Taking Leave of God* (1st ed. London: SCM, 1980). For Cupitt's relationship with Murdoch, see his 'Iris Murdoch: A Case of Star-Friendship', in Anne Rowe and Avril Horner (eds), *Iris Murdoch: Texts and Contexts* (New York: Palgrave Macmillan, 2012), 11–16.

12 Murdoch, *Metaphysics*, 127, 452–4.

13 Ibid., 454.

14 Conradi (ed.), *Existentialists and Mystics*, 226, 233. For a succinct account of what a religious life 'without illusions' might be, see 'My God: Iris Murdoch is Interviewed by Jonathan Miller', in Dooley (ed.), *From a Tiny Corner*, 209–17.

15 Meyers (ed.), *Remembering Iris Murdoch*, 97; Murdoch, *Metaphysics*, 419.

16 Meyers (ed.), *Remembering Iris Murdoch*, 109. David Robjant cautions against the tendency in Murdoch exegesis to claim her 'as either a reformist Christian theist, or a sort of Buddhist', saying that 'both of these approaches do violence' to her position: 'As A Buddhist Christian: The Misappropriation of Iris Murdoch', *Heythrop Journal* 52:6 (2011), 993–1008 (993).

17 'My God', 214–15.

18 For biographical information, I draw heavily throughout this essay on Peter Conradi's *Iris: The Life of Iris Murdoch* (New York: W.W. Norton and Company, 2001). See also the entry for Murdoch in the online *ODNB*. On Murdoch's ties to Anglicanism, Conradi observes that it was 'only within the framework of *that* Church [that she could] imagine a realization of the religious life', 335.

19 Meyers (ed.), *Remembering Iris Murdoch*, 88.

20 Conradi, *Iris*, 31.

21 Meyers (ed.), *Remembering Iris Murdoch*, 102; Conradi, *Iris*, 57.

22 Iris Murdoch, *The Red and the Green* (London: Chatto & Windus, 1965).

23 Conradi, *Iris*, 592, 249.

24 Ibid., 249.

25 Ibid., 248.

26 Ibid. Murdoch told Jonathan Miller, 'I think that a knowledge of Christianity in childhood is very important': 'My God', 217.

27 Conradi, *Iris*, 223. For Murdoch's visits to the Anglican Benedictine Malling Abbey (http://mallingabbey.org/ourhistory.html), and her contacts with the Roman Catholic Stanbrook Abbey and nuns in and out of convent life, see Conradi, *Iris*, 247–50, 418–23.

28 Conradi, *Iris*, 248. 'One of the joys of [*The Bell*] is the way its author, who later admitted to identifying "a little with the Abbess", in fact animates all of her characters' (Conradi, 421).

29 Ibid., 174.

30 For essays that grew out of these discussions, see *Faith and Logic: Oxford Essays in Philosophical Theology*, ed. Basil Mitchell (London: Allen & Unwin, 1957).

31 Conradi, *Iris*, 306.

32 According to Canon Brian Mountford, as cited by Conradi, 'in the early 1990s, [Murdoch] would occasionally be seen standing in the back of Oxford's University Church of St. Mary the Virgin, and gave one talk there, in the library: so many came to hear her that the doors had to be closed, to the vexation of those excluded'. Conradi goes on to say: 'while she could never entirely leave Christianity, she could never embrace its myths of Virgin Birth and Resurrection either; and God remained to her an anti-religious bribe, like the idea of an afterlife' (659, footnote 14).

33 *Henry and Cato* (London: Chatto & Windus, 1976); *Nuns and Soldiers* (1st ed. London: Chatto & Windus, 1980); *The Green Knight* (1st ed. London: Chatto & Windus, 1993).

34 *Nuns and Soldiers* (New York: Viking, 1980), 62.

35 Ibid., 60.

36 Conradi, *Iris*, 278, 298.

37 *Living on Paper: Letters from Iris Murdoch, 1934–1995*, eds Avril Horner and Anne Rowe (Princeton, NJ: Princeton University Press, 2015), 583.

38 *Paradise Lost*, book 4, line 110: quoted from *John Milton*, eds Stephen Orgel and Jonathan Goldberg (Oxford: Oxford University Press, 1991), 423.

39 *The Time of the Angels* (London: Penguin, 1966), 174. He is quoting the *Dies irae*, '*Nil inultum remanebit*' (nothing will remain unavenged).

40 In *Metaphysics*, 460, Murdoch writes, '"Spirituality" is always "breaking away", and is indeed at present "all over the place". (Spirit without the Absolute: the time of the angels.)'

41 E.g. *The Bell* (Frogmore, St. Albans, Herts: Triad Panther, [1958] 1976), 189–91.

42 *A Word Child* (New York: Viking, 1975). Hilary's diatribe against the 'sentimental old lie' of Christianity is given on 290–1.

43 *A Word Child*, 384, quoting from *Burnt Norton* I. See T.S. Eliot, *The Complete Poems and Plays, 1909–1950* (New York: Harcourt, Brace and

World, 1952), 117 (this edition has been used to reference all quotations from the *Four Quartets*).

44 *The Dry Salvages*, V (136).

45 *East Coker*, V (129).

46 *Little Gidding*, V (145). An earlier evocation of Dame Julian's words can be found in Section V (142–3).

47 I offer a fuller account of the novel in *The Language of Grace: Flannery O'Connor, Walker Percy, and Iris Murdoch* (New York: Seabury Classics, 2004), 85–124.

48 'A Collect or Prayer for all Conditions of Men', BCP, 267.

49 *The Bell*, 52. See the essay on P.D. James in this volume for a discussion of James's detective novel *The Black Tower* (1975), which bears interesting similarities to Murdoch's work.

50 Murdoch, *Metaphysics*, 496.

51 The Abbess is quoting Matthew 10:16.

52 *The Bell*, 270, 252.

53 'I am the voice of Love. I am called Gabriel.'

Chapter 12

1 See, for example, her opposition to the 'flying bishops' scheme created by the Church of England in 1993 following the approval of the ordination of women as priests. Monica Furlong (ed.), *Act of Synod, Act of Folly?* (London: SCM Press, 1998).

2 Michael De-la-Noy, 'Obituary: Monica Furlong', *Guardian* (17 January 2003).

3 Monica Furlong, *Travelling In* (London: Hodder and Stoughton, 1971), 88–93.

4 Monica Furlong, *With Love to the Church* (London: Hodder and Stoughton, 1965), 94. Emphasis in original.

5 See for example Monica Furlong, 'Introduction: A "Non-Sexist" Community' in the St Hilda Community, *Women Included: A Book of Services and Prayers* (London: SPCK, 1991), 5–15.

6 Furlong attributed this phrase to Joost de Blank: Monica Furlong, 'As if Love were True', *The Tablet* (5 December 1987), 10, 12.

7 For biographical details see Monica Furlong's entry in the online *ODNB*.

8 Graham James, *The Lent Factor* (London: Bloomsbury, 2015), ch. 5.

9 Monica Furlong, *Puritan's Progress: A Life of John Bunyan* (London: Hodder and Stoughton, 1975); Monica Furlong, *Merton: A Biography* (London: Collins, 1980).

10 Monica Furlong, *The Cat's Eye* (London: Magnum Books, 1976); Monica Furlong, *Cousins* (London: Weidenfeld and Nicolson, 1983). All citations below are from these editions.

11 Monica Furlong, *Divorce: One Woman's View* (London: Mothers' Union, 1981); Monica Furlong, *Shrinking and Clinging* (London: Friends Homosexual Fellowship, 1981).

12 Monica Furlong, *Bird of Paradise: Glimpses of Living Myth* (London: Mowbray, 1995), 89–94.

13 Margaret Webster, *A New Strength, A New Song: The Journey to Women's Priesthood* (London: Mowbray, 1994); Sean Gill, *Women and the Church of England from the Eighteenth Century to the Present* (London: SPCK, 1994), 232–76.

14 See for example *Women Included*; Monica Furlong, *A Dangerous Delight: Women and Power in the Church* (London: SPCK, 1991).

15 Monica Furlong, *Wise Child* (London: Victor Gollancz, 1987; New York: Knopf, 1987; German trans. Loewe Verlag, 2000); *A Year and a Day* (London: Victor Gollancz, 1990; New York: Random, 1991; released as *Juniper* (London: Corgi Books, 1992)); *Colman* (New York: Random, 2004).

16 Monica Furlong, *Robin's Country* (London: Hamish Hamilton, 1994; New York: Knopf, 1995, 1997; Puffin, 1996; Random House, 1998).

17 Furlong, *Bird of Paradise*; Monica Furlong, *Flight of the Kingfisher: A Journey Among the Kukatja Aborigines* (London: HarperCollins, 1996). For a critical examination of Furlong's attempt to engage with Aboriginal culture, see Mitchell Rolls, 'Cultural Colonisation: Monica Furlong and the Quest for Fulfilment', *Australian Feminist Law Journal* 11 (September 1998), 46–64.

18 Clare Herbert, 'Introduction', in Monica Furlong (ed.), *Prayers and Poems* (London: SPCK, 2004), vii–xvii.

19 Monica Furlong (ed.), *Our Childhood's Pattern: Memories of Growing Up Christian* (London: Mowbray, 1995), x–xix. This collection includes a chapter by P.D. James, the last author considered in this collection.

20 Furlong, *Our Childhood's Pattern*, xiv; Furlong, *Bird of Paradise*, 38. Sayers's radio plays are discussed in the chapter by Jessica Martin: see above, Chapter 6.

21 Furlong, *Our Childhood's Pattern*, xv.

22 John Peart-Binns, *Archbishop Joost de Blank: Scourge of Apartheid* (London: Muller, Blond and White, 1987), 56.

23 Furlong, *Bird of Paradise*, 58.

24 Furlong, *With Love to the Church*, 56.

25 *C of E: The State It's In* (London: Hodder and Stoughton, 2000), x.

26 Furlong, *Our Childhood's Pattern*, xix. For similar sentiments expressed in Rose Macaulay's fiction, see above, 106–7.

27 Monica Furlong, Erica F. Vere and David Blamires, *Shrinking and Clinging; Transition to Openness; Postscript to 'Homosexuality from the Inside'* (n.p.: Friends Homosexual Fellowship, 1981). This unpaginated pamphlet comprises three short articles by three different authors, of which Furlong's is the first. Quotations come from pp. [1] and [3].

28 Furlong, *Bird of Paradise*, 90.

29 Furlong, *Prayers and Poems*, xii.

30 Furlong, *Bird of Paradise*, 90–1.

31 For a discussion of the autobiographical elements to do with adultery in Rose Macaulay's *The Towers of Trebizond*, with which Furlong was familiar, see the chapter by Judith Maltby, above, Chapter 7. For similar treatment of these themes by Iris Murdoch, see the chapter by Peter Hawkins, above, Chapter 11.

32 Furlong, *Cousins*, 39; cf. 53.

33 Furlong, *With Love to the Church*, 78.

34 Furlong, *Bird of Paradise*, 120.

35 Furlong, *Flight of the Kingfisher*, 14.

36 Furlong discusses these in *Dangerous Delight*, 131–43.

37 Furlong, *Merton: A Biography*, xviii.

38 Furlong, *Bird of Paradise*, 8.

39 Furlong, *Travelling In*, 64.

40 Furlong, *Bird of Paradise*, 102.

41 Furlong, *With Love to the Church*, 16.

42 Furlong, *Dangerous Delight*, 7.

43 Monica Furlong, *Thérèse of Lisieux* (London: Darton, Longman and Todd, [1987] 2001), 4.

44 *C of E: The State It's In*, 3.

45 Furlong, *Bird of Paradise*, 11.

Chapter 13

1 On James's Anglicanism, see her essay 'As It Was in the Beginning', in Caroline Chartres (ed.), *Why I Am Still An Anglican: Essays and Conversations* (London: Continuum, 2006), ch. 2; on her public service, see her entry in the online *ODNB*. Famously, she interrogated the Director-General of the BBC over the misuse of public money: see John Plunkett, 'BBC Director General Mark Thompson Thrown by P.D. James's Detective Work', *Guardian*, 31 December 2009.

2 On James as a theological thinker, see Jo Ann Sharkey, 'Theology in Suspense: How the Detective Fiction of P.D. James Provokes Theological Thought' (M. Phil. thesis, University of St Andrews, 2011).

3 See ch. 6 in this volume, 94–6.

4 See introduction and ch. 7 in this volume.

5 *A Taste for Death* (London: Penguin, 1986), 92.

6 On James's admiration for Pym, see the account of her after-dinner speech to the Barbara Pym Society in its newsletter: *Green Leaves* 9:2 (November 2003), 2. On *Some Tame Gazelle*, see introduction, 7–8, and ch. 8, 123–4.

7 James pays tribute to Dorothy L. Sayers and Agatha Christie in *Talking about Detective Fiction* (Oxford: Bodleian Library, 2009), ch. 5. On Christie's

religious beliefs and practices, see Janet Morgan, *Agatha Christie: A Biography* (London: HarperCollins, [1985] 2017), especially chs 13–14.

8 *Nemesis* (London: HarperCollins, 2003), 91. Cf. Suzanne Bray, 'A New Generation of Anglican Crime Writers', ch. 5 in Linda Martz and Anita Higgie (eds), *Questions of Identity in Detective Fiction* (Newcastle: Cambridge Scholars' Publishing, 2007).

9 *See How They Run* (London: Samuel French, 1947), Act III.

10 Maxim Jakubowski, the owner of a bookshop specializing in crime fiction, has described the readership as 'the sort who don't touch anything with a stamp of realism – they like the murder to be a bit like in Agatha Christie, where it doesn't really feel real': quoted in Alison Flood, 'Murder Most Cosy', *The Guardian*, 3 August 2015.

11 On 15 April 2018, the Pan Macmillan website page recommending cosy crime fiction was illustrated by the picture of an English village, dominated by a church spire: https://www.panmacmillan.com/blogs/crime-thriller/cosy-crime-books-lavender-ladies-agatha-christie.

12 Detective novelists deploying an Anglican backdrop sometimes invoke Barbara Pym. Kate Charles, for instance, has described Pym as 'the most profound literary influence on my work': http://www.katecharles.com/about-the-author. See also Kathy Ackley, 'What is a "Pymish" Mystery Novel?', paper at the Barbara Pym Society of North America, Harvard University, 24–5 November 2007, available online at www.barbara-pym.org.

13 Cf. Ulrike Tancke, *Deceptive Fiction: Trauma and Violence in Contemporary Writing* (Newcastle: Cambridge Scholars' Publishing, 2015).

14 Avril Horner, '"Refinements of Evil": Iris Murdoch and the Gothic', in Anne Rowe and Avril Horner (eds), *Iris Murdoch and Morality* (London: Palgrave Macmillan, 2010), 70–84. *The Black Tower* recalls Iris Murdoch's earlier novel *The Bell* (1958), also set in an alternative religious community; see ch.11 in this volume, 170–3.

15 See the Introduction to this volume, 6.

16 The political adviser Alastair Campbell's remark, 'We don't do God', pre-empting comment from a Christian prime minister, Tony Blair, has come to emblematize this unease. See Colin Brown, 'Campbell Interrupted Blair As He Spoke of his Faith', *The Telegraph*, 4 May 2003.

17 Berowne's first name may allude to the conversion of St Paul (Acts 9).

18 Sigmund Freud, *The Uncanny*, trans. David McLintock, intro. Hugh Haughton (London: Penguin, 2003), 124.

19 *Death of an Expert Witness* (London: Faber and Faber, [1977] 2010), 143.

20 Given that James frequently spoke against the Prayer Book's liturgical sidelining and served as vice-president of the Prayer Book Society, this is a loaded comment. However, she also served on the Church of England's Liturgical Commission between 1991 and 2000, while the Church of England's current official liturgical resource, *Common Worship*, was being compiled. See Anthony Kilmister, 'Remembering P.D. James', *Prayer Book Society Journal*, Lent 2015, 18.

21 *BCP*, Psalm 39:14–15.

22 She described herself as reciting the 'Collect Against All Perils' every night (Kilmister).

23 *The Best Detective Stories of the Year, 1928*, eds Father Ronald Knox and H. Harrington (London: Faber & Gwyer, 1929), xi.

24 See Claire Jarvis, *Exquisite Masochism: Marriage, Sex and the Novel Form* (Baltimore: Johns Hopkins University Press, 2016).

25 However, when *The Black Tower* was adapted into a mini-series (dir. Ronald Wilson, Anglia Television, 1985), Father Baddeley appeared as a character.

26 Quoted from the edition in *The Lord Peter Omnibus* (London: Victor Gollancz, 1964).

27 A caricatured relationship of this kind features, for instance, in Ngaio Marsh's *Overture to Death* (1st ed. 1939).

28 'They are all gone into the world of light', *Henry Vaughan: The Complete Poems*, ed. Alan Rudrum (Harmondsworth: Penguin, [1976] 1983), 246–7.

29 Dalgliesh's eventual wife, Emma Lavenham (first featured in *Death in Holy Orders*), is a literary scholar specializing in the metaphysical poets.

30 A very similar scene figures in ch. 4 of *Death in Holy Orders*.

31 A famous elegiac use of the metaphor comes in Alfred, Lord Tennyson, *In Memoriam*: 'O life as futile, then, as frail! / O for thy voice to soothe and bless! / What hope of answer, or redress? / Behind the veil, behind the veil.' Quoted from *In Memoriam*, eds Susan Shatto and Marion Shaw (Oxford: Clarendon, 1982), LVI, 25–28.

32 'Outlook': outstare, look beyond (*OED*, *v*, 3).

33 See above, 195.

34 Matthew 27:46 and Mark 15:34, alluding to Psalm 22:1. See *On What Cannot Be Said: Apophatic Discourses in Theology, Philosophy, Literature and the Arts*, ed. William Franke (Notre Dame: Notre Dame University Press, 2007).

35 Susan Rowland, *From Agatha Christie to Ruth Rendell* (Basingstoke: Palgrave, 2001), 35.

36 See Jessica Martin's essay in this volume, esp. 94–8.

37 James appears to be conflating Jesus's self-characterization as the Good Shepherd (John 10:1–16) with the Parable of the Lost Sheep (Luke 15:1–6, Matthew 18:12–14); the intention may be to suggest both Miss Wharton's familiarity with Scripture and her mental agitation.

38 This adapts the centurion's words in Matthew 8:8: 'Lord, I am not worthy that thou shouldest come under my roof: but speak the word only, and my servant shall be healed'. Cf. the prayer before receiving Communion in *The Anglican Missal* (this ed. London: Society of SS. Peter and Paul, 1921), C 41, and the congregational response to the invitation to Holy Communion in Order 1 of *Common Worship* (available online at www.churchofengland.org) which post-dates *A Taste for Death*. 'But speak but the word' seems intended as Miss Wharton's personal adaptation, emphasizing her diffidence.

39   On liturgical modernization, see Jeremy Morris, 'Anglicanism in Britain and Ireland', ch. 16 in *The Oxford History of Anglicanism, Vol. IV: Global Western Anglicanism, c.1910–present*, ed. Jeremy Morris (Oxford: Oxford University Press, 2017), 425–6.

40   E.g. Hannah Furness, 'Modern Bible Is Too Dull, Says Philip Pullman', *Telegraph* (14 January 2015).

41   *The Skull Beneath the Skin* (London: Sphere Books, [1982] 1983), 254. James used the phrase 'devices and desires' as a title for a novel in 1989.

42   *The Alternative Service Book 1980* (London / Cambridge / Colchester: Clowes / SPCK / Cambridge University Press, 1980), Morning Prayer, 48. For the 1662 General Confession, see *BCP*, 240–1.

43   James is likely to have known C.S. Lewis's *Miserable Offenders: An Interpretation of Prayer Book Language* (Boston: Editorial Board Advent Paper, 1950): Beatrice Groves, personal communication. My thanks to Dr Groves for discussions relating to this point.

44   *OED*, 'miserable'.

45   Interview in *Observer*, 15 July 2012. James's interlocutors were the detective novelists Nicci Gerrard and Sean French, a husband-and-wife team who collaborate under the *nom de plume* 'Nicci French'.

46   The doctrine is best known for its importance in the life story of St Augustine, who converted from Manichaeism to Christianity: see *Confessions*, trans. & ed. Henry Chadwick (1st ed. Oxford: Oxford University Press, 1992).

47   *OED*, 'Manichaean', *n* and *adj*.

48   The Catholic Encyclopaedia describes it as a 'literary and refined' mode of thought (www.newadvent.org, under 'Manichaeism').

49   On Bloom's affinity with Gnosticism, see Douglas Robinson, *Exorcising Translation: Towards an Intercivilisational Turn* (New York: Bloomsbury, 2016), section 2:3:4.

50   On contemporary uses of the phrase 'Cool Britannia', see John Ayto, *Movers and Shakers: A Chronology of Words that Shaped our Age* (Oxford: Oxford University Press, 2006), 233.

51   See 'Mozley, James Bowling', online *ODNB*. On the Gorham Judgement, see Michael Wheeler, *The Old Enemies: Catholic and Protestant in Nineteenth-Century English Culture* (Cambridge: Cambridge University Press, 2006), ch. 7.

52   *England's Thousand Best Churches* (London: Penguin, 1999).

Afterword

1   Rumer Godden, *In This House of Brede* (London: Virago, [1969] 2013), 19.

FURTHER READING

Chapter 1

Brontë, Charlotte. *Jane Eyre*. 1847. Reprinted with notes and introduction. Ed. Margaret Smith, with introduction and notes by Sally Shuttleworth. Oxford: Oxford University Press, 2000.

Brontë, Charlotte. *The Professor*. 1857. Reprinted with notes and introduction. Ed. Margaret Smith and Herbert Rosengarten, with introduction by Margaret Smith. Oxford: Oxford University Press, 2008.

Brontë, Charlotte. *Shirley*. 1849. Reprinted with notes and introduction. Ed. Herbert Rosengarten and Margaret Smith, with introduction and notes by Janet Gezari. Oxford: Oxford University Press, 2007.

Brontë, Charlotte. *Villette*. 1853. Reprinted with notes and introduction. Ed. Margaret Smith and Herbert Rosengarten, with introduction by Tim Dolin. Oxford: Oxford University Press, 2000.

Gaskell, Elizabeth. *The Life of Charlotte Brontë*. Reprinted with notes and introduction. Ed. Angus Easson. Oxford: Oxford University Press, 1996.

Thormählen, Marianne. *The Brontës and Religion*. Cambridge: Cambridge University Press, 1999.

Thormählen, Marianne, ed. *The Brontës in Context*. Cambridge: Cambridge University Press, 2012.

Chapter 2

Cutt, Margaret Nancy. *Ministering Angels: A Study of Nineteenth-Century Evangelical Writing*. Wormley, Herts: Five Owls Press, 1979.

Giberne, Agnes. *A Lady of England: The Life and Letters of Charlotte Maria Tucker*. New York: A.C. Armstrong and Son, 1895.

Tucker, Charlotte Maria. *The Claremont Tales; Or, Illustrations of the Beatitudes*. London: Gall and Inglis, 1852.

Tucker, Charlotte Maria. *The Rambles of a Rat*. London: T. Nelson and Sons, 1857.

Tucker, Charlotte Maria. *The Story of a Needle*. London: T. Nelson and Sons, 1858.

Tucker, Charlotte Maria. *The Lady of Provence; Or, Humbled and Healed, A Tale of the First French Revolution*. London: Thomas Nelson and Sons, 1871.

Tucker, Charlotte Maria. *Daybreak in Britain*. London: Religious Tract Society, 1880.

Chapter 3

Coghill, Mrs Harry (Annie Louisa Walker). *The Autobiography and Letters of Mrs M.O.W. Oliphant*. Edinburgh and London: William Blackwood and Sons, 1899.

Jay, Elisabeth. *Mrs Oliphant: 'A Fiction to Herself', A Literary Life*. Oxford: Oxford University Press, 1995.

Levine, George. 'Reading Margaret Oliphant'. *Journal of Victorian Culture* 19:2 (2014): 232–46.

Milbank, Alison. *Dante and the Victorians*. Manchester: Manchester University Press, 1998.

Oliphant, Margaret. *The Autobiography of Margaret Oliphant*. Ed. Elisabeth Jay. Oxford: Oxford University Press, 1990.

Oliphant, Margaret. *A Beleaguered City and Other Stories*. Ed. Merryn Williams. Oxford: Oxford University Press, 1988.

Oliphant, Margaret. *The Perpetual Curate*. Intro. Penelope Fitzgerald. London: Virago, 1987.

Oliphant, Margaret. *The Rector / The Doctor's Family*. Intro. Penelope Fitzgerald. London: Virago, 1986.

Chapter 4

Novels

The Daisy Chain, or, Aspirations: A Family Chronicle. 2 vols. London: John W. Parker and Son, 1856.

Heartsease, or, The Brother's Wife. 2 vols. London: John W. Parker and Son, 1854.

The Heir of Redclyffe. 2 vols. London: John W. Parker and Son, 1853.

The Pillars of the House, or, Under Wode, Under Rode. 4 vols. London and New York: Macmillan and Company, 1873.

Criticism

The Charlotte Mary Yonge Fellowship maintains a useful website www.cmyf.org with links to primary and secondary material.

Courtney, Julia, and Clemence Schultze (eds). *Characters and Scenes: Studies in Charlotte M. Yonge*. Abingdon: Beechcroft Books, 2007.

Hayter, Alethea. *Charlotte Yonge*. Plymouth: Northcote House, 1996.

There is much biographical information and a bibliography in the online *Letters of Charlotte Mary Yonge*, ed. Ellen Jordan, Charlotte Mitchell and Helen Schinske https://c21ch.newcastle.edu.au/yonge/.

Chapter 5

Chapman, Raymond, ed. *The Practical Mystic: Evelyn Underhill and Her Writings*. Norwich: Canterbury Press, 2012.

Loades, Ann. *Evelyn Underhill*. London: Fount, 1997.

Stoeber, Michael. 'Evelyn Underhill on Magic, Sacrament and Spiritual Transformation'. *Worship* 77 (2003): 132–51.

Underhill, Evelyn. *Mysticism: A Study in the Nature of Man's Spiritual Consciousness*. London: Methuen, 1911. Several modern editions. Details of the Evelyn Underhill Association can be found at www.evelynunderhill.org.

Chapter 6

Hitchman, Janet. *Such a Strange Lady: An Introduction to Dorothy L. Sayers*. London: HarperCollins, 1975.

Latham, Sean. *Am I a Snob? Modernism and the Novel*. Ithaca, NY: Cornell University Press, 2003.

Leavis, Q.D. 'The Case of Miss Dorothy Sayers'. *Scrutiny* 6:3 (1937): 334–40.

The Letters of Dorothy L. Sayers. Ed. Barbara Reynolds. 5 vols. Sevenoaks: Hodder and Stoughton, 1996-2002.

Loades, Ann, ed. *Dorothy L. Sayers: Spiritual Writings*. London: SPCK, 1993.

Loades, Ann. 'Dorothy L. Sayers: War and Redemption', in *C.S. Lewis and Friends: Faith and the Power of Imagination*, ed. D. Hein and E. Henderson (London: SPCK, 2011): 53–70.

Reynolds, Barbara. *Dorothy L. Sayers: Her Life and Soul*. Sevenoaks: Hodder and Stoughton, 1993.

Chapter 7

Fiction

Macaulay, Rose. *They Were Defeated*. 1932. Reprinted with an introduction by Susan Howatch. Oxford: Oxford University Press, 1981.

Macaulay, Rose. *Told by an Idiot*. 1923. Reprinted with an introduction by A.N. Wilson. London: Virago, 1983.

Macaulay, Rose. *The Towers of Trebizond*. 1956. Reprinted London: Flamingo, 1993.

O'Donovan, Gerald. *Father Ralph*. 1913. Dingle: Brandon Book Publishers Ltd, 1993.

Non-fiction

Macaulay, Rose. *Some Religious Elements in English Literature*. London: Hogarth Press, 1931.

Macaulay, Rose. *Milton*. London: Duckworth, 1934.

Letters

Macaulay, Rose. *Letters to a Friend 1950–1952*. Ed. Constance Babington Smith. London: Collins, 1961.

Macaulay, Rose. *Last Letters to a Friend 1952–1958*. Ed. Constance Babington Smith. London: Collins, 1963.

Macaulay, Rose. *Letters to a Sister*. Ed. Constance Babington Smith. London: Collins, 1964.

Macaulay, Rose. *Dearest Jean: Rose Macaulay's Letters to a Cousin*. Ed. Martin Ferguson Smith. Manchester: Manchester University Press, 2011.

Chapter 8

Pym's novels:

Some Tame Gazelle. London: Jonathan Cape, 1950.

Excellent Women. London: Jonathan Cape, 1952.

Jane and Prudence. London: Jonathan Cape, 1953.

Less than Angels. London: Jonathan Cape, 1955.

A Glass of Blessings. London: Jonathan Cape, 1958.

No Fond Return of Love. London: Jonathan Cape, 1961.

Quartet in Autumn. London: Macmillan, 1977.

The Sweet Dove Died. London: Macmillan, 1978.

A Few Green Leaves. London: Macmillan, 1980.

An Unsuitable Attachment. London: Macmillan, 1982.

Crampton Hodnet. London: Macmillan, 1985.

An Academic Question. London: Macmillan, 1986.

Civil to Strangers. London: Macmillan, 1987.

All are widely available in reprints.

Biographical and critical material:

Allestree, Ann. *Barbara Pym: A Passionate Force*. Hove: Book Guild, 2015.

Bell, Hazel K., ed. *No Soft Incense: Barbara Pym and the Church*. Oxford: Barbara Pym Society/Anna Brown Associates, 2004.

Cotsell, Michael. *Barbara Pym*. Basingstoke: Palgrave Macmillan, 1989.

Holt, Hazel. *A Lot to Ask: A Life of Barbara Pym*. 1st ed. London: Macmillan, 1990.

A Very Private Eye: Barbara Pym, An Autobiography in Letters and Diaries. Ed. Hazel Holt and Hilary Pym. London: Macmillan, 1984. This contains excerpts from Pym's diaries in the Bodleian Library, Oxford.

See also www.barbara-pym.org for the Barbara Pym Society papers.

For Pym's own library, see LibraryThing, http://www.librarything.com/catalog/Barbara_Pym, maintained by Alison Felstead.

Chapter 9

Goudge, Elizabeth. *The Bird in the Tree*. London: Duckworth, 1940.

Goudge, Elizabeth. *The Castle on the Hill*. London: F.A. Thorpe, 1942.

Goudge, Elizabeth. *A City of Bells*. London: Duckworth, 1936.

Goudge, Elizabeth. *The Heart of the Family*. London: Hodder & Stoughton, 1953.

Goudge, Elizabeth. *The Herb of Grace* (Published in the US as *Pilgrim's Inn*). London: Hodder & Stoughton, 1948.

Goudge, Elizabeth. *The Joy of the Snow*. London: Hodder & Stoughton, 1974.

Goudge, Elizabeth. *The Little White Horse*. London: University of London Press, 1946.

Goudge, Elizabeth. *The Rosemary Tree*. London: Hodder & Stoughton, 1956.

Many of these books are available in recent editions, and in the UK, as ebooks. For the Elizabeth Goudge Society, see www.elizabethgoudge.org.

Chapter 10

Works by Noel Streatfeild

A Vicarage Family. London: Collins, 1963.
Away from the Vicarage. London: Collins, 1965.
Beyond the Vicarage. London: Collins, 1971.
Confirmation and After. London: Heinemann, 1963.
Luke. London: Heinemann, 1939; ebook available from Bello.
New Town. London: Collins, 1960.
Parson's Nine. London: Heinemann, 1932; reprinted [Edinburgh]: Greyladies, 2014.
Saplings. London: Collins, 1945; reprinted London: Persephone Books, 2000.
The Bell Family. London: Collins, 1954.
The Whicharts. London: Heinemann, 1931.

Works about Noel Streatfeild

Bull, Angela. *Noel Streatfeild. A Biography*. London: Collins, 1984.
Huse, Nancy. *Noel Streatfeild*. New York: Twayne, 1994.

Chapter 11

Bayley, John. *Iris: A Memoir of Iris Murdoch*. London: Duckworth, 1998.

Bayley, John. *Elegy for Iris*. New York: St. Martin's Press, 1990.

Bayley, John. *Iris Murdoch and Her Friends: A Year of Memories*. London: Duckworth, 2002.

Dipple, Elizabeth. *Iris Murdoch. Work for the Spirit*. Chicago: University of Chicago Press, 1982.

Dooley, Gillian, ed. *From a Tiny Corner in the House of Fiction: Conversations with Iris Murdoch*. Columbia, SC: University of South Carolina Press, 2003.

Eyre, Richard. *Iris: A Screenplay*. London: Bloomsbury, 2002.

Hawkins, Peter S. *The Language of Grace. Flannery O'Connor, Walker Percy, and Iris Murdoch*. New York: Seabury Classics, 2004.

Iris (2001), [Film] Dir. Richard Eyre, UK/USA: Buena Vista Pictures/Miramax Films.

Meyers, Jeffrey. *Remembering Iris Murdoch: Letters and Interviews*. New York: Palgrave Macmillan, 2013.

Murdoch, Iris. *A Writer at War: Letters and Diaries of Iris Murdoch, 1934–1945*. Ed. and intro. Peter J. Conradi. London: Short, 2010.

Murdoch, Iris. *Living on Paper: Letters from Iris Murdoch, 1934–1995*. Ed. Avril Horner and Anne Rowe. London: Chatto and Windus, 2015.

Chapter 12

Furlong, Monica. *Bird of Paradise: Glimpses of Living Myth*. London: Mowbray, 1995.

Furlong, Monica. *The Cat's Eye*. London: Magnum Books, 1976.

Furlong, Monica. *Cousins*. London: Weidenfeld and Nicolson, 1983.

Furlong, Monica. *A Dangerous Delight: Women and Power in the Church*. London: SPCK, 1991.

Furlong, Monica. *Merton: A Biography*. London: Collins, 1980; New York: Harper, 1980.

Furlong, Monica. *Prayers and Poems*. London: SPCK, 2004.

Furlong, Monica. *Wise Child*. London: Victor Gollancz, 1987.

Furlong, Monica. *With Love to the Church*. London: Hodder and Stoughton, 1965.

Chapter 13

In addition to the novels of James's discussed in this chapter, *An Unsuitable Job for a Woman* (1st ed. London: Faber and Faber, 1977) and the dystopian fantasy *The Children of Men* (1st ed. London: Faber and Faber, 1992) are particularly interesting in the context of her Anglicanism. Girton College, Cambridge, holds collection of James's personal papers (GCPP James).

See also:

James, P.D. 'As It Was in the Beginning', ch. 2 in *Why I Am Still an Anglican: Essays and Conversations*, ed. Caroline Chartres. London: Continuum, 2006.

James, P.D. *Talking about Detective Fiction*. Oxford: Bodleian Library, 2009.

Rowland, Susan. *From Agatha Christie to Ruth Rendell: British Women Writers in Detective and Crime Fiction*. Basingstoke: Palgrave, 2001.

Young, Laurel A., and Elizabeth Foxwell. *P.D. James: A Companion to the Mystery Fiction*. Jefferson, NC: McFarland, 2017.

INDEX